9

WITHDRAWN

The Kirkpatrick Mission

The Kirkpatrick Mission

Diplomacy Without Apology
America at the United Nations
1981–1985

ALLAN GERSON

THE FREE PRESS
A Division of Macmillan, Inc.
NEW YORK
Maxwell Macmillan Canada
TORONTO
MAXWELL MACMILLAN INTERNATIONAL
NEW YORK   OXFORD   SINGAPORE   SYDNEY

The Free Press
A Division of Macmillan, Inc.
866 Third Avenue, New York, N.Y. 10022

Maxwell Macmillan Canada, Inc.
1200 Eglinton Avenue East
Suite 200
Don Mills, Ontario M3C 3N1

Macmillan, Inc. is part of the Maxwell Communication Group of Companies.

Printed in the United States of America

printing number
1 2 3 4 5 6 7 8 9 10

Library of Congress Cataloging-in-Publication Data
Gerson, Allan.
    The Kirkpatrick mission: diplomacy without apology: America at the United Nations, 1981-1985 / Allan Gerson.
        p.   cm.
    Includes bibliographical references (p.) and index.
    ISBN 0-02-911611-2
    1. United Nations—United States.   2. United States—Foreign relations—1981-1989.   3. Kirkpatrick, Jeane J.   I. Title.
JX1977.2.U5G47   1991
341.23'73—dc20   90-26344
                                                                                    CIP

Marian Christy's interview with Jeane Kirkpatrick, published July 20, 1981, is reprinted courtesy of *The Boston Globe*.

To my children, Daniela, Merissa, and David,
so that they may understand
and in loving memory of my father, Morton Gerson,
who showed me the way

Contents

Preface

This book is about a critical moment in American and world history. Its central character is Jeane J. Kirkpatrick. My aim has been to portray both the woman with whom I worked and the issues that confronted us during her turbulent term as the U.S. Permanent Representative to the United Nations.

Writing about someone who is a national figure and a former boss, and who is also a friend, is not easy. Because of her position she always knew things that others on her team did not. She was a member of the National Security Council and frequently attended meetings in Washington of the NSPG, the National Security Planning Group. At the United Nations she often engaged in a very personal form of multilateral diplomacy—establishing networks that crisscrossed national and international lines; helping foreign officials find their way through the U.S. government; contacting Congressmen, Cabinet officials, Under-secretaries, and their subordinates in the pursuit of her daily tasks. I had little share in that whirl of activity. I approached matters as an international lawyer, as a legal counsel, special assistant, political adviser, speech-writer, travelling companion, and troubleshooter in Washington. But I knew what she wanted to accomplish and why, and I saw her particular genius at work.

Jeane Kirkpatrick read and commented on the manuscript. The views I express are, however, my own. I have relied largely on personal diary entries, interviews, and original source material. The result is an account, from that perspective, of the interplay between law and politics, personality and policy, in the shaping of U.S. foreign relations.

Completion of this work would not have been possible without the generous support and encouragement of a number of institutions and individuals, for which I am deeply indebted. The U.S. Institute of Peace, the Bradley Foundation, and the Ford Foundation provided financial support. The American Enterprise Institute for Public Policy Research in Washington provided a congenial setting for the progress of the work, and I owe a special note of thanks to its president, Chris DeMuth. At the Free Press, my editor, president and publisher Erwin A. Glikes, was present at the inception of the idea and helped see it through to the end. Noreen O'Connor, his editorial assistant, offered many useful suggestions, and Loretta Denner was instrumental in putting the manuscript into final form. I thank them warmly. There were many others whose help I relied upon in the creation of this work, and I thank them as well.

Of course, without the grace and encouragement of my wife, Joan, none of this might have been possible, and as always, I am especially indebted to her.

Washington, D.C.

Introduction

At the go-between post of the U.S. Mission to the United Nations I often sensed that we were on the divide between reality and make-believe and, at times, between the sane and insane. What happened there reminded me of a play that I had seen on Broadway a decade earlier, *The Persecution and Assassination of Marat As Performed by the Inmates of the Asylum at Charenton, under the Direction of the Marquis de Sade*. As the final curtain descended, the actors, playing the role of lunatics in an eighteenth century asylum, fanned out among the audience. For an instant it was impossible to tell which was which, or who was leading the wild applause.

Like the audience in New York, at the U.S. Mission we too were subtly but viscerally affected by a cadence set by others —the United Nations in New York and the State Department in Washington. The United Nations—the voice of the "international community"—did its best, or at least so it seemed in the beginning, to "ignore, deplore, despise, and revile" the United States, as Jeane Kirkpatrick put it. The State Department—"the Building"—extolled the virtues of patience, self-effacement, and collegiality. Patience because diplomacy could be expected to achieve little, and achieve nothing quickly; self-effacement because boldness made one a standing target; collegiality because style could be an end in itself.

Far from competing, these two voices actually complemented each other—twin bureaucracies that were suspicious, embarrassed, and resentful of the conservative policies advocated by the new President, Ronald Reagan. For Jeane Kirkpatrick and the members of her team chosen to represent those policies—the free-market system as a model for development, freedom and democracy as the keynotes of world order, and a single standard in judging the actions of nations— the predicament of the audience at *Marat/Sade*, caught between different visions of reality, often seemed close at hand. Our vision of America's role in the world seemed at times hopelessly at odds with that of either the United Nations or the State Department.

When we began we were told, above all, not to make the mistake of confusing the United Nations with the "real world." Yet Jeane Jordan Kirkpatrick—the relatively unknown professor of political science at Georgetown University whom President Reagan appointed as the first woman to hold the post of U.S. Permanent Representative to the United Nations, and the first woman to sit regularly in the National Security Council—could not accept this notion. She could not observe this distinction in practice, although clearly enough its effect was to make American diplomats complacent about the United Nations, willing to patronize it and ignore its abuses, and content that what went on there were mere "word games" not to be confused with the real "man's world" of bilateral diplomacy. But if the United Nations was not the real world, what was it?

Foreign ministers and heads of state came to the United Nations. Their emissaries in New York were their agents. They represented their governments. To be sure, the power of the blocs at the United Nations—the Soviet bloc, the African bloc, the Islamic Conference, the NAM or Non-Aligned Movement—was immense. It was immediately apparent that the Soviet bloc and the radical Third World dominated the agenda. But that too, it seemed to Jeane Kirkpatrick and the team she assembled, reflected—and affected—power realities in the world beyond the walls of the United Nations. The European and ASEAN blocs found it necessary to take account of majority votes, and thus even America's best friends and allies distanced themselves from us. The United States was the odd man out, and as long as bloc voting prevailed, causes and issues in which the United States had an interest could not expect to get a hearing, let alone fair consideration. This, it seemed, necessarily weakened the U.S. position in the "real world" and made a mockery of the idea that UN institutions and processes for conflict resolution could be made to work for the purposes for which they were intended.

What seemed beyond doubt in the winter and spring of 1981 was that the United Nations was at war with the United States, that the United States was not faring well, and that it was no accident that its fortunes around the world were at an equally low ebb. There were no shouts then of "Freedom" in the streets of Prague, Budapest, and East Berlin. Only a madman could have conceived of such a thing at the time. Equally beyond the scope of any rational imagination was the *New York Times* headline of October 24, 1989: "Moscow Says Afghan Role Was Illegal And Immoral; Admits Breaking Arms Pact." Instead there was the ubiquitous presence of Soviet, East German, or Vietnamese forces in Ethiopia, Angola, Yemen, Afghanistan, Nicaragua, Kampuchea, and Laos. The Communist goal of a worldwide "revolution without frontiers" did not seem mere rhetoric.

It was in this context that the meeting of Jeane Kirkpatrick and Ronald Reagan was so propitious. In him she saw relief from the Carter policies which she believed were responsible for causing the tragedies of Iran and Nicaragua, and for delivering, however involuntarily, our allies and friends into "the repression and horror of totalitarianism."

What had given rise to these convictions? Her roots gave few hints. She had grown up in Duncan, Oklahoma, when it was not much more than a frontier town. Her father was an oil man, a drilling contractor who had his share of ups and downs. The place and the man surely helped shape her independence. Both her parents took politics seriously—Democratic politics—and instilled in her a sense of civic duty. But her concern with America's place in the world was to come much later.

She went on to Stephens College, Missouri, for two years and then transferred to Barnard College in New York. It was there and in the continuation of her studies as a graduate student at Columbia from 1949 to 1952 that she came into contact with such works as Hannah Arendt's recently published *The Origins of Totalitarianism*.[1] She studied with Professor Franz Neumann and other political refugees from war-torn Europe, who were working on de-Nazification programs to insure that Germany would be democratized and the vestiges of totalitarianism buried.[2] Information and files on what had occurred were pouring in. The full extent of the tragedy was becoming known. Scholars were being given access to the massive files of Hitler's plans. The scope of Stalinist atrocities was also becoming evident. It was, as she put it, "all fresh. It would have been hard to have grown up in that climate and not developed an acute political consciousness."

Still, that awareness was held in abeyance, as if waiting for the proper event and change of circumstances to unleash itself. After getting an M.A. in political science from Columbia University, she worked in an intelligence and research bureau at the State Department headed by Evron Kirkpatrick, a former political science professor fifteen years her senior. One year later, in 1955, she married him and honeymooned at a political science conference at Northwestern University. For the next ten years much of her life was given over to being a housewife and raising three sons. But she found time to complete her doctorate and get a start in college teaching; and, together with her husband, "Kirk," she also became involved with Senator Hubert Humphrey (Kirk had been his teacher at the University of Minnesota and helped run his first campaign for public office) and the Senator Henry ("Scoop") Jackson wing of the Democratic Party. In 1971 she published a book, *Leader and Vanguard in Mass Society*. In 1974 she published *Political Woman*, dealing with women in state legislatures, followed in 1976 by *The New Presidential Elite*.[3] She was awarded an endowed chair in political science at Georgetown University, where since 1971 she had been teaching courses on political theory, the basic course in European government, and French politics, as well as a seminar on politics and personality.

She took little part in the Vietnam war debates that raged across campuses during the sixties and early seventies. But what she saw as a U.S. policy for abandoning South Vietnam under the cover of a peace treaty struck an old chord. In 1975 she wrote to Senator Hubert Humphrey of her "indescribable distress and anguish" over that decision. "I regard the U.S. refusal to provide material aid to South Vietnam today, in its hour of greatest need, as the most shameful display of irresponsibility and inhumanity in our history. . . . The quality of South Vietnam's beleaguered government—outnumbered, outgunned and overrun in a perfectly clear cut case of military aggression—is," she wrote, "no more relevant to whether this country should grant them aid than was the moral quality of individual Jews first imprisoned then exterminated by Adolf Hitler."

Four years later, in 1979, she wrote an article, her first of the kind, on why it was incumbent upon the United States to weave a careful course between support for "authoritarian" regimes and implacable opposition to those of the "totalitarian" stripe. The article caught the eye of presidential aspirant Ronald Reagan, and she was asked to sign on as a foreign-policy adviser in his campaign. It was a meteoric rise from there.

Interestingly, she at first thought that article unworthy of publication. It was a difficult piece to write, and somewhat more abstract than usual for her. After completing it at her summer place in St. Remy in southern France, she had put it away in the drawer of her desk until Kirk urged her to send it off to *Commentary*'s editor, Norman Podhoretz. It appeared in the November 1979 issue of *Commentary* under the title, "Dictatorships and Double Standards."[4]

What made that piece so attractive to Ronald Reagan was that it provided a road map and intellectual foundation for the argument he had been making on the campaign trail about the Carter policies as having resulted in weakening U.S. strength and influence abroad while at the same time abandoning friends and allies under the banner of advancing human rights. "Dictatorships and Double Standards" argued that "authoritarian" regimes need to be distinguished, for purposes of U.S. assistance and alliances, from those of a "totalitarian" character that denied their people all freedoms, including religious tolerance. Totalitarian regimes, she wrote, could not be expected to change: "authoritarian" regimes, by contrast, were more susceptible to reform and thus proper recipients of U.S. support. It was an argument that fit the tenor of the times and supplied exactly what Ronald Reagan was looking for in order to hold the Carter Administration responsible for replacing an "authoritarian" regime in Nicaragua (that of Sebastian Somoza) with the "totalitarian" rule of the Ortega brothers, and for likewise replacing, in the case of Iran, the regime of the pro-Western but authoritarian Shah with the rule of the Ayatollah Khomeini.

In late 1980, shortly after the national election, the Kirkpatricks were in Miami, where Jeane was addressing a gathering of the American Friends of the Hebrew University of Jerusalem. "Afterward, Kirk and I were having a long, leisurely dinner, just the two of us. When we came back to our hotel room there was a message to call Ronald Reagan. I asked how he was and he said, 'I'll be better if you agree to be our ambassador to the United Nations.' "

It was in many ways a curious choice. She had no political constituency of her own. And although she had taught political science and had lived in different cultures and spoke French and Spanish fluently, she had no direct experience in foreign affairs or in managing a diplomatic post. Her husband, recalling the phone call, said: "We had to know exactly what the job entailed—who she worked with, what were her responsibilities. Neither of us knew anything about it other than having seen Arthur Goldberg and Adlai Stevenson on television."

For the next year she would find herself under nearly total siege, harassed and beleaguered on all sides, struggling to make her views heard in a less than receptive bureaucracy, confronting a hostile Secretary of State, Alexander Haig, Jr., and never quite sure where his authority began and hers ended. The two institutions in which she was supposed to fulfill her responsibilities—the State Department in Washington and the United Nations in New York—would view her as the consummate outsider, untrained in the art of statecraft and nuances of diplomacy. The Chairman of the Senate Foreign Relations Committee would vilify her as "incompetent." Haig would spurn her as a mere "company commander." And the popular press would caricature her as a bomb-throwing ideologue from the right, a female Dr. Strangelove, who could not be expected to stay at her post for very long.[5]

But stay she would, serving longer than any other U. S. ambassador except Henry Cabot Lodge (1953–1960) and Adlai Stevenson (1961 to 1965). She would come to exercise greater influence over the formulation and articulation of U.S. foreign policy than any other U.S. Permanent Representative to the United Nations. Justice Arthur J. Goldberg came close, but early in his term he lost the confidence of the president he served, Lyndon Johnson (in disagreements over Vietnam), while she retained the confidence of President Reagan until the end.

She would be hailed as a national heroine by millions of Americans, denounced by others, but nearly universally respected for the strength and conviction she brought to the articulation of her views. The representatives who were so disdainful of her in the beginning would at her departure toast her night after night for two months at dinners in her honor. In her newly adopted Republican party she would be spoken of as a potential presidential candidate in the election of 1988. And, more than five years after having left office, she would remain celebrated in American political life, near the top on the national lecture circuit, and sought after for advice by heads of state and foreign ministers.

Jeane Kirkpatrick at the United Nations had become far different from Jeane Kirkpatrick the Georgetown University academic who was brought to power in 1981 because of an article she had published in *Commentary*. She was a far different Jeane Kirkpatrick from the woman I met in the summer of that same year. True, even then she spoke of a vision she shared with President Reagan of changing the direction of U.S. foreign policy. But the United Nations hardly seemed the place, nor did Jeane Kirkpatrick seem especially well cast for the part. Yet circumstance—events that made the United Nations a last major theater in the Cold War—would propel her and those around her to play a key role in shaping the transformation of world politics that was to come.

1

The Call

What's the difference if it's radiation and not Zyklon B gas? It's still aimed at our children and ourselves.

> Menachem Begin addressing a crowd of Holocaust survivors at the Western Wall, June 19, 1981 on why he ordered the bombing of Iraq's nuclear reactor.

On the afternoon of June 19, 1981, Jeane J. Kirkpatrick, sitting behind the United States nameplate at the large horseshoe UN Security Council table in New York, steadied herself to vote. Listlessly lifting her right hand, index and middle finger suspended in midair, she cast the decisive vote. That made it unanimous: 15 to 0, with no abstentions, in favor of condemning Israel for its pinpoint bombing of Iraq's Osirak nuclear reactor as a "clear violation of the United Nations Charter and the norms of international conduct."[1] Everyone seemed satisfied, even though in negotiations preceding the vote the phrase "aggression" had been deleted at the insistence of the U.S. ambassador. Only one thing seemed strangely out of place: unless the new U.S. ambassador was just very tired, there was something about her expression, carried live on video monitors around the world, that seemed to suggest disdain, if not contempt, for the entire exercise.

In Jerusalem, around midnight the same evening, I received a call from Eugene V. Rostow, the Director of the ACDA, the U.S. Arms Control and Disarmament Agency. A former dean of the Yale

Law School, Rostow had supervised the completion of my doctoral dissertation there and we had maintained close cordial relations ever since.

"Allan," he said with little of his usual ebullience, brushing aside my surprise at his call, "I have serious business to discuss. I had a talk the other day with Jeane Kirkpatrick, our UN ambassador, at a National Security Council meeting. It concerned the Iraqi nuclear reactor bombing. I assume you have been following these developments?"

I had in fact been reading the daily press accounts of negotiations in New York between Kirkpatrick and Iraq's Foreign Minister over the text of a draft UN Security Council resolution. I also knew that questions had been raised about whether the U.S. government had given Israel a green light for the operation. Apparently since 1979 the Israelis had been telling Washington that they were concerned that the reactor under construction with the help of French scientists could be used to produce nuclear weapons.

Indeed, earlier that evening, I had heard a revealing first-hand account by the man who ordered the bombing, Israel's Prime Minister, Menachem Begin. Addressing a crowd of 5,000 Holocaust survivors at the site of the Wailing Wall, he talked of the memory of one-and-a-half million Jewish children that perished in the Holocaust. "What's the difference," he asked, referring to the Iraqi reactor's capacity to produce nuclear weapons, "if it's radiation and not Zyklon B gas? It's still aimed at our children and ourselves."[2] One had to strain to catch all the words as his voice seemed intermittently to be drowned out by the amplified sound of an Arab muezzin from a nearby minaret calling the faithful to prayer.

Eugene Rostow came to the point of his call. "It's been a long haul in New York," he said. "Jeane Kirkpatrick has been doing a great job, but she needs help. She told me that she needs a good international lawyer, someone who sees things her way and, preferably, knows his way around the bureaucracy. Naturally, I recommended you."

"I'm flattered, Gene," I answered. "But you know I'm here trying to finish this book . . ."

"Look, Allan," he added, "I think your Justice Department experience was important. Don't get me wrong. You should do a book about it. But I'm not sure that this is the right time. You could make an important contribution in New York. Think it over and let me know what you decide." The experience he was referring to was my stint during the previous year and a half as a prosecutor with OSI, the U.S. Justice Department's Office of Special Investigations. Much of the time it was as if I was really living in 1942 or 1943 and only came up for air in 1979 or 1980. My role was to marshal the evidence, work with witnesses, and eventually bring to trial naturalized American citizens alleged to have collaborated with the Nazis in implementation of the "Final Solution." If found guilty, they would be stripped of their U.S. citizenship and deported. The usual destination was Lithuania, Estonia, or the Ukraine. There a quick trial, Soviet-style, awaited them, followed in all likelihood by a firing squad.

Some of these defendants were machine gunners attached to the SS Einsatzgruppen or mobile death squads. Others were concentration camp guards, chiefs of police, municipal officials, political leaders, and former cabinet officers in puppet governments who lent their high office to the processes of extermination. Their lives in the United States were largely uneventful and gave no hint of their pasts. My concern, having left OSI and the Justice Department a month earlier, was to reflect on what was their common denominator, and whether their collaboration with evil was a matter of time and place, a reaction—as they claimed—to particular circumstances. In Jerusalem I was seeking answers to these questions by reinterviewing some of the Israeli witnesses who had testified at a trial I had previously been involved in.

For the last year, therefore, I had been steeped in the past. Gene Rostow's call forced me to rethink things. Perhaps it was time to get back to international law, and contemporary international affairs. What I did not factor into my calculations was that the United Nations would provide me with little escape from the questions that then plagued me. I had not anticipated the degree to which charges of "Nazi" and "Nazi-like" behavior would be bandied about in UN bodies; only there it would be Israel that would be the object of these charges, with the Palestinian Arabs portrayed as Warsaw ghetto fighters rising up against the new twentieth-century incarnation of evil.[3]

I had mixed feelings. A career in "public international law"—not to be confused with its more lucrative cousins having to do with international commercial transactions—carried little attraction. "Peace and harmony through international law" was a banner that had lost much of its appeal. And I had seen enough of the UN's "deliberations" during my graduate school days—Charles Yost and George Bush were then the "U.S. Permanent Representatives"—to lead me to believe that there must be better ways for grown people to spend their time. Everyone had the angels on his side, but international law provided no single conception of heaven. There was no court—in any meaningful sense of the word—to determine which of the many contending views of international law might be correct. There were occasional cases heard by the World Court, the International Court of Justice sitting at The Hague, but only one case in the last forty years dealt with the primary issue with which the UN was supposed to deal: control of the use of force by states.[4] At the UN General Assembly the majority view always prevailed, and the majority had become notably anti-American and anti-Western.

I had studied international law in the hope that it would provide answers, signposts to justice, fair and universal standards for the equitable resolution of conflict. I looked to international law for a way out of the impasse of the Arab-Israeli conflict, for a solution to the anguish of Vietnam, for a basis for informed judgments as to who and what was right and wrong. I was disappointed. Increasingly, international law seemed a matter of choosing Arab international law or Israeli international law, Soviet or American, Indian or Pakistani, and so forth.

At the Yale Law School I tended toward the view of international law espoused by Professor Myres S. McDougal in conjunction with his long-term ally, the social scientist Harold Lasswell (who was also Jeane Kirkpatrick's mentor at Columbia). Together they derided traditional theories of international law as "make-believe universalism." They suggested instead a more policy-oriented approach which recognized that the world was composed of "diverse systems of public order."[5] It was a more modest view of the power of international law than that held by their contemporaries, but one that more closely coincided with the views of the founders of international law.

Hugo Grotius, the Dutch jurist, historian, diplomat, and poet who is known as the "father" of international law, wrote 400 years ago in his celebrated text *De Jure Belli ac Pacis*[6] (The Rights of War and Peace) that international law was "written reason," a code of intelligent precepts for diplomacy and the orderly and sensible conduct of international relations. Grotius did not examine the Koran and its commentaries on the Islamic law of war, nor the principles and practices of diplomacy and war prevalent in the Mogul Empire, nor the different Hindu and Buddhist kingdoms of India, nor the customs of Southeast Asia and China. All of them were irrelevant to the task Grotius had set for himself: to provide Christian Europe with a set of principles based on shared values and beliefs.

It was not that Grotius had not studied and was not aware of Islamic law, or Chinese law and history. He had, and *De Jure Belli ac Pacis* made ample reference to them. But he considered their principles radically different from the laws and philosophy common to the West. The twin pillars of Grotius' system of international law were state sovereignty and sovereign equality—the rights of states to be free from interference in their internal affairs or from external threats of attack, regardless of the ways in which they ruled their countries. Whether a regime was despotic or democratic, beneficent or uncaring, was beside the point to Grotius; each state was to be equal under the law. But he recognized that, for example, neither the Chinese nor the Islamic systems of justice saw the world in this way; each saw its universe as centered upon its leaders, the Emperor cast as the Son of Heaven, Mohammed as divine messenger, and the rest as either followers or as heathens and inferior barbarians (*der-el-Islam* or *der-el-harib* in the case of Islam).

It was only with the advent of the United Nations at the end of World War II that international law as it had traditionally been practiced for four hundred years—the "Grotian" view of international law—was revolutionized. The view of international law as a system for like-minded states under like-minded beliefs gave way to a new vision of international law as capable of overcoming different conceptions of justice and world order held by different cultures, by East and West, by the developed nations and the underdeveloped nations. Thus the Soviet vision of world order was seen capable of meeting the standards of legality upheld by the West. That law was seen, in the Soviet view, as an instrument of power in a world class struggle was somehow deemed compatible with the Western idea of keeping the legal system above political struggle in order to safeguard general order and liberty.

In the United States, international law increasingly became viewed as tantamount to foreign policy. President Dwight D. Eisenhower in the Suez Canal crisis of 1956 stated that he was willing to risk a rift in the Western alliance by condemning America's principal allies, Britain and France, as well as Israel, for their actions in Suez because the promotion of international law was more important.[7] The Carter Administration elevated international law to new heights by saying that human rights standards would be not merely a factor, but a principal component in U.S. foreign policy.[8] At the Department of State, the Office of Legal Adviser came to play a larger, grander role than its counterparts in other federal agencies. Its mission was perceived not only as representing and advising the Secretary of State but as aiding the progressive development of international law. Within the State Department it thus came to be accepted as conventional wisdom that U.S. foreign policy had to reflect not only the security interests and the obligations of the United States but the advancement of international law. Fealty to international law would bring about peace. Peace was increasingly seen, as Gene Rostow had put it in an earlier book on the subject, as "a problem of law."[9]

Thus, despite the inherent ambiguity of international law, it was being turned into a guide for the perplexed, offering a promised land of universal peace. It had become a new "ism" able to charm the minds of men by the promise of symmetry and world order. Overlooked in the rush to embrace international law were the issues of who defined it, where it was being defined, and the chasm between the law's aspirations and its realities.

Unlike lawyers who toiled in the everyday vineyards of commercial or criminal law, the new breed of "international lawyers" had trouble accepting the truth of Justice Charles Evans Hughes' observation that the law is simply "what the judges say it is."[10] They couldn't accept the notion that abstract questions of fairness were the province of the other branches of government—the legislative and executive—and that the law had its work cut out for itself in merely striving to see that its principles might be applied equally without too much questioning of whether they were intrinsically good or bad.

In the field of international law, there has always seemed to be a tendency to see law as something more fixed than the evolving application of neutral principles. Now it had assumed a touch of religion, and salvation. Its practitioners, such as they were, and supporters became "preoccupied," in McDougal and Lasswell's words, with the futile task "of establishing that the subject of their professional concern was in fact law and could not be dismissed as a miscellany of maxims principally useful for the admonishing of decision-makers to act ethically."[11]

McDougal and Lasswell nevertheless shared a belief in a conception of the common good. They believed it could be identified by subjecting decisions to their own elaborate scheme of policy preferences. I myself had come to view international law in a less sanguine light, as a tool used not so much for finding common ground as for cutting the ground out from under one's opposition. It was not a happy conclusion.

I had reached this awareness after having spent two years in the

well-stocked stacks of Yale's Sterling Law Library, digesting and analyzing all the international law I could find on the topic I had chosen
for my doctoral dissertation: "The Administration of Enemy Territory
and the Law of Belligerent Occupation."[12] I had read the rules and
commentary on whether an occupying power was entitled to exploit
natural resources, whether the ousted power had "reversionary interests" to the territory it had lost in war, whether the occupied
population could be expelled or arrested and under what conditions,
whether there was any reciprocal obligation between the occupied
and the occupying military power to respect each other, and on the
rights and duties of third states to contested areas. In the end, I left
convinced that more often than not international law could be as
flexible as one's imagination. Cloaked in the law's majesty, the villain
could become the victim, the victim the villain, and the accomplice
the good samaritan. It was a matter of what skill could be brought to
bear in shaping an amorphous body of rules, regulations, aspirations,
and resolutions called international law to suit one's desired objectives.

As if these reservations were not enough to give me pause before
returning to the field of public international law, there were other
concerns as well. A mastery of rules regulating state conduct on war
and peace issues was hardly an easily marketable skill. Employment
could be found mostly in the offices of legal advisers to foreign ministries where, if someone were so inclined, long hours could be spent
trying to churn out opinions that might put a blush of legality on
decisions already made and actions already taken. It was for that very
reason that I had opted for trial work, for dealing with visible injury
wherein clearer standards would guide me, for working in a world
where the prospect of meaningful redress of injury existed, and for
leaving public international law to the professors in academe.

Was there, I asked myself nevertheless, a future for me in the
maze of principles and learned commentary on the limits of permissible self-defense, impermissible aggression, on human rights to be
respected in times of peace and times of war, and in the twilight zone
of neither war nor peace? Could I now put to practical use the public
international law I had so assiduously learned and then abandoned?
More to the point, could I turn down an offer of public service in a
new administration for a president that I had voted for and whose call
for a restoration of American power and the promotion of freedom I
admired?

But first, who was Jeane Kirkpatrick? To be sure, Gene Rostow thought highly of her. She was, apparently, trying to chart her own course clear of the State Department bureaucracy. But was she some-one I could work with, and was there a method to her approach, a strategy, a well-defined line of thought?

I wanted to find out. The next morning I called the telephone number Gene Rostow had given me. But Jeane Kirkpatrick wasn't in. Carl Gershman, the Counselor to the U.S. Mission, answered the phone and said he had a message for me: "Jeane" would be delighted to meet me. We arranged to meet in New York two weeks later.

2

Encounter

People ask me how I got to this point, to this job, to this achievement. Well, I don't have the foggiest notion. . . . But there is only one reason, one, that I am doing this work. It's not the status perks, the prestige perks. I think it's my duty. I have a demanding conception of citizenship. I have an obligation to confront serious problems.

> Jeane J. Kirkpatrick to Marian Christy of the *Boston Globe*, July 19, 1981

Two weeks later, on an unusually breezy midsummer morning, I arrived at the U.S. Mission to the United Nations for a 10:30 A.M. appointment with Ambassador Kirkpatrick. The receptionist, Peggy Gregal, greeted me at the entrance after I had shown my identification and made my way past the bulletproof glass doors. On her desk were inscribed photographs of several former U.S. ambassadors. She told me she had seen six come and go in the last ten years.

With half an hour to spare before my scheduled meeting, I decided to first take a stroll across the street to see the UN grounds, to get a "feel" for the place where I might be spending much of my time. It was "off-season"—I knew the General Assembly session wouldn't begin until September. As I crossed the street to enter the UN complex, spanning the area between Forty-second and Forty-sixth streets and the East River and First Avenue, it seemed as if I had entered a deserted movie set, or an abandoned World's Fair. There were no chauffered limousines pulling up to the blue-canopied entrance to the UN General Assembly Hall, no hurrying diplomats, no reporters looking for scoops. The only sign of life seemed to be a small group of tourists at the visitors' entrance, and the sound of the flags lining the UN grounds flapping in the wind—too many to count, but I knew the number was 157, one for each member-nation, up from a count of 51 when the UN opened for business in 1945.

The sights that morning—the flags, the sunlight reflected off the massive marble and glass UN Secretariat building, the manicured lawns—and the sheer pleasure of a beautiful summer day all made for a giddy feeling recalling the day I toured here with my sixth-grade class as a twelve-year-old. Our guide, a beautiful Scandinavian woman, sported a ribbon of flags across her pale blue blouse. On her right sleeve was embossed the UN insignia—a world embraced in palm leaf clusters. Quoting from the preamble to the UN Charter, she told us, in the most reverential tones, that this place was dedicated to "save succeeding generations from the scourge of war, which twice in our lifetime had brought untold sorrow to mankind." It was to serve as a palace of peace, as the new Parliament of Man, embodying the hopes of a generation of great statesmen who had their fill of war and who looked to the UN to maintain peace and advance human rights. At that moment, I fell in love with her and with what she represented: progress, civility, and international brotherhood.

Now, bypassing the UN General Assembly hall, which seemed crowded with mostly Japanese, European, and Arab tourists, I made my way beyond the visitors' entrance toward a well-tended rose garden, a miniature park, squeezed between the UN building and a narrow boardwalk overlooking the East River. A sign across its entry said, "Use Reserved for UN Delegates." I ignored it and went past it into the garden, thinking that I might be a delegate soon enough. Toward the center of the lawn stood a solitary piece of sculpture, a black-marble configuration of a super-muscular man beating something into the ground. The bronze plate inscription at its base read: "Man beating sword into plowshare—Gift of the USSR." There was no mention of the author of that vision of wars being fought no more—the Old Testament prophet Isaiah, who said: "And they shall beat their swords into ploughshares, and their spears into pruning hooks."

I had just a few minutes left. At the boardwalk, the border of the UN grounds, a large Con Edison electric plant could be seen directly across the East River. Three tall smokestacks, silhouetted against the flat landscape of the factories and tenements of Queens, billowed gray-white smoke into the air. A huge neon sign across its front flashed "Pepsi-Cola." It occurred to me that the vision of America the thousands of UN delegates and workers in the UN Secretariat and adjoining buildings might have was affected by whether their glass walls faced east toward the workers' paradise of Queens or west toward the skyscrapers of Manhattan.

Upon my return to the Mission the receptionist told me that Carl Gershman would be down shortly to escort me. I remembered Carl's name from the 1960s; he had been President of the Students' Committee for Peace in the Middle East, and later a leader of Social Democrats USA, an organization of mildly socialist and fiercely anti-Communist convictions. For the last year or so he had been at Freedom House, an organization dedicated to charting those nations that were promoting freedom and democracy, and those that were trampling it. The scorecard didn't look promising.

As I waited for Carl, I looked around the reception area. There were two large color photographs, one of President Ronald Reagan, the other of Vice President George Bush, on either side of the elevators. On the wall in the center of the lobby was a floor-length mahogany plaque with the names of all U.S. UN Ambassadors since 1945, in gold letters. It was a long list. The last one was marked "Jeane J Kirkpatrick, OK(lahoma), 1981–   ."

Many of the names were immediately recognizable: Henry Cabot Lodge, 1953–1960, the handsome U.S. ambassador who served at the UN when I visited with my sixth-grade class in 1959, the year he was seen on television displaying the U.S. Moscow Embassy seal containing Soviet listening devices; Adlai Stevenson, 1961–1965, the eloquent intellectual who was all but ignored by the president, John F. Kennedy, whom he served. I recalled the 1962 television broadcast of his debate with Soviet Ambassador Valerian Zorin about the installation of nuclear missiles in Cuba. (UN proceedings were taken more seriously then and given greater coverage in the American media; the *New York Times*, for example, assigned four reporters to cover the UN.) I remembered his words: "You are in the courtroom of world opinion right now, and you can answer 'Yes' or 'No'. You have denied that they exist—and I want to understand whether I have understood you correctly." To which Zorin replied coldly, "You will receive answer in due course"; and Stevenson came back saying, "I am prepared to wait for my answer until hell freezes over, if that is your decision."[1]

There was Arthur J. Goldberg, 1965–1968, who gave up his seat on the U.S. Supreme Court for the UN post, believing that the

UN was as serious a place for peace-making as the Supreme Court was for resolving constitutional disputes. I had little doubt that he came to regret his decision. There were also George Ball, 1968, and James Russell Wiggins, 1968–1969; there were Charles Yost, 1969–1971; George Bush, 1971–1973; John Scali, 1973–1975. And then there was Daniel Patrick Moynihan, 1975–1976. I could recall his ruddy face on the cover of *Time*—flamboyant, defiant—when he rose to condemn the passage of the UN General Assembly's "Zionism is racism" resolution in 1975.[2] There was William Scranton, 1976–1977; and there was Andrew Young, 1977–1979, who met secretly with the PLO's UN representative in violation of U.S. assurances that there would be no meetings with the PLO until certain conditions had been met.[3] Last on the list, before Jeane Kirkpatrick, was Donald McHenry, 1979–1981, who failed to learn from his predecessor's mistakes and whose rush to vote in favor of declaring Jerusalem to be Israeli "occupied territory" very nearly cost him his job and, in the eyes of many observers, damaged President Jimmy Carter's quest for a second term.[4]

Of the early ambassadors—Edward Stettinius, 1946, Herschel Johnson 1946–1947, and Warren Austin, 1947–1953—only Senator Warren Austin's name rang a bell. During the UN Security Council's deliberations on the outbreak of war between the Arab states and Israel, he earned himself a place in history by his doleful appeal to Arabs and Jews to settle their differences "in the true Christian spirit."[5]

Gershman arrived wearing a rumpled jacket, scuffed brown shoes, and black horn-rimmed glasses of the type popular a decade ago, and looking more like the fiery young leader of some socialist cause than one active in diplomatic pursuits. Upstairs, on the eleventh floor, in the small waiting area outside the office reserved for the chief U.S. delegate to the United Nations, he introduced me to Joe Shattan, a portly younger fellow who spoke in bursts as if he did not have enough time to get his thoughts together. "Joe is supposed to write Jeane's speeches," Carl said. "That's if she ever lets me write a speech that she's prepared to use," Joe added.

They asked questions probing my views on the Arab-Israeli conflict, on U.S.-Soviet tensions, on my background in international law. In turn, I asked them about the other personnel at the Mission. They walked me around the eleventh-floor suite of ambassadorial offices. Ken Adelman, the deputy U.S. Permanent Representative, occupied the office adjacent to Kirkpatrick. Across the way was Chuck Lichenstein's office, a home away from home with pairs of polished shoes neatly lined up in shoe trees underneath a green leather sofa, and an assortment of ties lining the top of a corner chair next to a stack of laundered shirts. Chuck, said Carl, was an old friend of Kirkpatrick's and was responsible together with her for U.S. representation before the UN Security Council. He was about her age, mid-fifties.

Down the eleventh-floor corridor at the other end was the office of José Sorzano, its walls filled with original Norman Rockwell prints of family and community scenes embodying Roosevelt's Four Freedoms—freedom of worship, of speech, freedom from want, freedom from fear itself. Carl explained that José was around forty years old, had grown up in Havana, and had been a student of Kirkpatrick's at Georgetown before going on to join the political science faculty. At the mission he acted as the representative to ECOSOC, the Economic and Social Council. Bill Sherman, the only foreign service officer serving as one of the Mission's five ambassadors, had the office across from José and was in charge of General Assembly and Trusteeship Committee affairs. "And oh, yes," said Carl, "I nearly forgot Harvey Feldman. He's in the Washington office. He was formerly our Ambassador to Papua–New Guinea."

Twenty minutes later, Jeane Kirkpatrick arrived. Her right arm was folded up against her chest with half a dozen file folders, a yellow legal pad, and sheets of loose paper shooting out between. The shirttail of her white blouse, which she wore buttoned to the top under a blue serge suit, stuck out from a corner of her jacket. Her hair was blonde-gray, and cropped very short. She looked like an overburdened dean at a women's college.

She stood in the hallway continuing her conversation with a man in his sixties, kindly-looking, who I learned later was Bill Sherman. He had come to New York from Tokyo where he had served as DCM, the Deputy Chief of Mission. She turned to Carl and whispered, loud enough for me to hear, "Is that Allan Gerson?" Carl nodded. She extended her hand and invited me into her office.

Arranged neatly along the side of a black writing table were the latest issues of *Foreign Affairs*, *Political Science Review*, *Commentary*, and the French daily *Le Monde*. An assortment of manila file folders with the day's incoming cable traffic arranged by subject—Middle East, Disarmament, East-West, North-South Dialogue—lay neatly placed across the center. On top of them was a clipping from the *Jerusalem Post* international edition entitled "Joining the Jackals?"[6]

"Have you seen this?" she asked, catching my glance. I told her I had read it on the plane coming over from Israel. The title was a reference to Senator Daniel Patrick Moynihan's recent *Commentary* piece by that name, but without the question mark, in which he charged that the Carter administration, and in particular the State Department, had been complacent and indifferent to the anti-Israel campaign waged at the United Nations.[7] The *Jerusalem Post* article, noting that Kirkpatrick voted in favor of the resolution condemning Israel's raid on the Iraqi nuclear reactor, argued that she should have abstained. "Well, it's not true, not one word of it," she retorted. "In fact, if I may say so, I fought hard to delete the really bad language in that resolution when it first came up."

Then, lowering her voice to a near-hushed tone, she said: "The State Department wanted to keep the word 'aggression' in. Its Legal Adviser tried to convince me that Israel's bombing was a case of aggression. My lawyers here took the same position. That came as no surprise. Look, I'm not an international lawyer, but I studied with Harold Lasswell. I see that you went to Yale, so you know that he was Myres McDougal's partner in his treatises on international law. Lasswell believed in the importance of context, and so do I. If it takes one nuclear missile to wipe Israel off the map, and Iraq is developing the capacity to deliver such missiles, then context is not irrelevant. I negotiated to get the word 'aggression' deleted from the text of the Security Council resolution on the Osirak bombing incident. But I really couldn't do anything more. After getting 'aggression' out, we could hardly abstain from voting on the resolution. That would have made it appear that we were blessing the Israeli action, which we were not. I'm not at all sure, however, that what I have done is appreciated. What do you think?"

I was stunned that she would so immediately take me into her confidence, be so adamant in describing the Israeli bombing as reasonable, and take such pains to avoid being misunderstood by Israel's supporters. "What do you think?" she asked again, the words sounding now more like a command than a query.

I told her that it was hard to conceive of other countries in similar circumstances acting much differently; that, viewed from the vantage point of international law, had she not deleted "aggression" from the resolution, Iraq could have claimed that it had the UN's sanction to redress the consequences of the "aggression" by any means it chose. As to the *Jerusalem Post* article, I doubted, I said, that it represented anything more than the views of a junior staffer or copy editor bent on a catchy title. The fine nuances between being condemned for "aggression" or merely violation of the principles of international law might become lost to some of Israel's supporters, but surely it was a distinction that anyone familiar with the political dimension of the conflict recognized.

A door opened from a side entrance in the right corner of the room. Ken Adelman, the Deputy U.S. Representative, sauntered in. "Hi, Jeane," he said. "Thought I'd check to see what's happening."

"I'd appreciate it if you'd knock first." Whatever it was that bonded them was not immediately apparent. If she was cast as high sobriety, his first appearance was that of the jester. Ken waved good-bye and, with a lilt in his voice, said, "Catch you another time."

"Allan," she said then, "I'd like you to get acquainted with the legal staff here. Bob Rosenstock and Herb Reis have each been here for over 15 years. Why don't you come back and see me when you're done talking with them. I'm taking the 5 o'clock shuttle back to Washington. You can come along and go out to the airport with me, if that's a convenient time for you. The limo ought to be taking me at 4:25."

"Isn't that cutting it pretty close to the wire?" I asked.

"That's the way I like it," she answered.

On the seventh floor, Herb Reis, the Counselor for Legal Affairs to the Mission, occupied a spacious corner office. A green leather sofa and chair, standard government issue for mid-level bureaucrats, were in one corner. In front of them was a small brown wooden cocktail table; to the right of his desk was an American flag; to the left the blue flag of the United Nations; and all along the side stood rows of file cabinets with combination locks and red magnetic plates marked "Secret." Two long bookcases were crammed with the Marjorie Whiteman 21-volume *Digest of International Law*, various UN publications, legal treatises, texts, and stacks of reports. To the right of his desk hung a large map in raised relief of Israel and the Arab world. The office had the look of having been lived in for a long time.

Our discussion turned to the recent U.S. vote in favor of the UN Security Council resolution condemning Israel's bombing of the Iraqi nuclear reactor. Reis, a slender man in his early fifties who spoke in a high voice, said: "We advised her on that." Speaking as someone who considered himself a friend of Israel, he added that we dare not shy away from condemning the country when its actions are indefensible under international law. This led to a recitation, chapter and verse, of Article 51 of the UN Charter as permitting the use of force in self-defense only in response to an actual "armed attack" in the language of that Article.

"Is it reasonable," I asked, "to demand that a state wait until it is hit with a nuclear bomb before it may respond? Who would abide by such a standard? Doesn't the right of self-defense have to be measured against the gravity of the risk of inaction, the nature of the provocation, and the likelihood that the other party would in fact resort to terrible weapons of mass destruction? Or am I way off in thinking this?"

He thought I was "way off." This had nothing to do with disagreement over the facts. There was no disagreement between us that Iraq had developed the capability to make weapon-grade plutonium, and that Israel's calls for stopping production had been ignored. The issue was what the law required in such circumstances. For Reis the law was very clear, and had to be taken literally.

I bristled at the suggestion that the law was all that clear. Trial experience had taught me the perils of faith in the certainty of law. In litigation one could never be sure of the final judicial pronouncement. In international law, certainty was an even rarer commodity. Judges and judgments were few and far between. In the forty years of its existence, the International Court of Justice in the Hague had adjudicated only one case involving the use of force by states—its 1949 decision in the Corfu Channel dispute between Albania and Great Britain. Notions of international law appeared to be based more on argumentative assertions than on judicial pronouncements.[8] Thoughts about what international law ought to be became confusingly intermingled with what it actually was. The encounter between Herb Reis and myself did not augur well for the future.

Down the hall from Herb Reis' office was that of his colleague, Bob Rosenstock, the then Deputy Legal Counsel to the U.S. delegation. A half hour with Rosenstock made clear that he not only shared Reis' convictions fully, but that he was a more articulate and formidable advocate. Terrific, I said to myself, what am I getting into?

At 4:20 P.M., I caught up with Kirkpatrick as she dashed to the eleventh-floor elevator for her limousine outside the Mission's entrance for a sprint to La Guardia airport.

"Well," she asked, "what did you think of Herb Reis and Bob Rosenstock?" Then, before I could respond, "Oh yes, I should introduce you," she said, turning to the woman standing next to her in the elevator, "Marian Christy is a reporter from the *Boston Globe*. She's been trying to do an interview with me. We started upstairs but there was no time to finish so I asked if she would like to continue it on the way to the airport. We'll have a chance, Allan, to talk later on the plane."

I hopped into the limousine. Marian Christy squeezed into the center between Kirkpatrick and myself. Later, she wrote up that trip in a piece which succeeded in capturing the spirit of the moment:

New York. July 19, 1981. Is it possible to have an intelligent conversation with Jeane Kirkpatrick, United States Ambassador to the United Nations, while she is being whizzed to La Guardia at the height of late day traffic, flanked by two bodyguards and a male staffer, all of us squeezed into a chauffered Cadillac, fighting tricky Manhattan traffic, trying to get the ambassador to the White House party, on time?

What begins tensely, awkwardly as an interview in her private office, continues in a speeding car and ends at Eastern Air Lines shuttle at La Guardia.

The way it was:

The promised hour interview, in the works for weeks, is already running an hour late and, according to a U.N. aide, if it happens at all, it will be ten minutes duration. *Ten minutes?* Yes, and during the ten minutes, the ambassador will be going through stacks of files, deciding what papers will be "highly classified," what papers she will put in her briefcase. Ambassador Kirkpatrick will, in other words, be doing several things at one time.

The ambassador, who is multilingual, uses time well, uses her mind well, communicates well. This is evident as I watch her juggling the tardy 10 minute office-interview with sophisticated aplomb, simultaneously considering questions floating from in front of her desk and studying reports covering her desk. She is arranging papers in neat piles.

Ambassador, are you a fatalist? What are you, a registered Democrat, doing in Ronald Reagan's cabinet?

"Fatalist? No, no, not at all," she is saying, looking down at papers, scribbling little notes in the corners. "One's life is shaped by factors that one can control and a few that one cannot control. Success is a good deal of hard work and a little luck. Luck? Of course I believe in luck. Yes, my entry into this job was luck." She is still shuffling papers, still looking down.

"I had written an article on dictatorships" ["Dictatorships and Double Standards," *Commentary*, November 1987], she is saying. "Ronald Reagan was gearing up for his campaign. He liked what I wrote. Now suppose I had written the piece six months later? Probably I wouldn't have this appointment. Yes, there was an element of chance here. But it was not a chance that I wrote the article!"

We are going down on the elevator now, the minutes fading, the interview about to come to an untimely end. She is flanked by security officers but she is carrying her own briefcase.

Ambassador, you are a complex woman, a forthright woman, a woman who has shocked people with your frankness, your bluntness. But, ambassador, you are in the world of politics. No one really expects a politician to be frank, to be honest.

"Well," she says, smiling, a look of comprehension crossing her face, a face devoid of any artificiality, not even lipstick. "I have a habit of frankness and I have not broken the habit. Ever. I express myself very clearly, getting directly to the point. I suppose, yes, I am not in an arena of people who do that. I am not tactless. But I do not leave important things unsaid."

You once said that you have no drive. . . .

"I've had powerful interests all my life," she is saying. "Great intellectual interests. And I have pursued those interests. But compelling drive? No. I simply arranged my career around my interests. I have a deep, deep desire to understand political, social, cultural problems. And I'm terribly interested in writing. Things have fallen into place. I've never had any great secret ambitions. People ask me how I got to this point, to this job, to this achievement. Well, I don't have the foggiest notion."

Why, then, Ambassador, did you agree to take the job, knowing you'd have to be in New York, your husband in Washington? A moment ago, you told me that you hardly have time to talk to each other. Was it for the money? Was it for the prestige?

"Money! My take home pay is substantially less than what I was getting before this job. That's a fair question. Why do I pay the

price to hold this job? Well, when I got the job, a friend congratulated me, actually we congratulated ourselves because we,
the both of us, hardly ever did anything we didn't like to do. But
there is only one reason, one, that I am doing this work. It's not
the status perks, the prestige perks. I think it's my duty. I have
a demanding conception of citizenship. I have an obligation to
confront serious problems, to use whatever means are at my
disposal to strengthen this democracy."

*You are described as a workaholic and, from this time spent
with you, the picture fits.*

"Next to having children, work gives meaning to your life. I
told you that I am an existentialist. I like being in a job where
you have to think clearly. You build meaning for yourself by
committing yourself. Work is a way to do that. My fundamental
passion is to understand things, to figure things out. It's all part
of human history, how people live, how people organize their
lives."

The car is edging up to the airline. Suddenly the car is there,
at the curb, the bodyguards opening doors, gathering luggage
wordlessly. It is all very quick, very efficient, very natural. There
is only a split second to say goodbye, to say thank you, to say the
ride was a revelation.[9]

Marian Christy was taken by her interviewee. So was I. Her
openness was infectious. By the time we boarded the Eastern shuttle
for Washington, I felt as if I had known her for some time.

As the airplane made its ascent, Kirkpatrick, staring out the
window at the late afternoon light, said it reminded her of the lumi-
nescent quality of the air of Provence in southern France where she
vacationed each summer. I belonged, I told her, to a clan of people—
photographers—who worship this type of light. "That's very interest-
ing," she said and then turned back to my meetings with Reis and
Rosenstock.

"You mean to say, don't you," she said, after I gave her a run-
down of what had transpired, and my reactions to it, "that you thought
Rosenstock and Reis' views of international law to be unsophisticated?"

I supposed, I said, that "unsophisticated" was as good a way as
any of summing up my reaction. I tended to view the law as much
more complex, and as more adaptable. I believed in the importance

of context and gave less weight to UN resolutions, especially those of the General Assembly, as "law" by which the United States should consider itself bound. "And what's more," I said, "what they tend to see as black, I tend to see as white."

At that point, she leaned over her pile of file folders and pulled out from among them a copy of a signed letter addressed by her to Attorney General William French Smith. It was typed on stationery embossed with the seal of "the U.S. Permanent Representative to the United Nations."

"What do you think of it?" she asked, handing me the letter. It read essentially as follows:

Dear Bill,

The UN Secretariat has asked the U.S. Mission, in its capacity as Host Country to the UN, to agree to permit the entry into the United States of additional PLO representatives for the purpose of increasing the size of the PLO Observer Mission in New York. If we agree to this request it would mean a two-fold increase in the PLO's current representation from two to four permanently accredited delegates. This does not affect the standing of the dozen or so other PLO officials who regularly come to New York to attend General Assembly sessions on a non-permanent basis.

I understand that in signing the 1945 UN Headquarters Agreement, the United States reserved the right to refuse entry to individuals on grounds of national security. The legal staff at the U.S. Mission and the State Department's Legal Adviser have informed me we cannot deny the PLO's request on these grounds and that to do so would violate our legal obligations under the UN Headquarters Agreement.

I believe that U.S. national security considerations may not have been sufficiently taken into account in reaching this conclusion. Because U.S. national security interests are in fact affected by the disposition of this matter, I am forwarding it to you for review by the Justice Department, which may be inclined to take a more sympathetic view of these considerations.

I appreciate your help.

Jeane J. Kirkpatrick

enc. USUN Memorandum
of Law on PLO Observer Mission

I looked at the attachment. It was initialed by her legal staff in New York. Its conclusion: that the United States, as a matter of law, was precluded from denying the PLO's request.

"Well, Ambassador Kirkpatrick . . ."

"Call me Jeane," she demanded.

I told her that it was rather unusual to send a letter with this type of attachment to the Justice Department. I had worked at the Justice Department for the last several years. Before joining the Office of Special Investigations in 1979, I had done appellate litigation handling cases on behalf of various US agencies and departments that had lost at the district court level and were requesting appeal of that decision. We would receive, I told her, letters from agency heads with attached memoranda of law prepared by their subordinates arguing in favor of appeal. This was, I said, the first time I had seen a letter enclosing a memorandum of law that diametrically opposed the position of the principal.

"But that's my problem," she said. "That's why I need you, Allan. What I would appreciate from you is a legal memorandum in support of my position. The matter will probably be going up to Secretary Haig for a final decision, and I'd like to attach your memorandum."

"When do you need it?" I asked.

"Wednesday morning. You can take it to my assistant, Jackie Tillman, at the State Department. She'll make sure to get it to me in New York."

"That only gives me tomorrow. That's not much lead time."

"That's all the time I have. Now, there must be questions that you have to ask me. Here's your chance."

I did have a question in mind: Why, why was she doing this, why was she so unwilling to let the matter rest and so insistent on trying to get the Attorney General involved in a matter on which the State Department appeared to have already made up its mind against her? She was new to the job. Why didn't she just roll with the punches? It couldn't be that she alone in the Administration perceived the PLO as a key sponsor of terrorism around the globe. The Administration was plainly concerned about terrorism. Secretary of State Alexander Haig had repeatedly affirmed that fighting international terrorism was at the top of the U.S. foreign-policy agenda, and he had linked the PLO to the growth of terrorism. Why, I asked myself, was it that important to her that on this particular issue—where, even with the doubling of the size of the PLO Observer

Mission there would still be only four permanently accredited PLO representatives—she fight so hard? Was there, I wondered, something about Kirkpatrick's concern that went beyond the others'? Was it that she saw herself as more capable than those others of divining the will of the President she served—a view which saw the PLO's interests as incompatible with those of the United States, or was there something more to it, some personal fear or distrust that spurred her on? I thought back to a conversation I had with Dick Schifter the day before flying off to New York to meet with her.

Richard Schifter, a prominent Washington attorney, had known Kirkpatrick for nearly twenty years. He had been her ward leader in Montgomery County, Maryland Democratic politics, and in March of 1981 had been asked by her to serve on the U.S. delegation to the UN Human Rights Commission in Geneva. I asked Schifter if he might tell me a little bit about Kirkpatrick in advance of my meeting. Schifter told me of a conversation he had had with her when the Geneva post was suggested. "Dick, I just want you to know," she had said, "that I think the Holocaust is possible again. I didn't think so before I came to the UN, but I think so now."

What had led her to that conclusion? The answer might enable me to better deal with her concerns about the expansion of the PLO Observer Mission. So I asked her about what she had told Dick Schifter in that conversation. I received a long answer. Long answers were, I learned, her style.

"Well, first of all, because my name is Jeane Kirkpatrick many delegates open up to me in ways that they might not to Dick Schifter. In any event, it didn't take me long to learn that there are certain assumptions that are routinely made here and that are considered bad form to question otherwise. I learned this during the Security Council's consideration last month of Israel's' cross-border attack on PLO installations in southern Lebanon. No one denied that the PLO had fired first, sending rockets into Israel's northernmost town of Kiryat Shmona. But in the UN context, Israel was not permitted to fire back. It reminded me of the story in Pinocchio when he goes to the policeman and says, 'They robbed me,' and the policeman grabs him and takes him before a magistrate who gives him one month in a jail. 'I'll teach you to make trouble,' he says.

"The notion that victims cannot protest an injustice and have to end up acquiescing in it, the realization that there is a tacit understanding at the UN that victims can be blamed for disturbing others—this notion gripped me. Both because I was new and interested in learning the institutional culture as part of my socialization here and because they—the Europeans and our other friends—were eager to explain it to me, I learned quickly that they viewed Israel as a terrible embarrassment and nuisance. I don't mind telling you that some of the Americans in the U.S. Mission weren't very different. I would come to understand, they said, what Israelis are really like once I see them in operation at the UN. They had no hesitation in expressing to me their really negative feelings about Israel's ambassador, Yehuda Blum. You see, they were all confident that I would share them. Well, the juxtaposition of these views defining Israel as the offender and condemning it for defending itself, and the passivity and silence of everyone in the Security Council when confronted with outrageously unfair charges against Israel, shocked me. It was a very big shock. It was nothing that I was prepared for. And I guess that's what made me comment as I did to Dick Schifter. I still believe that."

And then she told me of another shock she received upon her arrival at the United Nations, that one Arab ambassador after another took her aside and spoke of Israel as a "Crusader remnant," as if it were a matter of time until Israel would disappear, expedited no doubt by their actions in New York at the United Nations. Thus, granting the request for enlargement of the PLO Observer Mission would, as she saw it, be another battle won toward making Israel a "Crusader remnant." It became patently clear from listening to her that she believed that neither her lawyers at the Mission nor at the State Department shared her stark vision; or if they did, that they didn't care much about it.

When I asked her why she hadn't simply taken her lawyers' advice and let matters rest there, she responded: "It's that I have a very powerful sense that a large number of people at the Mission and the State Department don't really approach issues from the viewpoint of U.S. interests and American policies, values, and concerns. My concern, to answer your question, is about the assumptions and commitments of people who represent the United States on UN matters. As they interpret it, there seems to be nothing that can be demanded of us that cannot be justified by the UN Headquarters Agreement. But the Headquarters Agreement also left the United States with rights. I'm concerned about this proclivity to bend over backwards to accommodate the demands of others. It's as if we are constantly prepared to place UN concerns over our own, to give more weight to obligations than rights given us under the Charter. That's why I am looking for a legal adviser who is ready to take account of American interests, who can analyze issues from a perspective that takes into account the legitimate interests of the American people. I know that's considered by many to be a very obnoxious concept. But my function, as I see it, is to represent the interests of the United States to the United Nations and not the other way around."

Later that evening I told my wife, Joan, about my meeting with Kirkpatrick: "She takes her job seriously, that's for sure. She's concerned about speaking out forcefully on behalf of U.S. interests. She's also very concerned about fair treatment for Israel. I like her, I like her a lot, but she has her problems. She is trying to buck the State Department. I don't get the impression that she's altogether comfortable with her deputy. And she's off to a running battle with her legal advisers."

"Where would you fit in?" Joan asked.

"Right in the middle. At first she mentioned she wanted me on the eleventh floor, the ambassadorial suite; then she talked of having me on the tenth floor instead, where the Political Section is housed, so that I could keep track of developments there as well. She doesn't trust anyone. All I know is that wherever it will be, it won't be an easy fit."

"What about moving?" she said. "If you were to take the job, doesn't it mean that we'd have to relocate to New York?"

I had asked about that, I told Joan, and what Kirkpatrick seemed to have in mind was that I play a role that would take me beyond New York to troubleshooting in Washington, to being based in the State Department part of the week, and also to serving as a liaison with Congress; that it would all be part of her ambition to revolutionize U.S. relations with the UN by institutionalizing a new relationship between Congress and the United Nations so that it would begin to take notice of what occurred there. "What do you think?" I asked.

"Sounds like you've already made up your mind," she answered.

Joan was right. In the limousine that afternoon on the way to the airport, hearing Kirkpatrick tell me that she believed it her duty to try to help "strengthen this democracy," I had made up my mind. I believed in what she was saying. She was prepared to take the UN very seriously, to view it as a forum in which U.S. national interests were affected. She was prepared to give it her all. But was she competent? She had the vision, but could she carry it through to fruition? I had my doubts. But of course I would join her. I could do no less. And I had my first assignment cut out for me: to help her stop the expansion of the PLO Observer Mission. The odds didn't look promising.

3

The PLO "Observer" Mission

Up Against the Bureaucratic Wall

We are expressing our faith in political and diplomatic struggle as complements, as enhancements of armed struggle.

Yasser Arafat addressing the UN General Assembly, November 13, 1974

The next morning, on the way up the marble steps to the U.S. Supreme Court library—open to those admitted to practice before the court—I worried about what I had gotten myself into. Earlier I had called Kirkpatrick to accept her offer. Now, thinking about my first assignment, it looked as though I was heading for a long uphill battle.

At best, the State Department seemed indifferent to her concerns. Her lawyers at the U.S. Mission—USUN—were supposed to report to her. In outlook, in shared expectations, and in regularity of communications the lawyers were integrated into the State Department system. She was the outsider, linked only to the President. She was the maverick who was expected to keep her instincts in check. If she had a special way of interpreting President Reagan's wishes, no one seemed to want to know about it. Unlike the permanent State Department, she had not come up the hard way, disciplined through a succession of minor consular posts, third secretary positions, desk

duty, and deputy assistant deputy slots before earning her ambassadorial stripes. What could she know of global politics? Of the importance of continuity in U.S. foreign policy?

Her desire to curb the growth of PLO influence at the UN was
in itself seen as shortsighted. It hadn't taken account of the reaction
of our allies, and whether we could count on their support. It hadn't
shown an appreciation of the diplomatic costs, the decline it would
cause in U.S. standing in the Arab world. It discounted the will of the
"international community" which had been wholeheartedly supporting the PLO ascent to power. Besides, her position on the PLO, and
the lengths to which she had gone to see it implemented, ignored the
advice of her lawyers at the Mission and those at the State Department; they had warned her that international law required the U.S.
Government to grant the PLO's request.

She had turned to Attorney General William French Smith for
help. She had talked to him in the past about this issue in particular,
and also on the problem of terrorism generally. Nevertheless, it was
a leap of faith to believe he could, or would, do much at this point to
influence the course of events. The Justice Department had little
interest or influence in international affairs, and no desire for a fracas
with the State Department. Once, the Justice Department controlled
most U.S. litigation before international tribunals, as well as U.S.
representation at the International Court of Justice in the Hague.
Over the last several years, however, the Justice Department had
allowed control to shift to the State Department. In 1985, when the
Iran-hostage case made its way to the International Court, it was the
State Department's Legal Adviser, and not the U.S. Attorney General, who was the principal representative before the Court.[1] Attorney General William French Smith complained about this to the
White House. In a letter to President Reagan's Counselor, Edwin E.
Meese III, he charged that he had been outflanked and that control
of the case should be in the hands of the Justice Department. But by
then it was too late. The State Department had taken control of
litigation in the World Court.

In tackling my assignment, I began at the beginning: the legislation enacted shortly after the establishment of the United Nations,
the UN Participation Act of 1945.[2] It defined the power and authority
of the U.S. Mission to the United Nations. Perhaps, I hoped, it would
give me a clue to what I was looking for: a legal basis for preventing
the expansion of the PLO's UN Observer Mission.

It was not simply that this was my first assignment; nor was it a wish to please my client that fueled my search for a valid basis for denial of the PLO's request. It was something which ran much deeper. I felt then that the PLO was part of the problem—not the solution. In my book, *Israel, the West Bank, and International Law* (my published doctoral dissertation) I had written in 1978: "Self-determination for the West Bank is a necessary condition for a just resolution of the Arab-Israeli conflict. The difficulty lies in achieving this goal without running the risk of either a PLO-controlled state, or a Palestinian West Bank canton which is autonomous in name only."[3]

That was my considered conclusion then, after much time spent on the West Bank and years spent in wrestling with the problem. And it was what I believed in 1981. I thought that the Carter Administration approach in brokering the Camp David Accords between Egypt and Israel was right. That scheme called for an interim solution, a period of local autonomy. Under it the residents of the West Bank and Gaza would have some measure of self-rule.[4] After a period of five years, this might lead to a breakthrough, perhaps even to discussions with the PLO, for the final resolution of those territories. But first the PLO had to renounce its commitment to solving the problem through "armed struggle," here meaning targeting civilians—terrorism—and not recognizing the legitimacy of Israel's right to exist. In 1981, when I came on board, the PLO denounced this approach entirely.

So did the UN General Assembly. It was phrased nicely; it opposed the Camp David Accords because they contemplated a "unilateral approach" to a problem that could only be solved through multilateral means. Behind that pleasantry, however, was the fact that in the summer of 1981 the PLO, and its most radical contingents, was the darling of the UN, embraced by its two major blocs—the NAM, or Non-Aligned Movement, and the Soviet/Eastern European bloc—who together with the Arab bloc pushed the PLO's cause. The Palestinians, above all other groups or peoples in the world, had come to symbolize the just struggle for self-determination.

That it was time to check the explosive growth of PLO influence at the United Nations, and that it was in the national interest to do so, was something about which I had no doubt. It was consonant with the anti-terrorism policy which President Reagan had announced as a key plank of his foreign policy program. Moreover, it seemed patently clear that events at the United Nations mirrored and shaped power realities in the world beyond its walls. Thus, in the absence of an airtight legal obligation to grant the additional PLO visas, I saw no reason for the U.S. government to sit idly by while they advanced their agenda at the United Nations.

The trouble was that Kirkpatrick didn't leave me with much time. I had all of one day, and knew no one that I could call on for help. Besides, it seemed to me that this was a matter that ought to be treated as confidential, although I wasn't yet officially back on the government payroll.

The UN Participation Act provided some help, but not much. Reflecting the high hopes and importance Congress and the American people first attached to the United Nations, the Act conferred on individuals appointed to the rank of U.S. Ambassador to the United Nations significantly greater authority than that accorded all other ambassadors. Others were required to report to and receive instructions from the Secretary of State. The U.S. Ambassador to the United Nations was to report directly to and receive instructions from the President "as might be transmitted through the Secretary of State."[5]

This was significant. It meant that as Ambassador to the United Nations, Jeane Kirkpatrick, as a matter of law, had powers exceeding those of any other U.S. ambassador. That fact might, I noted, prove useful should Kirkpatrick ever wish to challenge Secretary Haig's decisions as they affected her responsibilities at the United Nations. I had heard rumors that they did not get along with each other and that there was even some personal acrimony between them. But were she now to go on this issue to the President she would, it seemed, be fighting a losing battle. Even her own lawyers were lined up against her. Of course, if Attorney General Smith, who technically was the President's chief legal adviser on international as well as domestic matters, weighed in on her behalf, that might tip the scales in her favor. But his intervention seemed highly unlikely. The matter seemed to rest on whatever legal basis I could find by the end of the day.

I turned to the United Nations Headquarters Agreement of 1947, to see how it affected U.S. relations with the United Nations. Article 11(5) of the Agreement imposes on the United States the obligation, as host country, not to impede transit to and from UN Headquarters by "persons invited to the Headquarters District by the United Nations." To drive the point home, the next article (12) provides that hostile relations between the United States and invited states do not provide an exception to the rule. These were the articles relied on by State's Legal Adviser and the attorneys at the Mission.

The question I was left to ponder was whether these provisions necessarily governed.

Kirkpatrick had mentioned "national security considerations" in
her letter to the Attorney General. And there it was, Article 6 of
Annex 2 to the UN Headquarters Agreement: Where the host country has reason to object to the entry of a UN delegate on the basis of
risk to its own security, it may reject entry upon consultation with the
UN Secretary General.

But what risk, I asked myself, does accreditation of two additional PLO delegates pose to U.S. national security? Were the PLO
to send a known terrorist, someone who had actually planted bombs
and maimed or killed, and might do so in Coney Island, Minneapolis
or somewhere else in the U.S., then neither the State Department
nor the Secretary-General would have the slightest compunction
about finding a way to keep that individual out. But the PLO wasn't
that stupid; it was not about to send a known bomb-thrower as one of
its representatives at the United Nations. Undoubtedly, the new
representatives' records would reveal that they were as suave, well-
mannered, polished and nonviolent as most other UN delegates.

Perhaps, I thought, there was a way to argue that the individual
qualities of the new PLO delegates—whether or not they were bomb-
throwing terrorists—was totally beside the point; that the point was
that the PLO itself was a terrorist organization. Seen in this light any
bolstering of the PLO as an organization would run contrary to U.S.
national security considerations. But I doubted that argument would
fly. For all the Reagan Administration's rhetoric before and after the
campaign about getting tough with terrorists, I knew that the State
Department, if asked by a U.S. court or by the United Nations
whether it considered the PLO a terrorist organization, would say, as
it had under the Carter Administration, that the PLO was "an um-
brella organization which contains within it terrorist elements." Perhaps the Reagan Administration would take a stronger, less equivocal
position, but this did not look like the issue to force its hand. The
most the Reagan Administration seemed prepared to do then was to
exclude individual PLO members who were terrorists.

By noon I still had not developed an argument. "National security considerations" appeared to be too thin a reed on which to hang
our case. The provision, I concluded, related to threats to U.S. security within the United States, not to threats to U.S. national interests abroad. For a moment I toyed with the notion that the fact that
an expansion of the PLO presence in New York would engender

violent demonstrations from radical pro-Israel groups might provide a legal argument. But that strained the law beyond its limits. The law envisioned a curb on U.S. exclusion rights except where individuals applying for a visa posed a direct threat to the security of U.S. installations or to persons within the United States, and that simply did not seem to be the case here.

I returned to the stacks, retrieved an annotated copy of the UN Charter and read its provisions on UN membership. It contained no reference to observer mission status; it addressed only the admission of states to membership.[6] It also addressed the possibility, in rare circumstances, of expulsion of a member state on a finding by the UN Security Council that it was unwilling to abide by the generally accepted standards of international law set out in the UN Charter.[7] Observer status was a later invention of the UN General Assembly. The practice began at the inception of the organization with regard to Switzerland but it was first formally accorded by the United Nations only in 1963 to the Holy See, and then to North Korea in 1972. In all, I discovered, there were 14 states or entities that had observer status in 1981, including North and South Korea, Monaco, Switzerland, and Vatican City (the Holy See), as well as the Asian-African Legal Consultative Committee, the Council for Mutual Economic Assistance, the European Community, the League of Arab States, the Organization of African Unity, the Organization of American States, the Organization of the Islamic Conference, the PLO, and SWAPO, the South West Africa People's Organization.

The PLO obtained observer status on October 14, 1974, when it was invited by the General Assembly to participate in "the deliberations of the General Assembly on the question of Palestine."[8] The United States voted against that resolution on the ground that the PLO had little to contribute to the search for peace in the Middle-East; rather, that it was the responsibility of Israel and its Arab neighbors to negotiate peace according to the terms spelled out in Security Council resolutions 242 of 1967 and 338 of 1973. Moreover, as the United States viewed it, it was the Security Council, not the General Assembly, that provided the venue for serious discussions aimed at breaking the logjam in the Arab-Israeli conflict. This view was echoed by Ambassador Waldo E. Waldron-Ramsey of Barbados who declared that "the General Assembly is certainly not the place for settlement of the Palestinian question. . . . nowhere in the history of human conflict was a peace treaty elaborated and signed as a result of a vote taken by the parties not involved and their allies." Nor did Ambassador Waldron-Ramsey resort to euphemism in describing the PLO's ambitions; he characterized its vision of "any settlement of the Palestine question [as one] which contemplates the destruction of Israel as a State."[9]

One month later, on November 13, 1974, Yasser Arafat, chairman of the PLO, arrived to address the UN General Assembly. In September 1959, Soviet premier Nikita Khrushchev had come to the UN General Assembly, removed one of his shoes and used it as a gavel in an effort to stifle debate on an item he found disagreeable.[10] Arafat's contribution to changing styles was his neatly pressed battle dress with a holster on his hip. The message he delivered matched his choice of attire: in addressing the General Assembly he said, "We are expressing our faith in political and diplomatic struggle as complements, as enhancements of armed struggle."[11] It was a repeat of the message that had been delivered a few days earlier, at the close of the General Assembly's 1974 debate on the Question of Palestine, by the PLO's "foreign minister," Faruq Kaddumi: "We did not come here," he said, "to seek reconciliation with the Zionist terrorists and usurpers. We came here to bear witness to the historic differences between us and the Zionists. We regard diplomatic activities as a complement to our activities on the battlefield."[12] Arafat's speech in the Assembly hall occasioned another first: the vast majority of the delegates that had come to hear him rose to their feet to offer him a thunderous ovation. Flushed with the victory of seeing his views embraced by the United Nations, Arafat clasped his hands over his head to acknowledge the cheers of his audience.

The following year, on November 10, 1975, the General Assembly extended the terms of the invitation to the PLO to "participate in the efforts for peace in the Middle East" and "in all efforts, deliberations and conferences on the Middle East which are held under the auspices of the United Nations."[13] That same day the General Assembly, by a vote of 67 nations in favor, 55 opposed, and with 15 abstentions, voted to condemn Zionism "as a form of racism," and thus Israel as an inherently racist state.[14] And, in looking over the records of that day I learned that it was also on November 10, 1975, that the General Assembly, by a vote of 93 to 18 with 27 abstentions, elected to establish a Committee on the Exercise of the Inalienable Rights of the Palestinian People. The United States voted against both resolutions on the ground that they would take the United Nations further away from, rather than toward, a peaceful solution to the Arab-Israeli conflict.[15]

It took no gifts of prophecy to conclude from even a cursory review of the terms of the PLO's admission to observer status at the United Nations that the last thing either the PLO or the majority of the UN members expected was for the PLO to take a back seat as a quiet witness to events, "observing," and responding only when called upon to do so. An examination of the record of PLO activities at the United Nations since becoming an observer mission revealed how little "observing" the PLO did. In nearly every UN forum it had sought to make its presence known and to turn the subject under discussion into a basis for condemning Israel. It was clearly a very different observer mission than that of the Holy See or Switzerland.

Here lay the basis for my argument. It would rest on the context and general purposes of the law, rather than strict construction of black-letter provisions, on the supposition that the spirit breathes life, and the letter killeth. In international law circles, this approach was dubbed the "Yale Law School" method, named after Professor Myres S. McDougal who had emphasized the need for contextual analysis: for examining what purposes would be served by construing legislation in a particular way, which values would be furthered, whether those purposes or values were envisioned by the drafters of the legislation, and whether intervening circumstances had forced a change in those assumptions.[16] Critics of this approach said that it reminded them of the adage that when lawyers have the law on their side they argue the law; when the law is not on their side they argue the facts; and that when neither the law nor the facts are on their side they argue context and general purposes.

The key question, as I saw it, was whether enlargement of PLO UN representation, a doubling of its number, was necessary to fulfill the General Assembly's purpose in inviting PLO participation: to contribute to the search for a peaceful solution to the Arab-Israeli conflict. The record of UN activities in which the PLO had been participating revealed a long list of involvement in issues that had nothing to do with the purpose of the General Assembly's invitation: women's rights, disarmament, development, North-South dialogue, and so on. I could now argue that as the PLO Observer Mission already had more than enough manpower to fulfill the needs which the General Assembly had in mind in extending its initial invitation, there was no reason to permit a doubling of its size.

I reviewed the evidence I had marshalled. Since 1974 when Arafat was accorded the treatment due a head of state, the PLO had become the first nongovernmental organization permitted to address a plenary session of the General Assembly, the first to be welcomed as a permanent observer, and the first to demand a desk and a microphone instead of being seated in the theater seats on the side of the General Assembly hall like the other observer missions. It had succeeded in establishing within the UN Secretariat a Special Unit on Palestinian Rights and within two years had made its presence felt in nearly every UN organ and conference, transforming them into arenas for attacks on Israel. The only places where its efforts at gaining observer status seemed to have been successfully rebuffed were the International Monetary Fund and the World Bank. The leaders of these institutions perceived that Palestine and the world's monetary systems were separate subjects, and had the courage to act on their convictions. Everywhere else the problem of Palestine and problems of health care, development, women's issues, space exploration, or whatever seemed to become inextricably meshed.

The PLO was not a state, although it was treated as the equivalent. Yet if one looked at "context," it became clear that all the obligations and rights referred to in the UN Headquarters Agreement and other key legislative documents dealing with the purposes and intended functioning of the United Nations revolved around the idea that it was to be an organization of states. The record also revealed that the United States through successive administrations repeatedly stressed the importance of not treating the PLO as a member state.[17] But this was precisely the aim of the PLO: to be accorded the attributes of a state, all the privileges with none of the obligations. The PLO seemed to have gotten its way.

By late afternoon, using one of the two large manual typewriters that the U.S. Supreme Court library provides as a service to its users, I had prepared a memorandum of law arguing against enlargement of the PLO Observer Mission. "There appear," I said at the outset, "to be reasonable arguments [I could not say more than that] for denial, consistent with the United States commitments under the UN Headquarters Agreement, of the PLO request for issuance of visas for additional members to its UN Observer Mission."

Quoting from a report of the highly respected International Law Commission, a committee of jurists that meets annually under UN auspices in Geneva in an attempt to codify existing international law, I wrote that observer missions' representation must, in the words of the Commission, be "limited to specific purposes" relating to the circumstances of its invitation."[18] The role of the PLO observer mission was limited by the General Assembly to participation in Middle-

East peacemaking efforts. Moreover, the PLO's role was additionally circumscribed by the fact that, unlike observer missions of non-member states, the PLO represented neither a government nor a state. Tested by this standard, an examination of PLO activities within the UN since 1975 revealed that the PLO observer mission had gone beyond its mandate. Here I cited the PLO's participation in debates on human rights in Chile, the UN and the environment, international civil aviation, the UN conference on human settlements, Habitat, women's rights, rights to development, the independence of colonial countries, Namibia, and South Africa's apartheid policy.[19] Therefore, as the PLO's present mission size enabled it to devote substantial portions of its time to activities far beyond the sphere for which it was invited, increasing its representation would, I concluded, be inconsistent with the terms of its invitation.

Of course, there was nothing to prevent the United General Assembly from introducing and passing a new resolution the next day expanding the terms of the PLO's invitation to participate in UN functions, but they couldn't make it a member state. If the UN wished to challenge the determination by the United States not to grant the additional visas, it was free to do so, either by invoking compulsory arbitration provisions under the terms of the Headquarters Agreement, or by passing General Assembly resolutions widening the scope of the PLO's power to participate. In any event, the United States would have made the point that it was committed to the elimination of the scourge of international terrorism, that it viewed the PLO as playing a leading if not commanding role in that enterprise, and that independent legal considerations justified denial of the visa request.

That afternoon, on my way to see Kirkpatrick's executive assistant, Jackie Tillman, with my memorandum in hand, I still couldn't shake the thought of why Kirkpatrick was so determined on this issue. As far as I could tell, were she to go along with the State Department recommendation and that of her own lawyers for issuance of the visas, no one would so much as turn his head. To be sure, there might be a relatively low-level complaint by Israel or by pro-Israel supporters in Congress, but it wouldn't be directed at her personally. This seemed too small an event to attract much notice, and, even if it did, there was always the fallback argument that the U.S. Government's hands were tied by treaty obligations to the United Nations.

On the other hand, opposition to the recommendations of State Department lawyers and her own was sure to be a costly endeavor, especially so early in her tenure before she had established herself.

First, the odds were that she wouldn't get Secretary Haig to go along with her recommendation. No foundation had been laid, and the bureaucracy had already taken a position. I knew from my days at the Justice Department that once one of the Deputy Assistant Attorneys General had prepared a formal recommendation for action—for example, to appeal a lower court's decision—it would not be easy for the political appointees up the ladder—the Assistant, Associate, and Deputy Attorneys General—to reject it. I suspected that State functioned in much the same way, although Justice prided itself on being able to reach decisions on most matters without regard to politics. But, even if Kirkpatrick were to succeed in turning Haig around, it would be at the expense of an immediate confrontation with the State Department bureaucracy. Moreover, it would mean confrontation with the United Nations itself, which could be expected nearly unanimously to back the PLO appeal and deem the U.S. denial of the visa request an unlawful interference with its prerogatives. Here she would have no support, even from traditional American allies at the United Nations. And so in answer to the question I asked myself, as to why she was doing this, quite clearly, regardless of the odds, she wanted to make her case that the Reagan Administration could not afford to stand idly by and preside over the enhancement of PLO influence at the United Nations. And quite clearly she felt compelled to take the risk.

At the State Department, I took the elevator to the sixth floor and turned down a long, low-ceilinged corridor. The walls were bare except for a blue stripe down the center. It was a far cry from the look of the U.S. Justice Department, a prewar structure of high ceilings, thick walls, and halls graced by framed oil portraits of Attorneys General, and large offices with windows that opened to allow fresh air. No framed pictures or photographs or even posters adorned the State Department's halls, only the ubiquitous color-coded stripe to keep one from getting lost. For a moment, looking down at its tirelessly scrubbed linoleum floors and down its long white corridors I felt as though I might get to see a straitjacketed patient being wheeled down the halls. The blue-coded corridor came to an end. It turned into one with a yellow stripe. At the juncture of the two was the suite of offices with the shield on top marked "Jeane Kirkpatrick, U.S. Permanent Representative to the United Nations."

Jackie Tillman was on the phone when I arrived. Harvey Feldman was in the corner office reading the *Washington Post*. I walked in and introduced myself.

Harvey, a man in his early fifties, showed me to a comfortable beige-colored upholstered chair—a sign of ambassadorial rank, I supposed, one step up from the green leather sofa in Herb Reis' office in New York. Memorabilia from his recent ambassadorship in Papua–New Guinea in the West Pacific filled nearly every available spare inch of space: shrunken heads, masks, penis sheaths, shields, spears, photographs of sunsets, of meetings with tribal leaders, and of a young bare-chested Papuan beauty. The only reminder of his prior incarnation, a plaque given to him in recognition of his services as director of the State Department's Taiwan desk between 1976 and 1978, was nailed to the wall above his desk.

No one had told Harvey about my coming on board, so I announced myself. I told him that I had an urgent memorandum for dispatch to Ambassador Kirkpatrick. She had asked that it be sent as quickly as possible. "Oh," said Harvey, as if to say, "where in the world did you come from with an urgent memorandum for Ambassador Kirkpatrick?" Aloud he said: "May I see it?"

"Sure," I replied.

Harvey read it quickly. "I had better copy this," he said, walking down the hall to the Xerox machine. Then, with a copy in hand, he proceeded, unknown to me, to the offices of State's Legal Adviser, nearly a hundred lawyers in all—and handed a copy to Jim Michel, the Deputy Legal Adviser.

In the meantime, while Harvey was out making copies and distributing one for good measure, Jackie Tillman came out to say hello. She was a short woman, about 5'2", in her mid-thirties with prematurely gray hair, striking eyes, and an all-business gait. Later, I learned that she had previously been Jeane Kirkpatrick's research assistant at the American Enterprise Institute, a think tank in Washington where Kirkpatrick spent her time when not teaching political science courses at Georgetown University. Before that, Jackie had lived in Vermont where, as she put it, she was active in a variety of liberal and left-wing causes before becoming disenchanted and moving to the political right.

"Jeane mentioned to me," said Jackie, "that you would be bringing this memorandum. Gosh, Harvey certainly does seem to be taking his sweet time."

When Harvey returned, Jackie, with hardly a glance at him, took the original and copy of my memorandum and said, "I'll be right back. I'm going down to the IO [International Organizations] bureau to datafax this up to New York."

A few minutes later she returned and handed me a waxy copy of my memorandum marked "Secret" across the top and bottom of the page. "That's so it will get there more quickly," she said. Jackie and Harvey were clearly of two very different molds;, where he was cautious, she was adventurous. It was clear that she had the more intimate relationship with Kirkpatrick.

The next day I moved into the vacant middle office between Jackie Tillman and Harvey Feldman. Adjoining Jackie's office was the spacious but hardly elegant office reserved for Kirkpatrick in Washington. Behind her desk she had a very large poster marked Festival d' Aix-en-Provence, the scene of her regular summer excursions. Although I had been told that it might take as long as two months before I obtained formal security clearance—my prior Justice Department "Top Secret" clearance, which had very little to do with top secrets, would not satisfy State security, which insisted on doing the job all over again—I decided I might as well use whatever space was available at State to get started. Jackie Tillman or Harvey Feldman would arrange for my entry into the building. Thus I could begin familiarizing myself with the operations of USUN and prepare for the rush of business at the opening of the upcoming General Assembly session in September.

Jackie welcomed me and brought to my desk piles of Kirkpatrick's writings—her *Commentary* piece, "Dictatorships and Double Standards," which brought her to President Reagan's attention; "Latin America and U.S. National Security"; and copies of her books, *The New Presidential Elite* (1976), *Political Woman* (1974), and *Leader and Vanguard in Mass Society* (1971).[20] I could see her writing style evolve; the later pieces carried punch, even a touch of the polemic. I was especially intrigued by a lengthy address before the American Political Science Association which Jackie had brought to my attention.[21] It was an analysis of the work of Harold Lasswell and his contextual approach to policy-making. Jeane Kirkpatrick spoke of him as her mentor. It may not have been coincidence that had brought us together: she and I understood and spoke the same language— "Lasswellese."

Two days after I had settled in, Jackie handed me a copy of a note from Jeane Kirkpatrick to Secretary Alexander Haig. The subject was "PLO Observer Mission," and a copy of my memorandum was attached to it. "It looks like your work is on the way to the Secretary," said Jackie.

Kirkpatrick's note asked that Secretary Haig authorize her to deny the PLO request for the two additional visas. It had an odd quality. The note itself was personal and informal in tone, with none of the look or ring of official memoranda addressed to the Secretary. And yet it was clear that she was writing from a subordinate position as she was asking him to "authorize" her to undertake her proposed course of action—the denial of the PLO visa request.

She wrote that she was convinced that U.S. national security considerations would be prejudiced were the PLO request to be honored. To do so, she said, would send the wrong signal abroad that the United States was not serious about combatting international terrorism. Moreover, she added, sound legal grounds existed for denying the additional visas. She added that she knew that from the memorandum of law which she was attaching in support of her plea; it was from "an international law expert, Dr. Allan Gerson."

I was astounded. That endorsement was the last thing I or she needed. I had assumed that what I had said in my memorandum might be incorporated in her correspondence with Secretary Haig, but not that it would be attached in its entirety with me identified as an "international law expert." I was not yet formally on board. The Legal Adviser's office considered itself the international law expert, the institutional repository of wisdom on such matters. An independent voice on legal matters reporting directly to the U.S. Ambassador to the United Nations was an affront to its authority. It was also the last thing the other bureaus at the State Department desired. They wanted the U.S. Ambassador to the United Nations to take voting instructions from IO, the Bureau of International Organization Affairs, as coordinated with the regional bureaus at the Department; and to take legal advice from L, State's Office of the Legal Adviser, and the attorneys at USUN who indirectly reported to L. Attaching my memorandum to her note to Haig seemed extraordinarily provocative; and yet, I asked myself, short of that, what might have worked? Her own view on legal matters would simply have been disregarded.

Kirkpatrick's communication to Haig rang bells throughout the system. The two pieces of paper came to the attention of many at the Department, but not to its intended recipient, the Secretary of State. Although Kirkpatrick and her Executive Assistant in Washington, Jackie Tillman, had been on the job for nearly six months, neither of them had yet developed a clear sense of the paper flow. They couldn't anticipate that, instead of landing directly on Secretary Haig's desk, Kirkpatrick's personal note and memorandum to him would take a circuitous route, a "vetting" through the Department. It first had to "clear" IO, NEA, the Bureau of Near Eastern Affairs, and L, the

Legal Adviser's Office. S/S, the Secretary of State's outer guard, or Secretariat, was there to watch-dog the process.

The procedure had been established in the early 1950s, after the State Department bureau system had first been organized along its present lines. Interested bureaus were to be accorded an opportunity to "clear" on memoranda sent by other bureaus to the Secretary of State, thus preventing any bureau from being blindsided. It all worked relatively well, except when it came to the matter of communications to the Secretary of State from the U.S. Permanent Representative to the United Nations. Here confusion reigned. From the time of Henry Cabot Lodge, appointment to the rank of U.S. Ambassador to the United Nations carried with it Cabinet rank, and with it, at least in theory, access to the President. Whether it could be utilized, and how often, depended on an Ambassador's personal relationship with the President.

Of course, existing legislation, such as the UN Participation Act of 1945, already provided that the U.S. Ambassador to the United Nations was to report to the President and take instructions from him "as might be transmitted through the Secretary of State."[22] But this was honored more in the breach than in practice. Though the men appointed to the UN post usually came from backgrounds of independent political power, for one reason or another they usually conformed with State Department procedures in reporting to the Department for instructions, usually as transmitted by the Bureau of International Organization Affairs. Some representatives, like John Scali and George Bush, would almost invariably take their speeches as prepared by the State Department and deliver them without changing a comma. Others, like Adlai Stevenson and Patrick Moynihan, would draft their own speeches and only then send them to State for clearance, although claiming no similar independence when it came to voting instructions. Still a few others—Senator Warren Austin and, especially, Justice Arthur J. Goldberg among them—took advantage of their political clout to ensure that the State Department would act only as a servicing bureau, and sought to act independently of the State Department in matters at the United Nations. On such matters their line of authority would run directly to the President.

When Kirkpatrick arrived as the new U.S. Ambassador to the United Nations, she shared some of Justice Goldberg's ambitions. But she was operating under many more liabilities. She had next to no acquaintance with how the U.S. Government actually ran. She had a vision of executing the President's policies, having his ear, interpreting his views and articulating them. But in practice her aims were more modest: to be heard by the Secretary of State instead of having her views filtered through the mid-levels of the State's bureaucracy, while preserving the option of going directly to the President on exceptional issues of great national import. Although she had the confidence of President Reagan, and was told by him that he would treat her as a full-fledged Cabinet member and not simply as someone who held Cabinet rank, it was clear to those who met her at the State Department that she was a novice in the politics of government and that she had no political constituency of her own. The State Department was not aware of any special deals she had made with the President before assuming office because, unlike Justice Goldberg, she had made none. The professionals at the State Department expected, therefore, that she would follow the chain of command and that the Department would provide instructions to USUN in New York. If Kirkpatrick, the academic, wished to use her writing or rhetorical skills to add flourish or gravitas to what had been prepared for her—as "talking points" or as full texts of an address—well, she was free to do so, providing she stayed within the guidelines, and concentrated on style, not substance.

As Secretary of State, Alexander Haig relied on the tradition within the State Department of the "Decision Memorandum" as the key to making policy choices. A Decision Memorandum when properly drafted would succinctly state the issue or issues for resolution, and the pros and cons of the available options. To this, Alexander Haig, drawing on his military background, added his own refinements; Decision Memoranda were not to exceed two typewritten pages, unless this was clearly impossible, and everything of importance was to be underlined—a requirement that often kept secretaries busy underlining every word other than prepositions and definite articles.

S/S found Kirkpatrick's note to Haig on the PLO Observer Mission issue deficient on two grounds: it showed no "clearances" by interested bureaus, and it was not written in the form of a Decision Memorandum. To be sure, S/S could nevertheless have forwarded the note and memorandum to the Secretary, but, bureaucratic niceties aside, they knew, as did every one else in the building, that there was no love lost between Haig and Kirkpatrick. Haig was a stickler for a tight chain of command. A graduate of the Naval and Army War Colleges, he served as commander-in-chief of the U.S. European Command and supreme allied commander of Europe and was a brigade commander in Vietnam. He was also the recipient of a Bronze Star and Purple Heart. In describing the Al Haig of an earlier era when he worked at the White House under President Richard Nixon, Henry Kissinger had called him "a man of colossal self-confidence." "His methods were sometimes rough; his instincts on formal status could be grating."[23] By the time he arrived as Secretary of State in the new Reagan Administration, Haig had not mellowed. He described himself as the "vicar" of U.S. foreign policy. He was the General; Kirkpatrick, the company commander, was there to carry out his commands.

If accessibility to power is the highest reward in a bureaucracy, its flip-side—isolation—is the punishment for those who buck the system. An invisible wall suddenly arose, insulating the Secretary of State from Kirkpatrick. The female professor who had wandered into the department on Ronald Reagan's coattails needed to be shown that she could not escape formal procedures nor circumvent bureaucratic controls.

Thus, when Kirkpatrick's note on the PLO Observer Mission arrived at S/S, it was first "vetted" to L, the Legal Adviser's Office; to NEA, the Bureau of Near-Eastern Affairs; and to IO, the Bureau of International Organization Affairs for their reaction. IO had the responsibility for putting all these views, including its description of the points made by Kirkpatrick and in the attached memorandum, in one package in the form of a Decision Memorandum to the Secretary of State.

At L, the Legal Adviser's office, it fell to the Assistant Legal Adviser for Near-Eastern Affairs to pass judgment on Kirkpatrick's suggestion and, especially, on the attached memorandum of law. We had known and debated each other over the years, and it was no secret that the adviser tended to view the PLO as the answer and Israeli intransigence as the problem. My coming on board at State couldn't have been a welcome event. After all, it was at the United Nations in New York that the United States would have to take positions bearing on the legal aspects of the Arab-Israeli conflict: whether Jerusalem was "occupied territory"; which standard of law governed the administration of the occupied territories; whether Israel's settlement policy was unlawful; whether the requirements for peace-making were being complied with; whether actions of Israel or the Arab states were tantamount to aggression, and so on.

L/NEA, as the branch of the Legal Adviser's office which services NEA is called, therefore went after my memorandum intending, as one L attorney put it, to "blow me out of the water." Several days later, L/NEA forwarded its critique. It concluded that the U.S. Government's solemn obligations under the UN Headquarters Agreement ruled out any interference with the transit of accredited delegates to and from the United Nations. The Gerson memorandum of law was dismissed as a thinly disguised policy argument; the "law" was deemed crystal clear; the "major purposes" argument was derided as an effort to evade the clear intent of the law. Whether or not the PLO was engaged in terrorism abroad was treated as beside the point.

NEA had also forwarded a critique of the Kirkpatrick proposal bearing my attached memorandum. The reasoning was different from that of L, reflecting the political tone of one bureau and the legal tone of the other. NEA argued that denial of the PLO request would isolate the United States in the international community, that not even U.S. friends at the United Nations would support the move, and that the move would be interpreted as a pro-Israel tilt when we were trying to pursue a balanced approach to the Arab-Israeli conflict. Moreover, NEA warned that denial of the PLO visa request would encourage radical Arab states to undertake hostile acts against U.S. embassies and diplomatic personnel abroad, thus jeopardizing the Middle-East "peace process."

But NEA, sensitive as well to the prospect of Israel's outrage at permitting enlargement of the PLO Observer Mission, sought a less straightforward approach. It recommended compromise, an informal approach to the PLO through indirect channels to see whether it might agree to sending one, rather than two, additional accredited permanent delegates. If the PLO would agree not to publicize the expansion of its mission in New York, then perhaps the United States should be prepared to grant it an additional visa.

The IO bureau, having been apprised of all relevant views on the matter, then incorporated the various analyses and recommendations into a Decision Memorandum for Secretary Haig. Three options were listed and Secretary Haig was asked to check off and initial the one he favored. As drafted by IO, these options were to authorize the U.S. Mission to accede to the PLO request, favored by L as most consistent with our legal obligations under the UN Headquarters Agreement; or to authorize an informal effort at compromise with the PLO over the number of new PLO delegates, favored by NEA as most likely to avoid a flare-up with the Arab world; or, finally, to approve the proposal of Ambassador Kirkpatrick that she be authorized to deny the PLO request on the basis of U.S. national security considerations, favored only by Ambassador Kirkpatrick.

Several days later a document entitled "Decision Memorandum: PLO Observer Mission" was transmitted from Washington to Jeane Kirkpatrick. This was the first time she or anyone around her at USUN had seen a copy of it, although procedural protocol at State called for USUN to comment on the L and NEA proposals. At the end of the memorandum, next to the option summarizing NEA's recommendation and set off with two lines, one marked "Approve" and the other marked "Disapprove," appeared Secretary Alexander Haig's initials. They were on the line marked "Approve."

Given the way the issue was phrased for decision, Haig's choice was not surprising. The surprise was the Decision Memorandum itself. She had assumed that her personal note with my memorandum of law attached had made its way to Haig's desk and that the delay she was experiencing in getting a response was due simply to the press of other business.

Kirkpatrick vowed that her right to correspond directly with the Secretary of State would never be compromised again by State Department "clearance" procedures. I told her that I had recently become friendly with one of Haig's Special Assistants. "Good," she said, "you work with him. Maybe he can help make sure that in the future my memos get to Haig directly. He can do with my memoranda as he wishes, and if *he* wants to vet them through the system then that's his business. But he must get to see what I have written rather than some condensed, homogenized version put together by 'the Building.' I'll take this matter up with Haig directly, but I'd also appreciate it if you would continue to track it."

It was a very modest beginning. There was no intent to overcome the "system," only to be heard within it. That was the least she could expect, otherwise her role would be little more than that of a messenger. She wanted to change policies and direction, to give form to the broad general lines of policy espoused by President Ronald Reagan. That, in this instance, meant limiting the growth of the power and influence of the PLO. The State Department seemed to have a different agenda. If her recommendations were to be "vetted" through the system, all would be lost. If proof were needed, it was how Secretary Haig's decision to approve expansion of the PLO Observer Mission had come about.

4

UN Funding, Congress,
and the Restraints of
International Law

> The expenses of the Organization shall be borne by the
> Members as apportioned by the General Assembly.
>
> Article 17(2) of the UN Charter

I n mid-August 1981, about a month before the opening of the annual General Assembly session, Jeane Kirkpatrick received dis-
tressing news. It came from ECOSOC, the UN Economic and Social
Council. She already knew from firsthand experience what to expect
from the UN Security Council, having observed it at close quarters
during its lengthy consideration of Israel's bombing of the Iraqi nuclear reactor. She had read Daniel Patrick Moynihan's *A Dangerous
Place*[1] on the machinations of the UN General Assembly, and so had
a good idea of what to expect from that forum—trouble. What she
hadn't anticipated was that the other two organs of the United Nations in New York, the Trusteeship Council and ECOSOC, could
prove nearly as irksome.

She had been briefed and knew that ECOSOC would be the
forum for "global negotiations," a Third World effort aimed at redistribution of the world's wealth. She knew that it would also be the

arena for a fight over the status of Puerto Rico; Cuba was already spearheading an offensive against the United States, aimed at having the U.S. relationship with Puerto Rico condemned as that of a colonial power. That was what the United Nations was beginning to seem to be all about: the legitimation of one nation, and the de-legitimation of another.

The surprise, however, came neither from "global negotiations" nor from Cuba and Puerto Rico, but from ECOSOC's Statistics Committee—a committee little known to the general public and whose work would hardly arouse much fanfare. At the United Nations, however, it was recognized that what the Committee did and, equally importantly, who sat on it, mattered a great deal. The Committee's function was to compile and assess statistics for UN reports on economic and social development, higher education, employment, women's rights, social security, and the like. But the phrase "statistics don't lie, people do" was commonly recognized at the United Nations to mean that the make-up of the Statistics Committee could not be ignored; politics and statistics had much in common.

Under the so-called "Permanent Members' Convention," in effect since the founding of the United Nations, no permanent member of the UN Security Council—the United States, the USSR, the United Kingdom, France, and China—could be denied a seat on any Committee on which they wished to sit. In the summer of 1981, the Statistics Committee broke with this tradition. By a majority vote, it was decided to deny an American representative a seat on the Committee, despite the fact that an American had sat on the Committee since its inception.[2] The fact that 25 percent of ECOSOC's budget came from U.S. contributions was conveniently ignored. The United States, after all, had never before used its power of the purse to deny allocations to the United Nations when it disagreed with its practices.

For Jeane Kirkpatrick the action taken by the Statistics Committee was another indication of the steep decline of U.S. influence at the United Nations, a decline that appeared to be directly linked to the diminution of U.S. power and influence abroad. At the United Nations that decline was reflected not only in the realignment of blocs and in shifting voting patterns, which more often than not left the United States isolated on important resolutions, but was now being manifested in the composition of important committees. Moreover, it was being institutionalized on her watch, right before her first General Assembly session. She was determined to do something about it.

Congressman Mickey Edwards, a third-term Republican from a

district near Kirkpatrick's home-town of Duncan, Oklahoma, came to the rescue. A strong supporter of President Reagan's policy of strengthening U.S. defenses and adopting a more resolute posture in world affairs, Edwards, on being told of the problem, promptly prepared a draft bill which, if enacted, would require the U.S. Government to withhold 10 percent of its annual contribution of $90 million to ECOSOC until an American representative once again took a seat on the Committee.

A few days later, Kirkpatrick handed me a copy of Congressman Edwards' draft bill and asked for my comments. She mentioned that what the Statistics Committee had done was an assault not only on the United States but on all the Permanent Members of the UN Security Council (although none seemed anxious to join us in this fight) and a violation of the "Permanent Members Convention."

By this time, in addition to shuttling to New York for occasional dinners or receptions and meetings with the other members of the U.S. delegation, I had been doing my homework, brushing off my old law books, studying the UN Charter and its various commentaries, and reviewing relevant international law in anticipation of the fall General Assembly session. I knew of the "Permanent Members Convention" and that it had come under increasing attack from the Third World, which chafed at the special powers vested in the five permanent members on the UN Security Council—powers resulting in their ability, through use of the veto, to stop action from being taken or to prevent adoption of a Security Council resolution. But the "Permanent Members Convention" to which Kirkpatrick looked for a reversal of the Statistics Committee's action was not a treaty. It was merely an understanding among the five permanent members whereby each agreed to support the others for membership on any significant UN committee. It did not bind the other member-states of the UN system, nor take away their right to vote on memberships for any of the UN's constituent committees. Thus, withholding U.S. payments to express dissatisfaction with the ECOSOC election—Congressman Edwards' proposed remedy—was, arguably, unjustifiable. Regrettable as the Statistics Committee's decision to ignore the tradition of electing an American representative might be, there appeared to be little that we could do about it.

That evening Joan and I had dinner with Gene Rostow at Washington's celebrated Jean Louis restaurant in the Watergate. I had not seen him since his call to me in Jerusalem on June 19. Rostow knew that, although I was still awaiting formal security clearance, I had begun work with Jeane Kirkpatrick. I told him about the Mickey Edwards bill. Gene's response was immediate. "It will be up to you, Allan," he said, "to educate her about the role of law in international affairs. I'm not sure she has a sense of it."

I looked at him, somewhat puzzled, and he said, "The Certain Expenses Case, it rules out what Congressman Edwards and your new boss are trying to do."

Gene Rostow thought and talked in terms of "world order." It was in his blood. Perhaps it had been acquired from the socialist, universalist beliefs of his father, who raised the Rostow brothers— Walt, Ralph, and Gene—on a small collective farm outside New Haven, Connecticut, and named Walt for Walt Whitman, Ralph for Ralph Waldo Emerson, and Gene for Eugene V. Debs, the Socialist reformer.

In his work, *Peace in the Balance*, written after leaving the Johnson Administration in 1968 as Under-Secretary of State for Political Affairs, Gene Rostow expounded his view that law was the antidote to war.[3] The UN Charter's rules prohibiting the use of force in international relations could and had to be made to work;[4] what was required was iron will to exact a price from violators of the UN Charter's prohibitions. He thought it essential that the law be respected and that the United States, in the absence of an effective UN Security Council, had to be prepared to enforce it. It was here that he parted company with so many others in his field who were reluctant to give bite to the goal of reciprocal respect for international norms.

Rostow was not a "contextualist" like Myres McDougal, who thought in terms of "diverse systems of public order"[5] and detailed appraisals of an ever-changing legal and political climate. Neither was he of the pragmatic non-legal school of thought which measures the need for U.S. action by weighing costs and benefits with little thought to principle and consistency. Above all, Rostow was a "rules of the game" man. Vietnam was the paradigm. Like his brother Walt, who was Lyndon Johnson's National Security Adviser at the White House, Gene was most concerned that the United States draw lines. Crossing an international frontier, unless in the clear-cut exercise of self-defense, was the ultimate line. North Vietnam had transgressed it; a U.S. ally—South Vietnam, with whom the United States had a treaty—was affected; and so it was imperative, in Gene Rostow's view, that the United States respond, not simply for the sake of South Vietnam, or for U.S. interests in the region, but for the sake of world order and international law.

Here Gene Rostow differed from his mentor and role-model, Secretary of State Dean Acheson. In 1944, Gene Rostow was a protégé of Acheson when he was an Assistant Secretary of State and active in efforts at formulating conceptions of a postwar world. Reflecting Acheson's sartorial bearing and tastes, Gene Rostow's suits were all three-piece and custom-tailored in London to last forever, to be worn even after they became tattered around the edges. He was a gentleman and expected others in his company to be the same. Like Acheson, he wrote with style and wit. But, unlike Acheson, Rostow could never feel comfortable with the idea of a world order based solely on the balance of power, with little or no role for international law in maintaining that equilibrium.

In 1963, Dean Acheson—then an eminent lawyer reflecting on his experience as Secretary of State—told a hostile audience of the American Society of International Law that international law "simply does not deal with such questions of ultimate power." He was addressing the legal propriety of the U.S. "quarantine" in the Cuban missile crisis of 1962. He admonished international lawyers for wasting their time debating the matter. "The survival of states," he declared, "is not a matter of law."[6] Eugene Rostow saw things differently: power politics and international law could be combined; international law could be made to work if the United States was prepared to comply with it on a reciprocal basis, and to enforce it. Vietnam became the test case.

When he returned to his beloved Yale after his stint in the Johnson Administration, hushed whispers of "War Criminal" followed Rostow in the halls. He tried to defuse student anger through teas in the Faculty Lounge, but was rarely able to find common ground with his detractors. Then the sixties came to an end. By the fall of 1972, when I arrived for graduate work at Yale, students were crowding to register for Rostow's seminar on "International Law and the Regulation of Force." The course examined the rights and wrongs: legalities and illegalities of the Vietnam War, of the Arab-Israeli dispute, and other ongoing conflicts.

I took Rostow's course and later chose him to chair my doctoral dissertation committee: five professors guiding and cajoling me to completion of my doctoral dissertation on the law and practice of belligerent occupation.[7] I came to understand Rostow's view that peace was "a problem of law," but I never fully subscribed to it.

Now, as I listened to Rostow at Jean Louis' restaurant, these differences between us surfaced. I recalled the Certain Expenses

Case as a decision taken by the International Court of Justice in the mid-1960's relating to UN peacekeeping operations.[8] I drew a blank, however, on the details of the decision.

"You remember, Allan," Rostow said, "that's the case where the ICJ held that the Soviet Union had to pay its share of the cost of UN peace-keeping operations in the Congo in 1962. The International Court held that a country can't just pick and choose which UN activities it is going to contribute to. If that were the way things operated, the whole UN system would collapse. Article 17 of the UN Charter says: 'the expenses of the Organization shall be borne by the Members as apportioned by the General Assembly.' Well, it's the same with this Edwards bill. Congress can't tell the United States Government not to pay its UN bill just because it doesn't agree with the conduct of some UN agency. That sort of unilateral action is illegal under the UN Charter. And the UN Charter is, after all, part of the law of the land."

Rostow's remarks made me uneasy. I wasn't anxious to return to Kirkpatrick with, "Sorry, you had better go tell Congressman Edwards that neither he nor anyone else in Congress can help us; that a Congressionally ordered cutback in funds for ECOSOC because of the Statistics Committee's vote, reprehensible as that may be, would be illegal under the UN Charter." I was uneasy about the notion that Congress could not withhold money for the United Nations. It was not simply a matter of a lawyer's reluctance to tell a client "No, there's no legal way to solve your problem; you'll just have to accept defeat." The idea that the United States had necessarily forfeited all control over the money it contributed to the United Nations—one quarter of the UN's total budget—was repugnant.

"But, Gene," I protested, "surely you don't mean that the will of the UN General Assembly is supreme, come what may, in whatever use it decides to make of the U.S. contribution? What if the General Assembly votes to fund activities by terrorist groups, or at least groups that the United States considers to be responsible for international acts of terror? The PLO, for instance? Since 1979, there's been a law on the books requiring that the United States withhold from its annual assessed contribution an amount equal to funding for the two pro-PLO committees operating out of the UN Secretariat: the Committee on the Inalienable Rights of the Palestinian People and another special unit on Palestinian rights, whose name I now forget, that was set up in the UN Secretariat."

"Allan," Gene replied, "you're getting things confused. You're talking about withholding U.S. contributions to prevent the UN from funding activities that the United States Government or Congress may consider illegitimate. The Russians argued their right to make that type of decision in the Certain Expenses Case. Only there it wasn't withholding from the PLO or the UN Statistics Committee; UN peacekeeping operations were involved and the USSR maintained that they weren't a 'legitimate' activity that the United Nations could pay for through its assessed budget. The Russians then refused to comply with the World Court decision after the Court decided that peacekeeping was a legitimate UN activity. Now what Congressman Edwards and Jeane Kirkpatrick propose to do is simply to withhold a portion of the U.S. share of the UN assessed budget earmarked for ECOSOC because the United States was voted out of a seat on some committee. They're not interested in making an argument about legitimacy, they simply want to use U.S. power to bludgeon the UN into giving them the result they want. When they get what they want—our man back on the Statistics Committee—they're prepared to have the United States ante up once more."

I could see he hadn't yet finished.

"I'm afraid Congress can't do that, not legally," he continued, "and not if we want to retain our reputation as a country committed to the rule of law. That's terribly important, Allan. Never forget that we have a lot at stake in maintaining that reputation. We'd be giving up a great deal if we voted the way Edwards and, from what you tell me, Jeane Kirkpatrick, would like. People would say that there's no difference between us and the Russians. And the UN would never stand for this sort of unilateral action; they'd probably drag us before the International Court of Justice where we'd be bound to lose. Whatever advantage we secured in 1962 in having the Soviet Union condemned as a law-breaker would be dissipated. The United States would now be in the docket. No, it's no good, Allan. I'm afraid you'll have to tell her that bluntly."

The waitress brought us a white chocolate and raspberry mousse dessert, but by then I had lost my appetite. I wanted to get home and reread the "Certain Expenses" case. I needed to take a hard look at when, if ever, Congress could use its power of the purse to express disagreement with the UN. I needed to reexamine what limits, if any, international law imposed on the U.S. Congress's freedom of action.

At home that evening I looked at my textbook on United Nations law, edited by Professor Louis Sohn of Harvard, and its digest of the International Court's decision in the *Certain Expenses of the United Nations*.[9] Like many judicial opinions read in law school, this one made for dull reading. Court decisions—especially those of the International Court of Justice, with its panel of fifteen judges—aren't known for their literary merit. They come to life only when a client's fortune, or his or her lawyer's reputation, is on the line.

The Certain Expenses Case grew out of the civil war that raged in the Belgian Congo in the early 1960s. To bring that fighting to a close, it was arranged that a UN-sponsored cease-fire would be maintained by UN peacekeeping forces. The novelty in the call for the establishment of these forces was that it was not being done at the behest of the UN Security Council, which had authority under the terms of the UN Charter for peacekeeping arrangements, but at the behest of the UN General Assembly. The cost of the operation was then assessed to each member state as a part of its regularly assessed UN dues. (See Table 1 for an example of withholdings from the regular UN budget, and Table 2 for an example of special assessments.) On this occasion, however, the Soviets balked at paying. They argued that a UN General Assembly–sponsored peacekeeping force was not a legitimate UN activity, that this fell within the exclusive province of the UN Security Council, and hence that the cost was not an expense that they were obligated to pay.

The UN General Assembly asked the International Court of Justice for an "advisory opinion" on the legality of the Soviet withholding. On examination of the question, the Court ruled that peacekeeping operations were a legitimate General Assembly function and that, accordingly, the Soviets were required to pay their pro rata share of the cost. The Soviet Union ignored the Court's ruling.

Eventually the Secretariat separated "peacekeeping" expenses out of the "assessed" UN budget, as if not a part of it; but learning this did little to salvage the Edwards draft. It could not be argued that the Statistics Committee's vote to deny a seat to the U.S. representative was an "illegitimate" act. There seemed no way of getting around the fact that the Edwards bill would place the United States in violation of its obligations under the UN Charter.[10]

Still, there was something the United States Congress could do. Here the ultimate objective of Congress was to express its outrage and fire a warning shot across the bow. This, it seemed to me, could be accomplished without formally enacting any law. A Concurrent Sense of the Congress resolution might serve that purpose.

With that in mind I drafted a Concurrent Sense of the Congress resolution deploring the break in tradition of U.S. representation on the Statistics Committee as eliminating a necessary means of providing balance to the Committee's work and eliminating bias. Unlike the bill Congressman Mickey Edwards had proposed, it did not call for any punitive measures against ECOSOC. In my memo to Kirkpatrick on the matter, I wrote:

The Bill, even with addition of qualifying language, essentially calls for violation of our treaty commitments under UN Charter and is almost certain to be opposed by the State Department's Office of the Legal Adviser. This is because by Article 17, paragraph 1 of the Charter, the General Assembly is given the power to "approve" the budget of the UN and by paragraph 2 of Article 17 is given the power to apportion the expenses among the members. The International Court of Justice has made clear that the power of apportionment creates a legal obligation upon member states not to withdraw . . . assessed contributions as a response to UN action. . . . The Edwards draft is so broad in scope (automatic reduction of contributions and assistance for any denial of U.S. representation on any organ, commission, or other entity of the UN), that it simply cannot be reasonably reconciled with U.S. commitments under Article 17 of the Charter.

I then prepared to meet with Kirkpatrick the following day in her Washington office to tell her that I had concluded that the Edwards bill would, if challenged by the UN, be indefensible; that a UN challenge seemed likely, and that a fight over legality would ultimately not only prove futile but would distract our attention from more important matters. I presumed that her response would not be kindly; that she would point out that the Statistics Committee's actions were not only a slap at the authority of the United States, but aimed at weakening the authority of all the five permanent members; and that, moreover, it would be noted that for all her "tough talk" about stopping the decline of U.S. influence at the United Nations, this change was institutionalized under her watch before her first General Assembly session. It would be a bad omen.

Kirkpatrick listened carefully to my presentation, focusing her eyes, as she does at these moments, directly and unwaveringly on her interlocutor. There was none of the disappointment which I had expected. She calmly accepted my conclusion, as a patient might that of a physician when told that surgery won't help, when told that there were limits to how far even vague, nebulous international law could be stretched, and that here those limits had been reached. As long as we were part of the United Nations we had to live by its rules, which were of course the rules we had imposed on ourselves. I did, however, suggest an alternative that might accomplish the same end, although not as forcefully as the route Congressman Edwards was prepared to embark upon: a Sense of the Congress resolution expressing revulsion at the Committee's action. It didn't have the force of legislation, but it was the most that we could do under the circumstances.

Kirkpatrick thanked me and said that she respected my opinion, and that she would bring my proposal to Congressman Edwards' attention. I heard nothing further about Mickey Edwards' draft, however. Evidently the proposed Sense of the Congress resolution did not have enough bite to suit him. The incident was behind us, but not forgotten. We were not ready for a fight with the United Nations, not over this issue.

Yet the experience made clear that the issue of gaining control over UN financing would not go away. One Congressman had shown a determination to do something about it. We knew that there were others, and that they mirrored the sentiment of an American electorate that had become disenchanted both with the United Nations and with Congress's failure to check the decline of U.S. fortunes in that body. It seemed inevitable that the massive financial support provided by the U.S. for the UN system would have to be tied to curbing its abuses. There would have to be linkage between our nation's bilateral and multilateral relations so that what went on at the United Nations could no longer be cavalierly treated as unconsequential and cost-free. But now was not the time. That would come later.[11]

Table 1. Estimated Withholding by Member States from the Regular
Budget of the United Nations Projected to 31 December 1982
(Thousands of United States dollars)

	BOND ISSUE	*REGULAR PROGRAM OF TECHNICAL ASSISTANCE*	*OTHER BUDGET ITEMS*	*TOTAL*
Albania	36.0	—	—	36.0
Bulgaria	273.1	253.8	49.0	575.9
Byelorussian Soviet Socialist Republic	782.6	289.5	152.0	1,224.1
China	3,988.9	—	114.2	4,103.1
Czechoslovakia	1,542.5	—	216.9	1,759.4
Democratic Kampuchea	—	—	70.6	70.6
France	4,357.1	—	—	4,357.1
German Democratic Republic	1,046.2	1,391.8	147.8	2,585.8
Hungary	791.5	—	249.1	968.6
Mongolia	47.0	—	7.2	54.2
Poland	2,272.8	—	284.0	2,556.8
Romania	509.5	—	376.2	885.7
South Africa	814.5	—	15,895.7	16,710.2
Ukrainian Soviet Socialist Republic	2,933.8	2,031.9	571.5	5,537.2
Union of Soviet Socialist Republics	22,233.3	16,158.1	4,331.1	42,794.5
United States of America	—	—	612.6	612.6
Total	41,628.8	20,125.1	23,077.9	84,831.8

Table 2. Estimated Withholding by Member States from United Nations Emergency Force (UNEF), United Nations Disengagement Force (UNDOF), and United Nations Interim Force in Lebanon (UNIFIL)
(Thousands of United States dollars)

	UNEF/UNDOF[a]	UNIFIL[b]
Albania	20.2	12.7
Algeria	—	142.1
Benin	9.8	6.1
Bulgaria	27.5	195.5
Byelorussian Soviet Socialist Republic	566.7	2,536.0
Cuba	—	140.3
Czechoslovakia	397.7	5,325.0
Democratic Kampuchea	20.2	—
Democratic Yemen	4.5	6.1
German Democratic Republic	1,223.7	8,748.1
Hungary	—	421.4
Iraq	92.0	135.5
Lao People's Democratic Republic	—	6.1
Libyan Arab Jamahiriya	181.5	262.6
Mongolia	8.7	12.7
Poland	—	8,254.6
South Africa	2,719.9	2,683.4
Syrian Arab Republic	27.0	33.7
Ukrainian Soviet Socialist Republic	2,123.7	9,483.2
Union of Soviet Socialist Republics	18,826.8	85,795.8
Viet Nam	10.6	38.1
Yemen	9.4	—
Total	25,269.9	124,239.0

[a] Estimated cumulative withholding from inception of UNEF (1973) through the completion of its liquidation and from the inception of UNDOF in 1974 to 30 November 1982.

[b] Estimated cumulative withholdings from inception of UNIFIL on 19 March 1978 to 18 October 1982.

5

High Noon over Geneva Convention No. 4

There is the matter of the integrity of what we say and do at the UN.

Jeane J. Kirkpatrick, August 1981

Jeane Kirkpatrick may have heard of the Fourth Geneva Convention of 1949 on the Treatment of Civilian Populations in Time of War in the late summer of 1981.[1] If so, she gave no indication of it. Certainly she had no reason to know its particular provisions, nor of the controversy among a handful of legal specialists about when the Convention applied, particularly with regard to the Israeli-held West Bank and Gaza Strip. Yet, within weeks she would be prepared to make this arcane question the test of her already shaky relation with Secretary of State Alexander Haig and to ask President Reagan to decide between them on the merits of the issue.

For more than a century statesmen had tried to regulate the conduct of war through international agreements. If they could do little to prevent war they could, as civilized men representing civilized nations, at least agree—or so they thought—on the rules by which it was waged. Following World War II, spurred in its aftermath by the universal repulsion at the brutality and bestiality of Nazi occupation, the International Committee of the Red Cross oversaw a series of diplomatic conferences aimed at achieving a revised codification of international law governing the conduct of war and military occupation. The result was a series of four conventions, ratified in 1949: I, the Geneva Convention for the Amelioration of the Condition of the Wounded and Sick in Armed Forces in the Field; II, the Convention for Amelioration of the Condition of the Wounded, Sick and Shipwrecked Members of Armed Forces at Sea; III, the Convention Relative to the Treatment of Prisoners of War; and IV, the Convention Relative to the Protection of Civilian Persons in Time of War. All four conventions have been ratified, with various reservations, by most of the world's states. Yet for all their provisos and detailed clarifications of rights and duties, they rest on the questionable assumption that an aggressor would comply with their terms.

At the outbreak of World War II, there was no shortage of international treaties on the conduct of war. There was, most notably, the Hague Convention No. IV of 1907 Respecting the Laws and Customs of War on Land, the forerunner of the Fourth Geneva Convention of 1949. There were treaties on chemical warfare, especially the 1925 Protocol Prohibiting the Use of Asphyxiating, Poisonous, or Other Gases, and of Bacteriological Methods of Warfare. And there were other ancillary treaties and conventions on the permissible means of warfare and control of civilian populations under military occupation. It was not a paucity of international law that facilitated the Third Reich's aggression and destructiveness, but the lack of will or ability to enforce existing laws. Like the Hague Regulations of 1907, the Geneva Conventions of 1949 formed a gentleman's code for the conduct of war for those inclined to act like gentlemen in such matters.

Despite the advent of the United Nations, which had as its central purpose to save "succeeding generations from the scourge of war,"[2] war remained a fact of international life, though waged more by the surrogates of the great powers or independently of them than by the great powers themselves. Nearly one hundred such wars were waged in the last two decades alone. And when the fighting was over—either by cease-fire, truce, peace treaty, conquest or exhaustion—one state almost invariably found itself in possession of the territory of another, and in control of a hostile population.

The occupation of enemy territory is a normal by-product of war, and war is a norm of international life. Yet of the more than two dozen nations that have gone to war since World War II only one nation— Israel—has ever been cited, and repeatedly so, by the community of nations for violating the Fourth Geneva Convention. Nor was it for lack of questionable practices by other nations under the terms of this Convention[3] that Israel was singled out as a pariah state, contemptuous of international norms and law, a veritable "Nazi-like" entity.[4]

Toward the end of August 1981, in anticipation of the upcoming General Assembly session, the State Department's IO Bureau published its annual annotated compendium of the next UN General Assembly agenda. Listed near the top was the item entitled "Israeli Practices in the Occupied Areas." The annotation referred to a draft resolution then making the rounds in the General Assembly that "strongly deplored" Israel's refusal to acknowledge the applicability of the Fourth Geneva Convention of 1949 to its occupation of the West Bank and Gaza Strip. No specific abuses by the Israeli military government were cited; only the fact that Israel refused to acknowledge that, as a matter of law, the provisions of the Fourth Geneva Convention were indeed applicable to its military rule.

As a practical matter, little was at issue. The Government of Israel agreed to judge the actions of its military commanders by the standards stipulated in the Convention. Indeed, establishing a first in the annals of military occupation, Israel granted Palestinians on the West Bank and Gaza the right to appeal directly to the Israel Supreme Court to test the legality, under the terms of the Fourth Geneva Convention, of actions by military commanders that affected them adversely. But Israel, in an excess of legalistic purity, was unwilling to take the extra step and formally acknowledge that the Convention applied as a matter of law, and not simply as something it was willing to abide by ex gratia.

To understand why it was holding out on this point, one must look at the frame of mind that seemed to dominate so much of Israel's thinking at the time. The government was afraid that admission of legal applicability might be construed so as to weaken Israel's putative claim to sovereignty over the West Bank and Gaza Strip, which Israel referred to by their biblical (and geographic) terms as Judea and Samaria. Since the Fourth Geneva Convention applied to "occupied territory," accepting its legal applicability might weaken Israel's future claim that the territories weren't "occupied" at all, but "liberated." Of course, Israel might instead have acknowledged the applicability of the Fourth Geneva Convention while reaffirming its rights, as guaranteed under the Camp David Accords, to make whatever claim it chose to the West Bank and Gaza Strip after the conclusion of an interim autonomy period. Instead it chose a different, more legalistic, more contentious path.

When it became clear that the General Assembly would com-
mence with a resolution "strongly deploring" Israel's conduct regarding the Fourth Geneva Convention, it became equally clear
that the U.S. Government would have to take a stand. Once an
important issue is cast in the form of a resolution at the United
Nations, the United States is left with little choice. It becomes increasingly difficult to stay on the sidelines; the situation becomes
polarized, and even if policymakers in Washington prefer that the
issue be further drawn out, or left diffuse, they almost invariably
become drawn into choosing sides and taking positions. The U.S.
Mission at the UN had already had experience with this phenom-
enon in a number of Security Council sessions convened to deal
with the Arab-Israeli conflict. This, however, was to mark the first
General Assembly resolution on the Arab-Israeli conflict on which
the Reagan Administration would have to declare its position. The
U.S. vote would not go unnoticed, nor would the explanations of
our vote. Every sentence and nuance would be analyzed for telltale
signs of shifts in policy.

I brought this item to Kirkpatrick's attention. It was hard, I said,
to see the justification for condemning a nation, no less than an individual, for merely stating a belief, for construing the law in a particular way. There had to be more than that, there had to be tangible
action based on that interpretation, some act depriving others of
fundamental human rights, before the matter was ripe for the UN's
attention. Besides, Israel's position did not seem frivolous; acknowl-
edging the legal applicability of the Fourth Geneva Convention might
in fact prejudice any future Israeli claim to the West Bank and Gaza
Strip, providing of course that the Arabs could follow Israel in the
legalistic contortions the Israelis feared would flow from acknowledg-
ing the Convention's applicability.

There seemed, therefore, no good reason for the United States
to vote in favor of the proposed General Assembly resolution other
than the fact that the Carter Administration had done so in the past
with regard to a similar resolution. That did not seem reason
enough. It would be like condemning the United States for merely
stating that it had a legitimate right to provide aid to the Contras in
Nicaragua. Action had to be taken. In the parlance of U.S. constitutional law, there had to be a genuine "case or controversy" for
decision. Here no one had been hurt. As long as Israel applied the
Fourth Geneva Convention *de facto* the question of whether it was
de jure, or legally, applicable was beside the point. The question

arose only if one wanted to make political hay out of the matter, to use it as an opportunity to put Israel into the corner as an international miscreant.

Kirkpatrick listened attentively to my arguments, and then asked that I draft a memorandum from her to Secretary Haig, arguing along the lines I suggested—that at the most the United States should abstain rather than vote in favor of the General Assembly Israel/Fourth Geneva Convention resolution when put to a vote. I complied, and shortly before the opening of the UN General Assembly session submitted to her a 10-page single-spaced memorandum of law on the subject. My conclusions: (1) the question of the legal applicability of the Fourth Geneva Convention to the West Bank and Gaza Strip was in fact murky, with experts coming down on both sides of the issue; (2) the question was in any event moot as Israel was committed to *de facto* compliance with its terms; (3) Israel's action was consistent with the Camp David Accords which reserved for all participants in the Arab-Israel peace process their rights to make their respective claims to these territories after an interim period for the development of autonomous rule; and (4) that, regardless of the above, the UN General Assembly was not the place for these sorts of intricate legal arguments to be heard, as it was a political forum and not a court of law.

Kirkpatrick took my synopsis and added the following:

President Reagan has characterized the Israeli West Bank settlements as "not illegal." Abstaining is consistent with his position to eschew legalistic debate in favor of a more pragmatic approach. . . . Such resolutions are part of the ongoing campaign at the UN to equate Zionism with racism and Israeli practices in the occupied territories with Nazi atrocities. The U.S. should not even indirectly lend its support to efforts to apply to Israel alone the terms of a Convention aimed largely at preventing a recurrence of practices committed by the Nazis against civilian populations. . . . Recognizing that how we vote on this resolution could conceivably affect the Middle-East peace process, the U.S. abstention should be carefully explained in advance to all interested parties as in no way derogating from the U.S. commitment to the principles of Camp David. . . . There is the matter of the integrity of what we say and do at the UN.

This was my first exposure to what Kirkpatrick could do with an otherwise mundane memorandum to give it punch. It was characteristic of her approach. First, remind everyone that she is interpreting the President's will correctly. Second, place the discussion in a larger political context—here, as part of the ongoing effort that began with the 1975 General Assembly's "Zionism is Racism" resolution in an attempt to delegitimize the State of Israel. Thirdly, anticipate and minimize the diplomatic costs, or show that they are outweighed by other considerations—here, the need to consider the "integrity of what we say and do at the UN."

The memorandum, "Modification of U.S. Position on Israel/Geneva Convention Issue," was then given to Louise Siffin, Kirkpatrick's secretary in New York, for pouching to her Washington office. There her Washington secretary, Winnie Peterson, was to personally deliver it to Secretary Haig's front office, S/S, for his immediate attention.

Again, however, there were hurdles. S/S viewed this latest memorandum, like the earlier one on allowing expansion of the PLO Observer Mission, as intended to sidestep the "system." The fact that this time the memorandum was accompanied by a personal request that it go directly to the Secretary was hardly persuasive. First, it had to be "cleared" by the other bureaus, although there was no question of anyone being "blindsided" by Kirkpatrick's attempted direct communication with the Secretary since the other bureaus were already preparing Action Memoranda on this very point. The issue was whether the new U.S. Permanent Representative was to be permitted to establish herself as an equal within the system rather than subservient to it.

Kirkpatrick's memorandum to Haig was transmitted to the IO bureau to be synopsized and dissected as part of a larger Action Memorandum for Haig's signature. Again L was asked to analyze and offer comments on the Memorandum of Law I had prepared.

L quickly informed IO that the Fourth Geneva Convention was legally applicable, mainly because L had said so before and the prior Administration had acted on its recommendation and precedent was precedent. L also pointed out that the major Western nations were united in their belief that the Fourth Geneva Conventions applied, as a matter of law, to Israel's military occupation. This was something the Reagan Administration couldn't afford to ignore, L warned, if the United States wanted to maintain credibility as a country committed to respect for the rule of law in international affairs. The distinction between taking a legal position while in fact complying with a convention, and disregarding it altogether, was not discussed. The particulars were not allowed to interfere with the grand vision: the advancement of the "rule of law" through universal applicability of conventions.

NEA, the Bureau of Near Eastern Affairs, weighed in to argue that questions of law or justice aside, which were not its province, the politics of the "peace process," at which it was expert, required that the new Administration avoid being perceived as tilting toward Israel. Observers of the U.S. attitude toward the "peace process" would be sure to note an abstention on the Geneva Convention issue—in contrast to last year's Yes vote—as a signal of a shift. This, NEA warned, well-intentioned as the UN Ambassador's suggestion might have been, would be bound to hinder their efforts at advancing peace in the Middle East.

Several days after that memorandum had been submitted, Kirkpatrick, who was a rather late riser (after the diplomatic functions were over and the last guest had departed, she would usually take out her yellow pad, read cables, and write into the night) called me at 8:20 A.M. from her Waldorf Towers suite. I suspected that something was wrong.

"Allan," she said, "I've just received a copy of Haig's decision on the Geneva Conventions issue. Have you seen it?"

"No, I haven't."

"Well, it's awful. Just awful. I've been instructed to vote in favor of the resolution. I won't do it without instructions from the President. I'd like you to go to Communications and get a copy of the Action Memorandum. I'll be in at around 11 o'clock. I would like you to have a draft memo for me by then. Address it from me to President Reagan. Point out the reasons why I can't go along with Haig's decision, and why my views should be respected. Is that understood?"

"Yes, understood, a draft memorandum from you to President Reagan opposing Secretary Haig's decision. By 11:00 A.M. All right, I'll see you then."

The request had all the markings of a call to abet commission of an act of political hara-kiri. It seemed that, forced to choose between his Secretary of State and his chief UN delegate, the President would hardly choose the latter. I had little inkling then of the disdain at the White House in which Alexander Haig, Jr. was held by many of the senior presidential advisers. I only knew that the vehicle that Kirkpatrick now seemed ready to use for having the President resolve her difficulties with the Secretary of State and clarify his and her lines of authority was an incredibly abstruse issue of international law. And I knew it was a matter that could not easily be stated in a letter from her to the President. In any event, Haig would surely, it seemed, not roll over and yield his authority. If she lost this battle, she would be eating crow by the end of the day. Her prospects for playing a greater role in the U.S. foreign policy-making process would be vastly diminished. Still, I had my orders. By 11:00 A.M. I was to come up with a reasonably persuasive memorandum to the President on why he should listen to Jeane Kirkpatrick, rather than to Alexander Haig and the State Department, on how the United States should vote at the UN General Assembly.

The Communications officer on the sixth floor didn't make life any easier for me—he refused to share with me a copy of the signed Haig Action Memorandum that Kirkpatrick had referred to that morning. "I'm sorry, but we don't have you on the distribution list," he said. "You'll have to get Dirk Gleysteen to sign for its release before I can do anything."

Gleysteen, a career State Department foreign service officer in his early fifties, was the Mission's Counselor for Political Affairs and head of its political section. Neither he nor Kirkpatrick was a great fan of the other. To her, he was the Department within the Mission; to him, she was the undisciplined outsider. I knew that if I tried to get Gleysteen's approval, I would encounter a polished diplomatic stall. "Listen," I said to the Communications officer, "either contact Ambassador Kirkpatrick directly for confirmation that I am to get a copy or hand it to me." He opened the caged door and passed me the signed document.

The markings on the Memorandum showed that it was crafted by IO under the direction of its new Assistant Secretary, Elliott Abrams, a former staffer to Senator Daniel Patrick Moynihan of New York and son-in-law of *Commentary* editor Norman Podhoretz. The Memorandum had incorporated Kirkpatrick's recommendation for abstention. But it did so at the very end of its discussion of the issue, at which point her rationale had been ravaged.

As phrased by IO, the options for Secretary Haig were: (1) to vote "Yes," as recommended by L, NEA, and the IO bureaus. This would show continuity in U.S. foreign policy and enhance the image of the United States as a nation committed to the rule of law; or (2) to abstain, as suggested by Ambassador Kirkpatrick, which in the view of L, NEA, and IO, would endanger the Middle-East "peace process," disregard precedent, and unnecessarily aggravate friend and foe alike. As it was phrased, Secretary Haig would have had to be slightly balmy to do anything but acquiesce in Option 1. Reading the Action Memorandum and the transmutation Jeane Kirkpatrick's initial request had undergone was instructive—it was a blueprint of U.S. foreign policy directed from the bottom up, a testimony to bureaucratic skills in phrasing and framing foreign policy options to predetermine the decision.

But what was I to say in a letter on behalf of Jeane Kirkpatrick to President Reagan? To kindly ignore the calculus of costs and benefits described by the State Department, and to give preference to "the matter of the integrity of what we say and do at the United Nations" as determined by his chief UN delegate? Was this the occasion for bringing up the chronically tense relationship between the U.S. Mission to the United Nations and the State Department? Was this the place to argue that greater responsibility for day-to-day decisions should be given to the U.S. Ambassador, who had a better grasp of events at the United Nations, and that "instructions" from State should be considered as guidelines subject to interpretation and nothing more? How could I explain Israel's reasons for refusing to acknowledge the Fourth Geneva Convention in a way that the President (assuming he was willing to rack his wits over the issue) could be made to understand?

An hour and a half later my thinking had given rise to the following draft:

–DRAFT–

Memorandum for the President

Subject: Whether the U.S. Should Modify Its Previous Position of
           Voting in Favor of UN General Assembly Resolutions
           Condemning Israel for Refusal To Acknowledge the
           Applicability of the Fourth Geneva Convention To The
           West Bank and Gaza Strip.

Secretary of State Haig favors a "Yes" vote in support of an upcoming UN General Assembly resolution on this issue. I believe that such a vote would send the wrong signal. It would demonstrate indifference to unfair attacks on Israel at the United Nations. Coming at the opening of the first General Assembly session of the Reagan Administration, a "Yes" vote would raise questions about your pledge to do better than the Carter Administration in securing fair treatment of Israel at the United Nations.

The Camp David Accords preserved Israel's right to make territorial claims to the West Bank and Gaza at the end of a five year transitional period of autonomy. This resolution, by prejudicing Israel's right to assert such claims, would violate the spirit, if not letter, of the Camp David Accords.

States, if they are to be condemned, should be condemned on the basis of their conduct, not their beliefs. Moreover, while we disagree with the legal merits of Israel's reservations about the applicability of the fourth Geneva Convention, there are reasonable arguments to be made on both side of the issue.

For these reasons, Mr. President, I respectfully urge you to authorize me to abstain on the vote on this upcoming UN resolution.

Jeane J. Kirkpatrick

Kirkpatrick arrived at her office at 11:00 A.M., immediately took my draft, and began revising it: "Dear President Reagan," she wrote, "I believe that as a member of the Cabinet I have the right to bring to your attention matters which significantly affect the fulfillment of my responsibilities at the United Nations." She went on to state that continuation of business as usual in regard to Israel-bashing and the imposition of double standards at the United Nations should not be permitted, and that a "Yes" vote rather than abstention on this resolution would be a missed opportunity to demonstrate at an early and appropriate stage the Administration's opposition to such practices.

"All right, Allan, why don't you give this to Louise?" she said, handing me her note to the President. Looking at it, I concluded that, for whatever reason, she was prepared to stake her political future on the outcome of her battle over this issue with Secretary Haig. But, again, why? Victory was hardly assured. Defeat would mean that her relations with "the Building"—her term of non-endearment for the State Department, would be more miserable, if not unbearable. Her name might still be listed directly under that of Secretary of State Haig in the directory in the State Department's diplomatic entrance, but her actual power would be diminished to that of an Assistant Secretary, or less. Any idea of independence would be shelved. So why was she doing this? Could she really care that much about this particular issue, and about the double standard applied to Israel at the United Nations? Or had she seized on this issue to resolve her differences with Haig so that she would not be simply a mouthpiece for State Department policy? If so, I reasoned, then surely there were better vehicles than this for a showdown with Secretary of State Haig.

I thought back to a meeting with Elliott Abrams the previous week when, as a "courtesy," I handed him a copy of Kirkpatrick's note to Haig with the memorandum on the Geneva Convention issue. I assumed that he would go along with Kirkpatrick's aim of doing business directly with the Secretary of State, that as a fellow neo-conservative appointee coming from a similar political background, he would see eye-to-eye with her on this issue. In fact, unknown to me at the time, Abrams already had Kirkpatrick's note and memorandum—S/S had forwarded it to him—and was marshalling the efforts of L and NEA to defeat Kirkpatrick's proposal, determined to prevent her from using her post in New York to make policy in Washington.

Elliott Abrams evidently thought he would prevail and that in the end he, not Kirkpatrick, would control U.S. policy at the United Nations. He had a large standing army—a staff of over 100—compared to the handful of aides Kirkpatrick had assembled. He knew that L, the State Department's Legal Adviser's Office, was behind him; and that Jeane Kirkpatrick's lawyers in New York reported to the State Department. Abrams saw himself as part of the State Department; it was not "the Building" versus him. It was the other way around: "the Building" versus her. Substantively, there was no serious disagreement between them. They differed over power: who would control and who would be subservient to the other. At stake for Jeane Kirkpatrick was whether she could bypass IO and Abrams entirely, using them to service rather than direct the work of the Mission in New York. For Elliott Abrams it meant directing the show in New York out of Washington.

"What do you think?" Kirkpatrick asked, pointing to the note she had drafted directed to President Reagan. Seeing that I seemed less than enthusiastic, she said, "Call in Carl. Let's see what he thinks."

Carl had already conferred with her on this matter so that there was no need to brief him. As he read over her letter to President Reagan, an aide from the Political Section arrived with a note in hand addressed "For Ambassador's Kirkpatrick's immediate attention."

She smiled on reading it, and motioning to me and Carl said, "Take a look at this." The message read that word had just been received from the Arab sponsors of the draft UN General Assembly resolution on the Israel/Fourth Geneva Convention issue. The Arab sponsors had decided to amend the draft resolution, to toughen its stance by calling upon the UN General Assembly to "condemn" rather than, as previously drafted, to "strongly deplore" Israel's conduct in refusing . to acknowledge the Convention's applicability. The import of the change was immediately apparent. In diplomatic parlance, a vote to "condemn" is significantly more strident than a vote "to deplore." The upshot was that the showdown Kirkpatrick was about to precipitate between herself and Secretary Haig was no longer necessary. The language of the previous year's resolution having been suddenly changed, a U.S. "Yes" vote could no longer be justified on grounds of precedent. For a moment we thought of calling for a "No" vote in light of the changed circumstances, but decided not to press our luck. Victories at the United Nations, we had already come to realize, were administered in small doses.

Kirkpatrick asked whether I was still in touch with Haig's special assistant, the one who after the flap over the PLO Observer Mission promised to help smooth the paper-flow. "This time," she said in response to my affirmative reply, "I'd like you to make sure with him that Haig gets the message that a memorandum is coming his way from me, and that he needs to look at it directly and soon. Can you do that?"

I assured her I could and she then dictated a memorandum to be cabled to Haig informing him of the change in circumstances and arguing that a "Yes" vote would now be bound to embarrass President Reagan, and that she should accordingly be authorized to abstain on the upcoming vote. The next morning, at a meeting with Haig's special assistant in Washington, I told him that Kirkpatrick had been ready to go to the mat on this issue and to take it directly to the President, and that it all seemed a great pity as Haig and Kirkpatrick's views on the Middle East, as on Central America and Europe, did not differ, and that personality and bureaucratic high jinks were getting in the way of policy. He told me that word had gotten through to Haig of Kirkpatrick's pique, and that he had already read and acted on her cable of yesterday afternoon, having decided to go along with her request without first "vetting" it through the system. S/S had already been so informed. But for appearance' sake, they were instructed to go through the rigamarole of drafting an Action Memorandum for his signature, even though the decision had already been made, spelling out the changed circumstances that had persuaded all the interested bureaus to recommend "instructing" USUN to abstain from voting on the Geneva Convention resolution, rather than voting in favor of it as initially ordered. Form had to be maintained, but from now on, I was told, I could tell Kirkpatrick that Haig would personally see and react to whatever suggestions Kirkpatrick might make without first "vetting" them through the system.

The United States later abstained on that resolution,[5] and as it came up in the Special Political Committee where I was an alternate delegate, it fell to me to deliver the explanation of vote for our action. I argued that no matter how it was phrased the resolution had little to do with advancing the cause of peace or human rights. It was, at best, a distraction. What I did not say was that had overzealousness not overtaken the sponsors of the resolution, a showdown on this issue between Ambassador Jeane Kirkpatrick and Secretary of State Alexander Haig would have been almost inevitable.

Although the matter never reached President Reagan, it had the salutary effect of making clear to Secretary Haig and to the Department how strongly Kirkpatrick felt and to what lengths she was willing to go to preserve her independent voice in policy. For Elliott Abrams—who already had had multiple clashes with Carl Gershman, José Sorzano, and Chuck Lichenstein as well as Jeane Kirkpatrick— the incident did not augur well; before the end of his first General Assembly session, he would tire of trying to instruct Jeane Kirkpatrick, and instead move on to greener pastures as head of State's Human Rights Bureau. Jeane Kirkpatrick as Ambassador to the United Nations would fit no easy mold. Such was the message that had come across to the State Department. Perhaps more than any other U.S. Permanent Representative in the past, she would use her warm and sympathetic reception in the Oval Office to good political advantage.

6

"All Available Means"
The Abu Eain Resolution and the Legitimation of Terror

What this Assembly is dealing with is not the fate of one individual. . . . The case we are dealing with is a matter of principle. Where do we draw the line between legitimate resistance and criminal action and who decides where to draw that line?

> Z.L. Terzi, Chief Representative of the PLO, before the UN General Assembly, December 16, 1981

The indiscriminate bombing of a civilian populace is not recognized as a protected political act.

> Judgment of the U.S. Circuit Court of Appeals for the Seventh Circuit in the case of Ziyad Abu Eain vs. John J. Adams, February 20, 1981

The matter of Ziyad Abu Eain was our rough introduction into the state of the world, circa 1981, which had the promotion and legitimation of national liberation struggle at the top of its agenda. None of us at the U.S. Mission could have imagined that the major event at our first General Assembly session would be to witness the U.S. legal system put in the dock and denounced by a majority of the UN's member states for being out of step with the progressive development of international law. Nor could we have anticipated the reason: U.S. refusal to accept terrorism as a legitimate means of waging a national liberation struggle.

The case came up like a sudden summer squall through ECOSOC, the Economic and Social Committee, and soon reached hurricane proportions. In its wake all the other issues that one might have thought would occupy the fall 1981 General Assembly's attention—the Iran-Iraq war, Pol Pot's massacres in Cambodia, guerilla war in Central America, the Soviet invasion of Afghanistan, fighting in Angola—became of secondary concern as the UN General Assembly focused all of its attention on the "human rights" of a young Palestinian Arab, Ziyad Abu Eain.

Here the assessment of the PLO's chief UN delegate, I. Z. Terzi, was correct: "[what is at stake is] not the fate of one individual. . . . The case we are dealing with is a matter of principle. Where do we draw the line between legitimate resistance and criminal action and who decides where to draw that line?"[1] By the fall of 1981 the determination to answer this question in favor of legitimizing terrorism, as employed by the PLO and other select "national liberation movements," had become the top item on the agenda of the radical Arab bloc in collaboration with the Soviet and the Non-Aligned blocs.

On the afternoon of Friday, May 14, 1979, as Israelis in the lake-side resort town of Tiberias made their way home to celebrate the Sabbath, a bomb went off in a public trash basket near a bus stop adjacent to a public garden and refreshment stands. The street was crowded with Israeli schoolchildren. The explosion killed two of them and maimed and wounded 36 other children and adults. Israeli authorities investigating the bombing traced it to Abu Eain, a Palestinian living on the West Bank town of Ramallah. According to the confession of a captured accomplice, Eain had set the time-bomb and then gone home. Before he could be apprehended, Abu Eain succeeded in crossing the Allenby Bridge into Jordan. Israeli authorities asked for the help of INTERPOL, the international police organization, in tracking him down. Three months later, on August 17, FBI agents, acting on an INTERPOL warrant, located Abu Eain in Chicago and brought him before a local magistrate's court to show cause why he should not be extradited to Israel to stand trial for murder.[2]

When the hearing commenced on September 26, the issue confronting the U.S. Magistrate in Chicago seemed straightforward. A U.S.-Israel treaty for mutual extradition of persons charged with criminal offenses had been in effect since 1963. Like other treaties of this kind, it provided for extradition on a showing of probable cause that the requesting nation had sufficient evidence to warrant an indictment. Here Israel pointed to the signed confession by an accomplice, and to Abu Eain's efforts to elude apprehension. This was sufficient to warrant an indictment—though not necessarily a conviction—in a U.S. as well as an Israeli court. That would have to be left to trial— and so on this basis alone there were grounds for Abu Eain's extradition. Abu Eain's lawyers, however, introduced a new element into the case: even if their client planted the bomb—which he denied—he should nevertheless not be extradited because his act was politically motivated, and thus fell under the "political offense" exception to what would otherwise be an extraditable offense.

The U.S. Magistrate rejected both arguments. She found sufficient evidence linking Abu Eain to the bombing to warrant his extradition, and she found that political motives did not excuse the killing of innocent civilians. No sooner had the judgment been rendered than money began to pour in for Abu Eain's appeal. On May 28, 1980, the U.S. District Court for the Northern District of Illinois, after hearing argument, affirmed the Magistrate's decision. Dissatisfied by the ruling, Abu Eain's supporters retained the services of a former U.S. Attorney-General, Ramsey Clark, to appeal the District Court's decision to the U.S. Court of Appeals for the Seventh Circuit.

A brief was filed on behalf of the proposition that the "political offense" exception—the questionable doctrine that any act of violence related to the political objective of toppling a government was non-extraditable—applied in this case and mandated Abu Eain's release. On September 26, 1980, oral argument was heard, and on February 20, 1981, the three-member appeals panel rendered its ruling. It affirmed the lower court's order for extradition.[3]

In a lengthy opinion reviewing the history of the "political offense" doctrine, the Court ruled that, insofar as it still carried validity, it was meant to apply to acts aimed at the disruption of "the political structure of a State, and not the social structure that established the government," and thus had no bearing on Abu Eain. Writing for the Court of Appeals, Judge Harlington Wood concluded that "the indiscriminate bombing of a civilian populace is not recognized as a protected political act"; indeed, were he to construe the law as Ramsey Clark urged, "nothing would prevent an influx of terrorists seeking safe haven in America. Those terrorists who flee to this country would avoid having to answer to anyone. The law is not so utterly absurd."[4]

Undaunted, Abu Eain's supporters had Ramsey Clark seek review by the U.S. Supreme Court. The Supreme Court denied his petition for a writ of *certiorari* to review the Court of Appeals judgment.[5] At this point, all levels of the U.S. legal system—from the Magistrates Court to the U.S. Supreme Court—having been exhausted, the issue would, under normal circumstances, be resolved. But Ziyad Abu Eain's case went far beyond the fate of one individual. It concerned the struggle waged at the United Nations since the early 1970s to legitimate the use of terrorism by referring to it as "all available means" to "liberate" territory under "alien" rule. Over the course of the last decade, UN resolution after UN resolution had affirmed the principle that politically inspired violence—chiefly against South African or Israeli civilians—was a legitimate means of waging armed struggle. Terrorism, at the right time and against the right target, was to be treated as a legitimate exercise of political expression, or instrument of war, by those who found it to be the most expedient means to their ends. The proponents of that view—in 1981, a majority of the UN's member-states—were not about to let the U.S. Supreme Court stand in their way.

On October 28, several days after the Supreme Court had declined further review, Jordan's Ambassador Nuseibeh requested that the General Assembly's Third Committee, dealing with social, humanitarian, and cultural affairs, take up the matter of Abu Eain under agenda item 91: "Torture and Other Cruel, Inhuman or Degrading Treatment or Punishment." The treatment Nuseibeh was referring to was not that accorded the victims of the bombing in Tiberias, but Abu Eain's supposed "torture" or other "cruel, inhuman, or degrading treatment" at the hands of the U.S. judicial system.

Already back in May of 1981, after the U.S. Court of Appeals had handed down its decision, José Sorzano had gotten the first whiff of what was in store at the United Nations. When ECOSOC introduced a resolution stating that Abu Eain "had been illegally detained in a United States prison,"[6] Sorzano, who had never dealt with Middle-East issues before, and was a stranger to the Arab-Israeli conflict before taking leave from his Georgetown University post to join the U.S. Mission, couldn't believe what he was hearing. He thought that the claim that Abu Eain had been "detained illegally" in a U.S. prison was ludicrous. The only reason Abu Eain was in a U.S. prison was because for two years he had successfully fought extradition to Israel, through the fullest use of the legal protection afforded him by the U.S. legal system. And, as always, José had no hesitation about expressing himself forcefully. Nevertheless, on the last day of its spring session, before there had been any of the normally allotted time for consideration of pending resolutions, Algeria, Iraq, Jordan, and Libya forced the resolution on Abu Eain through ECOSOC. It was adopted by a vote of 24 to 14, with 12 abstentions and 5 absent.[7]

Now, on October 18, it was Carl Gershman's turn, in his capacity as the U.S. Representative to the UN General Assembly Third Committee, to take charge of the matter. He asked me to accompany him that day to the Third Committee to hear Nuseibeh make his charges, and to prepare our reply. I was then to receive my second lesson in the "rule of law" at the United Nations. The first had come several days earlier when, as the alternate U.S. delegate to the Special Political Committee, I had objected to the reopening of debate on a particular item on which debate had already been closed. The PLO delegate discovered that he had something more to say on this issue. I raised my hand and informed the Chairman that under the relevant rules of the Committee, once debate on an item is closed, it is closed and cannot be reopened. The Chairman, after thanking the "distinguished representative of the United States" for his observation—at the United Nations everyone is "distinguished"—then asked the delegates to vote on whether they wished their procedural rule to apply in this instance. This was flexible rule-making, UN style.

Now, as regards Jordan's request to have the UN take up the Abu Eain matter under the title "Torture and Other Cruel, Inhuman or Degrading Treatment or Punishment," Gershman had complained to the Third Committee's Chairman, Declan O'Donovan of Ireland, that it would be improper to consider the Abu Eain matter under item 91, the torture and other cruel or inhuman punishment provision. O'Donovan had promised to consult with the UN's Legal Counsel. After Ambassador Nuseibeh asked that the Abu Eain matter be raised under item 91, O'Donovan pointed out that the UN Legal Counsel had informed him that it would be inappropriate to do so; Abu Eain's treatment by American courts did not relate to torture or inhuman treatment. Ambassador Nuseibeh then asked that the members of the Committee vote on whether they wanted to abide by that ruling. By a vote of 65 to 19 with 31 abstentions, the members of the Third Committee decided to disregard the Chairman's ruling and the advice of the UN Legal Counsel. "Flexible" rule-making once again. I might be a lawyer, I observed to myself, but this place and its "procedures" bore little resemblance to that of any American forum where the rule of law prevailed.

The next day I accompanied Carl Gershman in addressing, in a small room adjacent to the UN General Assembly hall, the WEOG, the Western European Group Caucus. He wanted me to explain to them why the U.S. courts had rejected the argument that freeing one's homeland from "alien" rule, Abu Eain's proffered motivation, did not excuse the indiscriminate killing of civilians. Carl hoped that my presentation would help build a solid wall of American and European opposition to the UN effort to exonerate Abu Eain, and to take the U.S. Government to task for having impeded his freedom.

With the exception of the representative of France, all the other delegates at the WEOG meeting assured us of their support. They warned, however, that a resolution condoning Abu Eain's conduct and condemning that of the United States would be backed by a majority of states. The French representative "reluctantly" told the WEOG delegates that his government had to recognize that there was a divergence of views on whether the political motivations of a crime should result in making it a non-extraditable offense, and for that reason would abstain from voting for or against any resolution on the Abu Eain matter. He did not say that there was a reasonable basis for a divergence of views; only that the fact that, as a divergence did exist, it prevented France from voting according to its conscience and its perception of what the law requires.

Clearly France was bent on pursuing a course independent of the United States in its approach to the Middle East. In part this was a function of history and economics. As a former colonial power in the region and an administrator of the League of Nations Mandate over Lebanon, France always felt it had a special relationship with and understanding of the Arab world with which it had continued to foster strong economic ties. Here, France's independence would be at the expense of the U.S. position in the world; the United States was about to be condemned on charges France could hardly find credible, and the most it was prepared to do was abstain.

As the UN Third Committee began its "debate" and began to line up votes for a resolution condoning Abu Eain's actions while condemning extradition by the United States, the Abu Eain drama was also being played out in another arena: the State Department.

Under U.S. law, the Secretary of State is empowered to decline to enforce an otherwise valid court order authorizing extradition if it would adversely impact significant U.S. foreign policy objectives. After the U.S. Supreme Court declined to review the case, Secretary of State Alexander Haig asked his newly appointed Deputy Secretary,

William P. Clark, a former California Supreme Court judge and friend of the President, to make this determination. Within the State Department, those bureaus and individuals who wanted to have a say on the matter could bring their concerns and views to Judge Clark. Those who opposed extradition could bring their arguments to Judge Clark, providing they were careful not to overplay their hand. They could not be seen as lightly advocating noncompliance with treaties or court rulings. Their job would have to be limited to making Judge Clark understand prevailing political "facts," and the likely consequences extradition would have on U.S. military installations, diplomatic posts, and U.S. embassy personnel throughout the Middle East. Judge Clark was to be made aware that extradition might make these installations and individuals targets of Arab fury. From the field came warnings that the future of Abu Eain had become an emotional touchstone throughout the Arab world, and that this extradition would set off an uncontrollable stream of events. The future of the Arab-Israeli "peace process" itself might be at risk. All of these "facts" were presented to enable Judge Clark to reach his decision with a full awareness of the potential ramifications. It wasn't that any one bureau in the State Department bureaucracy wanted to see the United Nations condemn the U.S. legal system, or condone terrorism. They much preferred that the whole nasty business go away. If what it took to make it vanish was a way around the U.S. court decisions, a way for the Deputy Secretary of State to postpone indefinitely the extradition of Abu Eain and thus avert the risks that extradition carried, then that was an option worth exploring fully.

Kirkpatrick, from the start, saw the unfolding drama as a struggle over policy and direction—that of the United Nations and that of the United States. For the United Nations, at issue was whether it could bring to fulfillment a decade-long development of an intellectual and institutional infrastructure to justify terrorism and violent armed struggle when linked to the slogans of decolonization, national liberation, and an end to racism. For the United States— and the new Reagan Administration, which had proclaimed antiterrorism to be one of its chief foreign-policy goals—what was at stake was whether it would succumb to pressures to abort its antiterrorism policy. If it did, it would mark further proof of the connection between the decline of democratic ideals and principles at the United Nations, and the decline of U.S. power in the world. After all, the point of the Abu Eain resolution was not only to endorse the conduct of Abu Eain, but to condemn the United States and its legal system and procedures.

The issue for Kirkpatrick seemed therefore simple: whether to stand up to the threat of more terror to justify ongoing terror, or to fold our tents and declare—through the U.S. Deputy Secretary of State—that extraordinary foreign-policy considerations called for an indefinite postponement of the courts' order authorizing the extradition of Abu Eain. She asked that I help redress the balance caused by the influx of memoranda to Judge Clark on the prevailing political context—i.e., the threats of violence upon extradition—by providing him with a memorandum of law demonstrating why he should narrowly construe the exceptional foreign-policy considerations which might authorize him to override a court-approved and otherwise valid extradition request.

I did so, and on December 13, 1981, Clark made his decision. In a lengthy memorandum he provided reasoned conclusions as to why both policy and fidelity to the law—the 1963 U.S.-Israel Extradition Treaty and the relevant legal doctrines already examined by three levels of U.S. courts—dictated adherence to the principle that terrorism, regardless of motivation, could not be condoned. There were no extraordinary foreign-policy considerations that led to a countervailing result and he was therefore compelled, he said, to "sign the surrender warrant, and I have done so this date."

Kirkpatrick then asked that I summarize Clark's unclassified opinion in a one-page flyer to be distributed to all the delegations at the United Nations. Perhaps it would make a difference. Here for all to see would be the U.S. legal system at work from its lowest rung to the U.S. Supreme Court to further review by the Deputy Secretary of State giving the accused every benefit of the doubt and exhaustively dealing with the merits of each of his arguments.

The exercise proved to be futile. Seven days later, on December 22, seventy-five nations voted to condemn the U.S. legal system for ordering the extradition of Abu Eain. In its endorsement of "all available means" to combat "colonialism" and "alien" rule, there was no mistaking that the majority of the UN's members were openly endorsing the selective use of terrorism.[8]

It was a sobering—and sickening—spectacle as nation after nation cast its vote, each time causing a red or green light to go on next to its name on the giant tote board to the right of the General Assembly's podium identifying those for terrorism, and those against, and those who either hadn't made up their mind or were too intimidated to vote one way or another. The final tally ran as follows:

In favor: Afghanistan, Albania, Algeria, Angola, Bahrain, Bangladesh, Benin, Bhutan, Botswana (later advised the Secretariat it had intended to abstain in the vote), Bulgaria, Burundi, Byelorussia, Cape Verde, Chad, China, Congo, Cuba, Cyprus, Czechoslovakia, Democratic Yemen, Djibouti, Egypt, Ethiopia, Gambia, German Democratic Republic, Ghana, Grenada, Guinea, Guinea-Bissau, Hungary, India, Indonesia, Iran, Iraq, Jordan, Kuwait, Lao People's Democratic Republic, Lebanon, Libya, Madagascar, Malaysia, Maldives, Mali, Malta, Mauritania, Mauritius, Mexico, Mongolia, Morocco, Mozambique, Nicaragua, Oman, Pakistan, Poland, Qatar, Rwanda, Sao Tome and Principe, Saudi Arabia, Senegal, Seychelles, Sierra Leone, Somalia, Sri Lanka, Sudan, Syria, Tunisia, Uganda, Ukraine, USSR, United Arab Emirates, United Republic of Tanzania, Viet Nam, Yemen, Yugoslavia, Zimbabwe.

Against: Australia, Austria, Belgium, Canada, Costa Rica, Denmark, Finland, Federal Republic of Germany, Iceland, Ireland, Israel, Italy, Japan, Luxembourg, Netherlands, New Zealand, Norway, Portugal, Sweden, United Kingdom, United States.

Abstaining: Antigua and Barbuda, Argentina, Bahamas, Barbados, Belize, Bolivia, Brazil, Burma, Central African Republic, Chile, Colombia, Dominican Republic, Ecuador, El Salvador, Equatorial Guinea, France, Gabon, Greece, Guatemala, Guyana, Honduras, Ivory Coast, Jamaica, Kenya, Lesotho, Liberia, Nigeria, Panama, Paraguay, Peru, Philippines, Saint Lucia, Spain, Suriname, Thailand, Togo, Trinidad and Tobago, Turkey, Upper Volta, Uruguay, Venezuela, Zaire, Zambia.

Absent: Comoros, Democratic Kampuchea, Dominica, Fiji, Haiti, Malawi, Nepal, Niger, Papua New Guinea, Romania, Saint Vincent, Samoa, Singapore, Solomon Islands, Swaziland, United Republic of Cameroon, Vanuatu.[9]

The Abu Eain vote came as nearly the last item of business for the 36th session of the UN General Assembly. It was for us, the members of the UN delegation—as it was for the rest of the delegates—the most important single event of the session. We had all read and profited from Senator Patrick Moynihan's *Commentary* article, "Joining the Jackals," on the prevailing climate during his tenure at the United Nations, which saw passage of the Zionism as racism resolution and the decline of liberal values.[10] Still, for us at the U.S. Mission in the early fall of 1981, these were abstractions. We had not yet experienced what it meant and felt like to sit behind the nameplate marked "United States" and feel isolated in the world. We had not experienced the dimensions of the struggle to legitimate terrorism. It took the Abu Eain resolution to drive that home.

There were of course other events during that session that attuned us to the new political culture in which we were operating, though none with the dramatic impact of the Abu Eain resolution. There was the glamorous side to the rough edge of multilateral diplomacy. This came under the rubric of "representational functions," getting to know the other one hundred and fifty plus delegations at daily luncheons with two wines and champagne toasts to friendship and solidarity; two or three late afternoon receptions; and the concluding late evening dinners replete with cigars and after-dinner snifters and the hushed exchange of who was likely to do what on what vote. José Sorzano would say only half-jokingly that one had to train over the summer to get in shape for the gastronomic rigors of General Assembly diplomatic life. There would be mix-ups; none so embarrassing as the time Jeane Kirkpatrick and Chuck Lichenstein attended a reception hosted at one of the UN lounges by North Korea (with whom the United States had no diplomatic relations), thinking it was that of its more friendly neighbor to the south, only to realize their error by the attention they drew and the clicking of camera shutters. They beat a hasty retreat to the door to avoid the impression that they were presiding over a diplomatic breakthrough rather than a faux pas.

We learned to speed-read; we had to keep abreast of unfolding events not only at the UN but around the world. Time had to be set aside each day to read and digest the hundreds of cables sent from U.S. diplomatic posts around the globe. These cables, we discovered, would not only alert the Secretary of State and Assistant Secretaries, and everyone else who read them, to developments in those countries, but would also argue for adoption of policies in Washington. And then there was the enormous volume of data put out by the United Nations: UN Secretariat reports on forthcoming conferences, recommendations of the Secretary General, fact-finding missions, appointments, financial matters; transcripts of every word uttered in the Security Council and General Assembly proceedings, each translated into five different languages; and reports from the Special Committees on Palestinian rights, from UNDP—the UN Development Program—from ECOSOC, from the Trusteeship Council, and from the ancillary UN agencies abroad—IAEA, the International Atomic

Energy Agency, IPU, the International Postal Union; WHO, the World Health Organization. . . . The list went on and on.

There was no question that learning about this new world with its myriad and dazzling mirrors, its limousines, luncheons and dinners, and the realization of the sheer complexity of international life, was heady stuff. We were all new to this sort of life and learning quickly that, at the UN, style and substance easily meshed. Jeane Kirkpatrick's early choice of proper "academic" suits, which gave the impression of a teacher in search of a school (in 1981 she was voted by *People* magazine as one of the 10 worst-dressed women in America) soon gave way to the cosmopolitan look of silks and custom-made clothes. All of us adjusted. But through the glitter we could see something not as easily visible from afar—the UN agenda which legitimated Abu Eain's murders and condemned America's efforts to see him brought to trial.

Jeane Kirkpatrick had already given signals of her intent not to continue a "business as usual" policy: these included her stand in negotiations with the Iraqis in June to delete the word "aggression" from the text of the UN Security Council resolution on Israel's strike against the Osirak nuclear reactor; her defense of the free-market economic model at an overseas UN policy conference, even though her lack of any deference to the Third World's vision of a new economic order embarrassed some of her Western colleagues; and her response in October to a transcript of a communiqué issued by NAM, the Non-Aligned Movement, at a meeting in Havana.

The communiqué was sharply critical of U.S. policy around the world. On reading it she wrote to the representatives of twenty-one "non-aligned" nations considered as "friendly" to the United States, attacking the views expressed in that communique. "Such views are not an accurate reflection of your government's outlook," she said, "Yet what are we to believe when your government joins in such charges, for that is what you have done in failing to disassociate yourself from them."[11] To her surprise, her letter (encouraged by Ken Adelman, Carl, and José) elicited a large number of responses. Most said, in apologetic tones, that it was not their intention to malign the United States; indeed, they didn't even think that their communiqué would be taken seriously by U.S. officials; no prior U.S. Ambassador had ever read it, let alone thought enough about it to give it much bother. Those who received the letter realized that as she was taking their words seriously, she demanded the same of them. Her detractors deemed this attitude "combative." For better or worse it was a reputation that would stick to her, and the members of her team, until the end.

Carl Gershman helped fan that reputation. As the representative to the Third Committee—whose agenda encompassed self-determination, human rights, and colonialism—Carl took the battle to the other side. In delivering a speech on the annual item marked "self-determination," he decided not merely to defend the United States against attack but to explore in detail the flaws in the Marxist-Leninist approach. His speech set a record at the UN for the number of delegations—the entire Eastern bloc—requesting rights of reply. Indeed a special session had to be convened just to hear the responses generated by his speech.

But, more than anything else during the first session, it was the U.S. Mission's response to the Abu Eain matter that set the tone for what other delegates might expect from the new U.S. delegation. In May, José Sorzano had told the members of ECOSOC that the only thing "illegal" about the way the Abu Eain matter was handled was ECOSOC's conduct in not following its own rules of procedure before putting it to a vote. In the Third Committee, Carl did his best to solidify whatever support he could enlist from our Western colleagues. In Washington, working behind the scenes, Jeane Kirkpatrick acted to offset the pressure being put on the State Department to yield to demands from the United Nations, and from within the Department, to not extradite Abu Eain to stand trial for murder.[12]

The vote, when it came, though decidedly against the United States, made clear the nature of the struggle and the lineup of the sides. The United States would not be a willing victim. As Jeane Kirkpatrick later put it, it was time that the "kick me" sign be taken off the door of the U.S. Permanent Representative to the United Nations.

As to Abu Eain, in late December FBI officials put him on an Israeli airliner bound for Tel Aviv to stand trial for planting a bomb with intent to kill. Tried in a civilian court in the presence of U.S. embassy observers, he was convicted of murder and sentenced to life imprisonment. Three years later, in 1985, he was released as part of a swap of nearly 1,000 Palestinian and Arab prisoners in Israeli jails for three Israeli servicemen held in Syria.

7

Terror at
the Dome of the Rock
*Separating the Incident from
the Situation*

With the resolution now before us, the United Nations is being
pushed one step closer to a precipice beyond which looms a
political and moral abyss.

> U.S. Ambassador William Sherman addressing the UN General
> Assembly, April 28, 1982.

The magnificent Dome of the Rock Mosque, with its gold leaf
dome and dazzling tiles, has been the jewel of the Jerusalem
skyline since the seventh century when it was erected on the great
stone from which Moslems believe Mohammed ascended to heaven.
That same rock, referred to by Jews as the Temple Mount, is said to
be the stone of King Solomon's Temple, on which the Ark of the
Covenant stood. It is a place holy to Moslems and Jews alike. On
Easter Sunday, 1982, it became the scene of slaughter as a man
dressed in Israeli army fatigues entered the mosque and opened fire
on worshippers. That event triggered a month of debate at the United
Nations and in capitals around the world about who is entitled to rule
over Jerusalem, at least the Eastern part of it: Israelis or Arabs? It is
a debate that hasn't gone away.

After capturing East Jerusalem in the 1967 war, Israel placed the administration and security of the Dome of the Rock and the adjacent Al Aqsa Mosque under the jurisdiction of the Waqf—the Arab Society for the Holy Places, under the auspices of the Supreme Moslem Council. Unarmed Moslem guards and policemen were stationed at the entry. But they were unable to prevent a crazed Australian, Michael Rohan, a Christian, from entering the Al Aqsa Mosque and setting fire to it in 1969. Nor could they prevent Alan Harry Goodman, a 37-year-old Jew from Baltimore who had emigrated to Israel and was a reservist in the Israel Defence Forces, from entering the Dome of the Rock Mosque on April 11, 1982 with an M-16 automatic rifle, and opening fire. Before being subdued by Israeli police, who were immediately called to the scene, he had killed an unarmed Arab guard and an Arab youth, and had wounded 40 worshippers.[1]

The shooting shattered the peace of Easter Sunday. For the rest of the day, Israeli troops and police battled angry Arab crowds in East Jerusalem, repelling stone-throwing demonstrators with tear-gas grenades. Christian pilgrims in the Old City and Jewish worshippers at the nearby Wailing Wall left for safer ground. The next day, Palestinians throughout the West Bank and Gaza Strip staged a near-total general strike to protest the shootings, blaming the Israeli authorities for what had occurred. At least 20 Arab demonstrators were injured in clashes with Israeli troops.

On April 13, shouting "Justice for national liberation!" Alan Harry Goodman was led into an Israeli courtroom, arraigned, and charged with murder. Later that same day, the Supreme Moslem Council arranged a press conference to charge that more than one gunman had been involved in the attack and that the others were being shielded by Israeli authorities. Joining in the chorus of denunciation was Anwar Nuseibeh, the highly respected East Jerusalemite, former Jordanian Defense Minister and Ambassador to Britain, who maintained that "It is obvious from the nature of the damage that it was not only one person who fired the shots."

The following day, April 14, King Khalil of Saudi Arabia called on all Moslem countries in the Middle East, in Africa, and in Asia to join in a general strike to protest the "complicity" of Israeli authorities in the attack on the Dome of the Rock.[2]

In New York, the Security Council had already been convened on April 13 to deal with the incident. Israel's Prime Minister Menacham Begin called the charge of complicity by the Israeli Government a "blood libel" against the Jewish people; it was, he said, the crime of one crazed man who had already been arraigned and charged with murder.[3] Meanwhile a draft resolution condemning Israel for the incident was making the rounds at the UN.

For the Arab sponsors, it was important that they not overplay their hand. A U.S. veto would render the exercise useless. It was important for them to know how far they would have to go in toning down the language of the resolution in order to get a U.S. abstention rather than a veto. Journalists covering the United Nations were asking the same question. One of these, who was particularly well-informed and connected to the Arab caucus at the United Nations, was an attractive journalist of Lebanese origin. She wrote for a newspaper published in Beirut and for a London monthly which covered Middle-Eastern affairs. On April 13, the day the Security Council was to meet regarding the Dome of the Rock incident, she asked me out to lunch.

I felt certain, when I met her at a small Italian restaurant not far from the U.S. Mission near the corner of Forty-fifth Street and First Avenue, that whatever I might tell her would find its way back to the Arab caucus and the PLO. At the United Nations, information-gathering—which sometimes meant dissembling disinformation—was an essential part of the game. I wanted to learn from her which delegation and who within that delegation was the driving force behind the resolution; what their bottom line was; and what they expected in the form of compromise. She, I presumed, wanted to know the American bottom line: whether, if push came to shove and the sponsors of the resolution stood their ground, the United States would in fact veto the proposed resolution. We exchanged pleasantries, and over espresso the conversation turned serious.

"Will the U.S. really veto the resolution?" she asked, "The word is out that it will. But why?"

"Probably," I said. "We've already made that clear."

"But why?" she asked not at all disingenuously, as if trying to comprehend how we could do such a thing. "Because we don't consider the matter appropriate for a Security Council vote," I retorted. "A lone madman went berserk in a mosque. It's a terrible thing. But things like this happen around the world. It's not an earth-shattering event that threatens world peace. The sponsors of this resolution are trying to make something more out of it than it is."

"But he was an Israeli soldier!" she shot back, incredulous that I could believe that the shooting could have been a solitary act without official Israeli complicity.

"What difference does it make? An Israeli soldier, or reservist, can go crazy too."

"It shows that he wasn't a lunatic," she answered. "The Israeli army won't take lunatics. If it does, God help us all."

"But there's no proof, is there, that the Israeli government encouraged him, aided him, abetted him. . . . Is there?"

"And what about the way the soldiers reacted," she retorted, "shooting at kids afterwards; I saw them on TV when they were evacuating Jewish settlers from the Sinai. They carried them out tenderly, but they pulled out the hair of these young Arab boys they caught throwing stones in Jerusalem. Allan, it's a Zionist government."

Her face was saying it all: "I hate them. I hate them." And then she said, "I'll roll up my sleeves to work with anyone to build, to create, a better place for all people, but not to save the Jewish people at the expense of all other people, of my people. I am Lebanese, and I am Arab. I'll fight their autonomy schemes because it means the death of my country. There must be a Palestinian state. There must. Don't you understand that, Allan?"

There wasn't much more to be said, and it was time to head back. We knew where the other stood. One benefit of being at the United Nations was that one didn't have to travel far to get a sense of another's thinking. Everything was concentrated here; all one had to do was to listen carefully.

We returned to the Security Council, I to the horseshoe table around which the delegates and their aides sat, she to the gallery reserved for the press. The Security Council had been called to reconvene at 3:30 P.M., enough time for the diplomatic lunches to conclude. At a little after 4:00, the meeting was called to order.

The chief PLO representative, Terzi, spoke first. He began by citing an editorial in the day's *Washington Post* as proof that there was general agreement, even among informed American observers, that Israel bears responsibility for the shooting. In fact, the editorial merely made the common-place observation that Israel's occupation was bound to cause resentment and high emotions on both sides.[4]

The other delegates seemed uninterested in what Terzi had to say, as if they had heard it all before in a hundred different variations. Nisibori of Japan fought off falling asleep. The Soviet Union's deputy representative, Richard Ovinnikov, who was then occupying the absent chief delegate's seat, stared at the ceiling. Zaire's Kamanda read his copy of the *UN Diplomatic News*. Sir Anthony Parsons of the UK was busy brushing dandruff off his jacket, straightening his tie, and moving restlessly in his seat. Terzi continued undaunted: Goodman, he charged, was a member of an Israeli hit team; his role was to be the fall guy in order to give the operation the appearance of an isolated act.

The U.S. delegation had received instructions from the State Department to simply say "We are sorry the incident occurred," and not to comment on the impropriety of ever having brought the matter before the UN Security Council. Kirkpatrick was in New York that day but decided not to attend the Security Council session as a vote on the resolution was not expected for a few days. Chuck Lichenstein was asked to take her place. He did so with little enthusiasm, spending the bulk of his time at the Security Council opening session on the Dome of the Rock incident leafing through press clippings and *The Economist*, especially its account of Argentina's invasion on April 2 of the Falkland islands and the question of Britain's response. When it was his turn to speak, he delivered a short statement expressing his government's regret for the tragic loss of life. He then went on to say that his government did not view this as a matter appropriate for urgent Security Council consideration as all the available evidence pointed to the fact that the shooting was the act of a solitary deranged man. His statement completed, he returned to his reading.[5]

At 6:30 P.M. the meeting disbanded. As I headed back to the U.S. Mission, I spotted Professor Louis Sohn of the Harvard Law School. He was responsible for having elevated the study of UN resolutions to the level of a law school course, having edited the first casebook on the subject.[6] He was in New York to attend a UN-sponsored Law of the Sea Conference. "Was it always this bad?" I asked.

"No," he replied, "it's gotten much worse. The Security Council could now be doing constructive work in mediating the Argentine-UK Falklands dispute. It's not an issue complicated by East-West considerations and the Council could develop helpful legal principles—non-admissibility of the acquisition of territory by force, self-determination—but instead. . . . Yes, it's gotten worse."

On the 9:00 P.M. shuttle back to Washington, Kirkpatrick and I talked about the upcoming vote and about the deteriorating situation on the Israeli-held West Bank. Menachem Milson, a professor of Arab literature at the Hebrew University, had recently been appointed to serve as the civilian administrator of the West Bank. We talked about his chances of success in easing tensions.

Milson, who had written a recent *Commentary* piece on the subject,[7] believed that the best chance for a breakthrough was through the development and encouragement of dissident voices on the West Bank who might act independently of the PLO. I told her that the Israeli government's failure to find the individuals—suspected to be radical Jewish settlers—responsible for booby-trapping the cars of three West Bank mayors (one of whom, Bassam Shaka of Nablus, lost both his legs) was making matters much worse.

Kirkpatrick knew little about the complexities of the Arab-Israeli conflict when she started. But she was very quickly learning not only its politics, but also its legal aspects, and how the two intermeshed. The systematic Arab assault on Israel at the United Nations was consuming a great portion of her time simply because the matter dominated the UN agenda. Again and again the United States was being forced to take a position, with the point of the exercise invariably being to push U.S. policy, inch by inch, toward a harder stance vis-à-vis Israel. Whether we liked it or not, there was no escaping the anti-Israel campaign at the United Nations. To redress the imbalance required at times that mixed feelings or doubts about Israeli practices and policies held by Jeane Kirkpatrick, or myself, or other members of the team be put aside. The Arab, Soviet, and Non-Aligned blocs had succeeding in polarizing the situation, in eliminating room for ambiguity, and in forcing everyone to choose sides.

The next afternoon, April 14, back in New York at Carl Gershman's office, Herb Reis stopped by to discuss the U.S. response to the Dome of the Rock resolution. Reis told us that in 1969, when a similar incident occurred, things were different; Britain and France then refused to join in a Security Council resolution mildly condemnatory of Israel for the demented Australian's behavior at the Al Aqsa Mosque. Now, Britain and France had let it be known that they would vote in favor of the resolution, thus isolating the United States. Reis suggested we should take that factor—diplomatic isolation—into account in deciding how to vote.

Back in my office, I reviewed the latest news clippings and wire pieces pulled together by the Press section on the second floor. One item referred to Soviet Ambassador Dobrynin's warning to Washington against Israel's planned "new aggression" against Lebanon and Syria, and "terror and reprisals" against West Bank residents. "Israel's policies are universally condemned but sustained by America's indulgence," warned Dobrynin.[8] Another said that the U.S. ambassador in Tel Aviv, Sam Lewis, had warned the Israeli Government that the United States viewed the recent killing of two young Palestinian children by Israeli forces in quelling a disturbance as a demonstration of the self-defeating nature of Israel's continuing resort to lethal force to break up disturbances.[9] Israel was being told that its iron-hand occupation policies were "complicating" U.S. problems at the United Nations in dealing with the Dome of the Rock shooting.

Later that afternoon I was called to a meeting at Kirkpatrick's office to discuss the Islamic Conference's recently released draft Security Council resolution condemning Israel for the Dome of the Rock attack.[10] She showed me a message that had come to her from Under Secretary of State Larry Eagleburger. He had received messages from a number of ambassadors in Middle-Eastern posts urging the Department, in considering how to vote on the proposed Dome of the Rock resolution, to keep in mind that a U.S. veto at this highly charged moment could lead to violence against U.S. personnel and facilities in Islamic countries. Similar fears had been voiced earlier, when the Abu Eain matter came up in the 1981 General Assembly session. Now there seemed to be greater warrant for them. Eagleburger's message asked therefore that Kirkpatrick attempt to work with the Islamic sponsors to achieve a text which the United States could support; or, at least, abstain from rather than veto. A veto, which would render the whole Islamic exercise a nullity, would be seen as an unfriendly act: an abstention, rather than a "Yes" vote as an understandable act mandated by the needs of taking a "balanced" approach to Arab-Israeli issues.

I said that it was a pity that we had to become party to this sort of thing, of "negotiating" with the Arab sponsors, rather than simply telling them that we would veto any resolution that said, explicitly or implicitly, that the Goodman shooting was the product of Israeli governmental action. As this was the aim of their exercise, it would be better, I suggested, to simply tell them that their efforts were bound to go nowhere.

Kirkpatrick cut me off sharply: "Allan, I don't want to hear another word about it. You've read my instructions on the subject." I said I understood. But I didn't quite understand. She had shown no reluctance to play with "instructions" on other occasions, to draw attention to and make use of her Cabinet status and access to the President. What I did understand her to mean was that her effectiveness in shaping policy necessarily meant working within the ambit of instructions, following them, shaping them, and interpreting them her way if possible, but never disregarding them. Besides, there was another factor I was only now learning to appreciate. She preferred rounded corners. She liked keeping things in motion. She didn't relish giving a simple straight-forward "No"—not to other delegates, and certainly not to instructions.

Rosenstock and I then set to work to see if we could revise the Islamic draft resolution to make it compatible with a U.S. abstention, and perhaps even a "Yes" vote. We agreed that the resolution's preambular paragraph, which referred to the occupied territories as "Arab and Palestinian," had to be excised in favor of the phrase "occupied territories" so as not to prejudice any Israeli claims to the area. We agreed as well to delete the resolution's explicit reference to the Geneva Convention as applicable to Jerusalem. The Geneva Convention referred to enemy-held territory under belligerent occupation. Our understanding of the Camp David Accords was that the legal status of Jerusalem was to be differentiated from that of the West Bank and Gaza Strip and not be treated as "occupied territory" but as something undefined and in-between. Where we disagreed was in paragraph 3 of the proposed resolution, which called on Israel to observe and apply the Fourth Geneva Convention and the principles of international law governing military occupation. Rosenstock wanted it in so that the resolution remained strong enough "to get them to do something about the mess they've created."

"Israel," Rosenstock said, "is going crazy on all fronts at once."

Kirkpatrick suggested that we try to replace the paragraphs condemning Israel with a straightforward recitation that Israeli security measures proved inadequate for the protection of the Mosque. With that, our work on an acceptable proposal for compromise on the Islamic text was completed. Kirkpatrick thanked us and told us that she had to get ready to return to Washington. She asked if I was coming along. One foot in New York and one foot in Washington, that's the way things always were. I scurried to get papers together for another dash to La Guardia. To be sure, there was a schedule—of sorts, but it changed on a minute's notice—a Cabinet meeting, a quick convening of the NSC or NSPG (National Security Planning Group), or a Senator or Congressman or visiting parliamentarian, or whatever; my coat and bags always had to be ready for a switch in our vectors, to Washington or to New York.

Clearly, Kirkpatrick liked to juggle many matters at the same time. She didn't, however, necessarily communicate what she had in mind to do with what she had up in the air, even to those with whom she worked most closely. At times, neither Carl, Chuck, nor I knew with any degree of certainty what she was going to do. We did not delude ourselves into believing that our advice formed more than a part of the mosaic of her thought processes.

Back in Washington, it soon became apparent, however, that the revisions which Rosenstock and I had made in the Islamic Conference's draft resolution on the Dome of the Rock incident were not sufficient to meet some of the Department's concerns. The Department had already approved, I was told by the Legal Adviser's office, the use of the word "Arab" to describe the occupied territories and pointed out that its use was justified as a demographic expression without legal significance. As far as the Department was concerned, we should also have allowed the word "Palestinian" to remain and not made a fuss over Jerusalem as distinct from the West Bank. It seemed as if we might have another fight with State on our hands over acceptable compromise language.

I called Carl to let him know what was happening in Washington. Kirkpatrick, a breakfast meeting behind her, had already flown back to New York. Carl told me that she had gone into a meeting with a group from the Arab caucus pushing the resolution, and that he was not asked to attend. Michael Davis, the NEA officer assigned to the Political Section, was there. So were Bob Rosenstock and Chuck Lichenstein. The Arab group, said Carl, wanted the United States to agree to the phrase "Arab territories" and to refer to the applicability of the Fourth Geneva Convention to occupied territories "including Jerusalem." In return they would be prepared to revise the resolution to downplay Israel's responsibility for the shooting. Kirkpatrick had told them that she would pass on their suggestions.

It became apparent that she had spoken to someone in Washington that morning at State or the White House—probably Larry Eagleburger or William Clark at the NSC—and had received the message that the Department believed that the phrase "Arab occupied territories" and reference to Jerusalem as "occupied territory" was acceptable; the latter because it was only a "demographic" expression, and not related to the legal status of the West Bank, Gaza, or Jerusalem. That was, I reasoned, probably why she hadn't rejected out-of-hand the Arab caucus insistence on having the draft Dome of the Rock resolution refer to Jerusalem as part of the "occupied territories."

I decided that I had better make certain that Kirkpatrick was clear on the legal and political pitfalls involved in referring to Jerusalem as occupied territory, and so I drafted a note on the subject which I planned to present to her next morning as she arrived in Washington's National Airport. It read as follows:

As you know, there are two remaining troublesome aspects to the draft Dome of the Rock resolution: (1) the phrase 'reaffirms the applicability of the Geneva Convention to the territories occupied by Israel since 1967, including Jerusalem'; and (2) the phrase 'all Arab territories occupied by Israel since 1967, including Jerusalem.' You should know that it was reference to Jerusalem as 'occupied Arab territory' that got Don McHenry in trouble in connection with Security Council Resolution 465 of March 1, 1980. The U.S. vote in favor of that resolution was later repudiated by Secretary of State Cy Vance. To the best of my knowledge the United States has never since acquiesced in a Security Council resolution referring to Jerusalem as 'occupied Arab territory.'

With the memorandum typed and laid aside for the next morning, I turned my attention again to the news clippings and incoming cable traffic. The *New York Times* reported in a dispatch dated April 14, 1982 that "One million people packed the streets of Teheran to demonstrate against Israel as a result of the Dome of the Rock incident."[11] One million! It was hard to imagine. Towards the middle of the paper was another report: Syrian troops had shelled the Syrian town of Hama, a fundamentalist stronghold, killing at least 5,000 civilians. (Later the figure turned out to be closer to 20,000.)[12] No protests were reported. Another story in the morning's papers reported a broadcast from Damascus Radio that "all rifles should be directed at the Zionist heart." There was no mistake about it: the rhetoric was reflective of a new swell of hatred sweeping the region.

From our ambassadors in Moslem capitals came urgent requests that the United States not veto the Arab caucus resolution on the Dome of the Rock incident; and that it was good that the resolution should reflect the fact that Israeli occupation was the ultimate cause of the shooting. That reaction was not limited to the Middle-Eastern countries. From Indonesia—a Moslem but non-Arab country usually off the map on Arab-Israeli debates—came the message that its Parliament had condemned Israel on the grounds that the shooting proved that Israel was "not only the enemy of the Palestinian people, but of all Moslems because it is now trying to crush Islam."[13]

In the late afternoon, the Security Council convened once again to hear "debate" on the Dome of the Rock incident. In the Washington office there was a "squawk box" which could be tuned directly to the proceedings. Iran's representative was giving a long rambling speech which ended with his call to honor the memory of "martyrs"— those in Zionist-occupied territory, and those executed that day in Cairo for the assassination of Egyptian President Anwar Sadat. Jihad—holy war—was, he proclaimed, the only answer to the existence of the Zionist entity.

The U.S. vote on the proposed Dome of the Rock resolution was assuming major international significance. U.S. Deputy Secretary of State Walter Stoessel met on April 17 in Jerusalem with Israeli Prime Minister Menachem Begin to discuss potential U.S. support for the draft Security Council resolution. Begin replied that the issue was no longer Israeli responsibility for the incident—which was a non-issue to begin with, as "there are madmen everywhere"—but whether the United States would be a party to "the blood libel against the Jewish people and Israel" and to UN efforts to redefine the status of Jerusalem.[14]

At 10:00 A.M. on April 17, Kirkpatrick arrived at Washington's National Airport to attend an NSC meeting and a later meeting that afternoon between President Reagan and the Washington diplomatic corps of Arab ambassadors to discuss the U.S. position on the impending Dome of the Rock resolution. I met her with the memorandum I had drafted on this issue. She read it in the limousine on the way to the State Department. "I know this," she said, putting it down, "and, I hear you."

At the State Department, Phil Wilcox, the Director of IO's Political Section, came into Kirkpatrick's office carrying a sheaf of papers. He seemed pleased. One of those papers was a copy of a UN General Assembly resolution which had passed the previous year with the United States voting in favor. Wilcox, showing it to Kirkpatrick as if it were dispositive of the matter of how the United States should cast its vote on the Dome of the Rock resolution, pointed to the following language: "The General Assembly reaffirms that the Geneva Convention is applicable to Palestinian and other Arab territories, including Jerusalem."[15]

"What about this, Allan?" Kirkpatrick asked after Wilcox left. "I thought you said the United States never voted for a resolution deeming Jerusalem to be occupied territory, other than the Don McHenry flap, and yet there's this resolution. And I see that you raised your hand voting in favor of it. It came out of the Special Political Committee. I never knew about this. I would never have allowed it. I was on the alert for such language."

"Jeane," I said, "we abstained on that vote. It's no precedent for anything we're now called upon to do at the Security Council. It was part of a large omnibus Special Political Committee resolution dealing with Israeli practices in the occupied territories that worked its way up to the General Assembly. Reference to Jerusalem as encompassed in the area in which the Geneva Convention's rules on occupied territory were meant to apply was just one line in it; it was never a central focus. Here we're talking about a Security Council resolution whose heart is the question of Jerusalem as occupied Arab territory. It's a far different matter. We're not locked into an abstention rather than a veto because of that."

"You should have brought that resolution to my attention," she said.

"Yes, I suppose I should have, or Chuck should have, but it was part of an omnibus package, our voting instructions were clear, and, in any event, it doesn't determine what we have to do now. This is a Security Council resolution and the whole world will be looking to see how we vote on the Jerusalem issue. It's what the Dome of the Rock resolution is now all about. It hardly concerns the Goodman shooting any more."

"Look, Allan," Kirkpatrick said, "I'd like you to sit in on a meeting I'm going to have on this matter in a few minutes with Nick Platt (the Deputy Assistant Secretary of IO) and Phil Wilcox. Also with Watt Cluverius, do you know him?"

"Yes, he's NEA's all-purpose Middle-East hand."

"And, oh yes, the new Assistant Secretary for IO, Greg Newell, will be coming too."

The meeting had just begun later that afternoon when it was interrupted by a phone call from Hazem Nuseibeh, Jordan's UN representative. He was calling to check which way the wind was blowing on the likely U.S. vote on the draft resolution. Kirkpatrick answered, loudly enough for all assembled to hear, that her government remained "concerned" about joining the proposed resolution as currently phrased. She was pleased, she said, that the reference to Israeli governmental complicity had been dropped but there were still other troublesome aspects to the draft resolution. "Could you," she asked, "meet me at my Waldorf residence tomorrow morning with some of the other Arab representatives to discuss this further?"

Kirkpatrick was doing her best to appear very "diplomatic" to those in the room, as being cordial and on the best of terms with the other UN ambassadors, even those considered difficult if not hostile. She had already had several breakfasts with Ambassador Nuseibeh and the Arab caucus, and so the impression of smooth working relations came naturally.

Kirkpatrick seemed to relish stringing things out. It was, I thought, a risky course that could lead to the perception of irresolution by the United States and thus make us vulnerable and more prone to compromise or surrender on objectionable positions than might otherwise be the case. But Kirkpatrick seemed to have the knack for it, and it paid certain dividends; over time it helped defuse the anger of a hostile majority.

Then, after having placated Jordan's Nuseibeh, she turned to Platt, Wilcox, and the others, and said that the present resolution's language on Jerusalem was totally unacceptable; President Reagan and Secretary Haig would never buy it. But, said Platt, we have voted for similar language in the past. "We shouldn't have," Kirkpatrick answered abruptly, turning that suggestion aside. "The President will not agree. This is a Security Council resolution, not an obscure General Assembly resolution. The substance is wrong. The domestic political consequences are too great. I haven't forgotten what happened to Donald McHenry when he voted for this type of language, and neither should you."

The discussion then focused on the resolution's language which, although diluted, still implicitly attributed responsibility for the incident to Israel. Watt Cluverius argued that we could live with the resolution's language; "it's sufficiently ambiguous; the Arabs can make their claim, and we can make ours." I had the urge to say let's call a spade a spade and veto this resolution because it's based on trumped-up charges, but Kirkpatrick had taught me to keep that instinct in check. There were many ways to skin a resolution. I held my tongue, and Kirkpatrick registered no objection to Cluverius' suggestion.

The meeting adjourned shortly after 11:00 A.M., so that Kirkpatrick could attend an NSC meeting at the White House. As she was about to leave, I said to the group, "Can we stay for a few more minutes and talk this through?"

I raised the possibility of a deal with the Arab sponsors of the resolution. In return for removing reference to Jerusalem as an "occupied territory," perhaps we could offer a more accommodating statement about Jerusalem in our explanation of the vote while leaving it out of the text of the resolution. Platt, Wilcox, and the others seemed to like the idea. Platt said, "Let's draft changes we have to have, then ones we would like to have, and exchange copies in the afternoon."

But later that afternoon something occurred that made irrelevant the writing exercise Platt had proposed. The resolution's Arab sponsors made it clear that nothing could persuade them to remove reference to Jerusalem as occupied Arab territory. That, it became crystal clear, was the ultimate objective of the exercise—not the condemnation of the Israeli government for the Dome of the Rock shooting. Important as that was, it was only an incident, only a means to an end, and the end was the situation in the territories and the status of Jerusalem. Further proposals for revision by the resolution's sponsors—which had been wired to us from New York—showed that they were prepared to drop the reference to acts "by members of the Israeli army" and "Israel's failure to comply with the Geneva Conventions" in return for the United States' agreement to join in the resolution deeming Jerusalem to be "occupied Arab territory."

Kirkpatrick returned to the White House for the 4:00 P.M. meeting between President Reagan and the Arab ambassadors in Washington on the impending U.S. vote on the Dome of the Rock resolution. Before she left, we met for a final word. I told her of the information we had received from New York and suggested that she tell President Reagan—she would see him alone shortly before the meeting—that he inform the Arab ambassadors that unless reference to Jerusalem as "occupied Arab territory" were deleted the United States would not be able to join in the resolution. He might point out that no American administration had ever agreed to such a formulation in the context of a UN Security Council resolution. On this, I said, Cluverius, Wilcox, Platt, Newell, and I agreed. We differed insofar as they counseled a U.S. abstention if the Arab sponsors refused to make the changes we wanted, and I favored a veto. A veto would ensure that no party could claim that the description of Jerusalem as occupied Arab territory had the sanction of the UN Security Council, albeit without U.S. participation in the vote.

Much to the chagrin of the Arab ambassadors attending the meeting, President Reagan informed them that, although substantial improvements had been made in the initial text of the Dome of the Rock resolution, failure to delete Jerusalem as occupied Arab territory might force the United States into the unwelcome position of vetoing the resolution.

Two days later, on April 19, 1982, the Security Council was convened for a vote. At 11:20 A.M., when I arrived, most of the delegates were still standing about conversing with each other. Lichenstein was sitting alone in the seat reserved for the U.S. delegation; Kirkpatrick had decided to absent herself. Behind him stood Herb Reis and Michael Davis. I sat down next to Lichenstein in the adjacent seat, that of the UN Secretary-General Perez de Cuellar.

I asked Chuck where matters now stood. "Haig doesn't want to take responsibility for a veto. Jeane doesn't want to fall into a trap. That's all I can make of it. I assume she's still on the phone with Washington. Right now we're set for a veto but the language may soften up before the day is done, or Washington may cave."

The No. 3 man on the Soviet delegation came over to chat with Chuck, and said he was going to have lunch that day with Rosenstock. Chuck asked him about the delay in getting the meeting started. The Soviet delegate said that Djibouti was scheduled to speak first but now would not be ready to speak until 12:00.

"Why then don't we all go home?" Chuck asked.

The Soviet delegate chuckled and said, "Only Americans go home." I could see Chuck gearing up to say something like "It's 'Russians Go Home' signs that are having a run on the market," but suddenly De Cuellar arrived from a rear door and it was time for the meeting to convene.

The Soviet Deputy Permanent Representative, Richard Ovinnikov, began by declaring furiously that the Dome of the Rock shooting was "committed under cover provided by the Israeli occupying authorities." Could he, I asked myself, actually believe what he was saying? I doubted it, although certain that it was of no consequence to him. He continued: Israel's complicity in the shooting was part and parcel of the crimes committed "since the Israeli aggression against the Arab states in June 1967. . . . This is an act of terrorism. It was committed by a soldier of the Israeli army of occupation under cover provided by other Israeli soldiers. This is the real point: this was an act carried out by a terrorist under cover provided by other terrorists."

Then, Ovinnikov turned his thunder to the United States. It bore, he said, "equal responsibility."

It is precisely that assistance from the United States, which has now openly taken on the role of the strategic ally of Tel Aviv, that has given Israel the ability and the means to implement in the Middle East its expansionist designs against Arab lands, to assault the sovereignty and territorial integrity of neighboring States and, finally, unabashedly to disregard the will of the international community. It is precisely because of the complicity of the United States here in the Security Council that it has been impossible to take the necessary measures against the arbitrary rule of the Israeli occupiers in order to halt the annexationist ambitions of Israel.[16]

Jordan was second on the list of speakers. Its representative, Hazem Nuseibeh, was well-known for his eccentricities (even the PLO's delegates seemed taken aback by his antics, particularly the way he tried to argue his case by "reasoning" with Israel's UN representative). This time he began by quoting from a letter he had received from a widow of the late leader of the Naturei Karta, Israel's ultra-orthodox, anti-Zionist sect which opposed the establishment of the State of Israel on the ground that its creation was intended by divine command to await the coming of the Messiah; hence Israel's existence itself was a sacrilegious act. It was easy to see why Nuseibeh might have an affinity for the Naturei Karta.

A Zionist State has been created in 1948 in the Holy Land against the will of God and against the will of a great part of his creatures. The main thing for its leaders afterwards has been the building of the "Great Israel."

If Hitler wrote one book, *Mein Kampf*, to explain his Nazi ideas, there are a lot of Zionist books explaining Zionist ideals and ambitions and from the Israeli Parliament insults and threats are now raining on Western leaders' heads when they do not agree completely with Israeli leaders whose policies are based on hatred of the Arabs, whom they have turned into the universal enemies of the Jews. . . .

Why do people refuse to learn from the lessons of the past? Why do they close their eyes before the real danger while they mobilize all their energies to protect themselves against an eventual, more remote, danger—that one which may precisely proceed from the danger against which they remain inactive? On the way to Auschwitz, a Jew asked Rabbi Shlomo Zalman Ehrenreich, the Shimloer Rav, why the Holy One—blessed be He—had let this catastrophe fall upon the Jews of Europe. He answered him, "We are punished because we did not fight the Zionists enough."

"This," said Nuseibeh, commenting on this letter, "is a picture of how real Jews feel about what is happening."[17]

As Nuseibeh continued his relentless oratory, I heard Sir Anthony Parsons of the UK whisper to an aide, "He's filibustering. Djibouti is not ready and he's filibustering."

Terzi, the PLO representative, was then called to a seat at the Council table. How many times a day did I hear the announcement, "Mr. Terzi of the PLO, Mr. Terzi of the PLO, please contact your office" broadcast over the UN loudspeakers? Every hour or so, his secretary or someone else by prearrangement paged him to advertise the PLO presence at the UN. Terzi's theme was that if Alan Goodman was crazy, it was only because he represented the mentality of an entire people—the Israelis—who had "collectively gone mad."

> We are told it was a solitary maniac, and American citizen, who went there and, the moon over Jerusalem having made him moonstruck, shot at worshippers—perhaps he simply did not like the way they prayed? No, that is not true. Because who in his right mind opens fire at anybody, much less worshippers? And, for that matter, who in his right mind displaces millions of people, turning them out of their homes? Who in his right mind permanently mobilizes 30 per cent of the prime-age population, as the Israelis are doing, and keeps it constantly under arms? Who in his right mind has 60 per cent of the population on reserve and fighting? Who in his right mind would actually drag this Council into meeting on such issues?
>
> It is not that they are really maniacs. This is the implementation of a policy conceived, of course, in a criminal way. Right-thinking people cannot really accept that, but it seems to be a fact. We are dealing with the derivative of a policy of really persistent State terrorism. Shooting at worshippers in the Al Aqsa Mosque is a provocation to and a humiliation of not only the worshippers there, but all people of any faith—not just Moslems. . . .
>
> [And it is] the poor American taxpayer, who is forced to contribute to these acts of State terrorism. His Government is financing these acts of State terrorism.[18]

Finally, Ambassador Farah Dirir, the representative of Djibouti, a wedge of a nation between Ethiopia and Somalia on the Persian Gulf, arrived to take the seat reserved for him at the Council table. He cleared his throat, and began:

> It is extremely ironic that the shameful incidents of trigger-happy Israeli soldiers laughing at the wounded Arab worshippers in their agony of pain resulting from the shooting spree in Al Haram Al Sharif reminded us of the sadistic bouts of laughter and amusement of the Nazi Germans. . . .
>
> The Moslems of the world cannot accept that the profane act of violence inflicted on Al Haram Al Sharif was an isolated incident committed by a deranged individual. Rather it is the beginning of a dangerous exploit and a premeditated pattern of behavior aimed at

demolishing the holy shrines of Al Haram Al Sharif and other spiritual and cultural institutions in the Holy City of Arab Jerusalem. . . .

These sacrilegious acts perpetrated against the Moslem Holy Places in the Holy City of Jerusalem cannot be overlooked as an act of lunacy committed by a deranged individual. It is inconceivable that a sophisticated military establishment such as that of Israel would put an instrument of death into the hands of someone whose physical and mental condition had not been ascertained through prior routine checkups.[19]

With Dirir's emphasis on Israeli soldiers laughing like Nazis at the sight of their victims being put to death, the face and jaw of Israel's ambassador, Yehuda Blum, froze. Blum, a survivor of the Bergen-Belsen concentration camp—he had his Bar Mitzvah there— was doing all he could to restrain himself. Then it was Blum's turn to respond. He looked tormented. That's what the majority of the Council members seemed to have wanted; it wasn't lost on anyone that the Djibouti ambassador's comments took a personal toll on Blum.

Blum began by lashing out at the Arab speakers for "their valued theological insight into oppression." Blum was a master of understated cynicism, and a stickler for factual accuracy. Without mentioning the PLO directly, he charged them with attempting to falsify history once again. Addressing the PLO's statement that Israel had taken by force territory beyond that allocated to the Jewish state in the 1947 Partition Plan of the UN General Assembly (Res. 181, II), he said, "They talk of the Partition Plan, of the Israeli conquest of Eilat outside the Partition Plan. But Eilat was *inside* the borders of the Partition Plan."

The brunt of Blum's anger, however, was directed at the Soviets, who "today joined the list of bigots who have sponsored this debate." How ironic it is, he said, that they should now voice concern for the Holy Places in Jerusalem, given their own dismal record at home.

> I for one could not fail to be moved by the display of concern of the representative of the Soviet Union for the sanctity of holy places. After all, his country has an enviable record in preserving holy places all around the Soviet Union. I know, of course, that the Soviet Constitution guarantees freedom of religion—but, then, it also guarantees freedom of expression, freedom of association, freedom of movement, and virtually all basic freedoms. . . . Well, over the years the Soviet Union has closed tens of thousands of churches, synagogues and mosques. At best, they are used as barns or stables; at worst, as museums of atheism.

Soviet Deputy Permanent Representative Ovinnikov, who suffered from a nervous twitch, inhaled smoke from his long Canadian pipe as if gulping for air.

> For instance, those who have been to the former Cathedral of St. Isaac in Leningrad know what has happened to that Christian holy place. Those who have been to the former Khazan Cathedral in Leningrad know what has happened to that holy place; it is a museum of atheism.
>
> The Moslems of the Soviet Union have not fared any better. There are about 50 million of them—one of the largest Moslem communities in the world. . . .
>
> Now, what has happened to the mosques in the Soviet Union? There were about 25,000 mosques in the Soviet Union 60 years ago. There are 398 left—so-called working mosques—despite the fact that the Moslem population has increased considerably over the past 60 years. Religious publications are almost non-existent and copies of the Koran are in very short supply.
>
> If the representative of the Soviet Union wants to check on my figures, I have the honor to refer him to an article published in a book entitled *Religion in Communist Lands*, 1979; that article is by A. Benningsen and Chantal Lemercier-Quelquejay, entitled *"Official" Islam in the Soviet Union*.[20]

As Blum concluded his remarks, Ovinnikov quickly signalled that he wanted to exercise his right of reply. The "expansionist policy of Israel" was, he retorted, the crux of the problem. For peace to flow, he said, "it would be enough to withdraw all its troops from the occupied Arab territories and to ensure implementation of the inalienable rights of the Arab people of Palestine. Is Israel ready to do this or not? I should like the Permanent Representative of Israel to answer that question."[21]

Jordan's Nuseibeh raised his hand for a right of reply to speak of Israel's "spring hunting season, literally against the Palestinians."

> I think we are all aware that the Israeli troops and armed settlers— those armed settlers being the very same people who took over, usurped and confiscated the remnants of the Palestinian homeland and continue doing so, to the point where they now have almost 40 per cent of it—are enjoying the spring hunting season, literally. The only difference is that the hunted are not certain animal species. And not all animal species are accepted as being the objects of hunting. I am talking about those that are.[22]

Blum then had another turn to reply. He was more emotional than I had ever seen him. His voice quavered as he pointed a thin finger accusingly across the table at Ovinnikov. "The USSR now poses as an apostle of peace but no war in the Middle East was not preceded by Soviet incitement. They fish in the troubled waters of the Middle East. Note that the distinguished Soviet representative never replied to my statement about mosques destroyed."[23]

Ovinnikov replied once again, as if to say, "we can out-taunt you. You are one against the many." "It's true, as Ambassador Blum says, that we did not support the Camp David Accords, but that's because it contained a secret agreement with the United States that Arabs should not have any state! Even the United States has taken pains to call its new military alliance with Israel into question by stopping its proposed Memorandum of Understanding with Israel after its action on the Golan Heights."[24]

This galvanized Chuck into action. He had been observing the attacks on Blum with disgust. But there was little he could do under the Council rules. His government had not been directly attacked, and so he had no right of reply. Ovinnikov now gave him that opportunity. "The United States," Chuck said loudly, "makes no secret agreements or agreements that are secret for very long. U.S.-Israeli friendship is a fact of life and the inconclusiveness of the Memorandum of Understanding between Israel and the United States is but a lull."[25]

As we came down the escalator on our way back to the U.S. Mission, Syria's Ambassador Allah Fattal and Jordan's Nuseibeh were behind us with Mike Davis sandwiched in between them and Chuck and myself. El Fattal said to Davis, loud enough for us to hear, "Now we have the document that we would like in the form of your Ambassador Lichenstein's speech: the admission that U.S.-Israeli friendship and military cooperation is a fact of life." Neither of us bothered to respond. It had become worse than a circus. Perhaps, I mused, that's why Jeane Kirkpatrick had sent Chuck while she stayed behind at the U.S. Mission; she was trying to save herself from this.

I went up with Chuck to see Kirkpatrick. Ken and Carl were there, and she was in a good mood. She said we would veto the resolution when it was put up for a vote the following day. She had prevailed on the issue in Washington.

When the Security Council Session reconvened the following day, Jordan's Nuseibeh introduced the proposed resolution by telling the Council that the "mild form" the revised Arab-sponsored resolution had taken regarding the "outrageous Israeli armed attack on Easter Sunday" fell far short of "what would be commensurate with the enormity of the crime." Nevertheless, revisions had been made, he said, because "the sponsors thought it prudent to make it palatable to the Security Council"—a euphemism for gaining U.S. agreement not to veto the resolution.[26]

France's de la Barre de Nanteuil then took the floor to say that "France understands the reactions aroused by these acts, which are not only criminal but also sacrilegious." Then, waxing philosophical, he said that "the proclaimed best means of preventing such acts would be to infuse into people's minds a spirit of peace." France, courageously, would vote in favor of the proposed resolution not because it believed what it implied but because of humanitarian concerns: to impress upon Israeli authorities that they "must, in the future, take all necessary measures to prevent a repetition of such tragic events."[27]

Eugeniusz Wyzner, Poland's Permanent Representative, said that his country would vote in favor of the resolution to protest "once again the aggressive Israeli policies of creeping annexation of those territories, and the resulting methods of terror," and called on all the Council members to "live up to their high responsibilities."[28]

Kuwait, which, at its request, was invited by the President of the Council to participate in the debate without the right to vote, delivered the most vitriolic address. Its representative, Ambassador Abulhassan, recalled that in the United States habitual criminal offenders are called "repeaters," and he called Israel a " 'repeater' of the worst type." Then noting that the victims of fascism in another era have become its practitioners today, he went on to explain how his theory of history applied to Israeli-Palestinian relations:

> It is one of the ironies of our age that the victims of fascism in the first half of this century have become the neo-Fascists of the second half. It is yet another irony of the age that the "David" of the past has become the "Goliath" of the present. This has been so obviously manifested by the fact that the army with the most modern and most sophisticated United States-supplied arms is acting as though it was afraid of the oldest instrument of self-defence [sic]—the stone. . . . The upsurge of national feeling in the West Bank and the Gaza Strip, which sets a stone-armed people under occupation against the most ruthless and relentless occupying Power in memory, should be proof enough to the Israelis—who are apparently not good judges of history—that the Palestinians are determined to continue their struggle against their colonialist settlers until they achieve all their goals—goals which have been upheld by various resolutions of the United Nations.[29]

Ambassador Irumba of Uganda, one of the five temporary members of the Security Council that year, took the floor to explain why Uganda couldn't accept the idea of no official Israeli complicity in the Dome of the Rock shooting:

> My delegation shares the sense of outrage of the Islamic community at this senseless act of sacrilege.
>
> There have been attempts to explain the act as that of a lone mentally deranged individual. My delegation does not accept this explanation. . . . The general pattern of Israel's policy in the occupied Arab territories is that of violence against the Palestinian people. It is this policy which gave encouragement to the commission of this wanton and senseless act of 11 April 1982. It must be emphasized that the root of the turmoil in the Middle East is the denial of the right to self-determination of the Palestinian people and the continued illegal occupation of Arab lands by Israel.[30]

Finally it was Ambassador Yehuda Blum's turn. He called the Security Council debate over this draft resolution "glaring evidence of the double standard which Arab governments and their supporters seek to apply to Israel." It was, he asserted, also evidence of the abuse of the Security Council machinery by the sponsors of this debate:

> While their own countries are torn by dissension, internal strife and endless backbiting, the Arab Governments, in a rare display of togetherness, have gathered here to demonstrate their unity in hatred of Israel. They have fallen over each other in attributing to Israel crimes of which they themselves are guilty.
>
> A despicable act of sacrilege was committed by a single individual at the Dome of the Rock. That person has already been arraigned and will stand trial before an Israel court of law. The Government of Israel has expressed its dismay and shock and has acted swiftly, energetically and effectively. Yet, in a ritualistic outburst of frenzy, the Arab Governments and their fellow travellers have discerned in this affair a golden opportunity to stir up religious hatred and fanaticism. This has been done to mask Arab misdeeds and to project Arab guilt onto others. The mosque-destroyers and the church- and synagogue-demolishers have held forth sanctimoniously on the desecration of religious sites. The royal custodian of the holiest shrine of Islam, who for long suppressed details of a massive, politically motivated and costly raid on the great mosque at Mecca, asked for a work stoppage all over the Moslem world, to condemn an isolated act in Jerusalem.
>
> I mentioned before "fellow travellers." At least two of them spoke earlier in this debate today. The representative of the martial-law re-

gime of Poland saw fit to leap into this debate. So did the representative of Uganda.[31]

At this point Poland's Ambassador Wyzner interjected, objecting to the phrase "martial-law regime of Poland" as inconsistent with the Security Council rule that "representatives around this table should be addressed using the proper name of their countries."[32]

Thus admonished, Blum continued:

> The representative of Poland, who speaks for a country that is under a martial-law regime, and the representative of Uganda have leapt into this debate. Let me tell both of them: "Charity begins at home."[33]

Those on the receiving end of Blum's fury now had their chance to reply. Said Clovis Maksoud, the representative of the League of Arab States: "Israel claims that it is an aggrieved party and goes roaming around on a fishing trip in its strikes and attacks against those who criticize its policies. . . . If it cannot answer criticisms and condemnations, it resorts to trying to undermine the credibility and veracity of its critics and those who condemn its activities."[34] Uganda's Irumba added: Blum's statement typifies "the type of slander for which Ambassador Blum is well-known."[35]

Nisibori of Japan explained that his country would vote in favor of the draft resolution in the hope "that Israel, the occupying Power, will fulfill its responsibilities by protecting and safeguarding the sanctity of holy places in the occupied Arab territories."[36] Ambassador Karran of Guyana made the point more strongly:

> In my delegation's view, the Israeli authorities cannot escape blame for the violence and sacrilege committed on 11 April. That act has to be seen in the context of Israel's own deliberate policies of State-sponsored violence against the Arab peoples in the occupied territories, of colonialization and annexation, of expulsion and repression of the Palestinians.[37]

Finally it was the turn of the President of the Security Council for the month, the stylish, articulate, and sober-minded Kamanda wa Kamanda of Zaire, to wrap things up. Speaking in his capacity as the head of the Zaire delegation, he said, "[I]t is difficult for the parties, when carried away by emotion, to hold forth rationally and calmly on whether the act was an isolated one or not, or on whether it was accidental or planned as a provocation." Zaire, he said, would vote in favor of the draft resolution to express condemnation for the act "without necessarily linking this act of sacrilege and fanaticism to the Government of Israel, which has itself condemned it here in the Security Council."[38]

It was time to cast votes. Everyone except the U.S. representative raised their hand in favor of adopting the resolution. Secretary General Perez de Cuellar then asked if there were any "no" votes. Kirkpatrick raised her hand, thus vetoing the proposed resolution.

After the vote came the call for an explanation of vote. First, Anthony Parsons of the U.K. took the floor. "I think we need to ask ourselves whether in this case the interests of the international community were best served by having a resolution at all." The Israeli government, he pointed out, "has promptly and vigorously condemned the crime, and the people of Israel and Jewish people around the world share the sense of revulsion at this despicable act." Nevertheless, he said, Britain voted in favor of the resolution to "associate ourselves with the condemnation of the act of sacrilege which occurred," and "on the understanding that the draft resolution cannot prejudge the facts of the incident, which we understand is under investigation." But Parson's magisterial tone and talk of his government's "understanding" that its vote was not intended to "prejudge the facts of the incident" would fool no one;[39] Britain had joined the others in condemning Israel for the Dome of the Rock shooting.

Kirkpatrick spoke next and began by expressing on behalf of the United States Government profound regret and condolences for the victims of the attack. She then went on to state that "[This draft resolution] serves no constructive purposes, but will further embitter the peoples of the region and deepen the division that could lead to conflict. Thus, as much as we condemn the act of violence that occasioned this debate of the Security Council, we must oppose this draft resolution, which, in our view, would make new acts of violence more, not less, likely to take place in the future." Moreover, she pointed out, the draft resolution was flawed, in that it implied that responsibility rested with Israel, although there was no evidence to support the charge. She concluded by reaffirming the long-standing U.S. position that Jerusalem's future legal status was a matter that could only be finally determined by negotiations between the parties and not by UN fiat.[40]

She picked up her papers and then, starting to walk out, turned to me and asked, "Can you join me for lunch?" I nodded and rose. She was in no mood to listen to the other explanations of votes.

As we were leaving, the USSR's Ovinnikov could not restrain himself from a parting shot, not something said as an aside but as part of the official Security Council record: "It seems that the representative of the United States, Ambassador Kirkpatrick, has preferred to leave today's meeting already, no doubt on the principle known since the time of Shakespeare—the Moor, having finished his business, may leave."[41]

"Good statement," she said, as we descended the escalator leading us back to First Avenue and the U.S. Mission, "a good statement by Parsons for voting against the resolution if they were true to their convictions." She shook her head, as if beyond anger, even disgust, just glad to have the whole ugly mess behind her. It was now 1:45 P.M., and as we walked up Forty-fifth Street toward the Hunan Chinese restaurant on Second Avenue, one of her bodyguards approached her and asked, "Did you forget the 1:00 lunch you are scheduled to host for Nancy Reynolds?" Nancy Reynolds was one of Nancy Reagan's best friends and the newly appointed U.S. Commissioner to the UN for Women.

"Oh my God," she said, and ran back to the Mission to grab the limo to the Waldorf.

Late in the afternoon, I saw her again, this time looking much more relaxed. The storm had passed. The dreaded repercussions of the U.S. veto—the predicted anti-American demonstrations, the bombing of U.S. facilities abroad, and attacks on U.S. overseas personnel—had not come to pass. Nevertheless, the damage to U.S.-Arab relations was clear.

King Hussein of Jordan was reported to have felt as if he were having a heart attack when he heard of the U.S. veto, viewing it as an affront to the Arab world, a low point for U.S. credibility, and as an ominous harbinger of things to come. He was said to be concerned because it was the first time the United States had vetoed a draft Security Council resolution because of reference to Jerusalem as "occupied territory." He saw this as a change in President Reagan's assurance to him that American policy on Jerusalem would not change. He had believed that if the United States was not prepared to vote in favor of the Islamic Conference draft resolution, it would, at most, have abstained, not cast a veto.

Of course, Jeane Kirkpatrick, in meetings with the Arab sponsors of the resolution, had made clear that the United States would veto the resolution unless the phrase referring to the occupied territories as "including Jerusalem" was deleted. She reminded them that President Jimmy Carter had guaranteed Israel, at the signing of the Camp David Accords, that the subject of Jerusalem would never be raised until such time as all parties to the conflict were prepared to enter into final status negotiations, and that it would then be treated as a separate matter to be negotiated apart from the West Bank and Gaza. The Arab sponsors had apparently thought Jeane Kirkpatrick was bluffing, and that the United States would abstain, not vote against the resolution. They learned to take her more seriously.

For myself, there was scant sense of accomplishment. A resolution which should have never been introduced, which had half the world frothing against Israel for a crime it did not commit, had been vetoed. Perhaps that was a good thing if it fulfilled its intended purpose of convincing the Arab sponsors of the resolution that they would have to negotiate the future of Jerusalem's legal status directly, face-to-face, with the Israelis, and not try to achieve their purposes through UN fiat. But that lesson seemed not to have been driven home, and instead of accommodation violence seemed to be the wave of the future.

The next morning, April 22, as I arrived at the U.S. Mission, hoping to get my papers in order and perhaps enjoy a respite from the tension of Security Council meetings, another crisis had been taking shape. The situation in the Falklands was heating up. Secretary Haig had been shuttling back and forth between Buenos Aires and London, but the effort at mediation seemed futile. It looked as if we might have another war upon us soon, and more Security Council sessions. Still, I thought, Argentina and Britain, Westerners against Westerners, it couldn't be as bruising as the sessions on Israel.

On the way to my office I ran into Tom Windmuller, a junior political officer who had recently arrived with high grades from a tour of duty with Ambassador Sam Lewis in Tel Aviv. "What's happening, Tom?" I asked.

"The Israelis are bombing the shit out of Beirut," he answered. "The morning traffic is confusing. AP reports a wave of sixty airplanes; cables from Beirut speak of four planes."

At my desk I scanned the morning cable traffic and newspaper clippings, courtesy of the Mission's highly efficient Press section that provided, twice a day, neat clippings of everything of importance in the morning papers and wire services. The information indeed was confusing, but it was clear that there had been a major Israeli air attack on PLO strongholds in southern Lebanon hours after an Israeli soldier was killed by a land mine.

I then conferred with Carl. We had other business to take care of. The Dome of the Rock matter was not yet fully behind us. The

General Assembly was convening in special emergency session to protest the U.S. veto in the Security Council of the Dome of the Rock resolution. Carl was preparing the speech. We agreed that it had to make the point that the source of the problem was Jordan's refusal to make peace with Israel, that the General Assembly could pass resolutions until the end of time but that would not alter Security Council resolutions 242 and 338 as the framework for peace. They required direct negotiations; UN General Assembly resolutions do not short-circuit that route. But we both recognized that we'd be fighting on the General Assembly majority's turf, unable to take the offensive and make an affirmative case.

Nor did Menachem Begin seem to be in a conciliatory mood. Encouraged by the U.S. veto of the Dome of the Rock resolution, he was not inclined to go along with the urging of Deputy Secretary of State Walter Stoessel in Jerusalem for Israel to exercise maximum restraint and respect for the cease-fire lines in Lebanon. Instead, Begin replied that there were limits to Israel's tolerance, and that limit had been exceeded when a 21-year-old officer, the grandchild of one of his most beloved friends, had been killed by a land mine in Israel's security zone in southern Lebanon. Moreover, Begin asked Stoessel to convey to Secretary Haig that this had occurred one day after Holocaust Remembrance Day, as if the fact of that particular day dictated Arab restraint, and now mandated an Israeli response.

The situation, I reflected, is getting worse all around. Impending war in the Falklands. "Low-intensity" war in Lebanon. An Arab foreign minister arrives at the U.S. Mission and, in Kirkpatrick's absence, talks with Bill Sherman and Ken Adelman and informs them that all Egyptian leaders who do not repudiate Camp David will be assassinated.

Meanwhile at the United Nations, the UN General Assembly, bent on circumventing the Security Council veto, was employing the controversial "Uniting for Peace" procedure to condemn Israel for the Dome of the Rock incident and describe Jerusalem as occupied Arab territory. The United States, during the 1950 UN discussions of Korea, had taken advantage of the Soviet Union's walkout from the Security Council to move the venue to the General Assembly and get its blessings for concerted action, which otherwise was limited by the Charter to the UN Security Council. Now the United States was reaping the bitter fruit of that 1950 procedural victory as the General Assembly prepared to accomplish what the Security Council did not do.

I looked for good news, but didn't see any. A cable from Warsaw noted the celebration of the 39th anniversary of the Warsaw Ghetto Revolt. Next year, said the cable, the Warsaw Ghetto Revolt will be the centerpiece of the UN "Year of the Child." The legacy of the Warsaw Ghetto, the struggle of the remnants of Polish Jewry against their Nazi tormentors, would now be rediscovered and appropriated for "universal" purposes, as if the leaders of the Warsaw Ghetto uprising were not young Zionist leaders but Third-World liberationists.

At 3:30 P.M., I left New York for Washington. Seeing Washington from the air, I noted in my journal:

> Daffodils along the Potomac, cherry blossoms at the Basin, dogwoods blooming everywhere. A mirage? The "real world"—where? Here, in Washington? Or at the UN—mirroring deaths, torture, maimings, orphans, disasters? The UN must be getting to me. Maybe it's the World. Primitive instincts call the shots. I'm worn out.

In Washington, thinking that perhaps it would break my dark mood, I attended the annual convention of the American Society of International Law at the Capitol Hilton. Richard Falk, the Milbank Professor of International Law and Politics at Princeton, also of Hanoi fame for his expedition there with Jane Fonda during the Vietnam war, was debating Eugene V. Rostow on nuclear disarmament treaties. Rostow was arguing that, in the end, deterrence of Soviet aggression had to rest on U.S. willingness to destroy the Soviet Union in case of a Soviet first strike, and that the credibility of the U.S. willingness to so act was therefore necessarily a key piece of the quest for international peace.

Falk, asking how we can ever presume to know that we are "right," as one man's apprehension is another's self-defense, argued that resort to nuclear force is inherently immoral.

At the UN the world—for better or worse—seemed a lot clearer. Gray areas disappeared. Things were seen as right or wrong. The situation had become so polarized that the question of how one can presume to be correct was not a matter many thought about for very long.

I learned, however, that I was not alone in my feelings. On April 26, as the General Assembly Special Emergency Session ended its deliberations for the day, Michael Davis, our clean-cut Foreign Service officer fresh from Damascus, for whom taking the high road was an everyday occurrence, told me, "Allan, I'm beginning to share Jeane's views about the UN." Perhaps it was the speeches that he had been hearing the last few days that did him in. The last one was that of Democratic South Yemen (if the country's title has the phrase "democratic" in it, as, for example, the German Democratic Republic, it's likely to be undemocratic): "U.S. interests in the Middle East don't coincide with Israel; they are determined by Israel."

I checked in with Kirkpatrick on the eleventh floor. She asked me to quickly begin to refocus my attention from the Middle East to the Falklands. There was trouble afoot. Keep checking all the cables thoroughly, she said, for signs of new activity by Britain or Argentina. See if you can keep track of events at the OAS, the Organization of American States, its reactions to Argentina's claims, and how the sides stack up. She felt the matter would soon be back at the United Nations Security Council, which had taken a break from its deliberations to give Secretary Haig and Secretary General Perez de Cuellar an opportunity to resolve the dispute. Neither seemed to be doing very well at it.

Later that afternoon, one of Ambassador Yehuda Blum's aides stopped by to pass on the message that Blum had called Secretary General Perez de Cuellar to warn him that if the resolution of the GA Special Session, which was expected to conclude its deliberations on April 28, called for review of Israel's membership in the United Nations, that Israel would suspend all cooperation with the UN, including its peacekeeping operations. Perez de Cuellar, the aide said, then sent a message to King Hussein, asking that it be passed on to the PLO's Yasser Arafat, asking them to cool it at the UN. I informed him that in the meantime, U.S. embassies throughout the world had been instructed to make demarches on their host governments calling on them not to support any movement at the United Nations to "challenge the credentials of the Israeli delegation"—the euphemism for expulsion.

On April 27, in the interlude between the formal General Assembly Special Emergency debate and the vote scheduled for the next day, I was back in Washington accompanying Jeane Kirkpatrick to be interviewed by Israel's former Foreign Minister, Abba Eban. It was for a television series he was anchoring on conversations with world leaders, and taping was scheduled for noon at television studios in Georgetown. I showed up 15 minutes early. Abba Eban was already there. I had never met him before, but, of course, knew of his reputation for eloquence. His speech before the UN General Assembly in June 1967, at the outbreak of the Six Day War, had stirred the conscience of the world and left an indelible impression.

Eban, dressed in a light gray suit with a muted red and black striped regimental tie and his trademark large black-framed eyeglasses, seemed nervous. Trying to break the ice, I told him that I had taught international law at the Hebrew University in Jerusalem in the early 1970s, but he showed no interest. Then I said, "You must be glad that you're no longer at the United Nations."

"Yes," he replied, "matters have gotten immeasurably worse since I was there. In 1964, I was welcomed to the podium of the General Assembly as a prodigal son—something now unimaginable."

Kirkpatrick arrived. I introduced her to Eban. "I have always admired you," she said.

"Thank you," Eban replied, and then launched into a minispeech on the nature of the United Nations, the decline in expectations of what it was capable of achieving, and how the "conflictual" element of multilateral diplomacy has surmounted the impetus to conciliation. "Do you agree?" he asked.

"Yes, of course," she answered.

"So, the conclusion we reach," said Abba Eban, continuing his soliloquy, "is that Israel can only fight a holding action at the United Nations and that, therefore, as concerns both Israel and the United States, our best strategy at that forum is to downplay the UN's importance, to treat it as there, but as not very important. Do you agree?"

"Yes, I agree," she said.

The interview then began. Eban fidgeted, seemed ill-at-ease. He spoke as if his lines were memorized, straining to get them right. He seemed to fear that a serious exchange of ideas might mess up his script. During a pause in the taping, Kirkpatrick turned to him and said that she had been thinking of his reference to the new "conflictual" element of multilateral diplomacy. "You know," she said to Eban, "the average tenure of a U.S. 'Perm. Rep.' is 18 months. I have served 16 already. And while I enjoy the generally intelligent lot of people this job exposes me to, I'm basically not temperamentally suited for the 'conflictual' arena of multilateral diplomacy, as you put it."

It occurred to me that she had more than the "conflictual" element of international politics in mind. Chuck had recently mentioned a conversation he had with her in which she pointed out how impossible Haig had made life for her. I knew of their policy disagreements over how to handle the Falklands crisis, but I did not appreciate the personal rancor that ran between them. Chuck, who knew her best, surmised that she would probably go back to teaching soon, a calling better suited to her temperament.

It was something I myself couldn't have helped but observe over the course of the last year. Circumstances were forging her, making her tough and resilient, even unforgiving. But her natural leaning was not toward the "conflictual." Yet in both these arenas—the United Nations and the State Department—having a "conflictual" disposition seemed a prerequisite to success. I thought back again to the *Vogue* interview in July 1981 in which she said, "I think for a lot of people, commitment to intellectual clarity is associated with toughness. I am not someone who is personally tough. I'm not."[42]

She did a good job at disguising it. What I heard her tell Abba Eban that day was that, popular wisdom notwithstanding, she and her post as U.S. Ambassador to the United Nations were not made for each other—not in this era, not with day-to-day fighting and the back-biting at State.

The next morning, April 28, back in New York at the United Nations, I saw Bill Sherman rise to the rostrum of the UN General Assembly to speak on the proposed resolution holding Israel responsible for the Dome of the Rock shooting, and the status of Jerusalem as "occupied Arab territory":

> With the resolution now before us, the United Nations is being pushed one step closer to a precipice beyond which looms a political and moral abyss. . . . When a permanent member is condemned for its exercise of the veto, [it] is to assault the authority and effectiveness of the Security Council. It is one further step in the erosion of respect for the Charter and, indeed, in the perversion of the procedures and purposes of the United Nations.[43]

The resolution passed by a vote of 130 to 26 with 14 abstentions. The only surprises were Fiji and Japan, whom we expected would vote against the resolution, but whose resolve weakened to an abstention.

Later that day, Ken Adelman, who was not present at the General Assembly Special Emergency Session vote, and who generally steered clear of Arab-Israeli issues, told me that nothing he had seen at the United Nations had so shocked or repulsed him as the news of the General Assembly vote. For it was on that same day, he noted, that Israel had withdrawn its troops from the Sinai desert—taking a

major step, and risk, towards peace, only to have itself condemned in
New York by the General Assembly as a "non-peaceloving state."

That evening, back in my home in Washington, I couldn't help
but reflect about the impact of a solitary act by a man gone mad. Alan
Goodman, who later was to be adjudged insane at the time of the
shooting and committed to an asylum, had set in motion a downhill
spiral of events that reinforced the old stereotypes and prejudices,
and which seemed once again to be bringing the two sides to the
brink of war. Between Begin's compulsion to take action in memory
of the Holocaust, and Arab inability to come to grips with the reality
that Israel had the "credentials" to occupy a seat at the United Nations, loomed an enormous divide; and between them lay an ever-
present tinderbox. But no sooner had the vote been taken on the
Dome of the Rock shooting, than world attention was quickly refo-
cused on another crisis: in the Falklands at the tip of the South
Atlantic. An ominous vote dealing with the crisis had taken place on
April 28.

At the 20th Meeting of Consultation of the Organization of American States, attended by most of the foreign ministers of the Latin
American countries, a resolution was adopted by a vote of 17 to 0 with
4 abstentions fully supporting Argentina's claim to sovereignty over
the Falklands Islands.[44] It was clear that the action was now moving
back to the United Nations as large-scale military confrontation
seemed inevitable. The United States would no longer be able to bob
and weave, but would have to declare itself. The situation would put
to the test Jeane Kirkpatrick's new political and diplomatic skills. It
would also pit her against Secretary of State Alexander Haig. This
time there could be only one winner.

8

"Malvinas, Malvinas"
The Falklands Crisis

This is a war that should not have happened.

Ambassador Noel Dorr of Ireland before the 360th meeting of the
UN Security Council, May 2, 1982

We have been rent by the clash of values, loyalties, and friends.

Ambassador Jeane Kirkpatrick explaining the change of
instructions on the U.S. vote, before the 373rd meeting of the UN
Security Council, June 4, 1982

The Falklands/Malvinas crisis resembled nothing so much as a final
examination question drawn up by a law professor whose imagination had run amuck. Everything about it was improbable: that
Great Britain might send an armada, nineteenth-century style, 8,000
miles away to fight for the "self-determination" of 1,000 sheepherders
and kelp farmers living on a tiny island in the furthest reaches of the
South Atlantic; that Argentina could hope for U.S. neutrality; and
that both sides could claim in all sincerity that what was at stake was
fidelity to international law.

All the momentous issues of our times were there, neatly compressed in a small time-bomb: the definition of aggression; the limits
of legitimate self-defense; the requirements of proportionality and reasonableness in context; the attributes of sovereignty; the duty to exhaust peaceful remedies; the duty to negotiate in "good faith"; the

scope of self-determination; the interpretation of treaties; and the role of the United Nations, of the Secretary-General, and the International Court of Justice in the settlement of disputes. If ever a conflict lent itself to peaceful resolution, this was it, as traditional political cleavages and bloc alliances gave way to a consensus in favor of avoiding war.

There was no shortage of principles with which to fashion arguments. For Britain, foremost were the concepts that aggression must be punished; and that self-determination must be honored. For Argentina, the governing principle was that colonization in the Western hemisphere come to an end—by force of arms if necessary. Negotiations, argued the Argentinians, were being used as cover to deliberately stall the end of colonization. Britain's conquest of the Malvinas islands more than a hundred years ago could not be allowed to acquire legitimacy merely by the passage of time.

In the Security Council gallery, veterans of other skirmishes would fill the normally empty seats to see how clever the representatives of Britain or Argentina could be in explaining which of these principles took precedence over the other. To observers it became clear that if the United Nations could not play a useful role in resolving this dispute—one among friends—there was little else it could be expected to resolve.

For Jeane Kirkpatrick and Alexander Haig, the crisis would strain differences between them to the breaking point. While agreeing on overall points of policy—the need for a strong resurgent America—each nevertheless harbored a different vision of America's role in the world, and especially in Latin America. She prided herself on being an "Americanist"; he, the former commander of NATO, on being a Eurocentrist. In her *Commentary* essay of October 1981, "U.S. Security & Latin America,"[1] Kirkpatrick had warned that America was paying insufficient attention to "the deterioration of the U.S. position in the hemisphere (which) has already created serious vulnerabilities where none previously existed, and threatens now to confront this country with the unprecedented need to defend itself against a ring of Soviet bases on and around our southern and eastern borders." As she saw it, it was therefore in the strategic interest of the United States to maintain good relations with Argentina. If it did not, Central and South American support could no longer be expected for U.S. policies aimed at containing the spread of Communism in the Western hemisphere. She urged, therefore, a U.S. policy of neutrality. Haig, after a short-lived dalliance with neutrality, backed support for Britain.

The first hint to the U.S. Mission that a crisis might be looming in the South Atlantic came at a luncheon conversation in New York in late December 1981 between Jeane Kirkpatrick and Argentina's Foreign Minister, Nicanor Costa Mendez. Shortly afterwards, getting out of a limousine, she mentioned to me Costa Mendez's peculiar references to "Malvinas, Malvinas." Did I make anything of it, she asked. Not knowing the context in which it was said, and knowing little of the geography, I shook my head, not giving any further thought to the comment until Argentina's surprise invasion of the Falklands on April 2, 1982.

No one had expected the invasion. Negotiations with Great Britain over the future of the Falklands, an archipelago some 200 miles off the southern tip of Argentina, had been going on for nearly two decades. In 1964, the Argentinean Government, exasperated by its fruitless appeals to Britain for over a hundred and thirty-one years to peacefully relinquish control of the islands, filed its claim with the UN General Assembly's Special Committee on Decolonization. Ever since, Argentina and Britain had been meeting regularly, peaceably, and politely at UN Headquarters. The impression created by both sides was that they would go on for perhaps another decade: relaxed, civilized, and long-term diplomatic negotiations.

Thus in February, 1982, when Argentina abruptly called off further meetings, proclaiming that Britain had been negotiating in bad faith and purposefully stalling for years, it came as a shock. Still, no one in the U.S. Government expected an invasion.

On April 2, we heard the news that in the dawn hours several thousand Argentinean troops had invaded the Falklands, quickly overwhelmed the token British garrison on the islands, and declared Argentinean sovereignty.[2] My immediate assignment was to familiarize Kirkpatrick with the relevant facts of the dispute and the pertinent international law. Fortunately, I had the benefit of a little-known and little-used office: that of the State Department historian. The historian's synopsis of the dispute, gleaned from several learned treatises on the subject, made for fascinating reading.

Most scholars credited a Spaniard, Francisco Camargo, with the discovery in 1540 of two large islands (East and West Falkland) along with a couple of hundred smaller ones around 200 miles off the coast of Argentina. The first settlers were French who came in 1763 in the name of King Louis XV and used the islands as a base of operations for catching whales and seals. The King of Spain protested their arrival, claiming the islands as part of the Spanish settlement in

Buenos Aires by reason of "territorial proximity." France relinquished its claim in return for an agreed sum of money from Spain. Then, in 1765, ignoring Spanish claims, John Byron (grandfather of the poet) declared that he took possession of the islands for His Majesty George III of Great Britain and named them the "Falklands Islands." Twenty-five British marines were posted there. Five years later, they were ousted by a Spanish fleet from Buenos Aires.

In 1832 England sent two warships to the Falklands, compelled an Argentinean schooner anchored off its coast to surrender, and re-established control over the islands. Argentina lodged protests with Britain but they went unheeded; Britain viewed itself as the islands' rightful owner. In the next few years, some two thousand English men and women were settled on the Falklands, largely as employees of two British companies. At the time of the Argentinean invasion in 1982, one of these companies owned nearly a third of the island's ranch land and over a third of its sheep, while twenty-three other farms, mostly English-owned with resident managers, made up virtually the rest of the islands. The islanders themselves were not permitted to become residents of Great Britain without special permission.

This history had been repeatedly explored in sixteen years of negotiations between Britain and Argentina under the auspices of the UN Special Committee on Decolonization. Argentina relied heavily on the fact that, in 1965, the General Assembly had passed Resolution 2065 (XX) recognizing the colonial character of the islands "whose removal from that status should be negotiated as part of the process of implementing Resolution 1514 (XV)," the Assembly's omnibus decolonization resolution of 1960.[3]

I gave Kirkpatrick copies of the relevant historical materials and promised to give her a legal analysis of Britain's and Argentina's claims within the next day or two. I told her then that both sides seemed to have reasonable arguments to justify their positions, and that this was not a case of clear-cut "aggression" by Argentina.

The next morning, April 3, 1982, Britain won the support of the UN Security Council for a resolution demanding an immediate cessation of hostilities and the withdrawal of all Argentine forces from the Falklands. The vote was 10 in favor, 1 against (Panama), and 4 abstentions—USSR, Poland, China, and Spain. Guyana and all five Asian and African non-permanent members of the Council voted with Britain.[4] In part, the vote was a tribute to the diplomatic skills of Britain and its representative, Sir Anthony Parsons, in patiently nurturing relations with the Commonwealth nations. But there was more. The Falklands issue had not yet polarized the UN into a developed versus undeveloped nations conflict, or "colonialist" versus "anticolonialist." The members of the United Nations were in a mood to be helpful. No one wanted war. There was a general consensus in favor of resolving the crisis. So the first UN meeting was short on rhetoric and quick to authorize the newly elected UN Secretary General, Javier Perez de Cuellar, to use his good offices to resolve the conflict.

At first Perez de Cuellar deferred to U.S. Secretary of State Alexander Haig's frantic effort at "shuttle diplomacy" between Washington, London, and Buenos Aires in an effort to avoid war through mediation. Between April 8 and 20, Haig shuttled four times between Argentina and Britain, traveling over thirty thousand miles. Throughout this period, Kirkpatrick, with the support of National Security Council Adviser Bill Clark, Secretary Weinberger, and CIA Director Casey, agreed that a policy of U.S. semi-neutrality was the preferred course. Argentina was being helpful to the American effort to support the Contras fighting the Sandinista regime in Nicaragua; all of Latin America was lined up behind Argentina; and U.S. neutrality or semi-neutrality was consistent with the Monroe Doctrine and Pan-American alliances aimed at keeping the European powers out of Latin America. Alexander Haig had assumed center stage and others, therefore—like the UN Secretary General—would have to await the outcome of his "mediation" effort before considering alternative courses of action.

From her vantage point at the United Nations, Kirkpatrick was in a position to inform the U.S. National Security Council of the consequences of any decision to condemn Argentina at the UN—loss of support for U.S. Central American policy by the states of South America, and an end to the diplomatic isolation of Cuba's Fidel Castro. Kirkpatrick's view was shared by "Latin Americanists," who believed that "for America to sacrifice its new and hard-won position in South America, where a number of nations [teeter] on the brink of Marxism, all for the sake of the Falklands, [is] lunacy."[5] But while this view won support within the National Security Council, it was dismissed by the State Department as unmindful of the strategic importance of strong Anglo-American ties.

The prevention of war was a central objective on which the Administration was united. The Argentineans did not seem to be taking the threat of a British counterattack seriously enough. They may have thought that the United States would maintain neutrality and withhold intelligence and logistical support from Britain. Kirkpatrick was highly regarded by the Argentineans, who believed her "Dictatorships and Double Standards" article was an endorsement of their regime.[6] She spoke to them in New York and Washington to try to get them to understand that Britain was serious, and that U.S. neutrality should not be assumed. It was time, she said, that they understand this and be prepared to give thought to diplomatic alternatives to Argentinean control over the Falklands. Although her aims in meeting with Argentinean officials coincided with those of Alexander Haig, she also knew that, if he were informed of them, he would never approve. He wanted to retain exclusive control. So she undertook these meetings under the broad authorization of President Reagan and NSC Adviser Clark, but certainly not at the instructions of Secretary Haig.

Some of these meetings occurred in the apartment of José Sorzano with her Argentinean counterparts at the United Nations, with visiting Argentinean military officials, and with their Deputy Foreign Minister. Another, in which I participated, took place at the DuPont Plaza Hotel in Washington.

Late one afternoon during the period of the Haig shuttle mission, as I was walking out of the door of the State Department office, Jackie Tillman pulled me aside. "I think you should stick around until Jeane comes back," she said. Jeane Kirkpatrick had been at the White House Operations Room with Casey, Bush, and Haig. I hadn't expected her to come back to the office. "Sure, Jackie, I'll stay," I said, "just let me run down and tell my ride not to wait for me."

When I returned, Kirkpatrick was standing in the outer office of the State Department suite. "Allan, I want you to come with me, if you would." She always said, "if you would." "Sure," I said, "where are you going?"

"Just shut up and go," Jackie snapped, just out of earshot of Kirkpatrick. I rushed with Kirkpatrick to the elevator. Her sober bearing of a moment ago had given way to a great mischievous grin. "We're going to see the Argentinean military chargé d'affaires," she said.

We pulled up to the DuPont Plaza Hotel in her armor-plated bulletproof black limousine. For the last year she had been rumored to be on a Libyan "hit list," and State Department security was taking no chances. Fourteen agents were assigned to guard her. Bodyguards jumped out clutching Samsonite attaché cases loaded with Uzi submachine guns. As they buzzed into their walkie-talkies, Kirkpatrick barked, "No one is to recognize me here."

A short, nattily-attired man in his fifties appeared. He asked us to follow him to a small table next to the crowded bar. Kirkpatrick suggested that we move to a quieter spot. The maître d' pointed to the large empty dining room. Good. At the bar I had seen at least one head turn. I knew that if the papers got hold of this, Haig would blow a fuse.

She began by saying that he surely knew how she valued Argentina's relationship with the United States. The chargé d'affaires responded by saying that in Argentina everyone knew her as a friend. And then she came to the heart of her message: that Britain is serious in threatening to counterattack, and that U.S. "neutrality" is not in the cards. Could he, she asked, please get that message back to Argentinean President Galtieri.

Later, in the limousine as she gave me a ride to my Chevy Chase residence, she lamented how tragic it was: Britain had boxed itself in; if we lose the support of Argentina, our Central American policy will be in shambles. Haig is unsympathetic; and the people at IO seem incapable of figuring this all out. "Can you imagine, Allan, they are preparing a host of different scenarios for action at the United Nations if and when the counterattack comes, without consulting with me at all."

By the end of April, it had become apparent that Haig would not succeed in his mission. With the situation further polarized than the day he began, and the likelihood of war between Britain and Argentina greater than ever before, Haig declared on April 30 that the United States had no choice but to back Britain and maintain the strength of the NATO alliance.

Secretary General Perez de Cuellar then assumed the role of mediator, holding separate meetings each day with Sir Anthony Parsons of Britain and Argentinean Deputy Foreign Minister Enrique Ros in his thirty-eighth-floor suite at UN Headquarters. At one point a proposal emerged, either from Britain or the Secretary General, for a settlement involving the raising of three flags over the Falklands: those of Argentina, Great Britain, and the United Nations. When Kirkpatrick heard about the idea she was enthusiastic, believing that it might provide the breakthrough everyone was looking for. She approached the Argentineans, who had occasionally balked at the idea, to see if she could convince them that it was in their interest to accept it. She pointed out that the moment the UN flag went up over the Falklands, a return to the status quo which preceded the invasion would no longer be likely. It was only a matter of time. For the vast majority of the UN members the conflict had already become a case of Argentina trying to escape the yoke of a colonialist power. Then word came back from Buenos Aires. The three-flag solution was acceptable providing that Argentina's flag be a little higher than the other two. Britain refused to give an inch. And so the three-flagpole proposal, like the others emerging from the Secretary General's suite, foundered on the shoals of mutual distrust and the need by both sides to be seen as having gained the upper hand.

It went on like this inconclusively for 49 days after Argentinean troops landed at Port Stanley, the key outpost of the islands. Secretary General Perez de Cuellar then issued a detailed report to the UN Security Council of what he had tried to achieve in the interim. No one could fault him for trying.

> I met with Argentinean Foreign Minister Nicanor Costa Méndez and Francis Pym, the Foreign Minister of the United Kingdom on April 30. They both told me they were prepared to implement the following interim measures, all without prejudice to any claims to sovereignty over the island which they might wish to claim at a future date:
>
> 1. that Argentina begin withdrawing its troops from the area and that the UK redeploy its naval forces outside of the Falklands area.
> 2. that both sides commence negotiations.
> 3. that each side rescind its announcement of blockade and exclusive zones.
> 4. that both sides terminate economic sanctions.

"But then," de Cuellar concluded in his report to the Council: "I received texts which did not reflect this agreement. . . . I immediately telephoned President Galtieri in Buenos Aires and Prime Minister Thatcher in London and asked them to overcome their differences." Neither Britain's Thatcher nor Argentina's President Galtieri was, he discovered, in a conciliatory frame of mind. Both had staked their personal as well as national fortunes on the outcome of this confrontation. Neither could afford to lose, or, at this point, to be seen as amenable to any sort of compromise.[7] Britain had no interest in negotiating peace as long as Argentina's troops were still on the islands. Argentina was unwilling to withdraw its troops before negotiations commenced. The gulf was unbridgeable. Said Perez de Cuellar: "The efforts in which I have been engaged do not offer the present prospect of bringing about an end to the crisis nor, indeed, of preventing the intensification of the conflict."[8] The only solace the UN Secretary General could offer was that matters might be worse. "That I have ended my efforts does not mean the end of the world," he observed. No, not the end of the world, just the end of hopes for averting, as Ireland's Ambassador Noel Dorr put it, a "war between friends."

The idea that the Falklands/Malvinas dispute might possibly be ameliorated, if not resolved, by reference of the conflict to the International Court of Justice never emerged during Perez de Cuellar's mediation. True, neither Britain nor Argentina had accepted the "compulsory jurisdiction" of the World Court, and could as such not be compelled to participate in such a World Court adjudication. Still, there was nothing to prevent them from accepting the Court's jurisdiction in this particular dispute. Such a route, had it been suggested, might have provided a face-saving alternative to war. Both Britain and Argentina could then have been expected to say, regardless of the outcome, that they were bound by the Court's ruling. There would then be no need for anyone's national honor to be preserved by resort to armed force. Perez de Cuellar may have anticipated that neither Britain nor Argentina would have agreed to such a reasonable proposal. Both leaders knew that their country's legal claims were clouded, and neither seemed prepared to risk losing national title to the Falklands or Malvinas in a court battle. Yet, ironically, perhaps at no time in the post-World War II era was the World Court better positioned to avert war by adjudication of conflicting claims. That it was never seriously considered in the Secretary General's mediation efforts was a demonstration of how ineffective the World Court was and how hollow was the call for a world order based on the rule of law.

With the collapse of the Perez de Cuellar peacemaking efforts, and no move towards involvement of the International Court of Justice, the British armada was launched on an 8,000 mile, two-week, ocean journey to do battle with Argentinean forces. On May 1, British carrier-based Harrier aircraft were within striking distance and attacked airstrips at Port Stanley and Goose Green. The big blow came on May 2, when a British submarine sank the Argentinean cruiser, the *General Belgrano*. Three hundred and sixty-eight men perished at sea.[9] Thus, before the fighting on the island even started, Argentina had already lost nearly 400 men, a figure equal to roughly one-fourth of the 1,800 or so residents of the islands.

As twentieth-century aerial combat swirled over the South Atlantic, Jeane Kirkpatrick returned to New York for the UN Security Council "debate" on the Falklands scheduled to begin on May 22. The pattern was predictable as sides lined up for and against Britain and Argentina. The situation had polarized the world community as the momentary consensus in favor of peaceful resolution fell apart. The United States was caught in the middle, unable to decide with whom it wished to side.

Argentina's Enrique Ros opened the "debate." Argentina, he proclaimed, had been "victimized by aggression." But, he continued, the "resolute will of the entire Argentinean people to defend to the end our rights to the islands that are an inalienable part of our homeland will not be daunted."[10]

I had heard the "inalienable part of our homeland" language many times before at the United Nations, but always in reference to Palestinian rights. It was strange to now hear it invoked by Argentina in a different context. It would be stranger still to hear Britain invoke it on behalf of islands 8,000 miles away from the homeland, a speck of territory with no connection to Great Britain other than the fact that, after having colonized the islands in the mid-nineteenth century, Britain left 200 or so families behind to farm the area, and a naval garrison at Fort Stanley.

Sitting in the grandstand in the area immediately behind the Security Council horseshoe table, before the stretch of seats reserved for journalists and the section for spectators beyond, was Israel's Yehuda Blum. One row behind him was Syria's Allah Fattal, and next to him the PLO's deputy representative. They looked unusually relaxed. They were, it seemed, on a sportsman's holiday observing others now trying to manipulate as adroitly as they had on very different occasions the language of aggression, self-defense, self-determination, and "inalienable rights" to suit their purposes.

"Our commitment," Argentina's Ros concluded "is to justice and historic truth, which is in contrast to what Britain wants." Britain wants "the maintenance of a colonial situation. The islands belong to my country." Argentina had tried to negotiate in good faith, but Britain had "aborted any possibility of an interim solution."[11]

By "interim solution," he meant one which would have allowed a continuing British presence and autonomy for the islanders while salvaging Argentinean pride at not being able to recover what was considered rightfully theirs. If Britain were to agree that sovereignty over the islands rested with Argentina, then Argentina would in turn, he suggested, stretch its imagination to find ways of letting the islanders live as they had before. Yes, the flag of Argentina and not the Union Jack would be hoisted over Port Stanley each morning, and taxes would be paid to Argentina rather than to Great Britain, but otherwise the islanders could retain their independence, speak their own language and follow their own path of life. Argentina, Ros said, had no ambitions for its beloved Malvinas other than to excise the long-festering sore of colonialism in the American hemisphere.

The key issue, said Ross summing up, is "principle." "The corruption of principles is a grave crime."[12]

Not to be outdone in swearing allegiance to principle, the U.K.'s Sir Anthony Parsons pushed back his shock of graying hair and began his rebuttal. "The aggressor," he charged, "must withdraw. British territory has been invaded. Argentina's actions are unlawful because they constitute the first use of force." Parsons argued that there must therefore be the "total withdrawal of the aggressor": no buts, no in-betweens, no negotiations, no cease-fire in place, no face-saving scheme; nothing less than the immediate and total withdrawal of Argentinean forces.[13]

But the principles invoked were hardly all that clear. Were British Harrier jets sent to vindicate the rights of remote islanders against a tyrant? Were Argentinean troops in fact sent by a great liberator and foe of neocolonialism? Was not the real issue the maintenance of the symbols of power by nations whose manhood needed a shot in the arm? As long as the Union Jack flew over the islands, Britain was amenable to power-sharing solutions. If it meant that Argentina would in fact exercise control, that was all right. It was the symbol that mattered. As long as Argentina's flag was up an inch higher than the Union Jack, Argentina was amenable to power-sharing solutions. Symbols had to be preserved. Thatcher's and Galtieri's futures were riding on it. And so British citizens were told that a "fascist dictatorship" was demanding sovereignty over their kinsmen. Argentineans were told that their dignity was being threatened by a fanatical British woman bent on establishing a reputation for herself as the "iron lady."

In the speeches that followed the opening salvo between Argentina and Great Britain, all of the Latin American nations lined up, predictably, behind Argentina. "The Malvinas islands were clearly part of Argentinean national territory," the Ecuadoran representative asserted. "How could it be otherwise?" he asked. "How could it possibly be considered British territory? Just look at the map to see where Britain and Argentina are, and where the Malvinas are located."[14] The Europeans and most of the Commonwealth nations supported Britain.

Australia, on behalf of the U.K., tried vainly to make the counter-argument that it was "the will of the people, not geography," that was decisive. "The population of the Falklands," Australia's representative contended, "constitutes a permanent population with roots back to the early part of the last century."[15] It was unclear where the argument led. Colonial empires often leave their nationals settled on colonized territory. Did he mean by this that the Falkland Islanders were a permanent part of the British population?

It went on like this until the Security Council session came to an end at around 5:00 P.M. The Security Council had another "urgent matter" to consider. The Soviet Union had asked the Council to convene in emergency session to hear a complaint by the Seychelles islands.[16] It was island time at the United Nations, and the Soviets saw this as another opportunity to strike a blow at Western "imperialism."

That day a Security Council commission of inquiry, investigating an attack by an unknown handful of mercenaries against official installations of the Seychelles islands, had issued a report concluding that the mercenaries who had attacked the islands had been armed and trained in South Africa. Nothing else was known about the motives or actions of the government of South Africa in sponsoring or condoning the mercenaries' actions, but to the Soviets the occasion nevertheless seemed ripe for another emergency session of the Security Council, smack in the middle of its consideration of the Falklands crisis.

Ambassador Oleg Troyanovsky, the polished Soviet representative, took the floor to condemn the attack on the Seychelles as "a normal manifestation of the policy of the state-terrorist regime of Pretoria which intends to crush the aspirations of the people of Africa to freedom, independence, equal rights, and social progress." Then, to connect the actions of Pretoria with those of other "imperialists" around the world—i.e., the United States, Great Britain—he concluded his remarks by saying, "The rulers of South Africa could not persist in carrying out that reckless policy if it did not enjoy comprehensive assistance and support from the forces of imperialism."

Troyanovsky proposed a new international convention outlawing the training of "mercenaries." Of course, only the West had "mercenaries;" the Soviet bloc had "freedom fighters." But this wasn't the day to take his call seriously; a war was raging in the Falklands.[17]

The next day, May 22, the Security Council reconvened to discuss the situation. Uruguay and Venezuela had called for an immediate cease-fire. But Parsons, on behalf of the U.K., insisted that as the Falkland Islands were British territory, discussion of a cease-fire was out of the question until the withdrawal of all Argentine troops. The Soviet Union, echoing the call for a cease-fire, argued that the United Kingdom was merely insisting on maintaining its colonial status. Again, the meeting ended inconclusively with no resolution tabled. But a resolution would soon have to be put to a vote. The United States would have to declare itself: for Britain, for Argentina, or neutral. Haig's position had crystallized in favor of supporting Britain; Kirkpatrick was counseling neutrality in the form of an abstention from any vote.

On May 25, I noted:

Carl, José, Ken, Chuck, and I go with Jeane to the Szechuan Restaurant. She tells us, at some length, that Haig is impossible. How he called to yell at her for twenty minutes. How he did not want her to go independently to the President. Yesterday's telephone call was about going to see him at twelve noon on Memorial day. Yes, Haig is cut of such different cloth, certainly not of an academic background. He respects order and command structure. "You know, my father," she says, "used to yell at me, and at my brother. Now one of my sons, my middle son, has taken to yelling at me. And so, I've gotten used to it. I just let them press on and that's what I did to Haig. But clearly, it has gotten to a situation where the President will have to choose between the two of us."

Four days later, on May 26, the Security Council reconvened, this time to consider a modest plan of action proposed by the representatives of Uganda, Guyana, Ireland, Jordan, Togo, and Zaire. They had drafted a resolution which requested the Secretary General to "undertake a renewed mission of good offices," and which urged the parties to the conflict to fully cooperate with him to negotiate mutually acceptable terms to a cease-fire.[18]

But this still was not good enough for Britain. Sir Anthony Parsons pointed out that whereas Argentina had invaded the Falklands in defiance of international law, a "simple verbal agreement to withdraw" was not sufficient. Only an immediate Argentinean withdrawal, Parsons argued, was an acceptable starting point for a cease-fire. Some starting point, I thought: once there is withdrawal, there is a cease-fire.[19]

But it was not only the U.K. that opposed the effort led by

Uganda to find a solution through giving a greater role to the Secretary General. Panama, Argentina's staunchest supporter, announced that it would vote against the resolution because it did not contain the necessary element for real peace: a provision for decolonization of the Falklands. Nor could Panama resist the temptation to strike out at the United States for "providing weapons of extermination to be used against a country it once called its neighbor."[20] China, too, opposed the resolution on the grounds that it was too weak, that it had failed to demand that Britain accept a cease-fire, and asked of it only that it cooperate with the Secretary General.

Argentina, whose forces in the Falklands were now being badly beaten, pleaded for a stop to the fighting without any preconditions. The Argentinean representative insisted that the UN Charter required no less. Then, giving way to growing disenchantment with the United States, he argued that "a cease-fire is the necessary and responsible thing to do, but intransigence of more than one permanent member of this Council prevents it."[21]

It was then Ambassador Kirkpatrick's turn to reply. Mirroring the tug on her own emotions caused by the crisis, she said that the Falklands conflict was "particularly painful and poignant for us." She then urged adoption of the proposed resolution as it was "evidence of a serious desire to bring the fighting to a close." At the least, she told the Council, adoption of the resolution will allow it to save its own reputation as a force for peacemaking.[22] But her speech accomplished little. The resolution got nowhere. The United States voted in favor of it, only to see it vetoed by Great Britain and China.

In the remaining days of May and early days of June the Latin American states launched another try at a Security Council cease-fire resolution.[23] Argentina's forces in the islands had been nearly decimated. It became clear that there would have to be a withdrawal of the remaining Argentinean forces. The call for a cease-fire was intended as a face-saving gesture, nothing more. Nevertheless, Britain threatened to veto any resolution that called for a cease-fire without an explicit call for full withdrawal of Argentina's forces from the islands.

Knowing that the United States would be caught in a bind by this resolution, that this was the knell of the Falklands drama as played out at the United Nations, and that the U.S. vote would affect U.S.-Latin American relations for a long time to come, Kirkpatrick made several trips to Washington. At NSC and NSPG meetings convened at the White House she argued the case for U.S. abstention on the cease-fire resolution when finally put to a vote. The United Kingdom was, she maintained, perfectly capable of taking care of itself. Despite a good showing by the Argentine Air Force, the U.K. had in fact won the war.[24] At the United Nations it had been able to rely on Commonwealth ties to cut across bloc lines and thus reduce the hostile reaction it might have expected from the Non-Aligned Movement. The U.K. didn't need more U.S. support, at least not diplomatically, she argued. Besides, Kirkpatrick reasoned, Britain had always pursued its own interests at the United Nations—on the Middle East, and in Central-American affairs—and the United States owed it no debt. Finally, as Britain was certain to veto the proposed UN Security Council cease-fire resolution, a U.S. veto would, she maintained, be superfluous, and unnecessarily costly with our Central and Latin American allies.

Kirkpatrick pleaded with the Argentineans not to press the proposed cease-fire resolution to a vote, and to give her more time to work for a U.S. abstention. Argentina agreed. But Panama, a key backer of the proposed Security Council resolution, apparently believing that Kirkpatrick might be stalling to give Britain more time to complete its mopping-up operations, called for a vote on June 4.

On June 4, Secretary Haig was in France with President Reagan at the Versailles economic summit of industrialized nations. For the preceding two days Kirkpatrick had been in constant touch with Walter Stoessel, the Acting Secretary of State, and Tom Enders, the Assistant Secretary of State for Latin American Affairs, about the upcoming vote. The instructions left by Haig and communicated by Stoessel and Enders were clear: join Britain in vetoing the resolution.

The morning of the day the resolution was to be put to a vote— the Security Council was scheduled to meet late that afternoon— Kirkpatrick heard that France and Japan, who were expected to abstain, now appeared to be tilting in favor of a yes vote. That would leave the United States isolated in its support for Britain. Moreover, word had come from the representatives of five Latin American states that their governments would break diplomatic relations with Washington in the event it joined Britain in a veto instead of abstaining from the vote. Kirkpatrick cabled Enders and Stoessel requesting that they contact Haig and urge that he change his instructions to approve a U.S. abstention in light of these latest developments.

Four hours passed. Word came back that Haig had been informed, and was considering the issue. Kirkpatrick again conferred with Stoessel. It was agreed that, absent a clear change in instructions, she had to vote "No," and thus veto the resolution as initially instructed. Just outside the UN Security Council chambers a telephone line between the U.S. Mission, the State Department, and Haig's office at Versailles was established just in case there might be any last minute communication about a change in instructions.

At 4:00 P.M. the Security Council convened. Sir Anthony Parsons spoke first, explaining why Britain would veto the proposed cease-fire resolution:

> The draft resolution before the Council today in no way meets . . . [Britain's] criteria. There is no direct and inseparable link between the cease-fire and immediate Argentine withdrawal within a fixed limit. The wording of the draft resolution, without any shadow of a doubt, would enable Argentina to reopen the endless process of negotiation, thus leaving Argentine armed forces in illegal occupation of parts of the islands.[25]

Phrased differently, the proposed resolution would be vetoed by Britain because it would not leave the Argentines suffering from humiliating defeat.

Four other delegates asked to speak: Ambassadors Irumba of Uganda, Nisibori of Japan, Dorr of Ireland, and Kamanda of Zaire. Each made the point that they were supporting the call for a cease-fire because, as Dorr put it, the fighting had to stop before the "climactic battle" and, in the words of Irumba, because "there is no alternative to negotiations. Only through the mechanism of negotiations can a settlement emerge—a settlement which will preserve the national honor and prestige of each party to the conflict."[26] But the alternative of preserving the Argentines' national honor—something less than unconditional surrender and British victory—was what Britain sought to avert.

The vote was taken. China, Ireland, Japan, Panama, Poland, Spain, Uganda, the USSR, and Zaire voted in favor of the cease-fire resolution. France, Guyana, Jordan, and Togo abstained (more abstentions than Kirkpatrick had anticipated). Voting against the resolution were the United Kingdom, and the United States.

Within less than two minutes after the vote was cast I saw Carl Gershman, who together with Doug Kinney, the foreign service officer handling the Falklands issue, and George Moose, the deputy head of the Political Section, had been alternately manning the phone link-up with the State Department outside the Security Council. "There's been a change of instruction," Carl said as he huddled in the front with Kirkpatrick and Sorzano. "Haig wants us to abstain."

Kirkpatrick suspected foul play. It seemed peculiar to her that Haig, who had been inaccessible for the last four hours, and knew when the matter was coming to a vote in New York, should call a moment after she cast the vote. "I told him," Carl said, referring to Tom Enders, Assistant Secretary for ARA, "that you already voted."

"Tell him to tell Haig," said Kirkpatrick, "that there is no way we can change a vote once it has been cast, that it is impossible under the Security Council rules." Carl Gershman ran out to deliver the message.

Less than a moment later, he came running back with a new message: "They want you to announce that your instructions were to abstain."

"Tell them I won't do it," said Kirkpatrick, convinced that she was being set up by Haig to look incompetent, disorganized, and downright silly—a messenger whose clout in Washington was in fact much less than had been reputed. He was, she assumed, prepared to use her in this way in an effort to have it both ways—to side with Argentina and with Britain. "Tell them [Tom Enders and Alexander Haig] that it will make us look like disorganized fools, as if we can't manage our affairs. Tell them that we will be the laughing stock of the UN if we make such an announcement."

Carl came back with Haig's final word: "You are instructed to announce publicly that you were supposed to vote for an abstention."

Kirkpatrick took a moment to collect her thoughts and then asked Ambassador de la Barre de Nanteuil of France, the president of the Security Council, for an opportunity to deliver an explanation of her government's vote. Her words would astound the other members of the Council.

She began saying that the Security Council's decision against the proposed cease-fire resolution "marks one more failure in a series of failed efforts to mediate a conflict that is more than two hundred years old—one more failed attempt to substitute reason for force, negotiation for violence, words for bombs and bullets." But, as the representative of the United States, she had just voted to kill Security Council efforts to secure a cease-fire resolution. Was she, other members of the Security Council began to wonder, attacking the vote she had just cast on behalf of her government?

She went on: "Today's decision, then, marks one more step in a process of escalation whose end is not yet in sight. . . . Affirmed in the vote of the majority today is the will to negotiation and peace." Astonished, the other delegates wondered whether she would have nothing positive to say on behalf of her own government, which, she seemed to say, was opposed to negotiations.

Her next statement left no doubt as to where her personal sympathies lay. One of her sons, she said, had handed her that morning a poem of another man who disapproved of Argentina's forceful act against the Malvinas Islands. In some lines in a poem called 'An English Poem' the great Argentine writer Borges wrote:

> I offer you my ancestors, my dead men, the ghosts that living men have honored in marble, my father's father killed on the frontier of Buenos Aires, two bullets through his lungs, bearded and dead, wrapped by his soldiers in the hide of a cow; my mother's grandfather, just 24, heading a charge of 300 into Peru—now ghosts on vanished horses.

Her hope, she said, was "that Argentina will have few such offerings from this war." Nothing was said of England's dead.

Then she dropped the bombshell. "My government," she said, has "been rent by the clash of values, loyalties and friends. That clash continued down to the registration of the vote on this issue. I am told that it is impossible for a government to change a vote once cast, but I have been requested by my government to record the fact that were it possible to change our vote we should like to change it from a veto—a 'No', that is—to an abstention."[27]

Sir Anthony Parsons turned to Chuck Lichenstein, and said, "I will never understand you Americans." Other members of the Security Council and delegates of non-member states viewing the proceedings from the gallery shook their heads as if incredulous that with the President of the United States set to meet with Margaret Thatcher of Britain and other Western leaders, and with this sensitive issue certain to come up, communication of clear voting instructions would not have been possible for the White House or Secretary of State. After all, the vote had been pending for several days.

Kirkpatrick, convinced that she had been set up by Haig for public humiliation, did little to hide that belief. Whether Haig in fact knew she had already cast the vote when he ordered the change in instructions hardly lent itself to conclusive proof. Nevertheless, the incident removed any lingering hope that Kirkpatrick might have harbored that their differences were reconcilable. At no time had her relationship with Haig been easy. She felt certain that leaks disparaging her handling of the Iraqi nuclear reactor vote in June 1981 had come from his office. Now her relations with Haig had reached a breaking point.

On June 7 she talked by secure phone to Bill Clark, the National Security Adviser, who was in London with Haig and the rest of the President's entourage. The flap over the Security Council vote was causing President Reagan embarrassment; the press was asking just whom the United States actually supported—Argentina, or Britain? Kirkpatrick learned from Clark that Haig had informed neither him nor the President of the impending Security Council vote. Both had relied on Haig's daily briefings to keep them abreast of such matters. Clark then asked that she dispatch to him through back channels a full report of what had occurred in the handling of the Falklands vote, promising to bring it to President Reagan's attention.

International events, however, were moving at too rapid a pace for her to dwell on any single event, including the flap over the Falklands vote. On June 6 Israeli forces invaded Lebanon, ushering in a long and difficult period of diplomatic wrangling and negotiations for the U.S. Mission at the United Nations. Meanwhile the fighting in the Falklands continued until June 15, when Argentine forces surrendered at Port Stanley and President Leopoldo Galtieri accepted Britain's terms for a cease-fire.

The tragic drama of the Falklands had come to an end. It was a bad show all around. Britain's grandiose statements about the links of history and kinsmanship that tied it to the Falklands left it with no choice but to fight a bloody war for a worthless, but costly ($2.6 billion, and 255 lives lost) bit of remote real estate.[28] The number of combat casualties exceeded the number of Falklands Islanders for whose benefit the war had ostensibly been fought. Luck alone saved Great Britain from much greater potential calamities, such as would have occurred had an Argentinean missile hit the 67,000-ton *Queen Elizabeth 2*, which had been ferrying troops to the Falklands.[29]

Argentina's bravado led to national humiliation and the collapse of its government. The United Nations proved itself utterly impotent in resolving even a "dispute among friends." International law principles, though bandied about with great fanfare, were likewise of no value in resolving this dispute.

The United States suffered a setback to its Central America policy, exhausted its remaining influence in the Organization of American States, and created a picture of internal disarray. As a peacemaker, Alexander Haig showed himself to be not nearly as adept as his mentor, Henry Kissinger. Haig put it this way in his memoirs: "My efforts in the Falklands ultimately cost me my job as Secretary of State. . . . those in the Administration who had been looking for an issue on which to bring me down recognized that I had given them one." He was right. Of "the disagreements between Mrs. Kirkpatrick and me" he would only say this: "Our positions were irreconcilable . . . because each of us believed that the other's position was contrary to the interests of the United States. . . . Mrs. Kirkpatrick chose to keep on pushing her own view . . . because the concept of closing ranks had no meaning to the President's aides."[30]

Jeane Kirkpatrick, convinced that everything she did in handling the Falklands crisis had the blessing of President Reagan, and that he and his National Security adviser, Bill Clark, appreciated her sensitivity to the importance of maintaining cordial relations with Argentina, saw no need to report her many involvements in great detail to the Secretary of State. Thus, perhaps inevitably, the Falklands crisis became a test of Jeane Kirkpatrick's ability to establish her independent authority out of the strict confines of normal State Department chains of command. She risked meeting, without Haig's authorization, Argentine Air Force Brigadier José Miret, Deputy Foreign Minister Enrique Ros, and others in her Waldorf suite. It couldn't go on like this. Sooner or later either she or Haig would have to resign. She was prepared to bet that it would be Haig.

9

High-Stakes Poker
The Summer of 1982 and the Lebanon Crisis

"The PLO is finished as a military organization. We must not humiliate them." *Ambassador Luc de la Barre de Nanteuil of France*

"Oh. Why is that?" *Ambassador Charles Lichenstein of the United States*

> Late night session of "informal" UN Security Council Consultations, June 1982

For nearly a year, Israeli planners mapped the invasion of Lebanon. Its stated purpose would be to destroy the PLO's increasing military strength in Lebanon, and its capacity to launch terrorist attacks against Israel's northern frontier. Yet, for the last eleven months, since a PLO-Israel cease-fire had been negotiated by U.S. envoy Philip Habib, PLO infiltrations had been at a relative standstill. To seasoned observers, the purposes of the invasion seemed therefore more complex, with motives of political and military gain cited equally: by dealing a blow at the PLO's growing international stature, Israel might dampen its capacity to orchestrate the rising tide of nationalistic fervor on the Israeli-held West Bank and Gaza Strip;

and by ridding Lebanon of PLO control the prospects for another Arab-Israeli peace treaty—between Lebanon and Israel—would be immeasurably enhanced. Perhaps, too, policy planners in European capitals as well as in Washington might then abandon the idea of Israel negotiating with the PLO over the creation of an independent Palestinian state.[1]

When the invasion came on June 6, 1982, the initial American reaction was mixed. There were reports, which he himself denied, that Secretary Haig had earlier given Israelis an "amber" if not green light to go ahead with the invasion.[2] Whether true or not, there was a certain sympathy among Haig and his advisers for the fruits the invasion might bring: international terrorism would be dealt a major setback, the United States would be able to position itself to broker another peace treaty between Israel and an Arab State, and the moribund Camp David Accords for Palestinian autonomy might be revived. But among White House advisers, including, prominently, Vice President George Bush, the view was much less sanguine. They saw the already tenuous relationship between Israel and Egypt as being strained to the breaking point, and the chances for advancing the "peace process" under President Reagan's direction as significantly reduced. Instead of yielding to quiet American diplomatic missions aimed at moderating the PLO stance, the PLO would become bolder. International terrorism would take an upward surge and the prospects for that troublesome corner of the world would turn from bad to worse. These advisers would want Israel out—quickly! Others would look more to an elimination of the conditions that prompted the Israeli invasion.

The question of whether the PLO was part of the "solution" to the quest for Arab-Israeli peace or, rather, its greatest obstacle would cast its shadow over the Lebanon crisis almost from the start. It would pit the United States against France, and divide the U.S. Government. In New York and in Paris and Cairo, France and Egypt would conspire on ways of snatching victory from the jaws of the PLO's military defeat. At the United Nations Jeane Kirkpatrick would be caught between the tug of contending forces in the U.S. Government as she tried to engineer events so as to accord U.S. envoy Philip Habib the time and the leeway to accomplish his rescue of trapped PLO forces in West Beirut from a devastating Israeli onslaught and to provide them safe egress to Tunisia and other foreign shores. Kirkpatrick's rapidly acquired diplomatic skills and standing in Washington would confront a concerted campaign aimed not only at disgracing her as an incompetent, as a shrill-sounding academic unfit for the sophisticated world of multilateral diplomacy, but also ultimately at forcing her resignation.

The spark that set off the Lebanon crisis came on June 2. In London, assassins from the Abu Nidal faction of the PLO shot Israel's Ambassador to the Court of St. James, Shlomo Argov, leaving him paralyzed from the neck down. The next morning large concentrations of Israeli troops massed on the Lebanese frontier.

Jordan's UN representative, Ambassador Hazem Nuseibeh, representing the Arab caucus at the Security Council, called for an emergency session. He charged that Israeli troops were preparing to launch a massive attack. But at the time the session convened, little was known as to what was happening on the ground. The assembled delegates, recalled from their summer leisure without clear instructions from their governments, and never ready to take Ambassador Nuseibeh very seriously—his antics had often made him the butt of laughter within his own caucus—disbanded without taking any action.

The next day, June 4, Israel's Ambassador Yehuda Blum delivered a letter on behalf of his government to the Secretary General, making it clear that Israel held the PLO responsible for the attack in London; it was, the letter said, part of the "deliberate and vicious strategy of the PLO to cause the maximum loss of life and limb among Israelis and Jews everywhere." Although the PLO did not take direct responsibility for the attack, Blum warned that "the terrorist PLO seeks to deny its responsibility by resorting to the practice of hiding behind assumed names especially invented for such purposes—Black September, Eagles of the Revolution, etc., etc.,—all aliases for the same group of murderers." The letter, coming on the heels of a further build-up of Israeli armor and infantry on the northern frontier, gave an unmistakable signal: the PLO was in for a major punitive strike. Yet no one could predict the magnitude of the attack, or that this would be a war to destroy totally the military capability of the PLO and to drive the PLO out of Lebanon.

Two days later, on Sunday, June 6, fifteen years after Israeli jets thundered across the Sinai desert to strike Egyptian airfields in the opening round of the Six-Day War, Israel sent more than 250 tanks and thousands of infantrymen across the Lebanese border. The operation, called "Peace for Galilee," was hailed as having the limited purpose of insuring the safety of northern Israeli civilian settlements from shelling and sabotage by PLO strongholds in southern Lebanon. The size of the operation belied this "limited" aim. True, there were factors that called for an unusually large Israeli strike force. The build-up of the PLO's conventional military strength in southern Lebanon— particularly, its large-scale acquisition of tanks and armored personnel carriers— made punitive raids by Israel against the PLO riskier than they had been before. Also, because Syrian intervention was possible if fighting was prolonged, a large strike force was called for. Still, a punitive raid could hardly require the amount of armor and the number of men Israel deployed at the Lebanese frontier.[3]

The larger aim of the attack had been made clear in speeches preceding the invasion. Israel's Chief of Staff, General Raful Eitan, had told his forces on the eve of the invasion that "Operation Peace for Galilee" concerned much more than the Galilee. It was, he said, for the future of "Eretz Israel"—the Land of Israel, including the West Bank and Gaza Strip. At the same time, Israeli Defense Minister Ariel Sharon publicly acknowledged that "the more we damage the PLO infrastructure, the more the Arabs in Judea and Samaria and Gaza will be ready to negotiate with us and establish co-existence."[4]

On the morning of the Israeli invasion, June 6, Jeane Kirkpatrick was fighting her own battles. Her running feud with Secretary Haig had exploded into full public view. The flap over the U.S. vote on the Falkland Islands issue, and Secretary Haig's subsequent explanation, attracted intense media interest. His failure to communicate directly with Kirkpatrick was attributed to his notion that generals do not speak to "company commanders." Appearing that day on a nationally televised program, "Meet the Press," Kirkpatrick was asked about reports of personal acrimony between her and Haig. Did they, she was queried, signal substantive disagreement over policy?

She replied that policy had little to do with it, and that the problem largely stemmed from the fact that she was from "an egalitarian background—academia—and [Haig's] background is, after all, one based on rank." The questions then turned to the breaking story of the Israeli invasion of Lebanon, and she said that the Security Council would be meeting that afternoon to discuss the matter.

She then rushed from the "Meet the Press" studio in New York to the UN Security Council. I caught up with her later that afternoon. When I arrived on a flight from Washington the Security Council had already begun its "informal consultations." As always, they were being held in the long narrow rectangular room, barely wide enough to accommodate one representative and two aides from each delegation, that adjoined the formal and very august Security Council chambers. As usual, the room was smoke-filled, the long table in the center littered with boxes of the international brands—Dunhill, Benson & Hedges, Du Maurier, and Gitanes. Access was limited to UN delegates from countries that were then members of the Council. The press was not allowed to observe the proceedings. Nor would there be any tape recording or written record of what transpired in that room, although such a record would surely be more revealing and significant than the transcripts of formal Security Council sessions distributed world-wide in six different language editions. The formal UN Security Council proceedings would prove to be the staged event, the script already worked out in the "informal consultations." Rarely would the formal proceedings reveal a flash of genuine emotion or real dialogue. That is why Jeane Kirkpatrick could be so dazzling in that forum. Her speeches, like Adlai Stevenson's, conveyed authenticity and fresh analysis, not "canned" group think, the product of a bureaucracy hundreds of miles away.

Sitting behind Kirkpatrick was Chuck Lichenstein with a copy of the draft resolution Ireland had introduced.[5] He showed it to me. The first operative paragraph called for Israeli withdrawal across the Israel-Lebanon frontier and an end to violence by both sides. The Soviet Union's Oleg Troyanovsky was given the floor. In impeccable English, he suggested the necessity of several revisions—rather minor, was how he put it—for the sake of clarity and to give effect to the intent of the proposed resolution. It would be better, he suggested, to split paragraph 1 into two distinct paragraphs: one calling for an immediate and "unconditional" Israeli withdrawal to the Israel-Lebanon frontier; the other for a cease-fire and the cessation of all cross-border attacks—an oblique reference to PLO shelling and guerrilla incursions into Israel as well as Israeli troop movements into southern Lebanon.

Troyanovsky's aim was apparent. If we went along with his suggestion, no one would notice paragraph 2. Attention would be riveted on paragraph 1, and his paragraph 1 called for the "unconditional" withdrawal of Israeli forces. The Administration's position, as I understood it, was not to pressure Israel to withdraw from Lebanon until it could complete the job of giving the PLO a black eye. It couldn't oppose the call for a cease-fire—it wouldn't look right if it did—but it would tie withdrawal to the assurance that PLO attacks against Israel would cease and that some new form of order would be established in Lebanon to control the PLO's excesses.

I looked to Chuck. He shook his head, as if to say we'll never go ahead with this; Troyanovsky is simply spinning his wheels, or setting the U.S. up for a veto. We assumed that Kirkpatrick, when called upon to comment by the president of the Council, would say just that and urge the delegates to leave the Irish draft version unchanged if they expected American support.

The presiding president of the Security Council for the month of June, France's Ambassador Luc de la Barre de Nanteuil, canvassed the delegates for comments. Troyanovsky had already made clear that he was not amenable to changes in his proposal, and that it was a take-it-or-leave-it proposition. No one at the table raised any objections. Luc de Nanteuil turned to Kirkpatrick.

"No objection," she said in a still voice. Chuck and I couldn't believe what we had heard. Neither could many of the other delegates. They too had expected her to at least bob and weave, to say that while the Soviet Union's proposed revision was not objectionable in principle, it nevertheless created new problems which had to be ironed out. It had to account for PLO provocation and deal with the conditions that had given rise to the invasion. She had said this sort of thing often in the past, but said nothing of the kind now. With no delegate objecting to the draft resolution as amended by the Soviet delegate, the meeting was adjourned. Consensus had been reached. All that was left was to reconvene in formal chambers to cast votes. If any delegate wished, he or she could then make a speech "in explanation of vote."

Chuck gave Kirkpatrick a bewildered look. "What did you do?" he asked. "How could you go along with this resolution?"

"There are things I know that you don't," she snapped back.

Neither of us doubted that she might be subjected to pressures of which we were unaware—"instructions" that we knew nothing about. Still, in dealing with the State Department on this issue we had seen or heard nothing to suggest that Secretary Haig favored an immediate *unconditional* Israeli withdrawal. Yet, that was precisely what she had just voted for. And it was all done so quickly; no draft of the resolution had been sent to Washington for comment, which would have been the usual thing to do, to stall and ask for clarification before signing on to a resolution that seemed repugnant. We knew that she had been at NSPG meetings and Crisis Management Team meetings in Washington that day, dealing with the question of the United States reaction to the Israeli invasion. We had heard that Vice-President Bush had been particularly upset about the Israeli invasion and that he would be chairing the NSPG meetings. But even accounting for that, it seemed to Chuck and me that she would have the "wiggle room," to use her phrase, to maneuver at UN Security Council sessions. We found it hard to believe that "unconditional" and immediate Israeli withdrawal had become the White House position.

Jeane Kirkpatrick was looking awfully somber and dispirited. Perhaps something had occurred in Washington of which we were totally unaware. Perhaps we really didn't understand the determination of the White House to push for full Israeli withdrawal. Still, Chuck and I couldn't shake the thought that something else was going on. Had battle fatigue set in? It is not easy to say repeatedly "No" when everyone else is urging you to say "Yes." Endless negotiation and the strain of petty squabbling, a way of life for others, was not her métier. She didn't relish the fight. Public reputation aside, the "conflictual" element of her personality was not, we knew, as dominant as others might think. I recalled that Vogue interview in July 1981: "I think for a lot of people, commitment to intellectual clarity is associated with toughness, I am not someone who is personally tough. I'm not."[6]

"But," Chuck said, continuing to press his case, convinced that battle fatigue more than anything else was responsible for her decision not to challenge the Soviet draft, "if we don't draw a link between paragraphs 1 and 2 of the resolution, it will be seen as a straight call for unilateral Israeli withdrawal. The United States will then find itself behind the eight ball as to why it's not pushing Israel hard enough to withdraw."

"There are things I know that you don't," she shot back in admonishment. She intimated that there were other factors we didn't know about and didn't appreciate, and because it had happened so rapidly and so high up that there wasn't even reason to send a draft of the resolution back to State for comment. She knew what she had to do because her instructions were so sweeping and explicit: unconditional Israeli withdrawal, period! That she had neither choice nor appetite for what she was about to do was also apparent.

We took another step forward toward entering the Security Council and its formal session, and then she stopped on her heels, turned around, looked at Chuck and me, and said: "All right, I get your point," she said. "Try it. Draft an explanation of vote saying just that. I might ask you to deliver it, Chuck. It depends on how long this session goes on. I have a dinner engagement this evening at Henry Kissinger's which I can't break."

That Henry Kissinger would fail to understand that the call of duty kept her from being on time for a dinner engagement hardly seemed plausible, but if the U.S. explanation of vote were to state that our vote didn't mean what everyone would take it to mean—that the United States favored unconditional withdrawal, perhaps it would be better that Chuck deliver it. Overstatement by one's staff is, after all, easier to explain than that committed by oneself.

Chuck and I retired to a side room alongside the Delegates' Lounge. We didn't have much time. But how does one craft an explanation of vote to state that our vote didn't mean what common usage says it means? Chuck came up with the magic words: we would argue that an "inextricable linkage" existed between paragraphs one and two of the resolution, so that even though the first paragraph called for "unconditional" Israeli withdrawal, we would say it was conditional on the PLO's compliance with paragraph 2.

Kirkpatrick looked over the statement we had polished, expressed satisfaction, and then said she really had to run off to the Kissinger dinner. She asked Chuck to deliver the speech in explanation of the U.S. vote.

"Mr. President," said Chuck, when it was his turn to speak:

> We voted for this resolution because we believe that paragraphs 1 and 2 are inextricably linked. Paragraph 1 speaks of withdrawal of Israeli forces, paragraph 2 of cessation of cross-border hostilities. But there can be no Israeli withdrawal before there is a cessation of all cross-border hostilities. One cannot be without the other. There is an inextricable linkage between these two paragraphs.[7]

What other nations say at the United Nations may go unnoticed, but when the United States takes an official position at the UN Security Council—even through an explanation of vote where a sensitive issue is involved—other nations pay attention. They know they are hearing U.S. foreign policy articulated, and often it can come first at the United Nations. What is true for foreign delegates is also true for U.S. envoys abroad. Through cable traffic reporting U.S. positions and explanations of vote at the UN Security Council, U.S. foreign policy can be tracked.

That day the delegates at the Security Council had to rewrite the cables they were drafting for their foreign ministries. For despite the U.S. vote in favor of the Soviet-sponsored resolution, they realized, in light of Chuck's speech, that it would be a mistake to interpret this as a shift of the U.S. position to favor unconditional Israeli withdrawal. At the State Department our short explanation of vote also had its effect. Instead of a cable from the Secretary of State to U.S. envoys abroad informing them that U.S. policy, as articulated last evening at the UN Security Council, stood for unconditional Israeli withdrawal from Lebanon, the cable, as it went out, quoted the explanation of vote delivered by Chuck Lichenstein. It said, therefore, that the United States Government favored the withdrawal of Israel from Lebanon in a manner linked to the cessation of attacks directed against it from Lebanese territory. This became the official statement of U.S. policy which U.S. ambassadors in the field were asked to explain to their host governments. From that moment on, official U.S. policy did not espouse unconditional Israeli withdrawal. Rather, the emphasis had shifted to cessation of all cross-border violence and provocation so that there would be no going back to the conditions that led to the Israeli invasion.

The next day, June 7, the UN Security Council was reconvened to hear the report of Secretary General Perez de Cuellar. He informed the Council that the PLO was prepared to accept a cease-fire, but that Israel was not. He read from a communiqué received from Israel's Foreign Minister stating that Israel would not agree to withdrawal until the conclusion of "concrete arrangements which . . . permanently and reliably preclude hostile action against Israel's citizens."[8] "Concrete arrangements" was a euphemism for something more than PLO assurances against a repetition of cross-border incursions. It was diplomatic language for a formal accord, probably a peace treaty, with the Government of Lebanon. Clearly Israel's ambitions had gone beyond a punitive anti-PLO raid. It was upping the price of withdrawal from Lebanon to an accord institutionalizing a new relationship between Lebanon and Israel that would leave the PLO permanently out of the picture.

On June 8, the Security Council was called into emergency session to deal with further incursions of Israeli troops into Lebanon. Spain had introduced a draft resolution condemning Israel for noncompliance with resolutions 508 (the first call for a cease-fire issued immediately upon the start of the fighting) and 509 (the Irish-sponsored, Soviet- and U.S.-endorsed resolution). Spain was blunt: it called for the immediate and total withdrawal of all Israeli forces from Lebanon without any qualification. It omitted any of the earlier calls for mutual cessation of hostile activity.[9] There was no reference to provocation.

It was immediately apparent to Jeane Kirkpatrick, Chuck Lichenstein, and to me that the Spanish draft resolution was unacceptable. The State Department felt the same way. The "instructions" sent from the State Department—by this time they were more in the nature of "guidelines"—suggested that the U.S. Mission do whatever it could to avoid passage of resolutions that would call for a return to the chaotic prewar situation that prevailed in Lebanon. USUN should, we were told, stress that a key objective of U.S. policy in the crisis was "the restoration of the authority of the central government of Lebanon." In practical terms, this meant U.S. policy sanctioned the deployment of Israeli forces in Lebanon until Lebanon's new President-elect, Bashir Gemayel, could be installed and provided an opportunity to consolidate control.

Within the U.S. Government, "windows of opportunity" began to appear from out of the dark lining of the Lebanon crisis. The prospect of humbling the PLO took on a positive air. It would be a blow to Soviet influence in the region. It would weaken the stranglehold of international terrorism. It would enable the United States to assist at the birth of a new peace treaty between Israel and an Arab State.

In one respect, U.S. and Syrian interests, as seen by the State Department, were not that far apart. Both viewed the PLO as having grown too powerful in Lebanon. Syria, like the other Arab states, wanted the PLO to remain a thorn in Israel's side, with PLO terrorism directed to the West Bank and Gaza Strip and away from using Lebanon as a base of operations. Thus two different conceptions of the new "windows of opportunity" began to emerge in the State Department. For one group, a peace treaty between Israel and an Arab state was the objective. For another, the window of opportunity meant having the PLO's energies redirected toward a solution to the future of the West Bank and Gaza Strip, which would give the PLO political control. But if U.S.-Syrian differences over the future of the PLO began to diminish, differences remained over Syria's vision of the future of Lebanon. Damascus coveted Lebanon as part of "Southern Syria." The United States wanted to see the restoration of a central government in Lebanon. For this reason, on the night of June 8, when Spain's proposed Security Council resolution was put to a vote, the United States said it could not support it. Lebanon's future, warned Ambassador Kirkpatrick, had to encompass the restoration of the authority of the Goverment of Lebanon.

Meanwhile, Israeli troops continued to drive north. Syria threatened counteraction. The Soviets sent President Reagan a tersely written note urging him to control his client state. President Reagan obliged, sending a message to Israel's Menachem Begin asking him to curb his advance. It was a "Dear Menachem, you know how much I value our friendship, why spoil it?" type of letter. Begin responded in the same vein by saying that he had no desire to either spoil the U.S.-Israeli friendship, or to call off the invasion. The response left the White House furious, and aware of how limited, in the prevailing circumstances, was its control over Israel. There was little for the White House to do but publicly support Israel for routing the PLO, while privately fuming that Israel's advance was contributing to a decline in U.S. relations with the Soviet Union and the Arab world.

On June 9, reports came in that 20,000 Syrian troops had advanced south and that Israeli warplanes had bombed the suburbs of Beirut. In the afternoon, a report came in that Israel had shot down over two dozen Syrian MiGs. "That's marvelous, just marvelous," said Carl Gershman on hearing the news. His exuberance wasn't shared widely in the Administration.

Meanwhile, at the United Nations, while a major war flared in the Middle East, another event was taking place that was diverting the attention of the delegates as well as heads of state of the governments they represented. Its acronym was SSOD—the Special Session on Disarmament hosted by the Second, or Arms Control, Committee of the General Assembly. This was consuming all of Ken Adelman's time. Heads of state and foreign ministers were invited to attend. Prime Minister Zenko Suzuki of Japan came on June 9. And throughout the month of June, while the Security Council debated the deteriorating situation in Lebanon, and while fighting still raged in the Falklands, the limousines of visiting heads of state and foreign ministers who had come to attend the SSOD and speak of the connection between disarmament and world peace, between social and economic development and international stability, lined the roadway at the General Assembly.

Vice President George Bush came to New York to represent the United States. On June 9 he called on Secretary General Perez de Cuellar and attended the SSOD deliberations. I couldn't go across the street to attend that morning's session of the SSOD. It was not only fast-breaking events in the Middle East that demanded my attention that morning, it was the problem of self-determination in another remote corner of the globe—American Samoa in the West Pacific. The UN's Decolonization Committee was about to introduce a resolution deeming the U.S. administration of that island a vestige of colonialism. American Samoa's non-voting representative in the

U.S. Congress, Congressman Sunia, had come to see me about this; he wanted to personally explain to the Committee that American Samoa had voluntarily chosen its form of association with the United States. And so the greater part of that morning I spent with Congressman Sunia as he presented testimony and proffered documents to the Decolonization Committee showing that the local Samoan parliament was freely elected and voluntarily chose its form of association with the United States. The appeal was to little avail. The Committee affirmed its responsibility for looking after the future of the island and assuring that it not be abused through U.S. colonialist instincts.

But there was yet another matter to attend to on June 9—one which struck much closer to home. It concerned Ambassador Kirkpatrick's future: would she survive the protests and calls for resignation that followed in the wake of a speech she had given at the Heritage Foundation, a conservative, Washington-based think-tank?

It was the latest round in the Haig-Kirkpatrick feud, although she hardly had that in mind when she delivered her scholarly analysis of the causes of U.S. impotence at the United Nations. She observed that, having been at the United Nations for eighteen months, she had had ample time to study the problem. Its causes, she concluded, had less to do with changing world conditions than with the incompetence of successive American administrations in dealing with multilateral organizations. They had, she said, been ignoring a simple rule of politics: friends should be rewarded, and enemies punished. In this respect the United States had been incompetent and "amateurish."

The word "amateurish" was seized upon as constituting—which it did not—a personal attack on Secretary Haig's capacity to manage U.S. foreign policy. What she in fact said was that the decline of U.S. influence around the world could be traced to "our lack of skill in practicing international politics in multilateral arenas," and that that lack of skill was "a direct reflection of what has been a persistent U.S. ineptitude in international relations that has dogged us all our national life; an ineptitude that has persisted through centuries, through administrations headed by different parties, through different presidents, and is especially manifest in our multilateral politics. . . . We have not been effective in defining or projecting in international arenas a conception of our national purpose."[10] But the context of her remarks was conveniently ignored in the rush by pro-Haig forces to launch an assault on Kirkpatrick.

New York Times columnist James Reston wrote that her remarks at the Heritage Foundation were proof that she was unqualified for her post, and that she should resign. She misunderstood, he wrote, how things are supposed to work; it was the Secretary of State, not she, who was in charge; and it was she, not he, that was the "amateur." "So," Reston concluded, "Mrs. Kirkpatrick will probably have to go. Maybe this is not a bad idea considering the truth of Mrs. Kirkpatrick's reckless candor that the Reagan foreign policy is a disappointment and needs some changes."[11]

On the other side of that day's Opinion page, *New York Times* columnist Russell Baker denounced Kirkpatrick's lack of diplomatic skills and discipline. Wrote Baker: "She went to dinner with the Argentines [to discuss the Malvinas crisis] without approval from the President or the Secretary."[12]

It was a triple-header day—perhaps a first in *New York Times* history—as the lead editorial joined in the assault. Entitled "Amateurs on Parade," it called the Haig-Kirkpatrick dispute tomfoolery in the absence of diplomacy, and then placed the blame squarely on Kirkpatrick's shoulders.[13]

The *New York Daily News* ran an article entitled "Jeane Denies She Intends to Leave UN," reporting that she was denying the swirling rumors that she was ready to step down because of her dispute with Haig.[14] *Washington Post* columnist David Broder joined the fray. In an article entitled "Pulling Rank on the U.S. Envoy," Broder wrote that Kirkpatrick had embellished the tradition of trying to make the UN job the fulcrum of American foreign policy. But, Broder opined, "it ain't, and it can't and it shouldn't be. Foreign policy has to be run out of Washington by the Secretary of State and his representatives. The best ambassadors we have had at the UN . . . have been people the public rarely glimpsed."[15] Obviously Broder preferred that Kirkpatrick not only be rarely "glimpsed," but eclipsed. Clearly someone high up in the State Department or White House was orchestrating the anti-Kirkpatrick fanfare; it couldn't be that the press of three different major newspapers had coincidentally decided one day to gang up on Jeane Kirkpatrick for a relatively obscure speech that she had delivered to a small audience at a Washington think-tank.

When it appeared that matters couldn't get any worse that day, the news came that Senator Charles Percy, the chairman of the Senate Foreign Relations Committee, had just delivered a speech attributing the U.S. failure to prevent the Falklands crisis to "wrong signals" sent by Jeane Kirkpatrick to the Argentineans. There seemed nothing one could do to prevent the sniping, and little to correct the damage done. The next morning I made the following notes:

> I start the day thinking about her talk yesterday with me, Carl, and Mark Siegel (an associate from her days with the Democratic National Committee who had paid a call on her). Her talk of being in real trouble; her request, pleading, that we be on the alert to turn the tide; her worry that last Monday's *New York Times* article generated too much anti-Jeane sentiment not to be taken seriously; Senator Percy's joining the chorus. "It's all fed by Haig and exploited by his media cohorts. I don't know how to play the media at all." Perhaps she's right. Now that the issue has been raised, she's afraid that it will not go away easily, and that it will be necessary to gather Congressional support— discreetly—to retard the process. Ah, the awful power of suggestion. Amateurishness, impulsiveness, snappish judgment. All some element of truth. And the hiring of her staff, her support of Israel, Central America, well it has me wondering whether there isn't some connection. An excuse. Maybe she should just lie low, but she can't. . . . Joan asked me an interesting question: whether the action was necessary and whether it was smart. I thought she was referring to Jeane's Heritage speech. She was referring to Israel going into Lebanon. I had difficulty answering: no, it wasn't necessary in the sense that there were intolerable attacks upon Israel; only that it was getting intolerable that a guerilla gang was becoming a guerilla army on its border. What will the day bring?

There was little time left for thinking much about Kirkpatrick's new problems with the press, and little I could do about it. Consuming my attention was the immediate business at the UN Security Council, which had begun to meet in nearly continuous session.

By June 10 there had still been no sign of any let-up in the fighting in Lebanon. The Israeli casualty count had mounted to 40 dead and 150 wounded. Although President Assad of Syria had withdrawn his forces back to their positions of June 5 and away from advancing Israeli forces, Israel was now threatening to destroy Syrian SAM (Surface-to-Air Missile) sites unless they were dismantled. And, early that morning a Syrian SAM emplacement in the Bekaa valley was reported to have been destroyed by the Israeli air force. The SAM missile emplacements had been supplied by the Soviet Union and many were manned by Soviet technicians. There was no telling what Syria, or the Soviets, might do in response. In New York, Syria called for the Security Council to condemn the latest Israeli "aggression."

Drew Middleton, the *New York Times'* highly respected military analyst, wrote that the expanding Israeli drive was pushing Syria to the edge of crisis. Fighting between Israeli and Syrian air and ground units was spreading.[16] Middleton warned that what began as an Israeli attempt to sweep PLO forces out of their positions in south Lebanon was rapidly developing into a war between the two strongest military powers in the Middle East. Moreover, wrote Middleton, officers who know Israel's Defense Minister, Ariel Sharon, say that he is addicted to the doctrine of all-out offense, and that he may now see an opportunity to drive Syria as well as the PLO out of Lebanon in order to establish a neutral buffer state there. Later that day reports came in that Israeli troops had taken all the towns on the road to Beirut and had dropped leaflets in Beirut urging the Syrians to depart. Beirut airport had been bombed, and the situation in the city was approaching anarchy. From Damascus came news that our special Presidential envoy, Ambassador Philip Habib, had arrived and had met for inconclusive talks with Syria's Assad.

The next day, June 11, Ambassador Kirkpatrick received a courtesy call from a distinguished Arab official. Reports from the field had warned of a serious deterioration in U.S. relations with his nation because of the U.S. failure to halt the Israeli advance. The visitor, however, showed little enthusiasm for an Israeli halt. He spoke of a "breakthrough," providing that Israel did not succumb to pressure to withdraw before it completed its mission—a belief, Kirkpatrick noted, that hardly seemed to square with his country's public declarations on the subject.

"You know, Ambassador Kirkpatrick," the emissary replied, "we are part of the Arab world, but we are not certain that it would be most useful for the Israelis to simply withdraw precipitously. We were, of course, profoundly offended by Israel's violation of the sovereignty of another Arab state, but now that the Israelis are in Lebanon they should behave responsibly. A vacuum is not useful. It would be dangerous, Madam Ambassador, and would also mark a missed opportunity. Neither Syria nor the PLO should be allowed to control Lebanon. Power should be restored to a strong central government."

This, Kirkpatrick assured him, was precisely the aim of the U.S. Government.

Suddenly, everyone seemed to be seeing silver linings in Israel's war against the PLO in Lebanon. The *New York Times*, in its editorial of June 11, opined that: "Arrogantly, perhaps foolishly, the Israelis believe that they can by force create the stable environment that history has denied them." But, it concluded, reflecting the new attitude of the State Department, "one need not approve every facet of Israel's policies to see the opportunity that it has created. . . . A more forthcoming gesture towards the West Bank Palestinians would give Israel a more compelling moral case. But the peace of Lebanon is also a moral issue, whose world-wide evasion merely hardened Israel's resolve."[17]

New York Times columnist William Safire was less restrained. In his June 11 piece, titled "The Liberation of Lebanon," he wrote that the strategy of "the Reagan-Haig-Kirkpatrick faction (opposed by the Weinberger-Bush faction) has been to deplore the violence, to worriedly pass along the contents of the obligatory letter from Leonid Brezhnev, but to give the Israelis the six plus days they need to transform the chaos in Lebanon. . . . One new fact is that there is now a chance for a rebirth of an independent western-oriented Lebanon. . . . Another new fact is that terrorism will be set back to 'normal' [and] will find it harder to intimidate West Bank Palestinians interested in West Bank autonomy. . . . A third new fact is that the Israelis have now achieved an incredible credibility: peace-makers get peace, war-makers get war. . . . Liberation and not invasion is what is taking place in Lebanon today."[18]

Another point of view was expressed in a companion piece authored by Columbia University Professor Edward Said, a member of the PLO's governing Palestine National Council. Professor Said declared that Begin's interpretation of Zionism "reduces Palestinians either to pacified inhabitants of Judea and Samaria or to terrorists." "The invasion," he concluded, "is really the collision of two different views of reality. On one hand, Israel's severe and terrifying view that its neighbors exist only to destroy Jews, and on the other, a patchwork of sketchy, ambiguous and inarticulate Arab feelings that the modern world has not recognized the Arab nation. . . . The logic of Israel's action now has it that at some suitably distant date, the Palestinians in the occupied territories may have autonomy without land on exclusively Israeli terms; the other exiled Palestinians are to be exterminated. If extermination of the terrorists also includes killing of Lebanese civilians . . . then so much the worse for them. Now in Lebanon the Israels have tried to obliterate a disorderly Arab pattern of small-scale revolutions and petty squabbles with an apocalyptic logic of exterminism."[19]

What Edward Said hadn't mentioned was that those "small-scale revolutions and petty squabbles" had resulted in the death of more than 100,000 Lebanese civilians in the last ten years. But he was certainly correct in thinking that Israel and the Arabs were on a collision course of two different views of reality, each believing itself to be the victim of the other's unjustified nationalist ambitions.

At the U.S. Mission in New York and at the State Department in Washington our concerns remained focused on achieving a cease-fire. There were some encouraging signs. Moshe Arens, Israel's Ambassador in Washington, stated in an interview with the *Washington Post* that Israel's objective in Lebanon continued to be a 40-kilometer expanse clear of terrorists, and that it was Syria's intervention that made a temporary drive north by Israeli forces necessary.[20] But all the evidence seemed to point in the opposite direction.

From Beirut, the *New York Times*' Tom Friedman reported that the PLO was not yet ready to give up the fight. "We are like a piece of mercury," he quoted a PLO leader as saying. "Hit us and we just break up into smaller pieces, but we never really go away."[21]

It was becoming increasingly evident that a 40-km buffer zone was not what the Israelis now had in mind. Writing in *Newsday*, Professor Amos Perlmutter, a seasoned observer of Israeli politics and military affairs, observed that Israel's invasion of Lebanon was "quite simply a fight to the finish between Israel and the PLO. Israel means to destroy the threat of the Palestinians once and for all by destroying its political and military infrastructure."[22]

Stephen Rosenfeld, the *Washington Post* columnist, observed in a similar vein that "the purpose of the invasion was not simply to defeat the Palestinian armed forces, but to decimate its non-military structure, to shatter the sense of Palestinian corporateness. . . . The Israelis do not hope to turn the Palestinians toward peace; that would mean opening to it a path to statehood. They hope to destroy it as an organization, as an idea, and a cause, leaving the Palestinians as a small isolated bunch of individuals on the West Bank who can be intimidated, manipulated and perhaps eventually shuffled across the river into what the Begin government regards as the real Palestinian state—Jordan. In short the Begin government is using its legitimate purposes of self-defense to mask its illegitimate purpose of repressing another small, abused and persistent people."[23]

From Tel Aviv came more sobering news about the cost of the operation: Israeli casualty figures had climbed to over 100 dead, including among them Israel's Deputy Chief of Staff. Over 600 soldiers had been wounded. At this pace, Israel's casualty figures from what began as a punitive raid would soon exceed those of the 1967 war.

The text of the Israeli Cabinet's communique of June 11, translated by the U.S. Embassy in Tel Aviv and sent to major diplomatic posts, read: "The IDF fulfilled its mission with courage, sacrifice, and a great deal of resourcefulness. . . . The Cabinet is honoring the brave and holy sons who have given their lives for the peace of the Galilee and all the citizens of Israel." The Cabinet communique then listed two conditions for a cease-fire, and a subsequent Israeli withdrawal: 1) no PLO presence in a 40-kilometer zone north of Israel; and 2) the return of all Syrian forces to the positions they occupied before the Israelis moved into Lebanon.[24]

I noticed that the communique contained none of the earlier language of Israeli government communications that had referred to the need for "concrete arrangements" for a new political order in Lebanon to prevent a repetition of the circumstances that precipitated the invasion. Could this mean, I asked myself, that Israel now considered its mission accomplished? Israel now occupied more than 40 kilometers of Lebanese territory north of Israel. Moreover, the Israelis weren't asking for removal of Syrian forces from Lebanon, only a return to their previous positions. Perhaps something could be worked out along these lines, and the United Nations might be the place to do it after all.

From the U.S. ambassadors in the major Middle-East posts— Amman, Damascus, Beirut, Cairo, and Tel Aviv—all Middle-East hands who had grown up within the State Department system, largely within the Bureau of Near Eastern Affairs, came a common message for the Secretary of State: "opportunities" for creative Middle-East diplomacy had been created, but to take advantage of them, the Israelis had to be restrained from going too far in Lebanon. In addition, the U.S. Mission in New York had to be curbed in its continuing vetoes of UN Security Council resolutions aimed at getting the Israelis out of Lebanon. Otherwise the United States would be perceived throughout the Arab world as interested only in supporting Israel, and irreparable damage would be done to the "peace process."

The folders of incoming cables on our desks at the Mission kept growing thicker and thicker, oblivious to the fact that handling one major crisis at a time was about all that could be reasonably expected of any individual. Secretaries and assistants kept bringing in cables dealing with the world's other troubles, neatly labelled "Iran-Iraq war," "Africa," "Disarmament," "U.S.-Soviet relations," "Europe," and "the Falklands." The cables pertinent to whichever was the major ongoing crisis had to be digested first, and quickly. Were troops moving forward? Where? Were calls for a cease-fire being heeded? Was a cease-fire or other interim arrangement holding? Were press reports of atrocities to be believed? What was the view of our embassy in the field? Was there a reasonable chance for accommodation or peaceful settlement of the dispute? Any of these points could critically affect U.S. strategies at the United Nations: to push or not to push for adoption of a particular resolution, to opt for harsh condemnatory language or for softer methods of persuasion, to try to build alliances and share information with our allies or to tough it out alone. To fail to stay abreast of the cable traffic was the worst sin a U.S. foreign service officer or diplomat could be guilty of: to be uninformed.

On the evening of June 13, reports of mounting civilian casualties began to come in. Many civilians had been caught in the crossfire between Israeli and PLO forces. In the port city of Sidon alone over 10,000 civilian casualties were reported. The reports were compiled at the State Department's crisis management desk. There was no suggestion that the figures were exaggerated. The toll seemed staggeringly out of proportion to the peace the operation was to ensure.

The Security Council reconvened in yet another effort at a cease-fire. But no consensus could be reached. Chuck Lichenstein, who was standing in for Kirkpatrick while she was away in Washington, said that the United States would refuse to join in any cease-fire call unless it made reference to the need for restoration of the authority of the central government in Lebanon. On this point the cease-fire attempt foundered. Many of the delegates seemed too intimidated by the Syrians and their Soviet backers—neither of whom looked favorably upon the restoration of a pro-Western government in Lebanon. The diplomatic efforts launched by troubleshooter Philip Habib, who was making the rounds in Beirut, Damascus, and Jerusalem, seemed more promising. Michael Kozak, State's Deputy Legal Adviser, had just been dispatched to join him, creating a stir that some kind of agreement might be in the offing.

The following morning, Kirkpatrick returned to New York from Washington. No one could predict her real schedule, not even she. It seemed to be in constant flux, as she juggled several issues at the same time: the Lebanon crisis, an end to the Falklands fighting, curbing the sniping from Haig's quarters, maintaining relations with Congress and with the handful of individuals she could trust at the

State Department, shuttling back and forth for the NSPG meetings in Washington, arranging for diplomatic functions in New York, and for pre-General Assembly trips abroad, etc., etc. The list seemed endless. This particular morning her spirits were buoyed. She had received a letter of support from Senator Patrick Moynihan who said he was inspired to write by all the articles saying that she should be dumped. From Tom Dine, Executive Director of AIPAC, the American-Israel Public Affairs Committee, Israel's lobbying arm on Capitol Hill, came news that a bipartisan group of Senators had just given her a vote of confidence.

Four days later, on June 18, President Ronald Reagan arrived at the United Nations to address the still ongoing UN Special Session on Disarmament, accompanied by Secretary of State Alexander Haig. The President spoke about the need for improved bilateral relations as a conduit to nuclear disarmament. It sounded like the classic chicken and egg question: does disarmament make for improved relations, or do improved relations make for disarmament? But despite the occasional clumsy phrase, his speech was serious, and thoughtful. The other speeches seemed almost fungible: the obligatory call for an end to the arms race, the pronouncement that arms are no substitute for peace, the plea for a halt to nuclear proliferation. Most of the other world leaders had come to meet with their counterparts in the corridors of the United Nations and in hotel suites. But President Reagan was not delivering the expected anti-Soviet harangue; he was, it seemed, making an overture for improvement of bilateral relations between the two superpowers.

The following day, Israel's Prime Minister, Menachem Begin, arrived to address the Special Session on Disarmament. The timing was strange. Israeli forces were still locked in battle with the PLO in Lebanon, and threats of Syrian involvement had not abated. It was exactly one year ago that I had seen him last as he addressed a gathering of Holocaust survivors at Jerusalem's Western Wall and explained his reasons for ordering the bombing of the Iraqi Osirak reactor. Now he looked in good spirits, as if ready to show the world that things were going his way. More than two dozen world leaders had spoken. Why shouldn't he, Menachem Begin, have his chance as well?

My notes on the event:

Menachem Begin addressed the General Assembly this morning, what was left of it. After the walkout—leaving 123 out of a potential 900—I sat to the left of Jeane with Ken in between and Dirk absent. Begin came up to the podium with little hesitation, as if despite his disdain for the UN this was his big moment, a sort of graduation day ceremony, the successful businessman returning for his high school diploma. He respected international law, he said, but it had gone wrong in the Kellog-Briand pact by outlawing all war. I looked around the hall. Those that remained seemed the most junior members of their delegations—third or fourth rank. Then Begin lost whatever audience he had, as he launched into a discourse about a split of opinion among minor Hebrew prophets on the paths to universal disarmament. He tried to relate it to international law and why wars of self-defense are among "the noblest concepts of mankind." It became too abstruse for anyone to follow. Jeane applauded loudly after he finished. He grinned widely. Most of the other applause was coming from the visitors' gallery packed with supporters.

As Begin concluded his remarks, the delegates standing in the hall outside the chamber quickly returned to hear the next speaker, Prime Minister Trudeau of Canada. Israel's Yehuda Blum made his way to the podium to catch up with Begin, who was leaving. "What could I do?" Blum said, catching sight of me and throwing his hands up in despair. "He writes his own speeches and he lets no one see them before he delivers them, even me."

Jeane Kirkpatrick rushed out of the General Assembly hall and, catching up with Begin as he was about to enter his limousine in front of the UN delegates' entrance, gave him a warm embrace.

The next morning, June 20, Jeane Kirkpatrick boarded a government plane with staff, State Department desk officers, the wives of White House Counselor Edwin Meese and Transportation Secretary Andrew L. ("Drew") Lewis, Jr., as well as Nancy Reynolds, an old friend of the First Lady then serving on the U.N Commission on the Status of Women. Also going along was Elizabeth Dole, then a political liaison officer at the White House. They were leaving on a two-week, five-nation trip to central Africa, billed as pre–UN General Assembly consultations to consolidate relations with moderate Francophile African nations, to discuss problems faced by women in developing countries, and to prepare for the upcoming U.N. "Decade on Women."[25] There was nothing unusual about the trip (Ursula Meese and Marylin Lewis, because they were not government employees or on contract, reimbursed the government for the cost of their seats), other than its timing. Pre-UN General Assembly consultations were important but not so pressing that they couldn't be deferred until after a major crisis—here, the war in Lebanon and the nearly daily UN Security Council deliberations and meetings in Washington it engendered—had subsided. But for Jeane Kirkpatrick, it was also an opportunity to be away—preferably far away—to allow her feud with Haig to cool off.

Two days later, on June 22, while Kirkpatrick and company were in Rwanda, Jordan's King Hussein delivered an urgent plea through the Secretary General to the envoys of all the governments represented on the Security Council: "In the name of human decency, I appeal to you to exert your immediate and maximal effort on behalf of your nation to bring to an end the unprecedented Holocaust enacted on Lebanese soil today. . . . Israel is engaged in a continued war of genocide against the Lebanese and Palestinian people. . . . The blood of thousands of human beings who have fallen in Lebanon and in Beirut will never be forgotten. . . . Disassociate yourself and your nation for all time from any suggestions of tolerance of or acquiescence in the Israeli bloodbath created in Lebanon. I am, sir, your sincere friend, Hussein, the First."[26]

Israel countered the move by distributing a one-page paper on "The Truth About Civilian Casualties and Refugees in Southern Lebanon." It labelled as baseless the allegations that 10,000–15,000 civilian casualties had resulted from the fighting and that up to 500,000 individuals had been left homeless. The correct figure, it said, was that only about 1,000 civilians had died in the fighting; and that no more than 20,000 civilians had been left "temporarily homeless."

In the meantime, as world leaders gathered at the Disarmament session in New York, in Beirut the PLO's Yassar Arafat had run out of room to maneuver. It became obvious that the United Nations was not going to save him. On June 24, France had introduced yet another proposal for a cease-fire, arguing that unless it was accepted there was every reason to believe that in a matter of hours there would be a tragic bloodbath in Beirut. France suggested that provision be made for the neutralization of West Beirut under the supervision of UN observers after both sides disengaged. There was little enthusiasm from any quarter for UN observers in Beirut.

Arafat's options narrowed to acceptance of American terms for his total surrender and banishment from Beirut, or the risk of total annihilation at the hands of the massive Israeli forces at the gates of Beirut. As David Ottaway of the *Washington Post* put it in a June 24 dispatch from Beirut: "Arafat, 52, the miracle man of Palestinian politics, has to all appearances run out of allies or protectors, Arab or other nationalities. What has stung them [the PLO] to the quick and escaped their calculations is the abdication of the Soviet Union, their main arms provider and big power backer. Now Arafat has no fallback. He would have to give up totally the direct armed struggle and become purely a political figure—a role that he had already begun to try out before the Israeli invasion as he pushed for diplomatic recognition of the PLO in the capitals of the world."[27]

As Israeli troops stood poised to lay siege to Beirut, with America's capacity for effective diplomacy in the region on the line, the United States suddenly found itself without a Secretary of State. On the afternoon of June 25 Alexander Haig convened a hastily arranged news conference to announce his resignation, effective immediately. The stunned press corps was read a letter he presented to President Reagan a day earlier: "In recent months, it has become clear to me that the foreign policy on which we embarked together was shifting from that careful course which we had laid out. Under these circumstances, I felt it necessary that you accept my resignation."[28]

At the Versailles summit, the White House senior staff had embarrassed him by putting him in the wrong place at receiving lines and denying him appropriate travel accommodations and support. It was part of a pattern. He had expected his letter of "resignation" to serve as a means for venting his frustration at his treatment. But instead of a presidential vote of confidence and an invitation to stay on as a member of the Reagan team, Alexander Haig was fired. Worse, the manner of his firing made it apparent that it had been under consideration for some time. For, simultaneously with the announcement of Haig's departure, came the announcement of his replacement, George Shultz.

As syndicated columnists Evans and Novak said in the next day's *Washington Post*, Haig's departure had been predictable as early as the previous April. It was then, they reported, that National Security Adviser Bill Clark had told conservative Republican leaders, "Don't worry about Haig, he'll be gone in two months." It was not internal disagreements on issues that resulted in his downfall, concluded Evans and Novak, but his style—specifically his self-anointment as Reagan's "vicar" of foreign policy.[29] Haig himself was unaware of how his style and self-aggrandizing habits grated on others.

Kirkpatrick was unavailable for comment the day her nemesis was fired. She was in Togo at the time. But clearly a new "window of opportunity" had opened for her. The querulous Secretary of State Haig would no longer be breathing down her neck, the State Department bureaucracy would be preoccupied with briefing Shultz and thus hopefully staying out of her bailiwick in New York, and with Clark's power at the White House enhanced, her continued access to the President was assured. Bill Clark liked and respected her. From the beginning of his tenure as National Security Adviser, she had, at his request or at her own initiative, supplied him with a variety of memoranda on sensitive national security matters. Often I would do the international law component of such memoranda. Now she would be able to devote less time to worrying about the sniping from State and more to concentrating on what she preferred: the analysis of national security problems, and development of policy, particularly in regard to U.S.–Central American relations.

In New York, Haig's departure and Shultz's arrival had little effect on the Mission's work in dealing with the Lebanon crisis. Late evening meetings of the Security Council continued on until the early morning hours, resembling at times—with the United States often as the lone hold-out—nothing so much as a war of attrition to tire us out. We could understand, of course, the sense of urgency. The bloodletting was assuming enormous proportions, although hardly as staggering as the casualties sustained in the Iran-Iraq war—which rarely came to the Security Council's attention. But there were enough innocent civilian casualties to make many delegates at the United Nations want not only to be seen as doing something, but actually to do something. The trouble was that there was little that the United Nations could do to stop the fighting. Cease-fire resolutions were either not passed because of disagreements over what type of order should prevail, or, if a cease-fire was agreed upon, it was almost immediately violated.

It was in the course of these events that a shift, at first barely perceptible, took place in the focus of the UN Security Council deliberations. The lines of battle began to change. It became no longer a matter of warding off draft resolutions introduced by the Soviets or radical Arab states. Instead, we began to engage our European allies and Egypt over the blueprint for the resolution of the Arab-Israeli conflict. The crisis of Lebanon had suddenly been leapfrogged to the terms for settlement of the Arab-Israeli conflict.

It began on the afternoon of June 26 when France, with the support of Egypt, introduced a draft Security Council resolution calling for unilateral but not unconditional withdrawal of Israeli troops from Lebanon.[30] The PLO would have to withdraw from the Beirut area, but no more was expected of them.

Near midnight, the Council President, Luc de La Barre de Nanteuil of France, invited the U.S. and Egyptian delegations into his chambers to see if we couldn't reach agreement on the proposed resolution. "My government," said Chuck, "would be unable to support this resolution unless the phrase 'complete disarmament of the PLO and restoration of the authority of the Government of Lebanon' was inserted as a condition for Israeli withdrawal."

"Be reasonable," de Nanteuil retorted with unexpected intensity. "The PLO is finished as a military organization. We must not humiliate them."

"Oh. Why is that?" said Chuck, making it clear that it was beyond him what was wrong with the idea of "humiliating" the PLO.

Chuck remained adamant on the terms for U.S. acquiescence, and made it clear that if pushed to a vote, the United States would veto the resolution even though America's ally, France, was its key sponsor. Why, Chuck asked again, if France and Egypt were so insistent on getting this resolution passed and forcing Israel to withdraw, did they oppose the revisions he was proposing—disarmament of the PLO and the restoration of the authority of a central government in Lebanon?

Ambassador Esmet Abdel Meguid, Egypt's usually unflappable representative, replied emotionally. "This," he said, "is the view of my President. Egypt wants no reference to the laying down of arms by the Palestinians. It wants no humiliation of the PLO."

Chuck hesitated for a moment to reply, trying to keep his temper from flaring. Again Abdel Meguid pressed his point. Egypt's President Hosni Mubarak was, he said, unequivocally committed to no laying down of PLO arms. "It would be surrender if they did so, and there should be no surrender."

It was past midnight. De Nanteuil suggested that the Security Council be reconvened in formal chambers. He was disappointed. He had expected the United States to yield and go along with the French draft resolution. We took a half-an-hour recess. In the Delegates' Lounge Abdel Meguid, and his deputy, Amram Moussa, approached us. It seemed like a last-minute try at a compromise. No sooner had they begun to talk than Israel's Yehuda Blum and his aide, Yehuda Milo, who had been watching the action from the sidelines, came over to join the conversation. Seeing Blum and Milo approach, Abdel Meguid and Moussa quickly excused themselves, turned on their heels and walked away. "This is too much, the way Abdel Meguid dismisses me," Blum complained. There was little we could do to console him. It wasn't just that Egypt-Israel relations—never warm despite the signing of the peace treaty between them in 1979—had been severely strained by the Lebanon invasion. It was an open secret that Abdel Meguid detested Blum. Unfortunately, Blum chose what was probably the worst possible moment to make his approach. Whatever message it was that Abdel Meguid and Moussa wanted to convey to us remained a mystery. Around 1:00 A.M. the formal Security Council session was called to order to vote on the French draft resolution.

Chuck and I entered the Security Council chamber with an uneasy feeling. We couldn't recall a single instance when the United States had vetoed a resolution introduced by an ally. It helped to know that we weren't out of line with the State Department on this one. Chuck had remained in regular touch with Larry Eagleburger, the Under Secretary of State for Political Affairs. Now France and the United States seemed at loggerheads.

Earlier that day Eagleburger had called in France's Ambassador to Washington, Bernard Vernier-Palliez, in an effort to make clear to his government just how far the United States was prepared to go and where it drew the line on French efforts in New York to save the PLO from "humiliation." Eagleburger made it clear that the United States stood firm on the following points:

1. that the PLO had to hand over all arms to the Lebanese armed forces;
2. that in return the PLO leadership would be guaranteed safe conduct out of Lebanon;
3. that after such an agreement was reached, Israel would adjust its lines so that it wouldn't appear that the PLO was laying down its arms under threat.

That's as far as the United States was prepared to go. That apparently was not far enough, for word came back from Paris that Ambassador Luc de Nanteuil would introduce the draft French resolution at the UN Security Council. The die was cast for a U.S. veto.

The vote on the resolution was preceded by a tedious "debate"— speeches for the UN record duly delivered without any regard to the early morning hour. Besides the five permanent members of the UN Security Council—China, France, the USSR, the United Kingdom and the United States—there were ten nonpermanent members to be heard from: Guyana, Ireland, Japan, Jordan, Panama, Poland, Spain, Togo, Uganda, and Zaire. Nuseibeh of Jordan accused the United

States of doing everything it could to prolong the agony of Lebanon. Guyana's representative argued that the French draft resolution, which he supported, still did not go far enough to end the "Israeli aggression." Spain concurred. The Soviet representative, Ovinnikov, looked to Chuck and asked how it could be that the entire world supported the PLO but the United States always sided with Israel. Togo's representative called the whole exercise self-defeating as France's proposed solution, even if passed, did not offer a workable solution.

It was after 2:00 A.M. when Lebanon's Ghassan Tueni, the first of the invited non-Security Council member representatives, took the floor to speak. Beginning his oration with the observation that he was speaking on behalf of the country most affected by the proposed resolution, he said, to everyone's surprise, that the effort was misguided as it was likely to bring about exactly what France ostensibly sought to avoid: an Israeli attack on West Beirut. De la Barre de Nanteuil said, however, in defense of his proposed resolution, that the PLO would never voluntarily lay down arms and that something other than a "surrender or die" option had to be proposed.

By 3:00 A.M. no vote had yet been taken. We were worn out, but the speeches continued. France was pursuing a Middle-East policy at odds with that proposed by the United States. France saw as the key to resolution of the Arab-Israeli conflict the creation of an independent Palestinian state under PLO control. The United States viewed this as a formula for disaster, favoring instead a solution based on the Camp David Accords: autonomy for the Palestinians on the West Bank and Gaza Strip and peace treaties between Israel and its neighbors. Everyone else at the United Nations seemed to declare the Camp David approach dead and unworkable.

We had tried earlier in the week to understand the French position better. We had talked to other members of their delegation and they warned us that destroying the PLO would work against Western interests and would "renew the error of 1948." We took that to mean the failure to implement the UN's 1947 plan for partition of Palestine into independent Jewish and Arab states. The Arabs had rejected that formulation then. Apparently France believed that partition, or some variation of it based on the 1967 borders, was the only solution to the conflict. They also explained to us that the United States had made an "historical error" in concluding the Camp David Accords as they excluded the PLO. With the decimation of the PLO's military forces in Lebanon, France was now committed, we were told, to force a change in the West's approach to Middle-East peace-making efforts by focusing its attention on the need for direct Israel-PLO negotiations.

But why, we asked, was France pushing so hard in New York at the United Nations? Washington, not New York, was the proper venue for influencing U.S. policy. Besides, they knew that if push came to shove the United States would veto their draft resolution as inconsistent with U.S. commitments under the Camp David Accords, and also with U.S. assurances against dealing with the PLO. It never occurred to us that France would try to force a U.S. veto.

However, shortly before 3:00 A.M., as Chuck prepared to cast the U.S. vote, it became clear that provoking a U.S. veto, rather than working with the United States for a change in policy, was the object of French efforts. What seemed to matter most to France was the appearance of independence from the United States. Its ability to actually influence events in the region seemed secondary. That, it became clear, was why they had so fiercely resisted any efforts by the United States and several Arab states, and even by Lebanon—the putative beneficiary of these moves—to revise their proposal.

On the 9:00 A.M. shuttle back to Washington, after four hours of sleep, the intensity of the work and late night/early morning session began to catch up with me. Most other delegations waited for instructions from their foreign ministries. They were a step removed from the process. We made up our script as we went along. We worked with the State Department, but we were not directed by it. The "instructions" were cue cards; and often—as often as we could—we prepared them ourselves. But there was more to it than that. The problem lay in having to deal, day after day, with the awful no-win situation in Lebanon and the seemingly endless struggle between Israelis and Palestinians. The morning newspapers carried photographs of lines of cars heading south from Beirut, anticipating an Israeli onslaught against the PLO strongholds in East Beirut. On the basis of the information we had received in New York, we believed that if no solution was worked out by Phil Habib in the next 24 hours, Israel would storm East Beirut. The cause of Israeli security might take an awful toll.

In the meantime, as Israel consolidated control of territory south of Beirut, it discovered the extent of the PLO military build-up and infrastructure throughout Lebanon. UN refugee camps and vocational training centers were used for PLO military training purposes. Huge arms caches were found in schools run by UNRWA, the United Nations Relief and Works Agency for Palestine Refugees. One UNRWA-run vocational school near Sidon—the Siblin Technical and Teacher Training Institute—was used as a guerrilla training center. Since 1949, Palestinian refugees had received 1 billion dollars under the UNRWA program, with 25 percent coming directly from U.S. contributions. The U.S. Mission, which disburses these funds, on hearing about the Siblin Training Institute, decided to withhold further U.S. contributions to UNRWA until there was credible assurance of no repetition of the use of UN facilities for PLO training purposes. I took the check for $17,000,000 which I had received from State for disbursement to UNRWA and kept it in my safe until we received adequate assurances.

Several days later, France and Egypt, undeterred by the U.S. veto of June 26, undertook a more ambitious project. They shared "non-papers," precursors to draft resolutions, with the U.S. delegation. The purpose was nothing less than to rewrite the framework for Arab-Israeli peace which had been in effect since UN Security Council resolutions 242 and 338 terminating the 1967 and 1973 wars. That framework called for direct negotiations between the states that waged war in 1967 to end the state of belligerency, and to conclude treaties of peace. The Palestinian issue was, as the United States saw it, to be addressed as a matter of incremental steps toward autonomy with all future options left open.

France and Egypt had a very different view. They made clear in conversations with American and other delegates their conviction that had the Palestinians been given an opportunity to develop an independent state on the West Bank and Gaza, there would have been no need for the PLO to take control of Lebanon, or turn it into their base for attacks on Israel. The Camp David Accords had lost whatever vitality or promise they once possessed. Interim solutions had proven unworkable. It was time, they insisted, for the U.S. Government to push Israel to negotiate the final status of the West Bank and Gaza, and this had to be done directly with the PLO, the "legitimate representative of the Palestinian people." The Franco-Egyptian initiative called for three new developments along these lines:

1. mutual recognition between the PLO and Israel;
2. recognition of the Palestinians' right to "self-determination in all of its aspects;" and
3. recognition of the "national legitimate rights of the Palestinian people."

Kirkpatrick was still in Africa when the Franco-Egyptian draft was first floated, but she returned as the Mission and the State Department were determining how best to respond to the initiative. When Chuck and I first examined the Franco-Egyptian initiative it seemed a non-starter, destined for another U.S. veto. There was no mistaking that it was a departure from the Camp David Accords; and U.S. policy, as we understood it, was committed to preserving and promoting the Camp David Accords. Whereas the Camp David Accords studiously avoided any mention of "self-determination" in favor of interim measures for achieving Palestinian Arab autonomy, the Franco-Egyptian initiative spoke directly of "self-determination." Moreover, it called for self-determination "in all of its aspects"—a euphemism for an independent Palestinian state.

Final status negotiations under the Camp David formula were to occur only in the context of peace negotiations among Israel, Egypt, and Jordan after a preliminary five-year interim period for the implementation of autonomy. Thus the Camp David Accords referred to the "legitimate rights of the Palestinian people," carefully avoiding use of the word "political" rights. By contrast the Franco-Egyptian draft explicitly referred to the "national" legitimate rights of the Palestinians. The United States had set conditions for recognizing the PLO—renunciation of terrorism, and acceptance of resolutions 242 and 338 as a basis for peace-making. The Franco-Egyptian draft called for ignoring or abandoning these conditions. It was hard, therefore, to see how the United States could possibly support the Franco-Egyptian draft.

Yet Chuck and I continued to find it implausible that the point of the exercise was merely to provoke another U.S. veto. This was a far more significant diplomatic initiative than France's earlier proposal for Israeli withdrawal from Lebanon. This initiative was jointly sponsored by Egypt. It sought to redefine the terms of Arab-Israeli peace-making. France and Egypt must have thought that they could achieve U.S. acquiescence. They weren't pressing for a vote. They hadn't even reduced their initiative to "blue copy" resolution form. They had also made it clear that they were not demanding any immediate U.S. response to their proposal. This was something to be negotiated.

Ambassador Nicholas Veliotes was then the Assistant Secretary of NEA, the State Department's Bureau for Near Eastern Affairs. Together with Sam Lewis, the U.S. Ambassador to Israel who was at the State Department for consultations, he decided to pay a call on

Kirkpatrick to discuss the matter. He was concerned about the negative impact that yet another U.S. veto at the Security Council, especially of a resolution sponsored by friends, might have on U.S. relations with the moderate Arab world. At the same time, he was not anxious to travel down the road of the Franco-Egyptian initiative. Both Veliotes and Lewis, who had played a significant role in the process that led to the Camp David Accords, realized that negotiations on the basis of the Franco-Egyptian initiative would take the United States far afield from its commitments in those Accords. Moreover, the Camp David Accords were *the* foreign policy achievement of the Carter Administration—an achievement for which the State Department, particularly NEA, took deserved credit.

Veliotes and Lewis informed Kirkpatrick that NEA had not yet decided how to react to the Franco-Egyptian initiative, but that it would be best if nothing precipitous was done in New York. What they didn't realize is that they had little cause for worry: the last thing Kirkpatrick wanted was drastic U.S. action on a resolution introduced by two of her best friends at the United Nations—Luc de la Barre de Nanteuil of France, and Esmet Abdel Meguid of Egypt.

For the next two weeks, little was heard about the Franco-Egyptian initiative. Then, in mid-July, Harvey Feldman, with whom I had been working in the Washington office, showed me a proposed cable on the Franco-Egyptian draft that was about to be sent to all Middle-East posts over Secretary Shultz's signature. Neither Ambassador Kirkpatrick nor anyone else at the U.S. Mission had been informed about the draft cable. Harvey pointed to the line down at the end of the page which lauded the Franco-Egyptian initiative as providing "a serious basis for discussion."

"If this cable goes out," said Harvey, "then the message to Arafat—who will undoubtedly get wind of it—will be to hold out in Beirut, that a political victory is being worked out for him by the French and the Egyptians at the UN, and that he should therefore agree to evacuate his fighters from Lebanon only when it seems clear that the Franco-Egyptian draft will be accepted by the Americans. This gives Arafat a bargaining card."

I wasn't sure of Harvey's logic; news that the United States was working with France and Egypt on mutual recognition between Israel and the PLO might, I thought, have wholly unpredictable effects. What seemed certain was that should the Franco-Egyptian initiative became "a serious basis for discussion," it would mean the unravelling of whatever was left of the Camp David Accords. Instead of

discussing steps for interim solutions and confidence-building measures, the United States would become involved in trying to persuade
Israel to come to terms with the PLO. The goal of persuading Israel's
hostile Arab neighbors to come to terms with Israel would take on
secondary importance, if it did not vanish altogether.

The next morning, in New York, I briefed Kirkpatrick on the
cable State was preparing on the Franco-Egyptian initiative. "It
doesn't surprise me," she said. "Listen, I would like you and Harvey,
if you would, to do a redraft of that cable. It should express U.S.
concern over the Franco-Egyptian initiative, while not rejecting it
totally out of hand. But get out the phrase that it is 'a serious basis for
discussion'."

Harvey and I quickly began work. It was apparent that Kirkpatrick was ready to entertain and tinker with the Franco-Egyptian
initiative, but what that meant was uncertain. At the least it would
involve a stalling effort. But in the meantime she didn't want expectations built up around the world, especially in the American diplomatic community, that we were serious about renegotiating Middle-
East peace on Franco-Egyptian terms. She would have to walk a
tightrope, maintaining good relations with Ambassadors Luc de la
Barre de Nanteuil and Esmet Abdel Meguid at the United Nations,
while appearing to be co-operative at the State Department. Shultz
was still meeting with his advisers on setting up a new working team.
She wanted it known that any reported differences between her and
Haig had been exaggerated and were not of her doing, that she could
be counted on as a "team player."

Later that morning Kirkpatrick called Eagleburger to tell him
that she had some revisions to suggest in the cable. She was particularly concerned, she informed him, about reference to the initiative as "a serious basis for discussion." This, she suggested,
should be deleted, although the initiative should not be dismissed
out of hand.

The next day a revised cable was sent by the State Department
to all Middle-East posts reflecting Kirkpatrick's suggested changes.
Reference to the Franco-Egyptian initiative as providing "a serious
basis for discussion" was deleted. Should questions about the initiative arise, our embassies abroad were to explain: first, why the United
States remained concerned about the inconsistency between key
terms of the initiative and U.S. commitments under the Camp David
Accords; second, why it ran contrary to U.S. policy of not dealing
with the PLO unless certain conditions were met; and finally, in any

event, to express opposition to the creation of an independent Palestinian state.

Soon, however, a turnabout occurred. NEA began to see less and less merit in keeping the Franco-Egyptian initiative afloat. In its view, U.S. talks on the basis of that initiative would be bound to create an enormous outcry from Israel, at a time when Israeli goodwill was essential to the success of the Habib mission in securing the peaceful evacuation of PLO forces from Lebanon. Besides, NEA, more than anyone else, knew that the Franco-Egyptian effort could not be squared with U.S. commitment to the Camp David Accords. For these reasons, NEA decided it was better to halt any overtures to the French and Egyptians as such overtures would ultimately prove misleading. NEA recommended instead that the Administration forthrightly inform France and Egypt that there was no room for U.S. negotiations on the basis of their initiative. Kirkpatrick, however, still saw reasons to keep the initiative afloat without pronouncing a final American "No" to it.

Confident that she could handle the problem, Kirkpatrick decided it might be best to go a little longer without, insofar as possible, rebuking or offending any of the actors. If the United States needed to mollify the Israelis, it also needed, as she saw it, to assuage the French and the Egyptians. A U.S. veto would cost us French and Egyptian cooperation in persuading the PLO leadership to bite the bullet and leave Lebanon. Their support was also needed to restore order in a postwar Lebanon. On the other hand, if the Israelis became aware that the United States was prepared to support the Franco-Egyptian initiative, their cooperation in permitting the peaceful evacuation of the PLO would be at risk. "I'm buying time, Allan," she said. "I've already gotten Habib nearly three weeks."

"Time for what?" I asked.

"Time for Habib to get the PLO out by sea," she answered. "Any Security Council resolution can only hinder his efforts."

In late July, an Action Memorandum on the Franco-Egyptian initiative was prepared by the NEA and IO bureaus and sent to Secretary Shultz recommending that he instruct Ambassador Kirkpatrick to tell the French and Egyptians to call off their initiative, informing them that there was simply no room for the United States to negotiate over their proposal. The Decision Memorandum made no mention of Kirkpatrick's views. Again, we obtained a copy of the memorandum before Shultz had an opportunity to act on it.

It was unclear to Harvey and me whether Kirkpatrick had been bypassed purposely or inadvertently. It occurred to us that Gregory Newell, the 31-year-old White House aide who had been recently chosen to replace Elliott Abrams as Assistant Secretary for IO, had assumed that he was merely mirroring Kirkpatrick's views when he helped prepare and package the Decision Memorandum. After all, the previous week Kirkpatrick had intervened with Under-Secretary for Political Affairs Larry Eagleburger, to protest NEA's reference to the Franco-Egyptian initiative as "a serious basis for discussion." He may have thought that she surely would not object now to finally putting the initiative to rest.

There was another possibility, of course: Newell and his staff at IO may have thought that with a new Secretary of State on board they might succeed in a rerun of earlier attempts to bypass Kirkpatrick in making recommendations directly to the Secretary of State, without the UN Ambassador's input or "clearance." Whatever the case, Kirkpatrick was furious on seeing a copy of the NEA/IO Decision Memorandum that had been forwarded to Shultz.

"This can't go," she said, and proceeded to revise the Decision Memorandum to read that Ambassador Kirkpatrick recommends informing the French and Egyptians that the U.S. Government is prepared to work with them to eliminate "only that which is clearly objectionable." The problem was that everything of substance in the Franco-Egyptian initiative was "clearly objectionable."

Kirkpatrick was playing high-stakes poker. Of course it wasn't as if she on her own, without any cues or direction from above, had decided on this course. She understood the Administration's overall strategy: first and foremost to enable Phil Habib to work out an arrangement for the peaceful evacuation of PLO fighters from Lebanon. After that, other things could fall into place. She meant to implement that strategy as best she could from her vantage point at the United Nations; the middle level of the State Department was simply an obstacle in her way. She understood that if the French or Egyptians discovered that she was stalling for time—and it seemed almost inevitable that they would figure it out at some time—then her own credibility would be at stake; but she was prepared to take that risk. On the other hand, if the Israelis discovered that it was Ambassador Kirkpatrick—rather than, as they suspected, the other bureaus at the State Department—who was taking the lead in supporting negotiations on the basis of the Franco-Egyptian initiative, her credibility with the Israelis would also be at stake. She was prepared to take that risk too.

The strategy worked, up to a point. By July 29, the differences in French and American approaches to Middle-East peacemaking could no longer be contained. France called for a Security Council session to vote on the Franco-Egyptian initiative, which it had now put in blue ink as a draft resolution. Jeane Kirkpatrick happened, conveniently, to be abroad when the session convened.

Ambassador Luc de la Barre de Nanteuil, acting on direct instructions from French President Francois Mitterand through a phone link with Foreign Minister Claude Cheysson, was determined to advance the French agenda for a solution to the Arab-Israeli conflict: universal recognition of the PLO's legitimate right to form an independent state in the West Bank and Gaza. France and Egypt knew by this point that they had no chance of U.S. acquiescence, but again the prospect of a U.S. veto proved to be no deterrent. The important thing for France and Egypt at this point was to expose their ideas to the widest possible publicity.

De Nanteuil approached Chuck and me as we walked into the Delegates' Lounge outside the Security Council chambers. He had just gotten off the telephone with his foreign minister. His government was, he said, at a total loss to understand U.S. policy in the region.

"Don't you understand," Luc de Nanteuil said, exasperated, "that the PLO is essential to Arab-Israeli peace? You want to crush them politically as well as militarily."

Chuck simply said, "Yes," as if guilty as charged. "You are correct that my government does not see the PLO as the avenue to peace. Quite the contrary: my government holds the PLO responsible for much of Lebanon's present difficulties and for having created the situation that led to the Israeli invasion."

"But," said Luc de Nanteuil, exasperated, "don't you see? Without the PLO there is nothing. No solution is possible without them. They are needed if there ever is to be a negotiated peace."

"My government doesn't see it quite that way," Chuck replied coldly. "As we have already made clear, your government's approach is far afield of what is envisioned by Security Council resolutions 242 and 338, and by the Camp David Accords."

At 10:00 P.M. on July 29, Chuck and I walked into the formal chambers of the UN Security Council for a vote on the Franco-Egyptian draft. We sensed the isolation. Everyone but the United States would be voting in favor of the Franco-Egyptian draft. Every other member of the UN Security Council, including Great Britain, was prepared to endorse the idea that the PLO was the legitimate representative of the Palestinian people, and that Israel had to negotiate with it. In the past few weeks we had reiterated the American argument that in legitimizing the PLO, the UN was undercutting the prospects for direct peace talks between Lebanon and other Arab states and Israel. The argument fell on deaf ears. The other members of the Council had given up on bilateral peace talks between Israel and its Arab neighbors. Instead, despite the PLO's dismal record and its imminent military defeat, they placed their hopes on it, as the key to peace, on the terms proposed by France and Egypt.

The prospect of casting another U.S. veto—this time of a resolution sponsored by France and Egypt—was hardly appealing. What Chuck and I could not reconcile ourselves to was the idea that the rest of the world was prepared to look aside, to dismiss both the havoc wrought by the PLO in Lebanon and its record of terrorism as merely the growing pains of a national liberation movement. No one seemed to care much about seeing a replay of the turmoil and bloodshed that had become Lebanon in Israel's backyard: the West Bank and Gaza Strip. If the United States had to be the lone holdout again, then so be it. Secretary Shultz, through Larry Eagleburger, had approved the veto. This time we seemed to have nearly the entire State Department behind us; they weren't about to throw the Camp David Accords out of the window.

As we took our seats, ready to vote, France surprised us. They announced to the Council their decision to withdraw their draft resolution from a vote. Instead, said de Nanteuil, it was being introduced solely for the purpose of "discussion." This was a novel concept. Resolutions had never been introduced before in formal Security Council chambers solely for "discussion." But if this was what France and Egypt wanted, then it was better to have a discussion and avoid the prospect of a U.S. veto. For France and Egypt, it meant that they could accomplish one of their objectives. A U.S. veto would have set back the Franco-Egyptian effort to force a different approach to Arab-Israeli peacemaking. By allowing their draft resolution to be "discussed" instead and held in abeyance, the resolution could wait patiently in the wings to be resurrected at a more propitious time when U.S. policy, or a change in the situation on the ground, might result in a different reaction.

Speeches ensued. France, Egypt, and more than a dozen other countries spoke in favor of direct recognition between the PLO and Israel, leading to the creation of an independent PLO-run Palestinian state. Chuck, on behalf of the United States, argued that the best prospect for peace remained utilization of the Camp David Accords formula for interim measures. PLO participation in the peace process was a viable option, said Chuck, only if the PLO proved itself willing to live by the norms of civilized life: the renunciation of terrorism, and recognition of the right of Israel to live, like all other states, in secure and recognized borders. Finally Israel's Yehuda Blum spoke. Citing in detail recent PLO terrorist activities inside and outside Israel, he called the PLO a gang of unrepentant thugs and said that Israel would never negotiate with them; it would be a fight to the death.

On this note the grandiose idea of France and Egypt for a new framework for settling the Arab-Israeli conflict, hammered together in the middle of the Lebanon crisis, came to an end. The Security Council continued to meet throughout the first half of August, but the session had become perfunctory. The UN had proven its impotence in influencing events on the ground. Little was expected of the sessions that followed. Israel's Yehuda Blum continued to try to give back as much abuse as he received. To the Soviet representative's accusation of Israeli violations of international law, he would retort that the "Soviet government has been the greatest threat to peace and security since 1945." He would remind them of Stalin's pact with Hitler, and of the murder of Polish officers in the Katyn forest. He would do the same with the representatives of Poland, and each of the Arab and Non-Aligned states who dared to malign his country. It was one against the many, and a sad commentary on what the Security Council was reduced to in dealing with a war and the vast human tragedy that was Lebanon.

The situation in Beirut worsened. For Israel the risks inherent in routing PLO forces escalated as the PLO gained time to fortify its positions. West Beirut had become a giant bunker. Each day came reports that Philip Habib had succeeded in working out a plan for the PLO's evacuation and that all that was needed was a little more time for fine-tuning. Discussion centered on PLO fighters being allowed to go north to Syria. But Arafat and other PLO leaders feared any plan that would put their forces under Syrian control. Then on August 12, as fearful of falling under Syrian control as they were of an onslaught by Israeli troops, the PLO said it would accept an evacuation plan that would take them to Tunisia.

To ensure that the PLO would not change its mind, Israeli tanks moved into strategic positions in northern Lebanon, and its airplanes and artillery shelled Palestinian areas of West Beirut for the third consecutive day. The following day the PLO officially accepted the evacuation plan worked out by Phil Habib.

During the next week, PLO fighters, holding their Kalishnikov machine guns and light weapons in the air, boarded boats bound for Tunisia. No sooner had the evacuation begun than the State Department, in conjunction with the White House, began drafting a new American initiative for getting the stalled "peace process" going again. Writing in the August 12 edition of the *New York Times*, Leslie Gelb reported that: "With an agreement to end the Lebanon conflict reported near fruition, the Reagan Administration has begun working on a new plan for the Middle East. Officials described it as an expanded version of the Camp David Accords, capitalizing on the momentum of the PLO withdrawal. The American intention was to argue that since Israel's northern border was now secured against PLO attacks, Israel should be prepared to be more flexible on the broader issues of Palestinian self-determination."[31]

The major purpose of Israel's Lebanon operation had been less to secure its northern border than to destroy the PLO's political clout, and curb the growth of Palestinian nationalism on the West Bank and Gaza Strip with its demands for an independent state. Now Israel was about to reap more bitter fruit: a call by the American administration for greater flexibility on the issue of Palestinian self-determination, the very object Israel sought to quash by its expedition into Lebanon.

As to the fate of the PLO, within one month after the evacuation to Tunisia, on September 24, 1982, PLO Chairman Arafat was invited to address the European Interparliamentary Union in Rome. Israel, he charged, had left 70,000 persons killed, wounded, or missing—the actual figure was closer to 20,000—as a result of its "aggression," which had been made possible through the "unlimited" support of the American administration. He received a standing ovation.

The Near East Affairs Bureau had reason to be pleased. All along, as a long-range goal, they had welcomed the Franco-Egyptian initiative. They were interested in a realignment of the U.S. position towards eventual direct negotiations between Israel and the PLO. To accomplish this, the PLO's political credibility had to be maintained. Philip Habib's successful efforts to evacuate the PLO fighters, with their Kalashnikovs proudly held high over their heads, helped. NEA's opposition, such as it was, to the Franco-Egyptian initiative had centered not on its terms, but on its venue and timing. They wanted it kept out of the United Nations, where too many extraneous factors could cloud its realization. They preferred that it be left to bilateral negotiations.

As to Jeane Kirkpatrick's role during these developments, the first thing to be noted is that she was largely left out of the picture at the State Department. She did not have a part in the Habib mission's formulation for departure of the PLO fighters, but her stance at the UN helped keep it on track. Yet she kept the Franco-Egyptian initiative alive longer than the State Department would have liked, albeit for entirely different reasons: they welcomed its objectives, she did not, but she saw a tactical need to keep it afloat at the United Nations. At the White House, while her views on Central American relations were valued, her opinions on Middle-East policy were rarely solicited—no doubt because she was perceived as being a tad too pro-Israel.

Her role in the Lebanon crisis took shape only upon her return from her trip in the middle of that crisis to five small African republics to survey issues concerning women and development in preparation for the "U.N. Decade on Women." It was then that she sought to further—that is, "buy time" for—the Habib mission, through her own unique brand of diplomacy which evolved during this period.

The Habib mission couldn't stop the Israelis from going into West Beirut. They could have ignored the American entreaties, as they had in the past. In fact, they were of two minds about advancing into PLO strongholds in West Beirut and engaging in urban fighting to rout them. For the Administration, once the Habib effort was launched, it became essential that it succeed—regardless of whether its initial conception was or was not a good idea. For the Israelis to storm West Beirut after the PLO had an opportunity to shore up its defenses would have meant the bloodiest fighting of the war, with countless Arab civilians who lived in West Beirut being caught in the cross-fire. It would rupture U.S.–Israel relations. And there would have been little to gain, as even with total military defeat it was by no means certain that the PLO's political star would be extinguished.

For the Reagan Administration, therefore, Habib's success at the peaceful evacuation of the PLO from Beirut was a major diplomatic coup, saving both Israel and the PLO. The success, however, was overshadowed by the failures that followed in its wake: the misplaced hopes that Lebanon could be pressured into signing a peace treaty with Israel against Syrian wishes, and that Syrian domination of Lebanese politics could be replaced by a dominant central government.

But had the Habib mission failed, leaving Israel with no option but to enter West Beirut (it couldn't be seen as having bluffed), the badly frayed Egyptian-Israeli peace would have been strained to the breaking point; U.S. credibility in the Arab world would have reached an all-time low; and circumstances would certainly not have been propitious for President Reagan to launch a major peace initiative in his speech of September 1, 1982.[32]

If, then, the Habib mission was a significant diplomatic victory (irrespective of the string of failures that followed), Jeane Kirkpatrick's handling of the Franco-Egyptian initiative at the United Nations contributed to its achievement. There are no instructions that can be drafted with such specificity that would enable an ambassador to fulfill this type of an assignment. To help buy Habib the time he needed, she had to maintain cordial relations with the French and Egyptians whose support Habib needed; at the same time, she had to keep the Israelis, whose cooperation was equally crucial to Habib's plans, from becoming too fearful that the United States was actually considering the Franco-Egyptian initiative to be a "serious" basis for negotiations. It proved a high wire balancing act.

She had mastered her medium. At the State Department the paper-flow difficulties she had experienced initially ended with Larry Eagleburger's intervention and support in adopting her views on the tone and substance of outgoing cables. At the United Nations, the byzantine shadowy politics of Middle-East negotiations seemed to suit her; she found that she could play that game too, combining the political scientist's analysis of the "correlation of forces" with her innate ability to keep many balls in the air at once. Her nemesis, Alexander Haig, Jr., had left unceremoniously. By the end of the summer of 1982 she had learned her way in and around the United Nations, and the State Department. Forged in the crucible of struggle with Secretary of State Alexander Haig (although, unlike the Falklands crisis, the Lebanon crisis gave rise to no substantive disagreement between them); in a tug-of-war with a bureaucracy at the State Department that feared and opposed her; and confronted with a United Nations system that saw her as a highly unpleasant intrusion into its established ways of life, the Jeane Kirkpatrick that emerged commanded serious attention in New York and in Washington.

10

Defining "Illegitimate" Purposes

Expulsion as a Political Tool

"Improper Assessment"

> ... for if the Assembly had the power automatically to validate
> any expenditure ... this would mean that, merely by deciding
> to spend the money the Assembly could, in practice, do almost
> anything, even something wholly outside its function, or maybe
> those of the Organization as a whole.
>
> Judge Sir Gerald Fitzmaurice, Advisory Opinion of the
> International Court of Justice, The Certain Expenses of the United
> Nations case, 1962

A little more than a year after the experience with Congressman Mickey Edwards, who was trying to find a suitable way for Congress to manifest its irritation with obnoxious UN behavior—at that time, the UN Statistics Committee's unceremonious dumping of the U.S. representative—the problem was upon us once again. This time the stakes were higher. It was not an obscure UN committee that was involved. Rather, it was the UN General Assembly, and its move, in the fall of 1982, to expel Israel from its membership,[1] followed by the effort to make the United States share in the expenses of implementing the Law of the Sea Convention, despite President Reagan's opposition to any further U.S. involvement in that effort. In each instance the idea that the United States Government could choose to express its opposition to objectionable UN programs by withholding portions of its assessed UN budget stirred up a storm. The accepted wisdom dictated that regardless of the abuses to which U.S. dollars might be put, the nation had to pay—no questions asked. That, we were told, was what the UN Charter required.[2]

In January 1982 came signs of a major effort by the radical Arab states, in cooperation with the Soviet and Non-Aligned blocs, to expel Israel from the United Nations. The General Assembly had just passed a resolution condemning Israel's "annexation" of the Golan Heights (the extension of its civilian law and jurisdiction to the area) as demonstrating that Israel was not a "peace-loving state." It was a curious choice of phrase. It was only when one reflected on the fact that Article 4 of the UN Charter provided that membership in the United Nations was open to all "peaceloving states," that the intent in choosing those particular words became apparent: the expulsion of Israel as not peaceloving.

Under the terms of the UN Charter, expulsion required UN Security Council consensus. But this, like the idea of law generally, seemed just another formality that could easily be dispensed with when it was expedient to do so. There was precedent for this sort of thing: South Africa's expulsion by the General Assembly, without the requisite recommendation by the Security Council, on grounds that the "credentials" of its UN delegation were wanting. Of course, as everyone acknowledged, the credentials of South Africa's delegation were perfectly in order, but then if the law of the Charter was disregarded, twisted, and violated in the cause of isolating South Africa and treating it as illegitimate, as an entity that didn't exist, well then that was perfectly all right, because that was, after all, South Africa. And no one could raise objections to that. The United States did, but it didn't fight the issue very hard. Now it was Israel's turn.

As early as September of 1982 the tremors could be felt. On September 24 the International Atomic Energy Agency, a UN body, refused to acknowledge the Israeli delegation's credentials to sit at the Conference. The United States threatened to withhold its contribution to IAEA, and to review its relations with the agency, unless the Israeli delegation was seated. The IAEA relented, and the Israeli delegation was allowed in.

Then, on October 6, in a speech to the General Assembly, Libya's Foreign Minister called for removal of "the Zionist entity" from the United Nations.[3] Later that day the Credentials Committee voted not to accept the credentials of the Israel delegation. That this had nothing to do with the Committee's proper function—which was to decide which delegation's credentials were superior in disputes between rival delegations claiming to represent a single country—was beyond question. That the accreditation process was being used to judge the legitimacy of the government issuing the credentials, rather than the credentials themselves, was openly acknowledged.

Kirkpatrick consulted various Congressmen—placing more confidence in them than in her colleagues at State—about deterring the threat of expulsion through a declaration that U.S. funding of the United Nations (25 percent of the UN's annual budget) would be halted were the General Assembly to approve the recommendations of its Credentials Committee to unseat the Israeli delegation. In addition, with the cooperation of the State Department, a world-wide lobbying effort was launched, with cables drafted at the U.S. Mission and signed by the Secretary of State, directing American envoys abroad to warn their host governments that the United States would view seriously any vote abetting the effort at expulsion of Israel and readjust its bilateral relationship accordingly. My job was to work with several members of Congress, particularly Ben Gilman, Jack Kemp, and Tom Lantos, all of whom had expressed interest in enacting legislation requiring U.S. withdrawal from the United Nations and the withholding of further funds in the event of Israel's expulsion.

Differences between what Congress was trying to do and what the State Department wanted arose over only one point. Having agreed that the UN effort at expulsion was clearly in violation of the UN Charter, and pleased that it was Congress and not the Executive branch that was taking the lead, the State Department was nevertheless concerned that Congressional legislation might go too far. The Sense of the Congress resolution that had been proposed provided that if expulsion occurred, U.S. funding for the United Nations would cease—period. State, acting through the Legal Adviser, made clear its preference for a bill requiring, in such an eventuality, that U.S. funds earmarked for the UN be put in escrow; if Israel were subsequently reinstated to UN membership the withheld funds would be freed for payment to the United Nations. This would have created a penalty-free situation for those who would have Israel expelled. The proposal, however, foundered as steam for a bipartisan congressional consensus quickly formed around the proposition that the United Nations had to be made to pay for any such basic infraction of the UN rule of universality of membership.

As the U.S. Mission carefully tabulated the projected vote at the United Nations, the results looked ominous. We recalled how many nations had linked up in the Abu Eain matter to condemn the U.S. legal system. Despite our worldwide lobbying, it seemed that Israel was about to be expelled from the United Nations by a refusal to accept its credentials, the same mechanism used in 1974 to expel South Africa. On October 15 in Washington, the U.S. National Security Council took the matter under consideration. Kirkpatrick argued that the Mission's tally of the projected votes showed that we might not be able to forestall the expulsion; the majority of the world's nations would line up to endorse the recommendation of the UN Credentials Committee.

Some on the U.S. delegation mused that this might not be an unwelcome prospect: if Israel were expelled, it would give the United States all the reason it needed to get out of the United Nations. But the Government of Israel certainly didn't relish expulsion; it preferred to remain in the United Nations and fight back rather than be ousted as a pariah along with South Africa.

Kirkpatrick argued that what was needed was an unconditional statement by Secretary of State George Shultz of U.S. intentions in the event of Israel's expulsion, otherwise all the talk in Washington would be interpreted by the United Nations as mere rumbling by a Congress beset by the pressures of domestic constituencies, but lacking the support of the Executive branch. Congressional concern, she advocated, had to be publicized and matched by presidential commitment. President Reagan himself had to announce that the United States would withdraw from the UN General Assembly and withhold further payments until Israel's rights were restored. The following day, October 16, Shultz, speaking on behalf of President Reagan, made that unconditional declaration.[4]

On October 26, the Credentials Committee Report was presented to the General Assembly. Several days earlier, Herb Reis and I had gone together to the offices of Israel's envoy, Yehuda Blum, to discuss joint efforts at handling the matter before it was put to a vote. In separate consultations with the Nordic countries (Denmark, Finland, Iceland, Norway, and Sweden), we had agreed to make a point of order that no action could be taken on the Credential Committee's report (technically it constituted an amendment by Iran to the Credentials Committee report, adding the words "except with regards to the credentials of Israel" to the report for recognition of members' credentials). The Nordic Group would also ask that their motion be put to a vote immediately.

When the vote came in the General Assembly, the motion put forward by Finland was adopted by a large majority. The Arab Group, which had been meeting elsewhere at the time, complained that they had not been informed of the impending vote. No delegate assumed that their absence was anything but intentional. Clearly the Arab bloc was worried about the consequences of having taken this matter too far. If Israel were expelled from the UN, dire consequences would follow: U.S. efforts to activate the peace process, which had begun to take a more favorable stance toward Palestinian self-determination, would be stalled. The UN Secretary General had pointed out to the Arab sponsors of the resolution that the ouster of Israel would terminate the role of UNIFIL, the UN emergency peacekeeping forces in the Middle East, which depended on American dollars for their continued functioning. Also, UNRWA, the UN Relief Works Administration that since 1948 had provided relief, clothing, and shelter to Palestinian refugees, and those who were not quite "refugees," would cease to function; its support was dependent on American dollars as well.

Israel's expulsion from the United Nations had been averted, but only after the United States made unequivocally clear something it never stated in 1974 when South Africa's expulsion came up. Then too the United States delegation had made the same legal arguments as to why the Credentials Committee was abusing its power. This time, however, the United States was prepared to match its words with deeds: U.S. funds would be withheld, the UN would feel the pinch, and Palestinian programs in particular would suffer.

The following year Congress enacted legislation—introduced by Senator Moynihan on the Senate side, and by Congressman Kemp in the House of Representatives—providing that, in the event of Israel's expulsion from any UN agency U.S. participation would end, and that funding would be withheld—permanently, in the event of Israel's exclusion.[5] Nevertheless the campaign to expel Israel would continue through succeeding General Assembly session. But it would be reduced to ritual. But in 1982 the threat was real, and expulsion of Israel was averted, by a close margin, precisely because Congress, working in conjunction with the United States Government, demonstrated how costly such a move would be for the United Nations.

* * *

It was one thing to get Congressional support for withholding U.S. funds from the UN in the event of Israel's expulsion; getting Congressional support for U.S. withholding from the UN in regard to the Law of the Sea Preparatory Conference was quite another matter. President Reagan had vociferously opposed further U.S. participation in the Law of the Sea Conference once it became clear that it had split along an ideological divide, with the developing nations acting in concert with the Soviet Union to enact provisions detrimental to the deep seabed mining interests of the Western industrial nations.[6] Congressional reaction was mixed; there was no possibility of a bipartisan consensus evolving around this issue. If money earmarked for support of the Law of the Sea Conference was to be withheld from the United Nations, the Administration would have to go it alone.

At issue was funding for what was described as a Law of the Sea Preparatory Commission—LOS Prep. Comm., in short. It was to be the culmination of the Third UN Law of the Sea Conference, which ran from 1973 to 1982. As originally conceived by American participants, the aim of the Conference would be to stem the tide of "creeping jurisdiction" over the high seas whereby nations were increasingly extending the borders of their territorial sea. The LOS Conference proposed to fix the permissible scope of such claims. However, as the Conference progressed, technological developments in offshore drilling for petroleum exploration, and in mining in deep water for manganese nodules and other mineral deposits, suddenly opened the prospect of deep seabed exploitation by many less developed nations. Overestimating the possible profits, these developing nations began to claim extended sovereignty over seabed resources well beyond the national limits of the territorial sea and of the continental shelf agreed upon in the earlier major Law of the Sea Convention, the 1958 Continental Shelf Convention.

For the Group of 77, representing the developing countries of the world, the most important objective of the LOS Conference therefore became a "more equitable" allocation of the ocean's resources among the nations of the world. The Group of 77 called the deep seabed the "common heritage of mankind," and called for an international system to regulate seabed exploration and exploitation beyond the limits of coastal state jurisdiction. It called for the establishment of an international "Authority" to be the instrument for bridging the gap between rich and poor countries, and for initiating "industrial co-operation between the North and the South based not on aid but on sharing."[7] All activities in the deep seabed would be under the direct control of the Authority, which was authorized to conduct mining operations through its own commercial mining company, "the Enterprise." Thus, profits that would normally accrue only to industrialized nations, which alone had the capacity to begin immediate deep sea mining, would have to be shared with the nondeveloped world.

The United States had negotiated for an LOS Convention in the conviction that a global international agreement was essential to regulate maritime issues. And, despite its differences with the plan of the Group of 77, Nixon and Carter administration representatives had signalled that the United States would sign the Law of the Sea Convention. But when the Reagan Administration assumed office in January 1981, it took a dim view of the Convention.[8] The "Authority's" powers as well as the entire political structure of the LOS Convention for sharing wealth were perceived by the Reagan Administration as likely to cause economic distortion and the inefficient allocation of resources. President Reagan's negotiators attempted therefore to change the terms of the Law of the Sea Convention to convert its mining provisions into a free-enterprise system. The Reagan negotiating team succeeded in obtaining some changes, but the results were not sufficiently satisfactory to induce the Administration to endorse the Convention. In July 1982 President Reagan announced that he would ask the Senate to refuse to ratify the Law of the Sea Convention.[9] This, however, didn't prevent the UN from seeking U.S. funding for the implementation of the Law of the Sea Convention through the Law of the Sea Preparatory Commission, or LOS Prep. Comm.

Kirkpatrick saw the attempt of the UN General Assembly to force the United States to fund the LOS Preparatory Commission through its assessed UN contribution as a clear abuse of the power of the UN majority. The U.S. position on the Law of the Sea Convention was clear. Joining the Convention was a private matter. It couldn't be imposed upon states by fiat. Both the Law of the Sea Convention and LOS Prep. Comm. were not, properly speaking, United Nations activities as contemplated by the UN Charter. The Law of the Sea Convention and its offshoots, although conducted under the auspices of the United Nations, were activities outside the jurisdiction of the United Nations General Assembly; and the Convention was to operate as a wholly different authority separate from the UN as such.[10] How could it be, I was asked, that the United States could be held legally accountable for such expenses, imposing upon the United States the obligation to finance a private cooperative effort that it had fallen out of sympathy with?

To put the matter in perspective, the U.S. vote at the General Assembly counts for but 1 out of 159. Of the other 158 nations, 107 pay a total of about 1 percent of the UN's total budget, while the United States pays 25 percent. Yet those nations set the agenda of the United Nations and determine where its finances go. For example, the same year that the United Nations was decrying its worsening financial condition, the average cost of one page of the UN General Assembly summary record had grown larger than the annual per capita income of Tanzania, Haiti, Chad, or Bangladesh; and in 1982 the General Assembly was earmarking funds for nearly two billion pages of documents.

Moreover, the Soviet Union, the second largest contributor to the UN system, had refused since 1962 to comply with the judgment of the International Court of Justice to pay its share of UN peace-keeping expenses incurred in the UN's 1962 Congo operation. Angered by the Soviet's refusal to pay, Congress had considered withdrawing U.S. participation in the United Nations. Then Ambassador Arthur J. Goldberg devised a formula that gained Congressional acquiescence and laid the basis for future U.S. participation in the UN. He stated:

> . . . If any member can insist on making an exception to the principle of collective financial responsibility with respect to certain activities of the organization, the United States reserves the same option to make exceptions to the principle of collective responsibility if, in our view, strong and compelling reasons exist for doing so.

U.S. participation in the United Nations, said Goldberg, had to be based on the principle that there can be no carrying of benefits without an equal carrying of obligations. "There can be no double standard among the members of the organization."[11] Surely, Kirkpatrick noted when I briefed her about the Goldberg Reservation, that provides us with all the reason not to pay: to do otherwise would mean acquiescence to a system of financial double standards, a carrying of burdens without anything near equal benefits. It seemed particularly ironic that the Soviet Union, which for years had refused to pay its share of UN peacekeeping expenses, was now spearheading the effort to force the United States either to pay expenses for a Law of the Sea Conference it found repugnant, or be accused of being an international miscreant.

Kirkpatrick asked that I take the matter up with the State Department Legal Adviser's Office. That office, however, held to the view that international law prohibited U.S. withholding to protest particular funding decisions of the UN General Assembly. Israel's expulsion from the UN was pointed to as a different matter; there, Congress had forced the Administration's hand. The legal advisers pointed to Article 17 of the UN Charter providing that UN expenses were to be "collectively borne," and to the fact that the UN Charter made no provision for withholding portions of assessed contributions for particular activities considered to be "illegitimate." If every nation felt free to go along with Kirkpatrick's idea of withholding contributions for "illegitimate" activities, then, I was told, the UN financial system would collapse.

I recalled that Congress had already enacted legislation making it incumbent upon the Administration to withhold a pro rata share of the U.S. contribution to that portion of the UN budget that would be earmarked to support activities on behalf of the PLO, SWAPO, or Cuba. That, it seemed, provided the Administration with a rationale for withholding funds earmarked for LOS Prep. Comm.—both groups of activities were arguably illegitimate, outside the scope of permissible UN activities dedicated toward promoting international peace, and, on a voluntary basis, development programs. But, I was told, what Congress did was probably not compatible with what international law required, and insofar as Kirkpatrick was proposing that the Executive Branch, on its own initiative, withhold parts of the assessed U.S. contribution to the UN, this was something they could hardly support.

"But," I asked, "what of a situation where the UN General Assembly majority genuinely abuses its power of the purse by funding an activity clearly incompatible with the terms of the Charter—like terrorism, for instance? The aggrieved state has no recourse but unilateral action; it can't bring a lawsuit against the UN General Assembly. On the other hand, the General Assembly is free to ask the World Court for an advisory ruling on whether a state that withholds part of its assessed contribution has acted unlawfully."

My argument fell on deaf ears. The Legal Adviser's Office had no penchant for fighting the UN majority in a major legal challenge. Whatever the Administration's reservations about LOS Preparatory Commission might be, the U.S. Government, as the State Department's Legal Counsel saw it, had no recourse but to pay.

Kirkpatrick shook her head in dismay on being told the news.

She may not have had great respect for midlevel State Department opinion, but she needed its support, especially if the matter had legal overtones; otherwise her opposite numbers might easily argue that while they were prepared to go ahead with her suggestions, their hands were tied when it came to legal conclusions about what could or could not be properly done.

"There must be a way," she fumed. "It just cannot be that we have to fund whatever activity or group the UN wishes to give our money to. Expenses for *illegitimate* activities must be *illegitimate* expenses. Allan, you dealt with this issue, didn't you, in the memorandum you gave me on the Mickey Edwards Bill, the one dealing with the Statistics Committee action? The *Certain Expenses Case* of the International Court. Wasn't that the one you cited?"

"Yes," I said, "That case is on point here, too."

"What I would like you to do, then, is draft a memorandum for my signature to Secretary of State George Shultz making the argument for the U.S. withholding of its pro-rata share of the assessed UN contribution which they'll earmark for LOS Prep. Comm., as consistent with President Reagan's expressed opposition to the LOS Convention. Explain why such a finding would be consistent with our obligations under the UN Charter."

I had my work cut out. This time, however, she would be in a stronger position than when she was prepared to oppose the State Department on the Fourth Geneva Convention. Here, she wouldn't have to persuade President Reagan; she wouldn't have to try to shape policy, she would be following his call. Her biggest obstacle was that the Secretary of State, on matters of this sort, relied on his Legal Adviser's advice.

I began by reviewing the International Court of Justice's 1964 *Certain Expenses Case.*[12] The case had originated in 1962 with a General Assembly request for an advisory opinion on whether the cost of the peace-keeping forces stationed in Egypt (UNEF) and in the Congo (UNUC) were illegitimate expenses. As the Soviet Union viewed it, such forces could only be lawfully established by the UN Security Council (where the USSR had a veto), and not by General Assembly fiat. France also had refused at first to pay for UNEF expenses, but later dropped its objections.

The International Court of Justice ruled that the legitimacy of UN activities was to be determined "by their relations to the purposes of the United Nations in the sense that, if an expenditure were made for a purpose which is not one of the purposes of the United

Nations, it could not be considered an 'expense of the Organization.' " In this context, the Court determined that UN General Assembly peacekeeping operations in the Congo were "legitimate" UN activities related to the peacekeeping functions of the United Nations and, therefore, had to be borne collectively by all members.

That helped make my case. In the draft memorandum for Kirkpatrick to Shultz, I argued that there was no legal requirement that UN members must finance whatever activity the UN General Assembly majority decided to support. The activity had to be "legitimate." It had to be related to fulfillment of the purposes of the UN Charter. Members were not obligated to fund terrorist activities, to cite one example, simply because the UN majority decided to allocate portions of their assessed contributions to support such activities. By the same rationale, the United States did not have to help fund the activities of the LOS Prep. Comm. No provision of the UN Charter mandated the redistribution of the world's wealth in making this claim. The United States could withhold its assessed contribution until the International Court of Justice directed it to do otherwise.

There was also another aspect to the matter. As a treaty, the Law of the Sea Treaty could become effective under U.S. law only after executive signature and ratification by the Congress. The LOS Preparatory Commission sought a way around this impasse by securing the support of countries, like the United States, that had not signed or ratified the treaty.

Kirkpatrick made minor revisions in the draft I had prepared, signed it, and had it sent to Secretary of State Shultz through S/S, the Secretary's Secretariat. The response was quick. IO informed Ambassador Kirkpatrick that Secretary Shultz had been advised by the Legal Adviser that her suggestion for withholding LOS Prep. Comm. expenses would violate U.S. commitments under international law. The UN Charter, the Secretary was told, required the United States to pay its assessed share of the UN budget regardless of any opposition it might have to the ultimate recipients and uses of U.S. contributions. If Congress had decided to act vis-a-vis the PLO and require selective withholding of U.S. funds that the UN would allocate in their support, that was Congress's business and the Administration had to obey the will of Congress. It was quite another matter for the Administration to initiate an ostensibly "illegal" withholding. For these reasons, IO informed Kirkpatrick that Secretary Shultz unfortunately had no recourse but to put aside Ambassador Kirkpatrick's suggestion.

"I want to fight this, Allan," she said on hearing the news. "If George Shultz isn't going to do anything about it, Bill Clark will. I want a full-blown legal/political memorandum on the subject to go to him at the White House. I'll work with you. It has to be really good. I don't want to lose this one."

I began to draft the memorandum. It looked like the beginning of another showdown at the White House: the Secretary of State's authority versus that of the U.S. UN Permanent Representative over UN-related matters. "For over a decade," I wrote, "the United States had participated in good faith in the Law of the Sea Conference. However, when the Law of the Sea Convention created a framework of rules for redistribution of the world's wealth, the United States could not live with the imposition of that design. For that reason, it did not sign on to the LOS Convention. The LOS Preparatory Commission is designed to implement the LOS Convention. As there was no legal obligation imposed on the United States to join the LOS Convention, there can be no obligation to fund its implementation against the will of a member state. The United States had proposed an amendment to the LOS Convention requiring that financing come only from those states who signed the Convention. But that proposal was rejected by a vote of 134 against, 3 in favor, and 7 abstentions. Now the United Nations General Assembly is trying to force the United States to do through the back door what it couldn't do through the front door: to make the United States a party, or failing that, a contributor, to the Law of the Sea Convention."

Finally I turned to the "Goldberg Reservation:"

> . . . If any member can insist on making an exception to the principle of collective financial responsibility with respect to certain activities of the organization, the United States reserves the same option to make exceptions to the principle of collective financial responsibility if, in our view, strong and compelling reasons exist for doing so. There can be no double standard among members of the organization.[13]

The Goldberg Reservation, however, touched a sensitive nerve at the State Department. The idea of reciprocity in international relations, especially in dealing with the United Nations, was not acceptable. The State Department generally preferred that the United States take the "high road"—that is, pay, regardless of the abuses of others. Neither Kirkpatrick nor I saw anything appealing about that route.

The Goldberg Reservation was disparaged as reducing the

United States to the moral equivalent of the Soviets. For Kirkpatrick, however, the Goldberg Reservation provided the legal underpinning of her conviction that there should be no double standards, self-imposed or otherwise, on the conduct of U.S. foreign policy. She believed, as did Justice Goldberg, that there was no moral or legal imperative for the United States to be automatically bound to UN dictates—especially those of the General Assembly—no matter how they may have deviated from the norms of procedures set forth in the UN charter.

I called on Justice Goldberg at his northwest Washington residence. He said that experience had only confirmed his earlier stated views. He also agreed to provide the Mission with a formal letter detailing his conclusions that U.S. withholding for LOS Prep. Comm. expenses would be lawful. "There can," he wrote, "be no question that under the Goldberg Reservation the United States reserves the right to withhold assessment for the UN activities which, in our opinion, do not serve our national purpose."[14]

Then he went one step further. He wrote that it would "be improper and indeed illegal" under the U.S. Constitution for the United States to do differently and help finance the LOS Prep. Comm. as "the law of the Sea Treaty [which] had not been ratified by the U.S. Senate." We could now rely on the opinion of a former Supreme Court Justice to argue that U.S. withholding from LOS Prep. Comm. would not violate international law, and that, to the contrary, to pay for LOS Prep. Comm. expenses through the assessed U.S. contribution would violate the Constitution of the United States.

Kirkpatrick took my draft memorandum as well as materials Ken Adelman had given her on the nature of LOS Prep. Comm. and integrated our materials into a polished memorandum of her own. Leaving her memoranda on Central America aside—they were in a class of their own because of her special interest and expertise in the subject—this was by far the finest memorandum I had seen come from her desk. She knew she had to make the best case she could for Judge Bill Clark at the White House. At stake was the principle that the United States was not powerless to challenge the will of the UN majority; that it did not have to agree helplessly to fund 25 percent of the cost of any activity the UN majority deemed worthy. Her ability to influence policy within the new Shultz State Department was on the line.

The memorandum didn't miss an argument, marshalling history, law, and politics to drive home the points she was making. It concluded, in inimitable Kirkpatrick fashion, with a quote from the French paper *Le Monde,* which she read daily. "*Le Monde,*" she wrote, "estimates that such efforts to find LOS implementation expenses from the UN assessed budget will continue until LOS becomes financially self-sufficient which may not be for at least four to five years. It is therefore necessary to put the nail in the coffin of the LOS Prep. Comm. now, without delay."

The trick, however, was to get her memorandum to Bill Clark through formal channels. On an informal basis, memoranda had been passing routinely between her and Clark for some time. But this was something different: it would not do for her to initiate a memorandum to the White House saying she had taken issue with the position advocated by Secretary of State Shultz, and that a dispute had arisen between them requiring White House intervention. That would only go toward making an enemy out of Secretary Shultz, and she had had enough bruising matches with Alexander Haig to forego this route. Besides, George Shultz was infinitely more the political insider than Alexander Haig. Better to dance around this one: to have Bill Clark initiate the communication.

A less costly way was found: Bill Clark sent a memorandum from the White House on behalf of the President soliticing the views of both Kirkpatrick, as the U.S. Representative to the United Nations, and George Shultz as U.S. Secretary of State, so that President Reagan could reach an informed decision on the matter. It informed the recipients that President Reagan had determined that it was in the national interest to undertake all measures to prevent U.S. funding of the Law of the Sea Convention. This precluded funding LOS Prep. Comm., through UN-assessed United States contributions. Shultz and Kirkpatrick were asked to advise if there were any clear "countervailing legal considerations" which prevented implementation of the President's preferred policy.

Kirkpatrick quickly obliged, sending on her already-prepared memorandum to Judge Clark. For good measure, a copy of that memorandum was sent also to Edwin Meese III, Counselor to the President, so that there would be no mistaking that this was an issue of direct Presidential concern. Next came Secretary Shultz's response. This time the substance was markedly different from that indicated earlier. There were, he advised, no clear countervailing legal considerations that he could think of, although he couldn't guarantee that the UN might not think of some.

On December 30, President Reagan announced that the United

States would not pay its portion of the 1983 UN regular budget assessment to finance the Preparatory Commission of the Law of the Sea Convention. The White House pronouncement explained that the UN assessment for LOS expenses constituted "an improper assessment under the UN Charter that was not legally binding upon the Members."[15]

The announcement broke an unwritten tradition of the State Department and the Executive Branch of not questioning the UN General Assembly's use of American contributions to finance whatever activities it saw fit. The anticipated outcry and protests by the United Nations never came to be heard. Instead came grudging admiration for America's demonstration of the strength of its convictions. The United States had, after all, made it crystal clear that it would not join in a Convention that would hamper it from going after deep seabed riches, despite the wishes of the developing world. Had the United States caved in on the Law of the Sea Prep. Comm. issue and waved it off as something it was powerless to do anything about, it would have shown the world that with a little bit of ingenuity, one could almost always find a way, in multilateral fora, to get from the United States via the back door what one couldn't get from the front; in this instance, America's financial support for a project it despised.

For those who knew, the drama surrounding the arcane legal issue of U.S. funding for LOS Prep. Comm. showed the measure of Jeane Kirkpatrick's determination to, as she put it, "muck up the game" at the United Nations. It would also make it more difficult for the State Department to acquiesce on grounds that its lawyers advised it that this was what international law required. The assumption that the United States could always be counted on to pour out money for the United Nations, no questions asked, came to an end. A simple-minded interpretation of international law, one that ignored context and the intentions of one's adversaries, would no longer suffice to tap U.S. taxpayers' money at will without regard to the purpose toward which such money was being directed.

11

"It's 1979 All Over Again"
Ambassador Blum's Complaint

With her second General Assembly session behind her—the Falklands crisis, the Israeli invasion of Lebanon—and her bitter dispute with Secretary of State Alexander Haig now a thing of the past, Jeane Kirkpatrick could afford to heave a sigh of relief. She had survived. And, in the process, she had mastered the finer points of the multilateral diplomatic trade—which receptions to attend and which to avoid; whom to invite to dinners at her Waldorf Towers suite; which members of the press to court; even how to charm other diplomats. She had loosened up. Or so it seemed; inwardly, she remained as repelled as ever by what paraded as conflict-resolution at the palace of nations.

It didn't take her political scientist's acumen to realize that she was witnessing an unfair fight, the many against the few. Her instincts as a mother of three young boys, who had toughed it out in the schoolyards of Washington and France, had taught her about that. Witnessing it, she couldn't sit detached, content with understanding the process. The jurisprudential philosopher, Edmond Cahn, spoke of a "sense of injustice," of outrage, a sense that could manifest itself much more easily than a sense of justice, which was necessarily vague and diffused and difficult to be channeled. Kirkpatrick, whether she cared to acknowledge it or not, had a strong innate sense of injustice and the United Nations brought it out in full measure.

Central America was of special concern when she began. She would see in the speeches and actions of Nicaragua's representatives a cold-blooded effort to subvert U.S. interests in the Western hemisphere by arming guerillas trying to topple pro-American regimes in the region while at the same time, at the United Nations, decrying the United States as the big lone imperialist wolf bent on launching an ever-"imminent" invasion of their country. But more and more it became the perpetual attacks on Israel that aroused her sense of outrage. In early March of 1983, a confluence of both events—Nicaragua and Israel—impelled her to give vent to her feelings on the opinion page of a major American newspaper.

Nicaragua had called for a Security Council meeting to discuss an "imminent" U.S. invasion. At the same time "informal" Security Council discussions were in progress on Israeli practices in the occupied territories.[1] Neither event seemed directly related to any new occurrences. In the case of Israel, the alleged violations of the Fourth Geneva Convention—valid though they might be—had been the subject of prior resolutions. The only thing that seemed to have changed, and that provided some impetus for the meeting, was the announcement in Washington on March 21 that Israel had agreed to share with the United States the information about Soviet military equipment and tactics it had gained during the Lebanon war.

Kirkpatrick penned an op-ed piece for submission to the *New York Times* on similarities between Nicaragua's UN campaign, and that of the Arab bloc:

> [This] all too familiar scenario features one victim, many attackers, a great deal of verbal violence and a large number of indifferent and/or intimidated onlookers. . . . the Security Council serves as the stage, the presence of the world press insures an audience, the solidarity of the 'blocs' provides a long succession of speakers to echo, elaborate and expand on the original accusations. The goal is isolation and humiliation of the victim—creation of the impression that 'world opinion' is united in condemnation of the targeted nation. . . . In the process, states that have no economic, strategic, or political stake in the issue except their common bloc membership become involved. The charges become progressively outrageous, the denunciations progressively hyperbolic. Thus, Ghana, say, or Zimbabwe, Grenada or Vietnam may join the Arab bloc accusation against Israel for 'complicity' in an attack on Arab holy places, and before they are through 'discussing' the case the original charge may be lost entirely in accusations of 'genocide'. . . . the attackers encountering no obstacles, grow bolder, while other nations become progressively more reluctant to associate themselves with the accused—presumably out of fear that they themselves will become a target of bloc hostility.[2]

The process, she concluded, resembled nothing so much as mindless group violence.

Carl Gershman and I were shown and asked to comment on what she had written before she had it sent out. It was, we agreed, vintage Kirkpatrick: clear, strong, analytic, and passionate. The only thing that gave us pause was the title she had selected for the piece: "Gang Rape." It was not that the metaphor was not appropriate. It was that few would believe it. The number of individuals who had seen Security Council "informal consultations" in action was extremely limited—even accredited UN delegates who were not members of the UN Security Council were barred from attending these sessions—so few would know first-hand of what she spoke. Even knowledgeable readers would tend to view the phrase (insofar as it would be attributed directly to her and not to her editor) as hyperbolic, "unlady-like," un-diplomatic; it was bound, we feared, to confirm suspicions that she was a bit of a kook, out of place for the high position she held. Carl and I suggested that perhaps a slightly watered-down phrase might be more judicious if less apt. The *New York Times* editorial board did the thinking for us. They entitled the published piece, "UN Mugging Fails." But it was, we knew, more than mugging that Kirkpatrick saw taking place around her.

It was around this time, toward the end of March 1983, that Jeane Kirkpatrick called one morning asking if I could come to her office right away. I assumed it had something to do with the piece she was working on. I had no idea that what we would be talking about would involve me personally. "Allan," she said when I arrived at her office, "I need to talk to you about something very sensitive."

"All right," I said, wondering what it could be, and why she looked so agitated.

"It's 1979 all over again," she said in a subdued tone. "It's 1979 all over again." I had no idea what she was referring to. "Hear me out, Allan, please, if you would, without interrupting," she said. Then, looking nervously around the room, and especially at the window— we knew that voice vibrations could be picked up by outside listening devices—she added: "Perhaps we should go somewhere outside of my office. I'm afraid to talk to you here. The matter is too sensitive. The office might be bugged. Let's go next door to Ken Adelman's." I was still mystified. "Yehuda Blum came to see me early this morning," she continued. "He told me 'I have reason to believe that a member of your delegation has been having contact with the PLO.' "

So that's what the reference to its being 1979 was all about. In

August of 1979, Ambassador Andrew Young, Kirkpatrick's predecessor (Don McHenry served briefly between them), was forced to resign following the revelation that he had met secretly with the PLO's Terzi, its chief representative at the UN. He had gone to Yehuda Blum, Israel's emissary at the time, and asked that he try to keep a lid on the matter, and that it was in neither of their two countries' interests to further publicize the event or do anything more about it, that the meeting was more his peccadillo than sanctioned U.S. government policy. But Ambassador Yehuda Blum told him his conduct was in violation of the U.S. assurances given Israel in 1976. Secretary of State Henry Kissinger had then said that the United States would not recognize or negotiate with the PLO until such time as it renounced terrorism and recognized the State of Israel. Blum informed Young that, accordingly, he would have to bring the matter to his government's attention with the recommendation of a formal complaint to Secretary of State Cyrus Vance and President Jimmy Carter.[3]

Young had confessed to Israel's Blum that the meeting with the PLO's Terzi was not in fact "accidental" as initially claimed, but he nevertheless hoped that the matter could be put behind them by signalling that his meeting did not signal a derogation from U.S. policy. Israel nevertheless protested Young's meeting with Terzi as a violation of U.S. assurances. Secretary of State Vance was outraged, especially because Young had not initially provided the State Department with the full details of what had occurred, and told President Carter that he had the choice of accepting Young's resignation or his own. But what, I wondered, did this have to do with the present; what did Kirkpatrick, or Blum, whoever used it first, mean by "it's 1979 all over again"? Was he, I asked, alleging that a member of the US Mission was having secret meetings with the PLO?

"Naturally I was astonished by what Blum had to say," Kirkpatrick continued. "I told him so. He mentioned American assurances on this matter, and I told him we took our assurances seriously. I asked him if it might be Davis. Anyway, he said: 'No, it's someone higher up than that.' I asked him if it was Dirk Gleysteen. And he said, 'No, it's Gerson.' "

"Now hear me out," she went on, seeing my shock. "I want you to let me finish before you say anything. He told me that you had met with Farouk Kaddumi, the PLO's 'foreign minister.' You remember what happened in 1979 when Andrew Young met with the PLO's Terzi. This is just as serious. Perhaps worse. Kaddumi is a more important figure. I talked to Max Kampelman [a Washington attorney] about this. I trust his judgment. He knows the two of us well, and Shultz too. He suggested that the transition from private to official life might not have been an easy one for you. You entertain and you are gregarious. You were in academic life and may, he suggested, have tended to overlook the strictures of being in the government. Max told me I have to let Shultz know about this. He is right. Oh, yes, there's something else too. I don't mean to probe into your personal affairs. It's none of my business, but Blum also told me that you are having a romantic liaison with what's her name, the good-looking journalist who covers the UN for one of the Lebanese newspapers. Blum imputed that she might be a PLO operative. That's it, I'm finished. I have nothing else to say."

"Jeane," I said, stunned, not knowing where to begin, knowing only that Blum's complaint had impressed her as being sufficiently accurate for her to contact Max Kampelman for his advice as to how best to proceed—to call Secretary of State Shultz and explain that a member of her staff had, unbeknownst to her, overstepped his bounds. That would be the end of my job. Worse, rumors would follow. But it wouldn't be only my reputation that would be on the line. It would be difficult for anyone to accept that I had acted without the implicit, if not the explicit, authorization of Jeane Kirkpatrick. And would she have acted without the Secretary of State's authorization? It would be 1979 all over again. But it would not be Andrew Young that would be in the dock for actions he undertook in a misguided effort aimed at promoting understanding; it would be me, and for actions never undertaken or even contemplated.

I put aside an instinct to question her, to probe why she couldn't have been more assiduous in asking for the facts and the evidence to support the charges, before seemingly accepting them at face value. Instead, I simply said, "Jeane, it's not true, not a word of it," and told her that what she had heard was fabrication, imaginings, or the product of deliberate disinformation.

By way of background, and in an effort to make sense of what had occurred, I spoke of my days as a graduate student at the Hebrew University of Jerusalem. In my thesis for the Masters in Law degree I was quite critical of Blum, who was then teaching international law at the university, for his advocacy on behalf of Israel's legal right to annex the West Bank. Blum wasn't comfited by my piece, and an uneasiness with each other characterized our relationship. Perhaps it had affected his judgment; I didn't know. Of course, we worked together closely at the UN, but attitudes didn't change. As for Farouk

Kaddumi, I told Kirkpatrick, "I once stood within earshot of him at a reception thrown by the United Arab Emirates delegation. That was it. And, as for . . ."

"No, Allan, I don't want to hear or know about your personal business," Kirkpatrick said. "What you do off-hours is. . . ."

"No, Jeane," I said, raising my voice for the first time, "this *is* our business. Since he brought it up, we have to deal with it, I want you to hear me out. We met two or three times to exchange views and to trade information, or disinformation, about goings-on at the UN— who was likely to introduce what resolution, the likely vote, who stood to gain and who to lose—that sort of thing. I guess it was about three weeks ago when we shared a cup of coffee late one afternoon at a café on Second Avenue and Forty-third Street. It was raining outside, and as we departed I escorted her to a taxi. I think she may have kissed me on both cheeks, European-style, lightly, innocently, to say goodbye. That's the extent of our 'romantic liaison.' Perhaps an Israeli undercover agent or member of their Mission two blocks away spotted us and thought the worst."

Relieved by what I told her, she called Kampelman in Washington and told him that she wouldn't have to go to the Secretary after all on this and that I had cleared it all up for her. Then she said, "I have to run now. I have a meeting with Perez de Cuellar in less than five minutes," and dashed off.

That left me to ponder: if an Israeli Ambassador to the United Nations was willing to go to such lengths to have me fired—that was the only motive I could make out at the time, whether he acted on his own initiative or on the basis of reports from his intelligence service which didn't add up to a stack of beans—how much further might he be prepared to go? Would there be leaks of an alleged meeting with Kaddumi, or of a reputed affair? If such word got out, my continued presence at the Mission would be an embarrassment. If I left, the rumors that unauthorized contact with the PLO did me in would be bound to follow me. It would be a cruel twist of fate; most of my time had been taken up in the defense of Israel against its most determined attackers. This was by no means 1979 all over again. And yet if I left under a cloud of suspicion, charges of betrayal would fill the air. I felt they would surely extend beyond me to Jeane Kirkpatrick and color her efforts at securing fair treatment for Israel as mere camouflage for opening a U.S. dialogue with the PLO. If they couldn't trust Jeane Kirkpatrick, whom could they trust? The peace process itself might be affected. Or was I, I asked myself, blowing this totally out of proportion; was this not merely a personal incident with no greater significance?

For the rest of that day and late into the night that question and the overriding thought that something had to be done to prevent the rumor mills from starting up consumed me. I awoke convinced that a meeting had to be arranged with Blum before the start of the day's business. Otherwise, word of his meeting with Kirkpatrick might be leaked to the press, if it hadn't been leaked already. Either someone in Israel's secret service was feeding Blum false or misleading information, or Blum's judgment had taken a turn for the worse. Perhaps the pressure of constantly being on the defensive, and the personal attacks, had taken their toll. The matter had to be clarified, and quickly.

At 6:30 A.M. I rang Kirkpatrick at her Waldorf Towers suite. She was a rather late riser, accustomed to working late at night, and didn't relish being awoken early. But that morning I couldn't afford to wait.

"Hello, Jeane. I'm sorry to have gotten you this early, but it's about the Blum matter. I've been thinking about it all night. . . ."

"That's all right," she replied, "I couldn't sleep last night either. I keep thinking about it too."

"Can we arrange to see him first thing this morning? We can't let this simmer. Can you call him at home right away and arrange for a meeting at 8:00 A.M.?"

"Okay, I'll do it," she said. She called back several minutes later and said, "It's arranged. Come to my office at 8:00."

That morning, on the way to the U.S. Mission, I thought about how I could approach Blum. Not with anger, I decided; it had to be treated as a joint problem, perhaps one of misinformation being fed to him.

When I arrived Blum was already sitting on the sofa in Kirkpatrick's office looking agitated. I told him that I had never met with Farouk Kaddumi or any other PLO representative, and that the idea of a romantic liaison with someone having some vague link to the PLO was pure fiction. "Obviously someone is misinforming you," I said. I then asked, "Can you share with us the source of your information?"

"Yes," he said. "It was you."

"Me?" I said, incredulous.

"Yes. Hadn't you told Oren (disguised name—a former Israeli colonel then serving with the UN Secretariat) that you had attended a dinner party hosted by a Palestinian who is a member of the Palestinian National Council?"

"Yes, that's true," I said. "That person was Dr. Burhan Hammad, the legal adviser of the delegation of the United Arab Emirates, someone I knew from Yale Law School, and yes, he is a member of the PNC. In fact, in his dining room, staring at us during dinner, was a very large photograph of PLO Chairman Yasser Arafat embracing him. Professors Michael Reisman and Myres McDougal of Yale were both with me. So was the recently ousted dean of Teheran's law school. But you know that the United States Government draws a distinction between the PLO and the PNC and does not see the two as identical. Professor Edward Said of Columbia, for example, is a member of the PNC. You wouldn't meet with him, you see him as the same as the PLO, you see the PNC as a coordinating arm of the PLO, but the United States Government doesn't see it that way. As for Farouk Kaddumi, it's true that I was in the same room with him; so were about three hundred other people attending the reception hosted by the United Arab Emirates. I was never introduced to him—although, frankly, the offer was made, either in jest or not; nor did I have a word to say to him. And, again, as to . . . , there's nothing between us. One of your men may have seen her giving me a goodbye peck on the cheek. Harmless, I assure you."

"Well, if that's all there is to it, then I am very happy to hear that there is not more to it," said Blum, suddenly bringing the conversation to a close.

But later that morning Blum again reached Kirkpatrick expressing doubt that my assurances should be taken at face value. Kirkpatrick reminded him, no doubt uncharitably, of the importance in matters such as these of assuming innocence until proven guilty, a principle given as much currency in Israel as it is in the United States.

Shortly thereafter Kirkpatrick, myself, and Harvey Feldman left for our first fact-finding mission to the Middle East with stops scheduled for Israel, Egypt, Jordan, Morocco, and Tunisia. I brought some material on the Blum accusations and my countercharges. Kirkpatrick waved aside any thoughts of making reference to the matter on the trip. It was behind us. We would never discuss it again.

Less than a year later, Yehuda Blum was replaced as Israel's Ambassador to the United Nations by Benjamin ("Bibi") Netanyahu, the charismatic 36-year-old protégé of Israel's Ambassador to Washington, Moshe Arens, and the brother of Israel's slain national hero of the Entebbe rescue operation. Netanyahu was no less determined than Blum in defending Israel. But Netanyahu, who was not an international lawyer, focused less on legal rights and more on the facts and on using the international media, with whom he had fostered good relations, to tell his country's side of the story.

In a way, "Bibi" was lucky. The times had begun to change. Blum had already fought the tough wars. He had slogged through the attacks on Israel as a pariah state; he had been there alone when there was no U.S. ambassador to emphatically take sides with him; he had defended Israel during the long and darkest days that followed its invasion of Lebanon, and he had seen it narrowly avoid expulsion from the United Nations. The attacks against Israel at the UN—the really outrageous and baseless ones—now seemed to be on the decline, especially at the UN Security Council, as if the point of diminishing returns had been reached. The U.S. vetoes were instrumental in achieving that turnabout. And perhaps it was that very factor—the ebb tide of the intensity of the attacks against Israel at the United Nations—that led its UN representative to turn his attention to less worthwhile endeavors.

12

Reaching Bottom
The Soviets' KAL-007
Shoot-Down—
A "Characteristic" Act

It [the Soviet Union] has, in other words, behaved with complete—and I might add, characteristic—contempt for the international community and for even minimal standards of decency and civilized behavior.

> Ambassador Lichenstein's statement to the UN Security Council, September 2, 1983

We are reminded once again that the Soviet Union is a state based on the dual principles of callousness and mendacity.

> Ambassador Kirkpatrick's statement to the UN Security Council, September 6, 1983

The last four days of August, Jeane Kirkpatrick and her husband Kirk had been feted at the royal guest house of his Majesty, King Hassan II of Morocco. In Kirkpatrick's worldview, the maintenance of good relations with Morocco was essential. Because Morocco carried great weight with Francophile Africa, it could prove instrumental in achieving the realignment of U.S. strength and influence at the

United Nations where Francophile Africa played an essential and potentially pivotal role in the Non-Aligned bloc. Because Morocco maintained cordial relations with the radical as well as moderate Arab world, it could be the gateway to enhancement of U.S. relations with those countries. It had also already shown itself willing to be a go-between on the Arab-Israeli peace process. And then too Kirkpatrick considered Hassan to be a strategic thinker of world class proportions. Her affinity for Morocco and its scenic wonders ran deep. So for all these reasons she readily accepted King Hassan's invitation to come to Morocco to discuss a host of questions, including among them the downward turn in U.S.-Moroccan bilateral relations.

Relations had taken a turn for the worse since Ambassador Andrew Young had shunned Morocco in 1979 to visit the headquarters of the rebel Polisario group in Algeria (Morocco was at war with the guerilla group over control of a border strip adjoining Algeria). In the following three years, U.S. foreign aid to Morocco had dropped precipitously. By contrast, Algeria's stock had gone up after it helped broker the release in 1979 of U.S. hostages in Iran in exchange for the unfreezing of Iranian assets in U.S. banks. The bilateral issues to be discussed at their meeting were to focus on the improvement of these relations, ranging from the upgrading of USIA transmitters in Morocco to the role King Hassan II might play in getting the moribund Arab-Israeli peace process going again. The visit would be capped by attending the Mediterranean athletic games in Casablanca as the King's personal guest. There she would also get a chance to meet informally with other Arab heads of state.[1]

Before going to the Mediterranean games in Casablanca, she took a brief respite from her official duties. On September 1, 1983, she and Kirk checked in at the resplendent Mamouniah Hotel in Marakech. That evening, Chuck called from New York with the news that Soviet jets had shot down a Korean commercial airliner, KAL flight No. 007, a Boeing 747 jumbo jet, on a regularly scheduled route from New York to Seoul, South Korea.[2] That same day, the White House released a brief statement on the incident: "The President is very concerned and deeply disturbed about the loss of life aboard the Korean Air Lines flight overnight. There are no circumstances that can justify the unprecedented attack on an unarmed civilian aircraft. The Soviet Union owes an explanation to the world about how and why this tragedy has occurred." The airplane had inexplicably strayed off course into Soviet airspace over the Kamchatka Peninsula, the Sea of Okhotsk, and over Sakhalin Island. In all, Chuck told her, it had apparently flown two and a half hours over Soviet airspace, and had less than two minutes to go before leaving it, when Soviet interceptor jets fired missiles at it, destroying the aircraft and killing all 240 passengers, plus 29 flight crew members and cabin attendants. Congressman Lawrence P. McDonald (D-GA) was among the dead. From the State Department, Larry Eagleburger had asked that the U.S. Mission seek an emergency session of the UN Security Council to condemn the Soviets. When, Chuck asked, did she intend to come back?

She asked to be kept informed of developments, but said she saw no reason to return to attend the session; Chuck could handle it. Later that evening she received more bad news; her long-time friend and colleague, Senator Henry ("Scoop") Jackson—she was one of his delegates to the 1976 Democratic Convention—had died.

On September 2, Chuck prepared to address an evening session of the UN Security Council. All day he had been in touch with the State Department, the intelligence services, and the Japanese mission about what he could reveal regarding the sources the U.S. Government had relied on to obtain information about the circumstances of the shoot-down. An additional complicating factor was how to handle the fact that a U.S. reconnaissance plane with a markedly different configuration from a Boeing 747, one which the Soviets were well aware of, had regularly flown a route similar to that of KAL-007. As to the source of the U.S. information about the shoot-down, Chuck had learned that it was the Japanese; for years, by use of voice-actuated recorders in listening stations off the coast of Japan, they had been tracking radio transmissions between Soviet military ground control and its pilots. One of those recordings had picked up the conversation between the pilots who downed KAL-007 and ground control. In translation, it ran partly as follows:

> *Soviet SU-15 (805) at 1818:34 GMT:* The A.N.O. [air navigation lights] are burning. The strobe light is flashing.
> *MiG-23 (163) at 1818:56 GMT:* Roger, I'm at 7500, course 230.
> *SU-15 (805) at 1819:02 GMT:* I am closing on the target.
> *SU-15 (805) at 1826:20 GMT:* I have executed the launch.
> *SU-15 (805) at 1826:22 GMT:* The target is destroyed.
> *SU-15 (805) at 1826:27 GMT:* I am breaking off attack.

A copy of the tape had been turned over to U.S. intelligence. It revealed that the attack was deliberate, without prior warning, and was undertaken while the target craft was within sight of the attackers. US intelligence services were undecided, however, whether or not to reveal Japan's role in tracking Soviet military radio transmissions.[3]

Chuck, who in a previous incarnation had been with the CIA, decided to take the bull by the horns. On his own initiative, he went to see Japan's UN delegate to ask if the information about the shootdown, which he understood to have originated from Japanese sources, was accurate. If the Japanese Government could confirm the accuracy of that information, would they object to the disclosure, in Chuck's UN address, of the existence of such tapes? He recognized that this could be the greatest diplomatic coup against the Soviets since the debate in the UN Security Council 21 years earlier when Adlai Stevenson called the attention of the Council to "unmistakable evidence" that facilities for launching nuclear missiles were being installed in Cuba. Soviet representative Zorin had denied the charges, but Adlai Stevenson had the photographic evidence, as irrefutable then as the tapes of Soviet ground-to-air transmissions would be in the KAL-007 incident.

From Tokyo came the answer: no objection. Eagleburger, informed of this development, called back to approve reference to the existence of a recording. Chuck would say that the U.S. Government knew that the pilot who shot down the airliner "reported after the attack that he had fired a missile, that he had destroyed the target, and that he was breaking away—as he put it, 'I am breaking off attack.' " Chuck also provided Eagleburger and the State Department with a sketchy outline of the text he had drafted for his address that evening. It would begin with a recitation of the facts and end with a quotation supplied by Carl Gershman, who was spending the Labor Day weekend on Long Island and had called in with the quote. It was from Alexander Solzhenitsyn:

> Let us not forget that violence does not and cannot exist by itself. It is invariably intertwined with the lie. They are linked in the most intimate, most organic, and most profound fashion. Violence cannot conceal itself behind anything except lies. And lies have nothing to maintain them except violence. Anyone who has once proclaimed violence as his methods must inexorably choose the lie as his principle.

Beyond opening and closing, Chuck had little prepared. There hadn't been enough time that day to draft a commentary on what it all meant or portended. He would speak extemporaneously. There was no time left for further clearance. Nor did Chuck feel that he needed any; the White House and the State Department had made it clear that he needn't pull any punches in dealing with the Soviets' behavior; they had acted as callous murderers, and he could refer to them as such. Chuck was eager to oblige.

Upstairs in Chuck's office as we prepared for the Security Council meeting, I reviewed briefly with him the legal questions which Rosenstock and I had researched for his address. The main points were that both the UN Charter on the use of force and specific rules of international civil aviation had been violated. These set forth the procedures to be used when intercepting an aircraft not properly within the airspace of the intercepting country—radio communications, rocking of wings, and irregular flashing of lights. Only if the civil airliner ignored all efforts to communicate and was clearly on a hostile military mission might it be shot down. I had also supplied Chuck with a detailed log of some 75 documented instances in which Soviet aircraft had strayed into American airspace and that of its Western allies. Some of these unauthorized flight-patterns included Aeroflot commercial civil aircraft flying over security zones. Chuck said he would put all of this into his speech, but would I leave him alone for now—he wanted to take a few minutes to gather his thoughts on "preliminary conclusions" to be drawn from the incident.

It was early evening when the Security Council session was called to order. There was a great hubbub; this was the first time since the Soviets' 1979 invasion of Afghanistan that the Security Council was being formally convened to condemn Soviet behavior. No resolution had yet been tabled, but it seemed likely that one would be introduced shortly. The United States was deliberately staying in the background, encouraging Japan, South Korea, and the European nations to take the lead. Yet even this—the introduction of an anti-Soviet resolution, let alone the securing of the nine votes essential for its passage—could hardly be taken for granted. Soviet strength at the United Nations was too great to allow the introduction of a resolution condemnatory of Soviet behavior—even this outrage—to be taken for granted. Much more difficult to predict was whether the United States and the other sponsors of such a resolution could ever garner the nine votes needed for its adoption, thus setting up the necessity of a Soviet veto.

Chuck's address dwelt on a description of "the crime," and then moved on to drawing "some few, preliminary conclusions about the meaning of the tragedy" and the Soviet Union's refusal to acknowl-

edge responsibility for it. In terms rarely if ever before heard at the
Security Council in describing Soviet conduct, he charged:

> It [the Soviet Union] has . . . behaved with complete—and I must add,
> characteristic—contempt for the international community and for even
> minimal standards of decency and civilized behavior. Its refusal to
> admit the truth—to accept responsibility for this act—it is lying openly,
> brazenly, knowingly. In so doing it is—ironically—showing its true
> face to the world, the face that is so often hidden behind the peace
> offensive and the propaganda machine, behind all the talk of brother-
> hood and human solidarity, and international coexistence.
>
> It is the face of a ruthless totalitarian state, a state which has been
> responsible for the past six-and-one-half decades of killing more
> people—the latest estimate I have read is between 70 and 80 million—
> and enslaving more nations than any state in the history of mankind; a
> state that tailors its concept of truth to what will advance its own
> interest—that and nothing else; a state that does not accept responsi-
> bility for a minimally decent international order; a state whose ultimate
> objective is to reshape the world in its own images, which necessarily
> means a world in which it will control the lives of people and the fate
> of nations as completely and as ruthlessly as it exercises control over its
> own people—and I should add, even those who innocently stray into
> its airspace.
>
> If we are to learn anything from this awful tragedy, it is this mes-
> sage and this terrible warning.[4]

Even Adlai Stevenson's famed exchange with his Soviet counterpart during the height of the Cuban Missile Crisis was more restrained. Chuck's remarks marked a low point in U.S.-Soviet
relations. As we left a stunned UN Security Council chamber, I asked
Chuck about Kirkpatrick's plans. Had she given any indication to him
that she would be returning for the rest of the Security Council
debate and vote? Chuck, although relishing his moment in the lime-
light, could not put aside the thought that it was she, not he, who
should be there to represent the United States. He could only say, "I
hope so."

The next day, September 3, Bill Clark reached Kirkpatrick in
Marakesh. The President, he said, wanted her back in New York to
press America's case; her personal presence was necessary to give it
full effect. Later that day Clark's call was followed up by a cable,
drafted by Larry Eagleburger and bearing Secretary Shultz's signature, asking her to return to the United Nations. She said she would
be back on the 5th; she needed a day to wind up her business in

Morocco. September 4 was to be spent in Casablanca as King Hassan
II's guest at the Mediterranean games, where she would have an
opportunity to meet officials of other Arab countries informally. The
next day, around noon, her discussions completed, she was at Paris'
Charles DeGaulle International Airport boarding a Concorde jet for
Washington's Dulles airport.

On arrival she proceeded directly to her State Department office. I was on hand to greet her along with two senior USIA officials,
and an Air Force general with his aide who had come to brief her
about that other surveillance airplane that flew off the Russian coast.
It would be up to her to make sense of those facts and organize them
in a cohesive way for next morning's UN Security Council session.
She would be the key speaker. The USIA officials were there to help
her formulate the story by offering a videotape that was then being
produced, which provided a visual display of the typed English translation of communications between Soviet ground control and the interceptor pilots who shot down KAL-007. The audio portion would
consist of the actual voice communications in Russian, which U.S.
intelligence had obtained from the Japanese.

Placing video monitors in the UN Security Council chamber to
dramatize the event had been the brainchild of USIA Director
Charles Wick. The trouble was that video monitors had never before
been introduced or used in the Security Council chamber. That afternoon Chuck, anticipating the objections the Soviet delegation
would raise to the introduction of the video monitors, went to see that
month's president of the UN Security Council, Noel Sinclair of Guyana, an individual not known for his warm attitude toward the United
States. Chuck would try to convince him to permit the use of the
video monitors, relying in part on a memorandum I had prepared at
Chuck's request making the case in terms of legal and political precedent. The important thing was to convince Sinclair that video monitors were functionally indistinguishable from maps, graphs, and other
forms of demonstrative evidence that had always been allowed in the
Security Council chamber. TV monitors were merely a technological
advance aimed at achieving the same result. Sinclair, who was initially skeptical, in the end agreed to the idea, convinced that he could
use the fungibility argument to good advantage against the anticipated storm of objections by the Soviet representatives.

Tape recordings could have done the same job, but large video
monitors, four of them, placed high above the delegates' heads, offered the prospect of much greater drama. The "videotape" English

language transcriptions would be all that would be needed to cement the Administration's case. It would prove to the world that the Soviet interceptor jets gave no warning to the KAL airliner pilot before firing, and that Soviet ground control neither instructed the interceptor pilots to try to establish radio communications with KAL-007 through the emergency channel, nor used internationally accepted signals—wing movements—to get KAL-007 to land. The actual voice communications made clear that the interceptor jets were ordered, for unknown reasons, to destroy the airplane even though it was a civilian aircraft and had only moments to go before leaving Soviet airspace.

"But why did they do it?" Kirkpatrick asked, directing her question to the Air Force general. "If I understand correctly, KAL-007 had but a minute or two to go before leaving Soviet airspace."

That, the Air Force general explained, seemed to be precisely why the Soviets shot it down. They didn't want KAL-007 to leave Soviet airspace. They wanted it known that violations of Soviet airspace, even by commercial airliners straying off course, would be treated with "extreme prejudice." Then he explained that the Soviets' recent statements, that an American "spy" plane flying along a flight path similar to that of the KAL-007 flight had led them to believe that KAL-007 was the "spy" plane, were nonsense. A U.S. surveillance airplane regularly flew a route *adjacent* to Soviet airspace, and at one point crossed the route of KAL-007. But that airplane had landed at Guam by the time the shoot-down occurred, and it was impossible, he explained, for them to have mistaken KAL-007 for the U.S. surveillance plane. The Soviet interceptor jets were close enough to tell the difference between a "spy" plane and a commercial airliner—a Boeing 747 jumbo jet, no less, with passengers aboard visible even at night through some of the portholes. There was a full moon, the airplane's wing and fuselage strobe warning lights were functioning, and the silhouette of the 747 against a clear sky would have been unmistakable.

Chuck had already said as much in his statement before the UN Security Council on Friday, September 2. He hinted at the existence of tapes which proved that the Soviets had committed "wanton, calculated, deliberate murder."

"When will the videotape be ready for viewing?" Kirkpatrick asked.

"Late tonight, probably," answered the USIA official. "We have our technicians at USIA working on it. Could we meet again tomorrow at 7:00 A.M. here? Then we can catch the shuttle with you to New York. We can brief you on what we've put together and you'll have a chance to view it and ask questions."

"Good," said Kirkpatrick. "Now we need to make sure that we can set up those video monitors in the UN Security Council. I'll let you know if there's any hitch."

Late that afternoon, Noel Sinclair called Chuck with good news: it would be all right to place the four video monitors in the Security Council chamber. By this time we had a fallback plan. If we couldn't get the video monitors into the Security Council we would try to make use of them in a nearby room used for press conferences. But the effect would hardly be the same. For one thing, the room was quite small. Only a hundred individuals, at best, could fit in it. Secondly it wouldn't have the attention of the world riveted on it. That could only occur against the backdrop of the UN Security Council where all members of the Council, including the Soviet delegation, could view the videotapes, and the cameras and photographers would be there to pick up every expression on their faces. Good. Things seemed to be falling into place.

The only thing left to do was to provide whatever help I could toward completing the speech Kirkpatrick was then drafting for delivery tomorrow. Everything, of course, would be colored by the videotape. My assignment was to draft the "legal" component of the address, explaining the Soviet violation of accepted international law principles for interception of civilian aircraft which had crossed into another country's airspace without authorization. These guidelines were spelled out in the regulations of the International Civil Aviation Organization (ICAO). I went over some of the same principles I had digested in preparation for Chuck's address on September 2: interception of a civilian aircraft was prohibited unless it was on a military mission which posed a direct danger to the country whose airspace had been violated; if appropriate radio communications did not resolve the problem, the intruder could be forced to land after being signalled by wing movements. Although the rules left some ambiguity about what could be done if a civilian aircraft suspected of being on a military mission refused to heed signals to land, the issue was not germane here: KAL-007 was not on a military mission and there had been no emergency channel radio communication or signal that it should land.

For further details on the rules for intercepting civilian aircraft, I called Federal Aviation Administrator Lynn Helms. The Federal

Aviation Administration, I was told, had its own recordings relating to the episode, not as dramatic as the monitored interceptor jet communications, but relevant nonetheless.

The FAA had obtained the tapes of communications between KAL-007 and the Anchorage and Tokyo Control Centers before KAL-007 disappeared from their screens. Helms told me that, by FAA estimates, destruction of the aircraft must have occurred at 18:26 Greenwich Mean Time. There was no evidence, he said, of any Soviet communication to KAL-007. Such communication would have had to have been made on the universal emergency channel—Frequency 121.5 MHz—and that frequency is monitored and taped by numerous ground stations around the world. Hence, there would have been a record of it. Nor, I had been told in the earlier briefing that morning, was there any evidence of an attempt to establish ground communication on that channel. Had there been any such communication, KAL-007 or any other civil aircraft would immediately have transmitted a message that it was being intercepted. Helms concluded, as had the Air Force general that morning, that the Soviets had deliberately shot down KAL-007.

Nevertheless, despite the mounting evidence, the Soviets continued to deny that they bore any responsibility for the fate of KAL-007. At first, they said they had no information at all about the charges. Then, on the afternoon of September 1, the Soviet news agencies released reports that an airplane, which could not be identified, had flown deep into Soviet airspace without navigation lights, and had refused to respond to radio signals of the Soviet interceptor jets. Soviet interceptor jets had fired tracer warning shots along the flying route of the airplane, but the intruder aircraft headed toward the border of Soviet airspace and the Sea of Japan and then, once out of Soviet airspace, apparently escaped from their screens.

Shortly before 8:00 P.M. that evening, Kirkpatrick, who in the meantime had squeezed in a number of meetings at the White House and Pentagon, sat down with me in her office as we went over notes she had been drafting all day on the speech she planned to deliver the next morning. At 8:00 P.M. we turned on the small TV set in her office to hear President Reagan's address to the nation from the Oval Office. Describing the attack as a "crime against humanity," President Reagan then said, "Here is a brief segment of the tape [featuring a Soviet pilot confirming that the target has been destroyed] which we're going to play in its entirety for the UN Se-

curity Council tomorrow." The eyes of the nation would be upon
Jeane Kirkpatrick.

At 7:00 next morning, Kirkpatrick, myself, the Air Force general
and his aide, and the two USIA officials who had been present at
yesterday's meeting, met again in the conference room adjoining
Kirkpatrick's eighth floor State Department office to view the videotape USIA had produced. I looked at Kirkpatrick's speech. It was full
of many drafts and scratch lines and it was obvious that she had been
working on it long into the night. It was an infrastructure built around
a single core: what the videotranscript demonstrated, and the conclusions that could be drawn from it.

> The transcript we have just heard needs little explanation. Quite sim-
> ply, it establishes that the Soviets decided to shoot down this civilian
> airliner, shot it down, murdering the 269 persons aboard, and lied
> about it.
>
> The transcript of the pilots' cockpit conversations illuminates sev-
> eral key points.
>
> • The interceptor which shot KAL #007 down had the airliner in sight
>   for over 20 minutes before firing his missiles.
> • Contrary to what the Soviets have repeatedly stated, the interceptor
>   pilot saw the airliner's navigation lights and reported that fact to the
>   ground on three occasions.
> • Contrary to Soviet statements, the pilot makes no mention of firing
>   any warning shots, only the firing of the missiles which he said struck
>   the "target."
> • Contrary to Soviet statements, there is no indication whatsoever that
>   the interceptor pilot made any attempt either to communicate with
>   the airliner or to signal for it to land in accordance with accepted
>   international practice. Indeed, the Soviet interceptor planes may be
>   technically incapable of communicating by radio with civilian aircraft,
>   presumably out of fear of Soviet pilot defections.
> • Perhaps the most shocking fact learned from the transcript is that at
>   no point did the pilots raise the question of the identity of the target
>   aircraft nor at any time did the interceptor pilots refer to it as any-
>   thing other than the "target." The only activity bearing on the iden-
>   tity of the aircraft was a statement by the pilot of the attacking
>   interceptor that "the target isn't responding to IFF." This means the
>   aircraft did not respond to the electronic interrogation by which
>   military aircraft *identify friends* or *foes* (IFF). But, of course, the
>   Korean airliner could not have responded to IFF because commer-
>   cial aircraft are not equipped to do so.[5]

We then viewed the videotape. USIA had done as good a job as could be expected, and it seemed to fit perfectly with what she had prepared. Afterwards, we left for National Airport en route to New York. The USIA official had with him a black Samsonite attaché case. Inside was the videocassette.

When we arrived at La Guardia airport on the 8:00 A.M. Eastern shuttle, Carl, Kirkpatrick's driver in New York, was on hand to greet us. He escorted us to the bulletproof Lincoln limousine reserved for Kirkpatrick's use while in New York. Behind that was another limousine, a less ostentatious Chrysler with normal windows. "I'll go with the General in my limo," said Jeane. "Why don't you follow us in the other one."

I turned to the USIA officials and asked if they would join me in the backup limousine. "No, thanks," said one of them. "USIA has arranged for one of our own to come and pick us up. We'll just wait here until it shows. It ought to be here any moment."

Our flight from Washington had arrived a few minutes ahead of schedule and as there was none of the usual congestion at the airport that morning, we had made our way out a few minutes earlier than expected. I hopped into the waiting backup limousine, assuming it was one of the contract limousines the U.S. Mission employs during General Assembly sessions.

When I arrived at the U.S. Mission, Kirkpatrick had already made her way across to the UN Security Council. I caught up with her in the Delegates' Lounge. The corridors, the Council chamber, and the area reserved for the press were awash with the international press corps. I had never seen such a gathering. But then President Reagan himself had given the forthcoming performance star billing in his address the night before. It would be Ambassador Jeane Kirkpatrick, whom he had earlier spoken of as his "heroine," confronting the Soviets in their lair in New York with irrefutable evidence of their misdeeds.

"Where are the others?" Jeane asked as I caught up with her. "The UN people need the videocassette *now*."

"They ought to be here any moment," I said. "They're coming in a separate car."

"They had better be. We don't have much time."

But by 9:50 they had not arrived. The Security Council session was scheduled to begin in ten minutes.

At 9:55, panic was beginning to set in. Without the videotape we would have on our hand a major diplomatic embarrassment. It was not simply that the U.S. presentation centered around the videotape. Our speech could be changed at the last minute. But the international press corps waiting to see what had been touted as definitive proof of a deliberate Soviet shoot-down would be less kind. The TV monitors had been set up, expectations were running high, and if nothing was produced to show for it, it would seem as though the United States found that the videotape didn't make the case it was held out to make, or that it had been discovered to be bogus—all at the last minute. The moment might be rescued if the tape later showed up, but by then it might be too late; attention would have been deflected from Soviet conduct to what went wrong in the presentation of the American case.

"Where are they?" Kirkpatrick demanded. It was 10:00 A.M. and the delegates had assembled in the Security Council chamber. "You should have gone with them," she said. She was right. For it had by then become clear to me what must have occurred. I must have mistakenly taken their limousine: I had been driven by a USIA contract driver instructed to take people to the U.S. Mission; not by a U.S. Mission contract driver. I tried to assure myself that they surely would have had enough sense to have taken a taxi if their intended limousine didn't show after a few minutes of waiting. But they were not from New York. Perhaps they had no idea of how much time it takes to get into the city during rush-hour traffic. For all I knew they could still be there waiting for their intended limousine.

At the United Nations, word had gotten out that something appeared to be wrong; U.S. officials were not handing over the videotape to the UN technicians so that they could get things prepared and enable the session to begin. At 10:05 A.M. Kirkpatrick took her seat at the Security Council table.

A few minutes later Secretary General Perez de Cuellar arrived and took his chair. Guyana's Sinclair, the Security Council president, turned to an aide and chatted—thus giving us a little more time. I walked outside into the hall leading to the Security Council chamber. I was about to rush back to the Mission to ask Bob Moller, our chief of security, if he could give me a hand and run a special car back to La Guardia to see if he could see any sign of their whereabouts. And then I caught sight of them—the USIA man with the samsonite attaché case, puffing hard, rushing down the hall, his arms flailing, escorted by an aide from the U.S. Mission, and the other USIA official tracking behind him.

"You took the car intended for us!" he said in exasperation.

"I'm sorry for the mixup," I said, controlling myself from asking why it took them so long to figure that out.

At 10:20 A.M. Sinclair was about to call the session to order. I raced over to one of his aides near the TV control and said, "Here's the tape. We're ready to go." Sinclair commenced the proceedings.

The United States was the first scheduled speaker, to be followed by the USSR, Japan, the Philippines, Liberia, and Sweden.

I sat behind Kirkpatrick and studied the latest text of the resolution reflecting the consensus of the United States, Australia, and the other nations that had citizens aboard KAL-007 (South Korea, as a non–UN-member, could not join in the effort). I noticed that the Soviet Union was not mentioned by name. As with the previous year's General Assembly resolution, which condemned the Soviet invasion of Afghanistan, at the United Nations one had to read between the lines to discover that the Soviet Union was being condemned. Somehow the Soviet Union had managed to intimidate other nations into not mentioning it by name in a condemnatory resolution. The contrast between the treatment accorded the Soviet Union and that accorded the United States was striking. In 1981 the General Assembly, in its Abu Eain resolution, condemned the U.S. legal system for extraditing terrorists bent on liberating their homeland from "alien, colonial, or racist rule." In the Trusteeship Council the United States was castigated for its "colonialist" treatment of Puerto Rico. And here a civilian airliner with 269 people on board was deliberately shot down to prove a political point—the inviolability of Soviet borders—and no consensus would be reached on mentioning the Soviet Union by name.

The operative paragraph of the draft Security Council resolution merely said that the Security Council "deeply deplores the destruction of the Korean airliner and the tragic loss of civilian life therein"—as if no one in particular was responsible. It then declared "that such use of armed force against international civil aviation is incompatible with the norms governing international behavior and elementary considerations of humanity" and urged "all States to comply with the aims and objectives of the Chicago Convention on International Civil Aviation."[6] Little more than a slap on the wrist. But the text of the proposed resolution was less important than the U.S. presentation and what the videotape would reveal. That is what the world would remember.

The videotape was short—less than two minutes of running time. But that was all that was needed. Kirkpatrick's speech flowed naturally around what the videotape had demonstrated: that the Soviet interceptor pilots made no attempt at establishing either radio or visual contact with KAL-007 before blasting it out of the sky. Then she turned to a point that neither President Reagan nor the State Department—for all their natural inclinations—had previously dwelled on. She declared that the downing of the airliner was "characteristic" and showed the true face of Soviet policy: "contempt for the international community and for even minimal standards of decency and civilized behavior." These were the strongest lines Kirkpatrick had ever spoken at the United Nations in regard to Soviet behavior. She went on in the same tone: "Violence and lies are regular instruments of Soviet policy. . . . We are reminded once again that the Soviet Union is a state based on the dual principles of callousness and mendacity. It is dedicated to the rule of force."[7]

Kirkpatrick's statement provided a clear contrast to the statement issued that day by Larry Eagleburger on behalf of the State Department. The latter made no reference to the shoot-down as characteristic of Soviet behavior; only that it "raises the most serious questions about the competence of the Soviet air defense system, with all the danger that it implies. . . . The Soviet Union must accept the norms of civilized society in respecting the lives of innocent travelers. The world demands that the Soviet Union give assurances and take specific steps to ensure that the events of August 31 cannot occur again."[8] It was as if there was nothing systemic, or endemic, about what had occurred, as if it was a matter simply of correcting the Soviet air defense system's incompetence in a particular incident. Little wonder that President Reagan wanted Kirkpatrick back to take the lead in condemning the Soviet attack; even with the best of intentions, the State Department effort lacked conviction.

Soviet Ambassador Oleg Troyanovsky spoke next. It was not his finest moment. He denied that KAL-007 had been "downed" by the Soviets, but no one could possibly believe him. He was still echoing the party line. Soviet ambassadors do not have the same leeway to improvise as most of their Western counterparts, and Soviet communications between Moscow and New York seemed to be particularly slow that day. As he continued his speech, one of the U.S. UN press officers arrived with a copy of the latest release from TASS, the Soviet news agency. That report, hot off the wires, acknowledged that Soviet air force personnel had fired on the "unidentified" airplane. Troyanovsky, still in the dark as to what his government had in fact conceded, spoke as a man cut off from his moorings.

When Troyanovsky finished his remarks and the session adjourned for lunch, Chuck Lichenstein approached him with a copy of the TASS release. The normally unflappable Troyanovsky turned red, shook his head, and walked away.

The Security Council continued to meet in emergency session from September 2 to September 12 to discuss the KAL-007 incident. In addition to Japan, Korea, Canada, and Australia, 42 representatives lined up to address the Council and condemn the Soviet action. Of course, a Soviet veto was predictable, despite avoidance of any mention of the Soviet Union by name.

In later session, the Soviets acknowledged that their planes had downed KAL-007. But they defended their conduct, arguing that it was a legitimate act of self-defense. KAL-007 was on a spy mission, they insisted, carrying out intelligence operations for the United States.

It is dubious in the extreme that anyone at the UN Security Council believed the Soviet story. Nevertheless, the United States seemed incapable of mustering the requisite nine votes for adopting the resolution and forcing a Soviet veto. Nor was it for lack of trying. Indeed, improvement of the U.S. position at the UN Security Council through improvement of bilateral relations had been perhaps the overriding goal Kirkpatrick had set for herself as she assumed office. Still, the Soviet clout at the United Nations hardly seemed to be affected. Without nine votes in favor of the resolution, the Soviets would not be boxed into a corner, isolated on the world stage. The whole exercise would end in an anticlimax.

Attention focused on Zimbabwe as the swing vote. Its head of state, President Robert Mugabe, was scheduled to arrive shortly in the United States for a visit. Secretary Shultz and Senator Nancy Kassebaum met him at the airport. There were hints of improved relations if he would just back the Security Council resolution. President Reagan met with him. But Mugabe declined the overtures. He could not, he said, vote against the Soviet Union.

That left Malta as the only other potential swing vote. France, the UK, the Netherlands, Pakistan, Togo, and Zaire could be expected to join in voting in favor of the resolution. Poland and the USSR would definitely vote against. And China, Nicaragua, Guyana, and Zimbabwe were expected to abstain. But Malta was a long shot. Its representative at the United Nations, Ambassador Victor Gauci, was friendly with the United States, and pro-Western. His government was not, and had many ties with Libya, commercial and otherwise, that it preferred not to endanger. However, Larry Eagleburger had in the past developed a special relationship with Malta's foreign minister and so it was decided to give that channel a try. The response was peculiar: could the United States help Malta by convincing the UN Security Council to convene one of its sessions in Malta? Malta wanted to get its face on the world map, and there had been talk of holding UN Security Council sessions out of New York in a Third World state. But this was a promise to which Eagleburger could not commit his government.

Thus, on September 12, as we prepared to cross First Avenue en route to the final day Security Council deliberations and the impending vote, the mood of the U.S. delegation was glum.

All week long the text of UN Security Council Provisional Resolution S/15966/REV.1. had been subject to negotiations aimed at further diluting it to assure maximal possible acceptability. One of its preambular paragraphs stated that the Security Council was "gravely disturbed" by the fact that a Korean Airlines commercial jet with 269 people on board had been "shot down by Soviet military aircraft." But the operative condemnatory paragraphs of the resolution—the ones that really matter—made no mention of the Soviet Union. What was deplored was the loss of civilian life, not the Soviet role in causing the loss. The resolution was less than we thought we could live with. And yet the goal of putting the Soviets in a corner and forcing a veto seemed more remote than ever.

Then, minutes before the UN Security Council meeting convened, Ambassador Gauci of Malta approached Chuck Lichenstein with a peculiar request. "I have a message," he said, "from my government. If your government will give its agreement to reopening the suspended negotiations on civil aviation rights, then I am authorized to support the Security Council resolution." Chuck didn't know what Victor Gauci was talking about. He approached Kirkpatrick, who quickly penned a note that the U.S. government would give the request prompt consideration. A few minutes later at the UN Security Council Malta joined Pakistan, Togo, Jordan, and Zaire—the five undecided votes—in favor of a UN Security Council resolution condemning the Soviet downing of KAL-007. It was the first Security Council since 1979 that proved capable of mustering the requisite nine votes for adoption of a resolution that was in any way critical of Soviet behavior.

The Soviet Union, of course, vetoed the draft resolution. But the exercise had its intended effect. For the first time in the three years that we had been at the United Nations the Soviets were in retreat, knowing that they could no longer count on an automatic UN majority to protect the Soviet Union from condemnation no matter how heinous its behavior might be. The U.S. Mission had done its work. World attention was riveted on the incident as characteristic of Soviet behavior. It proved a turning point, but one that the United States secured by the narrowest of margins. A misstep by a U.S. Mission staffer—myself—in taking the wrong car almost led to an embarrassment that might have derailed the entire process. And then, had it not been for Malta's strange and totally unanticipated last-minute request, the exercise would have ended with the Soviet Union able to walk away unmarked, secure in the knowledge that its political clout at the United Nations remained unimpaired.

It became clear then, perhaps more dramatically than at any time in the past, what our mission at the United Nations was all about. The speeches were terribly important. The addresses delivered by Jeane Kirkpatrick and Chuck Lichenstein were different in tone from those presented by the State Department. The latter shook no one, and struck no popular chord of outrage. But the speeches alone without anything to show for them would have meant only that the venting of anger at Soviet behavior would have to extend to UN complicity in condoning that behavior. Soviet strength and influence at the United Nations buttressed Soviet strength and influence in other arenas. It had to be chipped at, and the means was to show others that we took their votes at the United Nations seriously, and were prepared to make a large personal and political investment in persuading noncommitted nations like Pakistan, Togo, Jordan, Zaire, and Malta not to be afraid to vote with the West. The medium was visits and careful demonstrations of good relations, and of the consequences of not taking U.S. interests into consideration on key UN votes. That investment paid off in the KAL-007 vote.

The rest was left for ICAO, the International Civil Aviation Organization, which then commenced an investigation of the facts of the incident. The Soviet Union refused, however, to allow any visit by an ICAO investigative team, and refused requests to turn over transcripts of its relevant radio communications and radar data. On December 30, 1983, ICAO released its final report.[9] It ridiculed the Soviet view that complete and exclusive sovereignty over airspace automatically included the right to force down intruding civil airliners. Interception, ICAO stated, is proper only where a real, imminent danger arises from the intrusion. As it was a matter of minutes before the KAL airliner would have departed Soviet airspace, the only damage KAL-007 was capable of doing had already been done. But even if the Soviet Union had grounds for concluding that KAL-007 was on an intelligence mission, it had to exhaust efforts to identify and communicate with KAL-007 before attempting interception. This it did not do. The ICAO message was, therefore, clear: the protection of innocent human life had to take precedence over concern for the inviolability of airspace.

KAL-007 proved in the saddest way possible that President Reagan was not, as his critics contended, a gun-slinging cowboy. In his address of September 2, he declared that the Soviet Union was "a regime that so broadly trumpets its vision of peace and global disarmament and yet so callously and quickly commits a terrorist act to sacrifice the lives of innocent human beings."[10] KAL-007 made Reagan's point: the Soviet regime was one the United States couldn't deal with responsibly—not on arms control, not on settlement of regional disputes, not on solving the problems of terrorism—in short, not on any of the major outstanding differences between the two systems.

As the 1984 presidential elections neared, presidential advisers like Michael Deaver wanted to make sure that their man ran as a peace candidate. The downhill spiral in U.S.-Soviet relations was now seen as a liability to the President. Jeane Kirkpatrick was viewed as being in the confrontationalist camp, after it had ceased being politically fashionable to be in that position. Moreover, for the first time since her assumption of office it could be noted that she had developed an increasingly large, appreciative, grass-roots constituency. She was warned to fall into line: confrontation had peaked, and it was time to move toward rapprochement and Big Power summitry.

13

Grenada, and the Emergence of a Reagan Doctrine

© 1989 *Seattle Post-Intelligencer*
Reprinted with special permission of North
America Syndicate, Inc.

The above cartoon—borrowing from the final scene of "Casablanca," in which Humphrey Bogart tells Ingrid Bergman that although they must part, "we will always have our Paris"—aptly shows the Grenada operation of October 1983 as Ronald Reagan's "Paris"; a starry-eyed United States as his lover. This American "Paris" came right after Reagan's greatest debacle, the death of over two hundred U.S. marines outside of Beirut's International Airport at the hands of a terrorist truck-bombing against which few precautions had been taken.[1]

Like Lebanon, Grenada involved the intervention of outside forces, violence of a new dimension, and near anarchy and chaos. Both Lebanon and Grenada demanded of U.S. policy-planners that they clearly define their objectives and the circumstances in which they were willing to commit American forces. In one instance it worked, in the other it failed.

Jeane Kirkpatrick was a student of power—how it was acquired and how it was lost, and what purposes it served. She concentrated on defining the purposes of American power: national security, and the encouragement of democracy and freedom abroad. These values stood in contrast and in opposition to the Soviet values of repression and expansionism. There was, in her worldview, no moral equivalence between the two camps; no duty of neutrality imposed by the UN Charter in the face of expansionist totalitarianism. Grenada would put to the test her beliefs, and those of the President whose views she mirrored.

When Grenada came, no one in the Administration, with the exception of President Reagan, seemed to be communicating more effectively than Jeane Kirkpatrick a conception of the purposes of American power. She did this at the rostrum of the United Nations and also through countless TV appearances, accepting every invitation she could, and soliciting others; in radio and press interviews; and, when the UN General Assembly was not in session, in a nearly non-stop succession of speaking engagements across the country. She was identified with her message: to be unapologetic, ready to act on the basis of convictions, and possessed of a firm belief in one's own values.[2]

As she spoke, as audiences warmed to her, and as relative successes were scored at the United Nations, she grew confident of her own powers. In the last two and a half years she had met nearly a hundred foreign ministers or heads of state and had travelled the world, in addition to weathering the storms at the United Nations and bureaucratic intrigues at State. But she wanted to shape U.S. foreign policy, not act under "instructions." No matter how skillful she could be at embellishing them, lending them her own interpretation, they were still the directives of others, and she was responsible for carrying them out. She believed that she understood the requirements of U.S. foreign policy as well as anyone else—better than Alexander Haig ever did, and probably better than George Shultz ever would. She had seen international politics from the inside out. For all the sordidness and distortions of the United Nations, it remained a place to meet foreign officials, to understand their ambitions, to observe them in action, and to negotiate differences.

The break came on the afternoon of October 13, when the White House announced that Bill Clark would leave his post as National Security Adviser to replace James Watt as head of the Department of the Interior. It came without warning. Earlier that day she had been with Bill Clark to see President Reagan on another matter—to report on her trip to Central America with Henry Kissinger and members of a newly established commission to examine the deepening crisis there. Bill Clark, however, had not mentioned his imminent departure. Later she was to learn it was because he hadn't known of it. It had been manufactured in the early afternoon between their morning meeting with the President and the end of the day, when an aide approached her at her UN office to say that a reporter was about to announce Clark's change of jobs.

At the White House two opposing factions had formed, separated not so much by ideology as personality and a sense of who was better serving the interests of the President. On one side were Bill Clark; Ed Meese, the President's Counselor; Caspar Weinberger, the Secretary of Defense; and Bill Casey, the Director of the Central Intelligence Agency. Jeane Kirkpatrick was closest to them. On the other side were Michael Deaver, then the President's senior White House aide; James Baker, the Chief-of-Staff; and Secretary of State George Shultz. Their prime target—at least as Jeane Kirkpatrick saw it and recalled it—was Bill Clark. He was too close to the President. James Baker wanted to replace him. On the day Watt was fired from the Department of the Interior, Deaver approached President Reagan and suggested that Clark, a committed outdoorsman, would be a logical successor. In the early afternoon of October 13, Clark met with the President in Deaver's presence and was asked by Reagan if he would be interested in the post. Clark replied that he would do whatever the President wished of him. Shortly after that, as the President was addressing a convention of women's clubs in the Rose Garden, Deaver handed President Reagan a slip of paper from which he could make the announcement that Clark would be replacing Watt at Interior. That set in motion a week of wrangling in Washington over who would be Clark's successor at the National Security Council.[3]

What had transpired quickly became apparent to Clark, Meese, Weinberger, and Casey. They saw the objective of the exercise as having James Baker fill Bill Clark's shoes. That caused them, all staunch Reagan loyalists, to take their case to the President. James Baker, they argued, would be the wrong man. He lacked any experience or background in foreign affairs. The Secretary of State, George Shultz, was still learning the ropes. A strong knowledgeable foreign affairs expert was needed at the White House, and they proposed Jeane Kirkpatrick. President Reagan agreed to reconsider.

Conservatives backed Kirkpatrick. She was their heroine: she had taken the "kick me" sign off the door of the office of the U.S. Ambassador to the United Nations. She was speaking out against Soviet totalitarianism and expansionism with freshness, wit, and determination. It was time to move her to the core of action, the White House.

The forces lined up against her, however, proved too strong to surmount. In Washington circles it became known that George Shultz had informed the President and others that if Kirkpatrick were named National Security Adviser, he would resign as Secretary of State. At the same time a spate of articles began to appear in the national press from unconfirmed sources that Kirkpatrick was threatening to resign unless she was awarded the NSC post.[4]

President Reagan asked Kirkpatrick to come to the Oval Office. A meeting was arranged for Monday of the following week. It lasted for over an hour. The President, fully believing the rumors of her intended resignation as reported in the press, tried to convince her to stay. He praised her UN performance, but told her that a decision had already been made to appoint Robert C. ("Bud") McFarlane—a former senior military staff aide on the National Security Council who was then serving as Counselor to the State Department—to succeed Bill Clark as National Security Adviser.

President Reagan again told Kirkpatrick that he hoped she would agree to stay on at her UN post. If not, he was prepared to create for her a new White House position of Adviser to the President for National Security Affairs, but what the job would entail was never clear. It was not a palatable choice. Her duties undefined, she could quickly disappear in the woodwork of White House officialdom. She told President Reagan that she would rather return to her post at the United Nations and stay through to the end of the present General Assembly session in December. Beyond that, she was making no promises.

In an interview with the *Washington Post* the following day, October 23, she was asked about her plans in light of the previous day's meeting. "I don't have any plans," she responded. "That doesn't mean anything except that I haven't made any decision beyond the General Assembly. I am not a long-range planner."[5]

An interview with one of her close associates was more revealing. "She feels," the *Washington Post* quoted him as saying, "like she was treated as a character in a novel or screenplay; first they wrote her into the script as a prototypical right-winger and then, after she served her purpose as a device for furthering the plot, they tried to write her out of the story by killing her off."[6] Inside the *Washington Post* that day, alongside the transcript of the interview, appeared a cartoon still caricaturing her as the prototypical right-winger, as a dragon lady with mischievous high eyebrows, smoking a cigarette (she doesn't smoke) from a long holder, reminiscent of Milton Caniff's "Terry and the Pirates" character.

It became clear that with Bill Clark out, and Bud McFarlane—with whom she had no special relationship—in, her influence in the White House had peaked. Moreover, McFarlane would not be running the show. Unlike Clark, he had no long personal relationship with the President. He would be doing George Shultz's bidding. George Shultz—pragmatic, competent, and presidential confidant—would be the ultimate insider, and she again the outsider.

Looming in the wings, however, was the first great crisis of the Reagan Administration—Grenada—and thoughts about the ups and downs of one's personal standing had to be set aside.[7] Two weeks earlier, Maurice Bishop—the radical leftist leader of Grenada, the Caribbean island furthest south in the Windward chain—had been deposed in a coup launched by an even more radical and violent group. Bishop, together with three members of his Cabinet, had been executed. Dawn to dusk shoot-on-sight curfews had been imposed throughout the island, and there were reports of soldiers firing into the crowds. No one knew much about the men who had engineered the coup. They called themselves "The People's Revolutionary Army." What was clear was that they had acted with the backing and support of Cuban advisers stationed in Grenada, and that the other nations of the eastern Caribbean viewed the developments in Grenada as security risks to their own countries.

On October 24, the Administration had to decide whether to honor a request it had received the previous day from the five member-nations of the OECS, the Organization of Eastern Caribbean States. It called for direct US military involvement in a joint effort to check the ominous developments in Grenada. The request came a day after the suicide bombing of the U.S. marine barracks outside Beirut. International crises do not defer to the ebb and flow of U.S. National Security Advisers, and, like Secretary Alexander Haig's departure at the outset of the Lebanon crisis, Grenada too was to find the United States at the crossroads of leadership in its foreign policy.

On the afternoon of October 24, the U.S. National Security Council Planning Group (NSPG) convened to decide what to do about Grenada. The meeting was chaired by President Reagan. When it was over, Reagan had another event to attend: in another wing of the White House, he declared the day "United Nations Day" as he proclaimed the UN remained "uniquely endowed to promote inter-national political economic, social, and technical cooperation." Not a second's thought was given, however, to bringing the crisis in Grenada to the United Nations.

Early the next morning, Prime Minister Eugenia Charles of Dominica, the chairperson of the OECS, arrived in Washington on an Air Force plane. Her message: developments in Grenada—the assas-sination of its leader, Maurice Bishop, and the takeover by a blood-thirsty anarchist group—boded ill for the whole of the eastern Caribbean region. By the time she arrived, the decision had already been reached: US forces would work with the joint military command of the OECS states to reverse the situation. No sooner had she landed than she was rushed to a hastily convened news conference at 9:00 A.M. to announce the landing on Grenada of 1,900 U.S. Army Rang-ers and Marines, supported by elements of the Air Force and Navy, in conjunction with a small cadre from the OECS member-states.

Prime Minister Eugenia Charles had come to tell President Rea-gan that "it doesn't take much—just a cell of twenty or so determined men, and they wouldn't have had any trouble finding recruits, to overthrow a state like Dominica."[8] Indeed, in 1981 two dozen mer-cenaries might have taken over Dominica were it not for the fact that the FBI had uncovered their plot and arrested the coup leaders as they were about to leave the U.S. mainland for the Caribbean. If the new Grenadan People's Revolutionary Army took Dominica, the rest of the small eastern Caribbean states—Antigua and Barbuda, Mont-serrat, Saint Christopher and Nevis, Saint Lucia, Saint Vincent, and the Grenadines—would not last long.

That was Eugenia Charles's message. It had been told earlier to U.S. ambassadors in the Eastern Caribbean, and it ran as follows: "Barbados and Jamaica, they're bigger than the other islands, but they still don't have much of a military force, not one ready to withstand air attacks and the army of Cuban advisers amassing in Grenada. The People's Revolutionary Army has access to an airstrip more than 9,000 feet long, which the Cubans have been building for some time, clearly for military use. A thousand armed Cuban advisers are there to help them. That's what it's all about: to point a dagger at the Eastern Caribbean states."[9]

As Prime Minister Eugenia Charles prepared to voice her concerns in Washington at a hastily convened joint news conference with President Reagan, I turned on the "squawk box" in my office connecting the U.S. Mission to the State Department. I heard President Reagan begin:

> Early this morning, forces from six Caribbean democracies and the United States began a landing on the island of Grenada on the Eastern Caribbean. We have taken this decisive action for three reasons. First, and overriding importance, to protect innocent lives, including up to a thousand Americans, whose personal safety is, of course, my paramount concern. Second, to forestall further chaos. And third, to assist in the restoration of conditions of law and order and of governmental institutions to the island of Grenada where a brutal group of leftist thugs violently seized power, killing the Prime Minister, three Cabinet members, two labor leaders, and other civilians, including children.[10]

It was the first I had heard of plans for an invasion. Information of the impending operation had been very closely held. U.S. Attorney General William French Smith learned of the operation shortly before it was launched, when two junior National Security Council staff members—Robert Kimmitt, the NSC's Legal Counsel and Secretary, and Constantine Menges, a Latin American specialist— arrived at his Justice Department office to brief him on the NSPG's decision.[11] Certainly there had been no prior consultations with the OAS, the Organization of American States, nor with the United Nations.

The UN and OAS Charters both require member-states to bring to the attention of those bodies situations calling for defensive military action unless circumstances of imminent attack make that impossible. Moreover, Article 54 of the UN Charter specifically provides that "The Security Council shall at all times be kept fully informed of activities undertaken or in contemplation under regional arrangements or by regional agencies for the maintenance of international peace and security." But, had these provisions on consultations and notice been complied with, OAS and UN opposition would likely have stymied the chances of any action being taken. Unlike 1962, when, during the Cuban Missile Crisis, the United States first sought to enlist OAS support before undertaking any operation, in 1983 there was little goodwill the United States could expect from the OAS; U.S. backing of Britain during the Falklands crisis had destroyed what was left of it. Advance consultations would, therefore, have telegraphed U.S. intentions without any offsetting gain. The U.S. medical students who were in a precarious position would have been further endangered. So too would Grenada's Governor-General, who was communicating with the United States in secret. Of course, in some vague sense, international law might have been declared the victor had the notice and consultation requirements of the UN and OAS Charters been complied with, but no one in the Administration thought in those terms. The last American president to consider, in a time of crisis, advancing the ends of international law above national interests was President Dwight D. Eisenhower in the Suez Crisis of 1956.[12]

At the U.S. Mission, we prepared ourselves for an onslaught of condemnation across the street as news of the invasion was announced. That afternoon, Tuesday, October 25, Nicaragua and Guyana called for an emergency UN Security Council session to introduce a resolution condemning the joint U.S.-OECS "aggression."[13] The session convened promptly at 10:00 A.M. the next morning with UN representatives of more than twenty countries—many considered friendly by the United States—lined up to register to speak out against the invasion.

The next morning, a member of the Egyptian delegation sought me out, knowing that what he had to say was likely to get back to my superiors. The conversation went like this:

We didn't mean it. We didn't mean what we said yesterday.

You mean to say now that all you said yesterday about the United States—that it had acted as an aggressor against a poor, hapless, defense-less Grenada, like a bully that ought to be reprimanded—you're now saying that you didn't mean that?

Yes, I'm saying just that. Of course, we didn't mean it. We know that the United States did what it had to do. We are glad of it.

After all, you are a great power. We know you can't afford another Nicaragua down there, not after the bombing of the U.S. Marine barracks in Beirut. How would it look if you, a great power, were now to run away again when being asked for help by the neighboring countries? Yes, of course we understood that your President couldn't do that.

Well, you seem to understand the American position. One question: why then did you come to the UN Security Council to speak out against the United States? After all, you are not a member of the UN Security Council this year, so it isn't as if you had to speak. So why did you volunteer to come and speak?

We did it for your sake.

For our sake? You'll have to explain that one to me. You rose to condemn us for our sake? How so?

You know, after we made peace with Israel we were ostracized from the Arab world of which we are the natural leader. And we were ostracized as well from the position of prominence which is naturally ours in the Non-Aligned Movement. We need to get back in. For your sake as well as for ours. Once we are back in the Non-Aligned Movement and the Islamic bloc, we can then act to moderate their radical excesses. But you know, both the NAM and the Islamic bloc are firm in their opposition to the Grenada operation. It's a matter of ideology, isn't it? We are against invasions. We are against interventions. After what the Israelis did in 1967, how could we be otherwise? So we have to go along, but not forever. So please try to understand, it's for your sake as well as ours.

I'll pass your thinking along as best I can.

My interlocutor also offered a bit of friendly advice: Don't take things so seriously, don't get so concerned with the rights and wrongs of your case, you are a superpower, you can afford to be above the bloc politics that drive us, so grow up, and don't be disappointed when we, or others, act differently at the UN from when we meet with you in bilateral sessions; don't take it so seriously, it's only the UN, and you are a great power.

Well-meaning as this advice might be, our job at the U.S. Mission was to present the facts and the best legal rationales on behalf of our government. What we said in our speeches might not affect the voting patterns of other countries at the United Nations, but it could establish precedent and guidelines for use by American ambassadors around the world. How we chose to characterize the Grenada operation—whether as a fluke, as an isolated incident in U.S. foreign relations reflecting no more than the reaction to one set of unique circumstance, or whether we chose to cast the matter in larger terms as part of the pattern and strategy of U.S. foreign policy—would help determine U.S. foreign policy.[14] Our explanations in New York would give the world notice on how the Administration perceived the Grenada operation, and whether other "Grenadas" might be in store for the future.[15]

In the early afternoon of October 26, the second day of the special Security Council session on Grenada, Kirkpatrick turned to me and said, "Allan, we're scheduled to speak tomorrow morning. I'd like to deliver a major address. I'd like you to make the strongest case possible in international law on behalf of the Grenada operation." Until now I had expected that our speech would be big on the facts and little on the law, and that we would follow the script laid out at White House briefings. "Do you wish," I asked, "to go beyond what the President said at the news briefing? He's already spelled out our legal defense: protection of the lives of U.S. nationals, forestalling further chaos and anarchy, and the restoration of conditions of law and order on the island. It's not a defense in any doctrinal sense of international law, but apparently it's the case the White House, and presumably the State Department, want to make. They haven't come out with any other legal defense. Do you want to go beyond that?"

"I don't care if the State Department hasn't done so," she answered. "I'd like you to do it, if you would."

"When are you inscribed to speak?"

"First speaker on the list, tomorrow morning at 10:00 A.M."

I called to cancel a dinner engagement, went to my typewriter, and prepared for a long night. I also called the Deputy Legal Adviser at the State Department to keep him abreast of what I was doing, and to enlist his support in bringing to bear whatever international law arguments we could in our defense of the Grenada operation.

I told him I thought we might argue that the joint U.S./OECS operation in Grenada was justified under international law and the law of the UN Charter as an act of collective self-defense, permissible under Article 51 of the UN Charter, which provides for the inherent right of individual and collective self-defense in response to an "armed attack." Although there was no armed attack in the literal sense, less than this was arguably sufficient under international law. In justifying bombing of the Iraqi nuclear reactor, Israel, for example, contended that there were reasonable grounds for fearing that unless action was taken promptly, it would be too late to do so later. Events would get out of control and later action would become prohibitively costly. Along these lines, I was prepared to point to the reasons why the OECS states feared for their safety from the turn of events in Grenada: the ease with which these islands could be taken over, and the physical capacity, as well as inclination, of the revolutionary group in Grenada for developing and exporting subversion. The OECS States had, it seemed, valid legal grounds for acting before the men and women responsible for the killing of Prime Minister Maurice Bishop could consolidate their control of Grenada with the help of 1,000 or more Cuban advisers on the island. It was in this context that we would argue that United States assistance was based on concern for the safety of the region and for the stability of the Western Hemisphere, as well as an interest in serving the safety of the American medical students left stranded on the island. These, I thought, could be the central themes of our argument.

"You can't say that," the Deputy Legal Adviser said to my surprise.

Asked why not, he replied that were we to rely on the self-defense argument here, where there was, in fact, no imminent threat of an armed attack, we would be doing serious damage to the UN Charter's prohibition (Article 51) of the use of force except in instances of genuine self-defense against an "armed attack." The explanation, I recalled, was similar to the one offered two years earlier with regard to the Israeli bombing of the Osirak reactor. The adviser's primary concern seemed to be the effect such an interpretation would have on other states who might then claim an expanded notion of self-defense to justify their own preemptive military adventures. Were the United States, he warned, to endorse self-defense as a rationale for the Grenada operation, it would be enlarging an exception to the UN Charter's prohibition on the use of force to the point that armies could march through it.

I countered by saying that no nation would have to go so far as to look to an expansive definition of self-defense in the U.S. justification of its Grenada operation as giving them license to do whatever they had decided to do in their national interest. Besides, I said, President Reagan, in pointing to the Cuban role in the takeover of Grenada, had as much as endorsed the self-defense argument.

Again, I was counseled to stay clear of the self-defense argument; the State Department was opposed to it because it would send the wrong signal. The Department's "instructions" were to limit USUN's legal defense of the Grenada operation to the argument that the operation was predicated on the need for protection of U.S. nationals abroad.

"You can't be serious," I retorted. "The whole world knows that that's not what the operation was really about. If it was, it would have been much more limited, without the need for OECS involvement. If protection of nationals is what we were truly interested in, we would have done an Entebbe-style rescue. Here U.S. national security interests in the region were involved. We didn't want another Cuba or Nicaragua in the Caribbean, especially one led by the likes of the group that killed Maurice Bishop. And we had reason to act: the OECS states felt threatened. Isn't that why we did what we did? If so, why not say it?"

The answer put to me was very simple: the Department felt it necessary that our case for intervention in Grenada not be linked to stopping the expansion of Cuban or Soviet influence in the Hemisphere. It was proposed that we exchange drafts of our respective approaches and see what we might piece together.

The next few hours were spent receiving and analyzing data-faxed material: the chronology of events, the public statements of other East Caribbean leaders in defense of the operation, the request by the Governor-General of Grenada for assistance, and the analysis by State Department lawyers of what legal weight to accord, under British Commonwealth law, to the Governor-General's request for assistance. With the latter document came also the admonition not to refer to the Governor-General's request; it had been smuggled out of the island, and as the Governor-General was still there in hiding, revelation of the request would only endanger his life. We could inform the UN Secretary General privately of this development, but were asked not to make it public.

The more I thought about it the more it became apparent that, to meet the State Department's concerns, a sound legal defense of the Grenada operation would have to rest not on a single argument—like individual and collective self-defense—but on the cumulative weight of several arguments which, if taken individually, might be insufficient to make our case. These arguments were protection of nationals, restoration of conditions of law and order, and an end to anarchy.

Around 2:00 A.M. a draft of that portion of the speech outlining legal arguments for the Grenada operation had been prepared. The emphasis would be on the facts, not the law. My colleague at the State Department suggested that stress be placed on the "unique combination of circumstances" presented by Grenada; the emphasis on "unique" serving to indicate that the United States did not consider the Grenada operation as a precedent for the use of U.S. force, whether against Cuba or Nicaragua or anyone else. But that, I said, was probably not the impression that President Reagan wanted to convey.

Early the next morning Kirkpatrick received an urgent call from Deputy Secretary of State Kenneth Dam on behalf of Secretary Shultz. He would like her, he said, to emphasize that the U.S. operation in Grenada was based on a unique combination of circumstances, that it was a reaction to very particular and compelling circumstances, and avoid any reference to self-defense as a legal justification.

When I reached her later that morning shortly before she was to deliver her speech, she told me that she had my draft and my notes but that she had already talked with Ken Dam that morning and was all set.

Her speech at the UN Security Council table began by describing the events that had precipitated the crisis and then moved on to an articulation of the legal defense. Looking from behind her at the text she was reading, I could see some lines pencilled in reflecting her conversation with Ken Dam.

> Ambassador Kirkpatrick:
> It was, indeed, *a unique combination of circumstances* prevailing in Grenada that led the United States to respond positively to the OECS request that we assist them in their decision to undertake collective action to secure peace and stability in the Caribbean region. Those circumstances included danger to innocent U.S. nationals, the absence of a minimally responsible government in Grenada, and the danger posed to the OECS by the relatively awesome military might those responsible for the murder of the Bishop government now had at their disposal. The U.S. response, we believe, was fully compatible with relevant international law and practice. . . .
> There was, indeed, a *unique situation* in which there existed a vacuum of responsible governmental authority. . . . Though a small

island, Grenada, because of its massive build-up of arms and material, had become capable of gravely affecting the security of the entire Caribbean region. . . .

In assessing this danger, the states of the OECS—most of which have no army at all or armies of less than 200 men—concluded that the military potential of Grenada in the hands of the madmen who engineered the coup had reached threatening proportions. For example, although Jamaica's population exceeds by twenty-fold that of Grenada, Grenada's army—its indigenous forces alone—exceeded by one and one-half times the size of Jamaica's Armed Forces. Moreover, a new airstrip was in the final stages of completion by over 600 armed Cubans. . . .

It was in this context that the OECS, viewing with the greatest alarm this combination of brutal men with awesome might, decided to undertake collective action pursuant to its charter. Such action fully comported with relevant provisions of the UN Charter, which accord regional organizations the authority to undertake collective action. When asked to assist this effort, the United States, whose own nationals and vital interests were independently affected, joined the effort to restore minimal conditions of law and order in Grenada and eliminate the threat posed to the security of the entire region. . . .

In the context of these *very particular, very unusual, perhaps unique, circumstances*, the United States decided to accede to the request of the OECS for aiding its collective efforts aimed at securing peace and stability in the Caribbean region.[16]

On October 28, the UN Security Council voted—11 nations in favor to 1 against (the United States), and 3 abstentions—to condemn the U.S. and OECS intervention in Grenada as a "flagrant violation of international law and of the independence, sovereignty and territorial integrity" of Grenada.[17] The U.S. veto prevented adoption of the resolution and formal reprobation of the United States by the international community. However, four days later, on November 2, the UN General Assembly did what the Security Council had been prevented from doing by the U.S. veto. By a vote of 108 in favor to 9 against, with 27 abstentions, the General Assembly adopted a resolution condemning the U.S./OECS action as a "flagrant violation of international law."

Other than the Eastern Caribbean states and El Salvador, only Israel voted with the United States against the resolution. Even British Prime Minister Margaret Thatcher sharply criticized the U.S. intervention in Grenada. She did this despite the fact that the United States had made a controversial decision to support the United Kingdom in the Falklands War.[18] Kirkpatrick prepared to take the podium to respond to the charge. But before she could do so, the General Assembly, acting on a motion introduced by the People's Democratic Republic of Yemen (the undemocratic one), decided by a vote of 60 to 54, with 24 abstentions, to close debate on the issue before giving her an opportunity to be heard.[19] It was a clear violation of a member's right to be heard.

The reception by the popular press was not much kinder. It ridiculed the U.S. legal justification of the Grenada operation.[20] Indignant that the Grenada operation hadn't been described and defended for what it ostensibly was—a warning to the Soviets, Cubans, and Nicaraguans that the forceful expansion of their influence in the Western Hemisphere would not be tolerated—the *New York Times'* October 30 lead editorial, "Goliath in Grenada," deemed the Administration's legal justifications for the Grenada operation a "sham."

> If there is an argument at all for the way the United States invaded Grenada, President Reagan has been clumsy in making it. The rescue of medical students was, almost by his own admission, only a pretext. Their evacuation, if necessary, could have been accomplished by lesser means. The legal justifications were a sham. Such breaches of treaties and sovereignty can only be rationalized by the aggressions of others.
>
> Four days after the landings, Mr. Reagan finally pointed to a valid question, conceding his underlying concern: What *were* all those Cubans doing in Grenada? . . .
>
> If Cubans, on behalf of the Soviet Union, were subverting Grenada's Government and establishing a base 'to export terror and undermine democracy' in Latin America, their expulsion is surely a proper American objective.[21]

Indeed, subsequent explanations of the reasons for the U.S. intervention in Grenada were broader than the justifications initially relied upon. In subsequent public briefings, for example, Kenneth Dam relied heavily on the danger posed to the Eastern Caribbean by Grenada. In a major address on November 3, before the Associated Press Managing Editors' Conference, he provided the Administration's fullest justification for the U.S. action.

> The evidence that we have found suggests that Grenada would have become a fortified Cuban/Soviet military outpost. . . . we had been concerned—well before the events that brought about our collective action—that Grenada could be used as a staging area for subversion of nearby countries, for interdiction of shipping lanes, and for transit of troops and supplies from Cuba to Africa and from Eastern Europe and

Libya to Central America. . . . What we found in Grenada may be summed up as the military underpinnings for just such uses. . . .

Think about the facilities that all this would have secured—the Point Salines Airport, which would have enabled a MIG 23 carrying four 1,000 pound bombs to strike and return from Puerto Rico in the north to Venezuela in the south; the Calivigny military training area; a 75,000 watt radio transmitter capable of blanketing the entire Caribbean Basin; the potential for a deep-water harbor. . . .

A final lesson of the events in Grenada is that neighbors have a clear, ongoing responsibility to act in ways consistent with each other's legitimate security needs.[22]

Good arguments. Still, for one reason or another, the State Department still did not want to justify the Grenada operation in terms that could be used to show its opposition to the creation of another Cuba or Nicaragua, or its prototype, in the eastern Caribbean.

The community of international law scholars seemed less incensed and more embarrassed by the legal justification offered on behalf of the Grenada operation.[23] In an interview with the *New York Times*, Professor Don Wallace Jr., Director of the International Law Institute at Georgetown University, mirrored this feeling: "Although I don't think we can square what we did in Grenada with the UN Charter system, it may be that the system is now somewhat out of date. The policy justification was a lot more substantial than the legal justification." The legal justification "forced [us] into a sort of hypocrisy which embarrassed people who believe in law."[24]

The State Department persisted, however, in eschewing use of the word self-defense to characterize the Grenada operation. In a letter dated February 10, 1984, to the American Bar Association Committee on the Grenada operation, the State Department's Legal Adviser, Davis Robinson, explained his reasons.

We did not contend that the action on Grenada was an exercise in the inherent right of self-defense recognized in Article 51 of the UN Charter . . . for fear of a weakening of established international legal restraints concerning the use of force.[25]

What was being said by President Reagan seemed more and more out of tune with timid legal justifications being proffered on behalf of his actions. In a televised address to the nation on October 27, President Reagan tied together events in Lebanon and Grenada. In both countries, he charged, the Soviet Union had "assisted and encouraged the recent violence." There were, he said, 30 Soviet advisers and "hundreds" of Cuban military and paramilitary troops in Grenada; the evidence of Soviet/Cuban intentions was clear—to use it as a base for encouraging subversion throughout the region. Later he would equate intervention in Grenada with support for "freedom fighters."

> We only did our duty, as a responsible neighbor and a lover of peace, the day we went in and returned the government to the people and rescued our own students. We restored that island to liberty. Yes, it's only a small island, but that's what the world is made of—small islands yearning for freedom.[26]

For many at the State Department, President Reagan's unabashed assertion of an American *right* to aid freedom fighters—what came to be known as the Reagan Doctrine—was cause for embarrassment. Many treated that notion or doctrine derisively as the moral equivalent of Soviet support for Daniel Ortega, Fidel Castro, and Yasser Arafat; as the counterpart of the Soviet's Brezhnev Doctrine. The fact that the Brezhnev doctrine sanctioned the expansion of power and the repression of rights, while Reagan's view imposed limitations on power and sought the furtherance of democracy, was ignored.

In this light, the insistence that "self-defense" not be relied on to justify the American intervention in Grenada took on new significance. At stake was not some obscure point of international law. The issue was whether Grenada would stand for the reassertion of American power in the Western hemisphere. Kirkpatrick saw nothing wrong with putting Nicaragua's Daniel Ortega on notice about the capabilities of U.S. power and the limits of U.S. patience. She assumed that was what the President wanted. But few in the State Department sought the accolade of being shock troops for the Reagan Doctrine. That job would be left to Kirkpatrick. Speaking on the Hill, in a seemingly endless stream of public forums, addresses, and through opinion pieces, interviews, and short articles, she made the point that America had no apologies to make in supporting the cause of freedom around the world. In that struggle Grenada would be only one example; a reaction to unique circumstances, but not a "fluke" of policy.

Years later Kirkpatrick and I would argue in a jointly authored piece:

> Ironically, the articulation of the Reagan Doctrine is nearly as offensive to its opponents as its implementation is. Most opponents of the doc-

trine attack the notion that U.S. use of counterforce in support of democratic self-determination is legitimate rather than argue about the prudence of support for this or that insurgency. The idea that American power can be usefully and morally utilized in support of a world of independent, self-governing nations still seems implausible to those who define an appropriate world role for the United States in the shadow of their interpretation of the Vietnam War.[27]

The Reagan Doctrine did not emerge full-blown from the Grenada operation. That operation involved the direct use of force, and the Reagan Doctrine stressed indirect U.S. support for indigenous forces fighting for freedom when all other means of expression had been closed to them. Had, however, the Grenada operation been limited to its peculiar circumstances—a fluke occurrence providing neither precedent nor guide-posts for future conduct—there would have been little basis and scant confidence for the emergence of the larger Reagan Doctrine.

14

Winding Down
The 39th General Assembly Session

Confrontations in the [UN's] deliberative organs [are] carried too far.

UN Secretary General Perez de Cuellar's Annual Report, 1984

The 39th UN General Assembly session, Jeane Kirkpatrick's fourth as head of the US delegation, was to be her last. In the world beyond the UN's walls, these were stirrings of momentous change. Inside the institution where change often came last, the United Nations, its reverberations were being dimly felt.

At the U.S. Mission change of a different order was taking place. Carl Gershman had left to become president of the newly established National Endowment for Democracy. Funded by Congress, it would provide financial support to overseas groups and individuals struggling for greater personal and political freedom. Carl was the perfect choice. The cause of freedom had been the preoccupation of his adult life. Chuck Lichenstein left too. More than any of the rest of us, he had trouble controlling the gall he felt on seeing the reality of the international "Parliament of Man" in action. Our loss was a gain for the Heritage Foundation, a conservative Washington-based think-tank. Ken Adelman was tapped to replace Arms Control and Disarmament Agency head Eugene V. Rostow, whose professorial bearing

234

had grated on colleagues in the Reagan Administration who preferred Adelman's more casual manner.

With their departures came their replacements. Alan Keyes, a brilliant articulate young foreign service officer, whom Kirkpatrick discovered in India where he was serving as a consular official, took over José Sorzano's post as representative to ECOSOC. José moved up to take Ken's slot as Deputy Permanent Representative. Replacing Chuck Lichenstein as alternate delegate to the Security Council was Richard Schifter, Kirkpatrick's friend and former ward chief in Maryland's Montgomery County Democratic political machine.

Everyone, newcomer and old-timer alike, sensed the makings of a shift in world politics. Although we had been warned not to confuse the United Nations with the "real world," in fact the United Nations gave one a fantastic vantage point for viewing and anticipating the changing correlation of world forces. Ideological shifts and the gravitation of nations to and away from alliances and blocs could, with some experience, be easily discerned at the United Nations.

In the fall of 1984 there were faint signals that perhaps we had seen the worst. The concert of attacks-for-attack's-sake on Israel seemed to have reached its zenith. The downhill spiral in U.S.-Soviet relations seemed to have bottomed out with the KAL-007 airliner incident. The American intervention in Grenada, while condemned at the United Nations, earned America new respect for its capacity to act on the basis of its convictions. The United Nations was shaking off its self-complacency, recognizing that it had to reform itself, to contribute meaningfully, and get its financial house in order if it was not to be dismissed as an expensive irrelevancy.

In Washington came feelers of a Soviet desire to ease superpower tensions. President Reagan's successful launch of the Strategic Defense Initiative seemed to have convinced the Soviets that a prolonged competition for more technologically sophisticated strategic space-based weaponry was not in their interest. Besides, the Soviets had their hands full in Afghanistan, where the tide of battle was turning against them. In Central America, U.S. support for the Contras was taking the war to the enemy's side, greatly complicating Soviet support for Nicaragua's hopes to "export" revolution on the American continent.

President Reagan and his key White House advisers were eager not to let opportunities slip for a superpower thaw. The United Nations became the venue for testing and probing. From the rostrum of the General Assembly, President Reagan could project a new more

generous tone, eschewing earlier references to the "evil empire." In
private meetings between President Reagan and Soviet Foreign Minister Andrei Gromyko at the U.S. Mission to the UN, personal diplomacy could augment the more formal signals of a receptivity to
deal.

Thus President Reagan's 1984 address to the U.N. General Assembly, his fourth, spoke of a "political settlement" of regional disputes in Central America and elsewhere. No longer were the Soviet
Union and its proxies portrayed and treated as if they were committed to the perpetuation of conflict, with no option left for U.S. leadership except a long twilight struggle. Instead, the President
suggested, they might if they wished join with the United States in
serious discussions aimed at a resolution of their differences. The new
optimism was apparent in President Reagan's concluding reference to
Thomas Paine's aphorism: "We have it in our power to begin the
world again."[1]

Mirroring the official Kremlin view, the Soviet press dismissed
President Reagan's overtures as "a vessel with nothing inside it." But
to seasoned observers it was apparent that something new was going
on. The tone of President Reagan's UN meeting with the dour Soviet
Foreign Minister, Andrei Gromyko, was noticeably more pleasant
than that of previous years.

But if there was a warming trend, Jeane Kirkpatrick was not part
of it. National Security Adviser William Clark had moved to the
Department of the Interior, and in doing so had exchanged daily early
morning presidential briefings on the state of the world for the company of U.S. Park Police riding horseback through Rock Creek Park.
With Bud McFarlane, and later with Admiral John Poindexter filling
Clark's shoes, Jeane Kirkpatrick's ease of access to President Reagan
could no longer be assured. At the White House, power shifted to the
Chief of Staff, James Baker, III, who would soon be able to maintain
and consolidate his power within the Administration from another
base, that of Secretary of the Treasury. For Baker, as for President
Reagan's other top White House aides, the opportunity of a U.S.-
Soviet summit became the overriding goal. A face-to-face meeting between President Reagan and his Soviet counterpart—in time for the
1984 elections—could project Ronald Reagan as the peace candidate.
Kirkpatrick and her close ally, CIA Director Bill Casey, were seen as
potential obstacles to this goal, as part of the old order that may have
outlived its usefulness now that a summit was within reach.

At the United Nations, Secretary General Javier Perez de Cuellar took careful note of international developments. He saw the United Nations lagging behind positive developments in superpower relations, and facing the danger of rapidly becoming obsolete. In his 1984 Annual Secretary General's Report on the workings of the UN, he warned that the organization was spending money and expending resources at a geometrically increasing rate with little to show for it. The Security Council's failure to contribute to the peaceful resolution of either the Falklands or Lebanon crises had severely impaired its image as a responsible, effective body. The UN General Assembly had become a factory for the production of frivolous resolutions that had eroded "the seriousness with which governments and the public take the decisions of the United Nations."

"Why," he asked, "has there been a retreat from multilateralism at a time when actual developments, both in relation to world peace and the world economy, would seem to demand their strengthening?" His answer: "Confrontations in the [UN's] deliberative organs [are] carried too far."[2]

But the General Assembly agenda for 1984 showed a body with little inclination for reform. Instead, the agenda provided testimony to the staying power of the old issues and fixed perspectives.

Items 1 to 9 of the General Assembly's 142-item agenda for 1984 concerned largely administrative matters: the opening of the session by the chairman of the delegation of Panama; elections to subsidiary organs of the UN; reports on vacancies in subcommittees—the International Civil Service Commission, Board of Auditors, Investments Committee, Administrative Tribunal, Committee on Contributions, and so on. But Item No. 3 certainly was not. Entitled "The Credentials Committee Report," it was the euphemism for a repeat of the last two General Assembly attempts to expel Israel.

Item 10 concerned the ongoing situation in Kampuchea. Presumably the question would be what the United Nations could do to put a stop to the fighting that had been going on since December 1978, when the North Vietnamese had invaded Cambodia to oust the Pol Pot regime. Not much had been done in the past, and there was little reason to believe 1984 would prove much different.

Items 21 to 23 of the agenda paid tribute to the power of UN blocs. Item 21 was the Report on Cooperation Between the UN and the Organization of the Islamic Conference; Item 22, the Report on Cooperation Between the UN and the Organization of African Unity; Item 23, the Report on Cooperation Between the UN and the League of Arab States.

Item 24, "Armed Israeli Aggression against the Iraqi nuclear installations and its grave consequences for the established international system concerning the peaceful uses of nuclear energy, the nonproliferation of nuclear weapons and international peace and security," was a replay of the efforts to condemn Israel for aggression for the 1981 bombing.

Item 25, "The situation in Central America: threats to international peace and security and peace initiatives," was intended to give the General Assembly an opportunity to do what the Security Council would not: condemn America's Central America policy. Nicaragua had already presented a letter to the Security Council president complaining that U.S. threats and aggressive actions had intensified in recent weeks with "the assassination and kidnapping of children, men and women, extensive damage to the economy and destruction of the country's modest resources." Responding to these charges would be Jeane Kirkpatrick, who recently had the distinction of having a Contra combat unit named after her—the Nicaraguan Democratic Forces (FDN) "Jeane Kirkpatrick brigade." After the anticipated veto in the Security Council the action would move to the General Assembly, where Nicaragua would again command a clear majority.

Item 28, "The situation in Afghanistan and its implications for international peace and security," marked the U.S. effort to turn the table around by seeking to condemn the Soviet Union for its invasion of Afghanistan. The resolution seemed likely to pass again this year, as it had in the past. But the Soviet Union would not be mentioned by name. It was impossible to muster a UN majority to do that. There was never a similar inhibition about condemning U.S. actions in Central America and elsewhere.

Item 29 was "The Question of Namibia," and item 31, "The Policies of apartheid of the government of South Africa." In both items the United States would join the majority in again condemning apartheid and urging independence for Namibia.

Item 32: "The International Year of Peace." Item 33, the "Report of The Special Committee on the Inalienable Rights of the Palestinian People." This would be the precursor to item 36, "The Situation in the Middle-East"—i.e., the Arab-Israeli conflict, to which three to four times as much attention would be devoted as to any other single item.

Some of the other items on the agenda included: the Law of the Sea; the UN Conference on the Promotion of International Cooperation on the Peaceful Uses of Nuclear Energy; the question of peace,

stability, and cooperation in South-East Asia; the launching of global
negotiations on international economic cooperation for development
(on spreading the world's wealth from the rich to the poor nations);
the question of equitable representation (action on eliminating the
superpower Security Council veto); the observance of the quincen-
tenary of the discovery of America; the question of Cyprus (like the
Falklands, an ideal case for UN resolution, as both are on the same
side of the ideological dividing line, but little progress could be expected); the implementation of the resolutions of the United Nations
(discussing what the point of these resolutions was if they would not
be enforced); the consequences of the prolongation of the armed
conflict between Iran and Iraq, (the world's major ongoing war finally
made it onto the UN's agenda as item 44); nuclear-free zones, disarmament, relations between disarmament and development; the implementation of General Assembly resolutions on the immediate
cessation and prohibition of nuclear weapons tests (which obviously
have not been implemented); the implementation of the declaration
on the denuclearization of Africa (declaring South Africa's nuclear
program to be illegitimate); the prohibition on the development and
manufacture of new types of weapons of mass destruction, chemical,
and bacteriological weapons; general and complete disarmament; the
question of Antarctica; reports of committees on disaster relief assistance; the UN Institute for Training and Research; International Research and Training Institute for the Advancement of Women; UN
Decade for Women; the elimination of all forms of discrimination
against women; the question of a Convention on the Rights of the
Child; the implementation of the Declaration of Granting Independence to Colonial Countries and Peoples by the Specialized Agencies
and the International Institutions Associated with the UN; the pattern of conferences; the UN pension system; the financing of the UN
peacekeeping forces in the Middle East; the progressive development of the principles and norms of international law relating to the
new international economic order; observer status of national liberation movements recognized by the Organization of African Unity or
by the League of Arab States; the status of the Protocols Additional to
the Geneva Conventions of 1949; the Rights of Peoples to Peace; and
the celebration of the 150th anniversary of the emancipation of the
slaves in the British Empire; countries stricken by dysentery and
drought.

Those were the highlights of the agenda. If something didn't
make the list, it didn't warrant international attention. Little on the

list hadn't been there the year before, or the year before that. Some new crises were added, but no old ones had been deleted, or checked off as resolved.

The day after President Reagan's address to the opening of the 39th session of the UN General Assembly came another truck bombing outside of Beirut. This time the target was the U.S. Embassy. Two Americans were killed. The next day syndicated columnists Rowland Evans and Robert Novak connected their deaths to Ambassador Kirkpatrick's vote at the United Nations earlier that month: "the veto by the United States in the UN Security Council this month of a Lebanese-sponsored resolution condemning Israel's occupation almost certainly helped trigger the terrorist attack in presumably secure Christian Beirut."[3] There was some truth in the charge. Various groups in Lebanon had threatened action against American men and facilities in the event the U.S. exercised its veto power.

The veto had taken place on September 6. Kirkpatrick voted "No" to an Arab-sponsored resolution calling for an end to "objectionable" practices in the Israeli occupation zone of southern Lebanon. Kirkpatrick had insisted that the draft resolution make some reference to context or provocation. When the sponsors refused to budge, Kirkpatrick vetoed the resolution. Now a terrorist bomb in Beirut was being attributed to her actions in New York.

The "new" UN General Assembly agenda, the sniping from Evans and Novak and other columnists, the leaks and what they said about the sources of the leaks, cued Kirkpatrick that she was in for a replay of the dramas of earlier years. Nicaragua would ask the UN Security Council to condemn another "imminent" invasion. Israel's expulsion would be attempted once again and the same procedural rigmarole to defeat the motion would have to be put into play, although with much greater assurance of success than in previous years. Life at the United Nations had become predictable, and shabby. She had weathered the storm; now she stood in danger of becoming a regular feature on the political landscape, the loyal opposition.

At this juncture of the UN's and Jeane Kirkpatrick's fortunes, Richard Schifter appeared on the scene, providing a link between Kirkpatrick's difficult first three years and the more accommodating term of her successor, General Vernon A. Walters.

Dick Schifter had grown up in Vienna. His parents sent him to safe haven in the United States, but they themselves perished in concentration camps. During the war Schifter went on to serve in U.S. military intelligence, and then, after graduating Yale Law

School, established a successful law practice. In the 1960s he chaired the Democratic Party's Central Committee in Montgomery County, Maryland, where he honed his political skills, had occasion to work closely with Senator Hubert Humphrey, and met and worked with Jeane Kirkpatrick.

In the late fall of 1980, shortly after Kirkpatrick's appointment to the UN post, Schifter called her to tell her that with his children grown and with his financial situation secure, he would welcome an opportunity to serve in the Administration. A month later, she called. "Dick," she said, "can you be in Geneva next Monday?"

The post she had in mind was that of an alternate U.S. delegate to the UN Human Rights Commission, a suborgan of the United Nations whose meetings are held in Geneva in February and March of each year. Schifter seemed ideal as a backup and lawyer to Michael Novak, a theologian and political philosopher and colleague of Kirkpatrick's at the American Enterprise Institute. In February 1981, Schifter was appointed the Principal U.S. Alternate Delegate to the Human Rights Commission. He was reappointed to this post in 1982. In 1983 he replaced Novak as the chief U.S. delegate to the Human Rights Commission, a post he held through 1986. In addition, he began to pick up other odd jobs as a diplomatic troubleshooter for the Administration, as a delegate to UNESCO in Paris one year, and as U.S. delegate to the U.S.-Soviet Conference on Cooperation and Security held in Europe in the spring of 1984.

The first major event in the greening of Dick Schifter occurred in the beginning of the Human Rights Commission's 1982 session. Reports had come in that the Syrian army had razed an entire town, Hama, a fundamentalist stronghold in central Syria. Upwards of 20,000 civilian deaths were reported, although since the area was closed off by the Syrians and access was denied to the outside world there was no quick way of getting verification of the reports. To Schifter's surprise, the Human Rights Commission displayed little interest in getting at the facts; no one seemed anxious to explore Syrian responsibility. When Michael Novak asked about it, he was told that the United States would be unlikely to get enough votes to secure adoption of a resolution condemning the Syrians; therefore, he needn't bother. Novak nevertheless tried, but the predictions were correct. Syria could kill tens of thousands of civilians without any risk of having the matter put on the UN Human Rights Commission's agenda.

Schifter soon learned another lesson: it wasn't good form to complain about double standards in judging Israel's human rights record. At the Human Rights Commission's 1984 session in Geneva a draft resolution deemed Israel's treatment of captured Arab guerrillas to be in violation of the relevant 1949 Geneva Conventions. Schifter called on the Europeans to join the United States in opposing the resolution on the grounds that it was imbalanced since it made no reference to known abuses, in violation of the Geneva Conventions, in the treatment of Israeli soldiers held captive in Lebanon by Syria and the PLO. The Europeans refused to budge. Frustrated, Schifter asked what possible rationale could justify voting in favor of a resolution condemning the Israeli treatment of Arab prisoners while ignoring Arab treatment of Israeli prisoners.

The response was embarrassed silence. Did this new American diplomat really have to have the rules of engagement spelled out for him in detail? For them, the fact that the Arab-sponsored resolution was destined to pass by sheer weight of numbers was decisive. Putting up a fight in these circumstances seemed pointless. To Schifter it smacked of appeasement.

It went on like this for Schifter until early spring of 1984, when Kirkpatrick called to say that Lichenstein had just quit, and invited Schifter to New York to replace him. Schifter quickly accepted. He would soon learn that what he witnessed in Geneva was but a more gentrified version of what awaited him in New York.

The 1984 UN General Assembly session, Schifter's first, was tamer than those of the previous three years weathered by the Kirkpatrick team. Anti-Americanism and its progeny, name-calling, was no longer as flagrant, no longer flaunted as it had been in the past. Endorsement of terrorism was less pronounced, and left more to innuendo and to reading between the lines. The incessant late-night Security Council sessions, month after month, which had followed the Israeli invasion of Lebanon were a practice now largely discarded. The drama of the Grenada invasion was gone. There was no mad incident, like the Soviet shoot-down of the airliner KAL-007 to galvanize world attention and outrage. The challenge to the credentials of the Israeli delegation would continue, but it had become ritual. In the General Assembly, condemnation of the Soviet intervention in Afghanistan would pick up more votes, but only at the price of never mentioning the Soviet Union by name. Nicaragua would ask the Security Council to condemn U.S. policy in Latin America, but here too there was little that was new. The battle lines were the same, the skirmishes followed a set pattern, and the speeches had all the appeal of a late-night movie that had been seen several times over.

Perhaps not surprisingly, Schifter's focus turned to procedure, particularly the upcoming elections for new members of the Security Council. Each year the Security Council votes to elect five new non-permanent members. The results determine how many friendly votes the United States can count on in that forum. Each of the regional groups—the Africans, the Latins, the Arabs—nominates one of their own for a Security Council seat. In the late summer of 1984, the African bloc nominated Marxist-run Ethiopia, which was bound to vote in tandem with the Soviet bloc. The selection was done on the basis of a random rotational system. But under the African bloc's rules of procedure, unanimity was required for a nomination to go forward. Somalia, Ethiopia's neighbor with whom it was having a border war, had voted against Ethiopia's nomination. Nevertheless, Ethiopia's nomination went forward to the UN General Assembly, where a two-thirds majority, voting in secret ballot, was necessary for adoption of the nomination.

No one at the State Department was happy at the thought of Ethiopia occupying a UN Security Council seat. The State Department preferred Madagascar, the runner-up for nomination on the Africans' list, but assumed there was nothing one could do about it at this point. Schifter calculated, however, that it would be possible, with extensive lobbying, especially among the African states, to put together the one-third required to block adoption of the nomination. If successful, it would demonstrate to the General Assembly that it needn't feel bound to go along with the nomination of Ethiopia as the Africans had been unable to secure consensus on the vote. Schifter discovered that Senegal, Gambia, and Niger, in addition to Somalia, were willing to help bring about the defeat of Ethiopia's nomination.

Schifter set to work making detailed charts of the voting patterns of the African states, trying to focus on who might be turned around. He discovered that what he had learned in Geneva was also true in New York; that West European delegates, for all their talk of understanding the concerns of Third World countries, rarely met with Third World representatives on a one-to-one basis. Their contacts were normally through the receptions circuit. As in Geneva, Schifter decided that this was a mistake, and arranged luncheon dates over the next several months with nearly every delegate from an African country. He organized a massive lobbying operation, both in New York and in capitals around the world. Of course, we at the Mission had been doing the same thing for four years. Every ambassador had a regional responsibility to cultivate, but Dick Schifter went about it more systematically, as if nothing mattered more than buttonholing that extra vote. And every day his arithmetic looked better. He kept getting closer to getting the one-third vote that was needed to defeat Ethiopia's nomination.

In pursuing his cause, there was one arrow Schifter could pull from his quiver which hadn't previously been available to American diplomats. He could assure those votes he was seeking that Congress would be looking to their votes, not as an acid test of U.S. bilateral relations with that country and a determinant of its share of U.S. economic and military assistance, but as one important factor to be considered in adjusting U.S. bilateral ties. Congress had recently enacted into law PL 99–500 and PL 98–164 requiring the President and the Secretary of State to submit annual reports to Congress highlighting the UN voting practices of all countries on issues of importance to the United States.[4] The legislation was the outgrowth of the efforts of Jeane Kirkpatrick to tie bilateral and multilateral relations, and was made possible through the work of Senator Robert Kasten, who served with the U.S. Mission as a public delegate at the General Assembly's 1983 session.

In early December, the secret balloting for membership on the UN Security Council began. Ethiopia failed to get the required two-thirds majority. The Africans then put Madagascar forward. Madagascar received the two-thirds vote, thus eliminating a Soviet proxy state that would otherwise have sat on the Security Council.

Dick Schifter's hard lobbying had paid off. Jeane Kirkpatrick had given him full support. So had José Sorzano, with whom he had worked closely. But still something was amiss. It wasn't that Kirkpatrick and Sorzano lacked Schifter's capacity to methodically plot and pursue votes and to track the numbers relentlessly. This is the stuff of politics; and UN politics was no exception. Indeed, Kirkpatrick had lobbied assiduously to make possible legislation requiring annual reports to Congress on country-by-country voting practices at the United Nations. Securing an extra vote, even for something as potentially important as a Security Council seat, seemed however to have become an end in itself, as if the larger system in which votes were pursued was rational and sensible. The hard fighting over the restoration of U.S. influence and strength in the world body appeared to have reached an anti-climax.

Perhaps it was time to move on.

Before that, however, two matters had to be dealt with at the 1984 session: one reminded us of the danger of letting our guard down; the other, of the risk of underestimating our adversaries' capacity to manipulate international law.

15

Legitimating Terrorism Once Again
The Case of the 1977 Protocols

> We must not, and need not, give recognition and protection to terrorist groups as a price for progress in humanitarian law.
>
> President Ronald Reagan urging Congress to reject ratification of the 1977 Protocols to the Geneva Conventions on the Laws of War, February 15, 1987

At the United Nations every maneuver was related to a larger purpose. Nearly invariably—the condemnation of Soviet actions in Afghanistan, and the shoot-down of the KAL airliner providing notable exceptions—that larger purpose was not determined by the West. This was, of course, especially true at the UN General Assembly, where the West's capacity to marshal the majorities necessary to win support for resolutions was nearly nonexistent. Instead, initiatives came from the Non-Aligned Movement, the Soviet blocs, and the radical Arab states. The legitimation of terrorism against select targets was one of those purposes. It had first surfaced on the agenda in 1981 with the matter of Abu Eain dominating that year's General Assembly session. At the 1984 session the legitimation of terrorism reared its head again. This time the issue was handled more deftly. Indeed, the United States came close to being party to the effort.

When the matter arose in the fall of 1984, I had just assumed new responsibilities. Until then, in my capacity as counsel to Jeane Kirkpatrick, I was involved as much in policy as in "law" in any narrow sense of the word. I was not responsible for the day-to-day legal work of the Mission: preparing guidelines on procedural aspects of U.S. representation at the UN; representing the United States on the UN's Sixth (Legal) Committee; examining what restrictions could be imposed on the size and travel of personnel attached to the Cuban, Libyan, or Soviet UN missions; dealing with host-country relations, with New York municipal authorities over unpaid parking tickets, with drunk-driving charges, abuse of secretaries, or whatever, by diplomats who claimed immunity from U.S. legal processes; or dealing with the UN Secretariat over such matters as disbursement of funds and "secondment"—whether the Soviets and others could continue to keep on their payroll and control their own nationals who had been hired by the UN Secretariat, and who were supposed to be independent international civil servants. All of these matters fell under the responsibility of Herb Reis, the Mission's Legal Counselor, and Bob Rosenstock, his deputy, who reported to him; the Mission's attorney for host-country affairs; and the young lawyers from the Legal Adviser's Office in Washington who would come to help out during General Assembly sessions.

However, Reis, who had been with the Mission for nineteen years, was retiring in the fall of 1984. Kirkpatrick asked if I would take his place while continuing to retain my existing portfolio. I agreed to do so.

The first thing I did was to inform Rosenstock and the legal staff that I had no desire to intervene in the performance of its routine daily functions, particularly as concerned U.S. representation in the Sixth (Legal) Committee. The bulk of the Committee's time was devoted to such matters as subcommittees dealing with UN Charter reform; or the promulgation of conventions on the highjacking of aircraft; diplomatic immunity; status of mercenaries; the law of the sea, or of outer space, and review of the International Law Commission's efforts in Geneva to codify international law. As with everything else at the United Nations, there was a heavy political, or ideological, dimension to this work. Any time a significant resolution was introduced or passed, a cable on the subject would have to be sent to the State Department. My job was to review these cables and, if they were not objectionable, to "clear" them by affixing my signature for transmission to Washington. I had no need or desire to see every single cable that went out: Rosenstock would initial routine transmissions for me; I wanted to see any matters that had significant political overtones.

About a month after assuming my additional duties, I received a surprising telephone call from the Pentagon. It was from Douglas Feith, Deputy Assistant Secretary of Defense for International Negotiations. I had known him briefly in his former position during the first two years of the Reagan Administration as a staff-member of the National Security Council. "I assume," he said with a hint of incredulity, "that you saw this cable which went out over your signature regarding the '77 Protocols. Do you realize what you are doing?"

I did not know what he was referring to. Perhaps I should have known—but I did not—that the 1977 Protocols to revise the 1949 Geneva Conventions on the laws of war had made their way to the Sixth Committee. A resolution had been introduced before that Committee[1] urging all nations—but here clearly directed at the United States—to ratify the 1977 Protocols. Since the United States was the key hold-out, the purpose of the resolution was to push the United States further along the road to ratification. If it did not vote in favor of the proposed resolution, it would find itself isolated. The United States would be the one country (besides Israel) out of step with the "progressive" development of humanitarian law. If the U.S. voted for the resolution, continued hemming and hawing by the Pentagon over ratification could only prove an embarrassment. The cable Feith referred to, and which I had not seen, asked that the State Department "instruct" the U.S. Mission to vote in favor of adoption of the proposed resolution.

Superficially, the '77 Protocols seemed innocuous. They contained many provisions that were purely humanitarian in scope. They had been arrived at as a result of three years of deliberations at an international conference convened with the backing of the United Nations and under the sponsorship of the International Committee of the Red Cross, with the aim of conforming the Geneva Conventions with the requirements of developing international law and current needs. Towards that end, two protocols were adopted by the conferees on behalf of, but subject to ratification by, their governments— Protocol I and Protocol II. The latter extended to victims and combatants in internal civil or revolutionary conflicts many of the rights previously applicable only to international conflicts. Protocol I presented more difficulties.

On the operational side, Protocol I gave the Pentagon pause by making a whole category of quasi-military targets off-limits for aerial bombardment. I was more familiar with the political objections to Protocol I. These fell into two categories. The first stemmed from the Protocol's definition of "national liberation movement" struggles as "international conflicts." With that definition, outside powers could legitimately provide assistance to "national liberation" insurgent groups, whereas under traditional international law this would have been a violation of the principle of non-intervention in the internal affairs of another country.

The second objection concerned abandonment of the traditional rule that guerrillas are not entitled to be treated as belligerents— internment in prisoner-of-war camps and repatriation at the conclusion of hostilities, rather than jailed and incarcerated as ordinary criminals—unless they meet certain conditions. To qualify, they had to use distinctive insignia—the equivalent of wearing uniforms—and to carry arms openly. This was necessary to distinguish guerrillas from civilians in order to minimize casualties to the latter. If civilians couldn't be distinguished from combatants, they would necessarily be in the line of fire from those responding to shots or bombardment from their vicinity. Taking the lead in pushing for adoption of these revisions of the old standards in the laws of war was the PLO, and a host of other "national liberation movements" that followed in its trail.

When these revisions were first suggested in 1974 and 1975, they were strongly objected to by the U.S. and by other Western delegations. They pointed to the problems raised by the proposed elevation of the status of "national liberation movements." The first was that it was incompatible with the UN Charter's prohibition of intervention in the internal affairs of other states. The second was that "national liberation movements" were being defined in a skewed way. As proposed by the sponsors of the revisions, "national liberation movements" were to be defined as those seeking to overthrow "colonial," "alien," or "racist" regimes. The targets were clearly pro-Western regimes.

Regional organizations were to decide whether the country being liberated was "alien," "colonial" or "racist." Thus regional organizations like the Arab League, or the OAU, the Organization of African Unity, could decide that any group seeking to overthrow the regimes in South Africa or Israel was entitled to outside assistance from Libya,

Syria, the Soviet Union, or any other power that cared to intervene. Similarly, Soviet help to the guerrillas attempting to overthrow El Salvador's government would, under this theory, presumably be considered to be lawful assistance in the national liberation of a "colonial" regime—i.e., one tied to the United States, while U.S. assistance to the guerrillas opposing, for example, the regime in Nicaragua would have no similar justification and therefore would be illegitimate.

If Protocol I's proposed redefinition of international conflict to include certain "national liberation movements" was designed to tilt the law against Western interests in stability and the sovereign equality of all nations, the other proposed provision of Protocol I— blurring the distinction between guerrillas and civilians—was designed to destroy the traditional protection accorded by the law to civilians; protecting civilians was important, but advancing revolution came first.

In 1974, when the Conference first convened, the U.S. delegation opposed the recommended amendments to be incorporated as Protocol I to the First Geneva Convention. In 1974 it had spoken out vociferously against them; and the United States, along with every other Western nation, had voted against their adoption.[2] But in 1977, the United States and every Western country except Israel changed their earlier "No" vote to an abstention, thus facilitating adoption of the '77 Protocols.

Why the U.S. delegation changed its tune is not revealed in the diplomatic record. What seems likely is that the familiar ailment to which U.S. diplomats are exposed when operating in multinational arenas took root; without the support of any bloc, and faced with repeated charges that America's arrogance was impeding international progress, U.S. self-assurance gave way to self-doubt. As for America's Western allies, they were always ready to swim with the tide, and capitulation to the will of the majority was the normal result. Rosenstock surely knew that the White House had not yet made up its mind on whether to ratify the '77 Protocols and that some quarters within the U.S. government were firmly opposed to ratification.

"Look, Allan," said Doug Feith, "were it not for the fact that the State Department Secretariat automatically forwards to the Pentagon copies of incoming cables related to military issues, I would never have seen this cable. I called Mike Matheson (State's Deputy Legal Adviser for Political-Military Affairs) and he told me that he was preparing the cable to instruct the Mission to vote in favor of the resolution. If we vote in favor of it, that's the end of the show. With a declaration at the UN of U.S. intent to support ratification of the '77 Protocols, Congress is not going to be inclined to listen to any of the problems some of us here at the Pentagon may have with specific provisions of the Protocols. It will then be a matter of honoring a national commitment."

I said that I was sure that this was the purpose behind introduction of the resolution—to affect national policy in Washington through commitments made in New York at the United Nations, perhaps without our being fully aware of what they meant. I had seen this process at work at the Security Council level, but never very effectively on the General Assembly Committee level.

"I don't know if you know it, Allan," Feith continued, "but a review is now going on in the Pentagon as to whether the Secretary of Defense should recommend ratification. The President will have to deliver a message to Congress later this year on the Administration's position and I can tell you that the brass here doesn't like Protocol I one bit. If the Mission votes in favor of this resolution at the United Nations, that will settle the issue before the Joint Chiefs of Staff can conclude the review. I don't know if you know the whole history of this, but apparently the Carter White House was anxious to urge the Senate to ratify the Protocols the first day they were open for signature. Carter wanted to show he favored "humanitarian" agreements. When the Joint Chiefs of Staff voiced reservations, he agreed not to recommend ratification until the JCS had completed its review. That's what we're about to conclude now; the text of Protocol I covers more than 150 pages and it takes a long time for the services to analyze all the provisions and make their recommendations. Does Jeane Kirkpatrick know about this?"

I explained that was hardly possible since I myself was not informed, although it was manifest that neither I nor Kirkpatrick would have cleared any cable requesting instructions to vote in a way calling for ratification of the Protocols. Had the issue been presented in context we would never have cleared the cable. After all, this resolution was but a more sophisticated replay of the Abu Eain matter of 1981. I asked Feith to send me a note that the Joint Chiefs of Staff were presently undertaking a review of the '77 Protocols with a view to recommending against U.S. ratification.

Later that afternoon the following unclassified cable arrived on my desk from Fred Ikle, the Under Secretary of Defense:

MEMORANDUM TO ALAN GERSON [sic], ACTING LEGAL
COUNSEL, USUN MISSION

SUBJECT: UNGA Sixth Committee—Item 122—Status of the Protocols Additional to the Geneva Convention of 1949 and
Relating to the Protection of Victims of Armed Conflicts

Reference: USUN New York 02797, 16 Oct 84

DOD has serious misgivings about the 1977 protocols. OSD and
OJCS are both conducting reviews.

Some of our objections are: The discarding of the classical rule of
proportionality through the granting of special protection against attack to certain facilities "even where these objects are military objectives" (Article 56(1)), the prohibition against reprisals in kind against
such facilities (Article 56(4)) (i.e., even if they attack our dams, we
cannot attack theirs), and the prohibition against making use of the
uniforms or insignia of adverse parties.

Equally troubling is the easily inferred political and philosophical intent of the protocols, as reflected in Article 1(4), which highlights "armed conflicts in which peoples are fighting against colonial
domination and alien occupation and against racist regimes in the
exercise of their right of self-determination." The protocols aim to
encourage and give legal sanction not only to radical "national liberation" movements in general, but in particular to their most dubious
tactics. Article 44(3), in a single subordinate clause, sweeps away
hundreds of years of law and morality by "recognizing" that an armed
combatant "cannot" always distinguish himself from non-combatants
and granting him the status of combatant anyway. As the essence of
terroristic criminality is the obliteration of the distinction between
combatants and non-combatants, it would be hard to square ratification of the protocols with our policy of combatting terrorism.

It is by no means certain that we shall find ways of fixing the
gravest problems the protocols would create. Hence, it may ultimately prove impossible for the USG to ratify. For this reason we
cannot support voting "yes" or joining a consensus on any resolution
which, like the subject resolution, encourages ratification.

Fred C. Ikle

I immediately brought Ikle's cable to Kirkpatrick's attention,
and told her the history of the whole matter. "They never give up, do
they?" she said. I wasn't sure if she was referring to the General
Assembly, or something closer to home.

"Unless you have any objections," I said, "I'm going to instruct Rosenstock, on the basis of the Ikle letter, to vote 'No' on this matter when it comes up later this week at the Sixth Committee on the ground that the matter is still under review by the U.S. government, and that each country should feel free to make up its mind without the urging of the UN as a whole. I'll also send a cable to State informing them of our decision."

"Neat work." she said. "I surely don't have any objection."

"Oh, there's one other matter, Jeane," I said, referring to the fact that the person responsible for sending the cable should have known that in asking State to instruct the Mission to vote for the '77 Protocols, the request was for something neither of us would have authorized.

"Look, Allan, it's no good firing people. It's too messy, especially if you're dealing with people who have been around the system for a long time. Just stay on top of things."

A few days later Fred Ikle received a letter from Davis Robinson, State's Legal Adviser, taking issue with the conclusions reached in Ikle's memorandum. Ikle responded by informing him that opposition by the Joint Chiefs of Staff to ratification of the Protocols was a virtual certainty. At the United Nations the Sixth Committee resolution did not gain the U.S. "Yes" vote the sponsors of the resolution were looking for.[3] And within the United States Government the matter continued to simmer inconclusively through interagency reviews, re-reviews, and NSC appraisals.

Finally, on February 15, 1987, President Reagan took the unusual step of recommending that the Senate not ratify the Protocols, although initially entered into and approved by envoys of the United States. "We must not and need not," he said, "give recognition and protection to terrorist groups as a price for progress in humanitarian law."[4]

This result would have been unlikely had U.S. support for the General Assembly resolution favoring the 1977 Protocols not been blocked. A U.S. vote at the UN in favor of the ratification resolution would, at the least, have complicated President Reagan's position of avoiding ratification of the Protocols. At the United Nations those forces that had two years earlier pushed for adoption of the Abu Eain resolution were continuing to push their agenda. Their means had become more sophisticated. In the U.S. government those who had advocated "the high road"—more often than not a euphemism for acquiescence, we later learned—had not given up their supportive role.

President Reagan's unusual advice to the Senate to not ratify a convention negotiated by American diplomats received enthusiastic support—some, from unexpected quarters. In a lead editorial the *New York Times* described the 1977 Protocols as "a pro-terrorist document."[5] And yet, the Reagan Administration had been only a hair's breadth away from endorsing ratification of that convention, and from thus permitting terrorist organizations to shape America's view of the requirements of international law as it pertained to their legal status and the legitimacy or illegitimacy of the way they conducted their business.

16

The Last Illusion
The International Court of Justice

The Court's decision ranks in folly with that of the Supreme
Court of the United States in the *Dred Scott* decision as an act
of hubris and abuse of power.

> Eugene V. Rostow commenting on the International Court of
> Justice's decision in the Nicaragua case.

The International Court of Justice had become, over time, the
chief deity in the system revered as international law. That its
caseload on important issues of war and peace, aggression and self-
defense, was practically nil seemed not to matter. That the struc-
tures around it might be crumbling, that the UN General Assembly
had become petty and venal, that the UN Security Council had
strayed far from its appointed purpose as guardian of international
peace and security, hardly diminished the esteem in which the International Court was held. It stood—or so its supporters thought—
above world politics, above the stresses and strains of bloc voting
and ideological warfare that had infected the rest of the UN
system.[1]

To labor daily in the UN system was to know otherwise. To
witness General Assembly elections for selection of World Court
judges was to see the pervasive role of politics—bloc politics—in

255

everything the United Nations did. At the State Department, removed from the center of action, illusions would be held onto tena-
ciously. It was as if in letting go of one's idealized notions of the
International Court of Justice, seeing it instead as an institution not
removed from the environment in which it operated, one ran the risk
of letting go as well of the dream of peace through international
organizations on which so many had been reared.

Appropriately enough, the modern idea of a world court to resolve international differences by a system of universal justice first
took hold largely among American lawyers. In 1895, U.S. Supreme
Court Justice David Brewer called upon the members of the American Bar Association to join him in working for a new era where:

> the lawyer will work out the final peace, and bring in the glad day
> when the spear shall be turned into a plowshare and the sword into a
> pruning hook, and nations learn war no more. . . . International courts
> will soon be a part of the common life of the world . . . whose judg-
> ments shall determine all controversies between nations and by such
> determinations bid the world's farewell to the soldier.[2]

In his inaugural address of 1897, President William McKinley,
interpreting American history liberally, declared that the "leading
feature of American foreign policy throughout our entire national
history" has been the insistence on "the adjustment of difficulties by
judicial methods rather than by force of arms."[3]

In 1921, that vision came to partial fruition with the establishment of the Permanent Court of International Justice in The Hague,
a semi-independent institution, parallel to but not an organ of the
League of Nations. But, despite various attempts by Presidents Har-
ding and Coolidge to have the Senate approve U.S. acceptance of the
Permanent Court's jurisdiction, the Senate remained hostile to the
idea. President Franklin D. Roosevelt made another attempt at Senate approval, arguing that "For years Republican and Democratic
administrations and party platforms alike have advocated a court of
justice to which nations might voluntarily bring their disputes for
judicial decisions."[4] But again the U.S. Senate failed to provide the
two-thirds majority necessary for U.S. acceptance of the Court's jurisdiction.

From the start, therefore, the Permanent Court of International
Justice's viability was jeopardized by the nonparticipation of the coun-
try that had played the leading part in its establishment—the United
States. Two strains of American thought fought each other: the ide-

alist versus the hardboiled legislator who felt that subordinating American supremacy to a world judiciary would never sit well with his constituency. With the United States on the outside, few nations were willing to make the leap and subject themselves to the World Court's jurisdication. So many reservations to the Court's jurisdiction were attached by those ostensibly accepting it that acceptance became an exercise in cosmetics, and the effect was to pare the Court's actual powers down to a bare minimum.

Apart from one case—the Austro-German Customs Union case,[5] on whether a customs union could be considered to conflict with certain security provisions (the Versailles Treaty relating to the "Anschluss" between Germany and Austria)—the Permanent Court never adjudicated any "sensitive" case concerning the national security interests of states, let alone cases involving larger questions of aggression and the unlawful use of force. When the League of Nations system collapsed in the late 1930s, the Permanent Court of International Justice closed its doors as well.

Yet the idea of an effective international court continued to excite the American imagination. World War II, far from diminishing that hope, spurred it to greater heights. In the summer of 1943, when Allied victory was still far from assured, a committee within the State Department, at the request of Secretary of State Edward Stettinius, began to work on a draft constitution for a new world court. It was part of the larger plan for a new United Nations system at the conclusion of the war. The committee concluded that the new court would have to have compulsory jurisdiction; that is, member states would be obliged to submit their disputes to the court and be bound by its judgments. Otherwise, warned the committee, if member states were free to use the court or ignore it, the envisioned UN system would be unable to achieve its prime objective: to bring the rule of law to bear on an unruly world.

A few days after taking the oath of office, President Harry Truman announced that the United States would participate in the Conference on International Organization in San Francisco on April 25, 1945 to establish the new United Nations system. From that moment, Truman became personally committed to pushing for a new world court with meaningful powers.

> I disapproved the recommendation that we should insist on voluntary jurisdiction for the World Court. I felt that if we were going to have a court it ought to be a court that would work with compulsory jurisdiction. Consequently, [Secretary of State] Stettinius was instructed to

strive for a formula that would make possible, at least eventually, compulsory jurisdiction of the International Court of Justice.[6]

At San Francisco, the majority favored granting the Court compulsory jurisdiction. Nevertheless, the United States and the Soviet Union, each for their own reasons, joined in opposing the idea. The American representative, mindful of U.S. Congressional opposition to the idea of making the United States subservient to an international body (despite President Truman's personal endorsement), warned the Conference that the U.S. Senate would never ratify a charter that included compulsory jurisdiction. The Soviet representative stated that compulsory jurisdiction was "absolutely unacceptable" to his government.[7] Together, the Soviet and American delegates prevailed in making the Court's jurisdiction voluntary. Every state could thus determine for itself whether or not it wanted to be subject to the Court's jurisdiction, and in what instances.

The issue of U.S. acceptance of the jurisdiction of the newly established International Court of Justice reached the U.S. Senate in the summer of 1946. Senator Tom Connally of Texas, then Chairman of the Senate Foreign Relations Committee, introduced a resolution providing that U.S. acceptance of the Court's jurisdiction would exclude "disputes with regard to matters which are essentially within the domestic jurisdiction of the United States, *as determined by the United States*" [emphasis added]. In addressing the Senate, he stated:

> I am in favor of the International Court of Justice. I am in favor of the United Nations, but I am also for the United States of America. I do not want to surrender the sovereignty or the prestige of the United States with regard to any question which may be merely domestic in character, and contained within the boundaries of this Republic. Our ancestors fought with fortitude and with sacrifice in order to establish our Government. We must preserve it because the best hope of the world lies in the survival of the United States with its concepts of democracy, liberty, freedom, and advancement under its institutions.[8]

Senator Arthur Vandenberg introduced another significant reservation. U.S. acceptance of the Court's jurisdiction regarding disputes arising under a treaty would be limited to controversies where all parties to the treaty had also agreed to be bound by the court's decision in that dispute. On August 2, 1946, the U.S. Senate voluntarily accepted the compulsory jurisdiction of the International Court, with the reservations introduced by Senators Connally and Vandenberg.

Beyond these concerns was another fear, having to do with the nature of the law the Court would be called upon to apply. Secretary of State John Foster Dulles, a latter-day critic of U.S. acquiescence to the Court's jurisdiction, put it this way:

> Courts are designed to apply law, not make it, and international law has not yet developed the scope and definiteness necessary to permit international disputes generally to be resolved by judicial rather than political tests.[9]

John Foster Dulles argued that the United States should not subject itself to international law as determined by judges from 15 different countries sitting at The Hague. He warned that even if they were inclined to be fair and objective, the fact remained that international law was "so uncertain that resort must be had to alleged custom and teachings . . . in which case the court can scarcely avoid indulging in a large amount of judicial legislation or political expediency."[10]

Two decades later Dulles' premonitions about the Court were revived as Nicaragua filed its complaint seeking to end U.S. support for the Contras by a judicial declaration that it was in violation of international law. For damages already sustained through U.S. actions, Nicaragua sought reparations of over 12 billion dollars.

Until the Nicaragua case, the ICJ had never dealt with a political crisis in which there was an ongoing use of force. The Court's Corfu Channel case of 1949—involving the laying of mines by Albania in the waters of the Corfu Channel, which resulted in injury to a British vessel—is the closest example of such an adjudication. But in that case hostilities had ceased by the time the matter reached the Court. Since 1949, the Soviet Union and Eastern bloc countries had rejected the jurisdiction of the Court six times. No crisis involving hostilities or guerrilla war—not Korea, Vietnam, the Middle East, Angola, or Afghanistan, to name but a few trouble-spots—ever reached the ICJ.

In another major area of political conflict, decolonization, the Court also had been ineffective. Despite the flurry of activity in this area since 1945, the Court had heard only three cases regarding decolonization.[11] In none did the Court contribute to the settlement of the dispute: one case was settled independently, another was dismissed by the Court, and, in the final case, the Court decided that it could not adjudicate the issue.

By 1984, almost 80 percent of the UN's members had either rejected the Court's jurisdiction or accepted it with severe reservations. Only a handful of states had accepted its jurisdiction without qualification. Of the five permanent members of the Security Council, only the United Kingdom and the United States had subjected themselves to the Court's mandatory jurisdiction; but Britain's acceptance was replete with qualifications including its right to terminate its acceptance at any time without prior notice.[12] As a result of the optional nature of its jurisdiction, the Court became like other organs of the UN—the creature of a double standard; states like the Soviet Union, which had not accepted its jurisdiction, could not be held legally accountable for their actions, while countries such as the United States, which had accepted its jurisdiction, had to defend their actions before it.

At the U.S. Mission to the United Nations the question of the International Court's jurisdiction lost its academic innocence on April 6, 1984. That afternoon a junior attorney from the State Department's Legal Adviser's Office had ascended the elevator to the 38th floor of the UN Secretariat building to deliver the following note to the UN Secretary General:

Excellency:

I have the honor on behalf of the Government of the United States of America to refer to the Declaration of my Government of August 26, 1946, concerning the acceptance by the United States of America of the compulsory jurisdiction of the International Court of Justice, and to state that the aforesaid Declaration shall not apply to disputes with any Central American state or arising out of or related to events in Central America, any of which disputes shall be settled in such manner as the parties to them may agree.

Notwithstanding the terms of the aforesaid Declaration, this proviso shall take effect immediately and shall remain in force for two years, so as to foster the continuing regional dispute settlement process which seeks a negotiated solution to the interrelated political, economic and security problems of Central America.

[signed] George P. Shultz
Secretary of State of the United States of America

The U.S. Mission had not been given advance warning of the State Department's decision. Indeed, neither had Davis Robinson, the Legal Adviser, who was in the Hague at the International Court of Justice dealing with the Maine-Canada boundary dispute. The decision had been left to others higher up in the State Department hierarchy. Like Davis Robinson, Jeane Kirkpatrick was abroad at the time the decision was made. She too had not been informed of the notification making its way that day from the Secretary of State to the UN Secretary General.

Perhaps it was only the pressure of events that led to the way in which the matter was handled. The State Department had come upon information that Nicaragua, acting on the advice of its lawyers—Abram Chayes, the former State Department legal adviser during the 1962 Cuban missile crisis and now Felix Frankfurter Professor of Law at Harvard, and Paul Reichler of the Washington, D.C. bar—was planning to file suit against the United States. The suit, to be filed in the International Court of Justice in three days' time, would seek to enjoin and declare illegal any further U.S. aid to the anti-Sandinista forces.

The last thing that anyone concerned with the implementation of U.S. policy in Central America welcomed was the prospect of an ICJ ruling on the propriety of U.S. assistance to the Contras. Anticipating that Nicaragua was about to file its complaint, the State Department decided to pull the rug from under that nation's feet by withdrawing the U.S. acceptance of the Court's compulsory jurisdiction; Nicaragua's complaint would thus be without effect as the United States, no longer a party to the Court's compulsory jurisdiction, could not be subject to suit.

The following day, Kirkpatrick returned to New York. Livid on hearing the news, she asked that I draft a short but pointed note from her to Secretary Shultz reminding him that the International Court of Justice is part and parcel of the UN system, that her job is to preside over relations within that system, and that it was, accordingly, inexplicable how a decision of this magnitude affecting the UN system could have been made without anyone having bothered to have first informed her.

That day, as news of the U.S. decision broke, Nicaragua charged that the U.S. move was invalid, and could not therefore affect the Court's jurisdiction to adjudicate its complaint. It pointed to the fact that in accepting the ICJ's jurisdiction in 1946 the United States had stipulated that it would give six months' notice prior to any subsequent action to terminate its acceptance of the Court's jurisdiction. Here the United States gave three days notice.

Editorial writers in major U.S. newspapers picked up on the same theme. The Reagan Administration was charged with "disre-

spect" and "contempt" for the rule of law, of acting like shyster lawyers pretending to respect the law but ready to jerk back their
acceptance of a court's jurisdiction the moment it really mattered.

In Washington, the American Society of International Law,
which was then holding its annual convention, joined in the chorus.
The American Society of International Law viewed itself as *the* guardian of the U.S. commitment to "the rule of law" in international
affairs. The Society prided itself on the fact that its birth had coincided with the conclusion of the first major convention regulating the
conduct of war, the 1907 Hague Regulations on Land Warfare. Ever
since, it had been in the forefront of those groups promoting respect
for international law and the development of its institutions, particularly the Permanent Court of Justice at The Hague and its progenitor, the International Court of Justice. The Reagan Administration's
action was thus seen as a slap at its guardianship and a challenge to its
leadership. The Society responded by doing something it had never
done before: by convening a special session to pass a resolution condemning the U.S. Government's decision. As a scholarly society it
had in the past refrained from taking partisan stands or seeking consensus on political issues.

On hearing of the impending move—I was at the time attending
the Society's annual meeting—I appealed to its president to delay the
vote scheduled for Friday afternoon. The Society had had an opportunity to hear Jeane Kirkpatrick at a luncheon on Thursday. Yet
Michael Kozak, the State Department's Deputy Legal Adviser, would
not have a chance to explain the legal basis of the U.S. action until a
specially convened panel on Sunday morning—after the impending
vote.

Professor Covey Oliver, the Society's president, politely but
firmly let me know that its members were in no mood for a delay of
their scheduled vote. That Friday afternoon, acting with near unanimity, the American Society of International Law adopted a resolution condemning the Administration's action as inconsistent with the
U.S. commitment to the rule of law in international affairs.

The next morning I spoke by phone with Mike Kozak. He expressed regret at the Society's vote, seeing it as not only unfortu-
nate but misguided insofar as it was based on the assumption that
the Administration had decided to have nothing more to do with
the World Court's compulsory jurisdiction, that the United States
would now allow itself to be sued in that forum only if it so vol-
unteered, and that Nicaragua would, accordingly, never get to have

its day in court. I told Kozak that I shared that assumption. I too had assumed that that was the Administration's intent. But I was mistaken. For Kozak explained that at the next morning's panel discussion he would say that the Reagan Administration had made no such decision. It had only decided to "modify" the U.S. acceptance of the Court's jurisdiction. It would be left to the International Court of Justice to determine whether that modification comported with America's legal obligations. Thus, in fact, the Reagan Administration had done no more than posit a "claim"; nothing had been done by unilateral fiat. Everything was left open for the Court to decide.

I was shocked. If the State Department was merely making a "claim," that was certainly not what it had signalled. Or, had it decided to change signals after catching so much flak for its decision? I received no clear answer, only that this was State Department policy and that it had been cleared with Ken Dam.

I called Kirkpatrick at her Bethesda home. She was outraged. "Don't they understand," she asked, "that to allow the International Court of Justice to rule now on whether U.S. revocation of jurisdiction was proper is just crazy? How do they expect to prevail? They understand nothing about the politics of the Court." And, she asked, assuming that we lost, what then? "Is the U.S. Government prepared to then allow the International Court of Justice to tell it whether the use of force in Nicaragua is or is not in the U.S. national interest? I thought that the whole purpose of the exercise was to keep that question away from the Court."

I had assumed likewise. So had the critics who had condemned the Reagan Adminstration's "contempt" for international law. The common understanding was that the U.S. announcement was intended to end the matter of Nicaragua's suit, and that the United States would take no part in any Court proceedings on that complaint. It was not, it seemed, much different from the way France responded when Australia and New Zealand went to the International Court in the 1974 *Nuclear Test Cases* to challenge France's right to engage in nuclear testing in the South Pacific.[13] France promptly invoked national defense considerations to justify its refusal to participate in those proceedings, then withdrew its acceptance of the Court's jurisdiction and refused to appear for any further argument on the matter. By contrast, the State Department now seemed prepared to have the United States go to the International Court of Justice to contest the jurisdictional question out of "respect for the rule of law."

"This makes no sense whatsoever," Kirkpatrick continued, "We can't win. There's no use trying to persuade the International Court of Justice with logic, and law, to rule in our favor. The International Court is elected by the General Assembly. We have already been condemned in the newspapers, in public opinion, in the media, and now apparently, you tell me, in the American Society of International Law, for withdrawing from the Court. And now we want to say we haven't done that at all, that we've merely posed the question as to whether we are permitted to do so, and are prepared to go to the Court and have them second-guess us. This is only going to make matters worse. I have got to reach Shultz and Dam right away."

She reached Ken Dam and later George Shultz, who apologized for the oversight in not having informed her of the timing of the letter to Secretary General Perez de Cuellar. Both men tried to persuade her that she was overwrought; that the decision to appear before the Court to argue the legality of the U.S. withdrawal of jurisdiction was based on the fact that the United States had a solid legal case to make. She tried to explain that no mere technicality was at issue, that the merits of Nicaragua's claim about the illegality of U.S. actions in Central America would inevitably be the focus of attention, and that she knew as much as, if not more than, anyone else about the likely outcome of the International Court's deliberations: they were not going to rule in favor of the United States. She made little headway. The decision, she was told, had already been made. Ken Dam, whose background was in the commercial or non-"public" side of international law and who had very limited experience with the United Nations, had apparently persuaded Shultz that the United States had to argue the matter before the International Court, and could win.

Some time later a meeting convened in the White House Special Situations Room to discuss the best means of handling Nicaragua's complaint. The National Security Council Adviser, Admiral John Poindexter, presided. Ken Dam and Davis Robinson were the first to speak. They began by pointing out that they had already reserved a date on the International Court's calendar to argue the legality of the U.S. action in withdrawing from the Court's jurisdiction. "We have assembled," Robinson said, "an absolutely first-class team." He was right. He had recruited some of the ablest and best-known American professors of international law—Louis Sohn of Harvard and Georgia, Myres McDougal of Yale, Stefan Reisenfeld of Berkeley, Fred Morrison of Minnesota, and John Norton Moore of Virginia. But their

individual and collective talent was not what would make the difference.

When called upon to comment I said that I believed there was
no reasonable chance of obtaining a favorable verdict, of having the
Syrian judge or the Algerian judge or the Polish judge, distinguished
jurist though he was, or the Africans on the bench, rule in our favor.
What, I asked, would we do were we to lose on the question of the
Court's jurisdiction? If we picked up our marbles and ran at that
point, it would be worse; we would be seen as having tried to have it
both ways—to go to the Court and seek its blessings, but ready to flee
if they were withheld. And if, instead, we proceeded to argue the
case on the merits, we would then be doing precisely what we tried
to avoid in the first place. Only this time we would have succeeded in
focusing world attention on the happenings in The Hague. Or do you,
I said, directing my question to Dam and Robinson, believe it likely
that we might get a favorable verdict from the Court on the merits
after they have ruled against us on the jurisdictional issue?

Robinson stressed that the U.S. legal arguments were airtight,
that we had the best team to advocate our cause—something I never
questioned—and that we could expect to prevail. He was ready for a
hard fair fight, and excited by the prospect of devoting himself to it.
Exuding confidence, he proceeded to outline the proposed basis of
the U.S. defense. First, the U.S. stipulation to six months' notice
prior to withdrawal of acceptance of the Court's jurisdiction would be
argued to apply only to U.S. "termination" of any ICJ jurisdiction. He
would, accordingly, point out that in its note of April 6, 1984, to the
UN Secretary General, the United States stated that it "did not terminate or purport to terminate the 1946 declaration," but rather
sought only to "modify" it. Thus, the six-months' notice "withdrawal"
provision would be deemed irrelevant as the United States only
"modified" its acceptance of the Court's jurisdiction.

Secondly, he would argue that Nicaragua never accepted the
Court's jurisdiction as its filing with the clerk of the Permanent Court
of Justice in the 1920s was procedurally faulty. It hadn't been filed with
the proper clerk, and the appropriate notations hadn't been made. In
any event, even if Nicaragua had properly accepted the Court's jurisdiction, Nicaragua had not bound itself to a six-months' notice provision similar to the one contained in the American declaration, and, on
the basis of the principle of reciprocity, was now precluded from arguing that the United States was bound to provide such notice.

Assuming the Court rejected these arguments, Robinson and his team would then proceed to a secondary line of defense: that the resolution of the Central American dispute was within the purview of the political organs of the United Nations, particularly the UN Security Council, and its regional organization, the Organization of American States; not the International Court of Justice. He would point out that the Court was not equipped to address such disputes because it lacked the wherewithal to collect the facts in a context of ongoing armed struggle, and, besides, it had no experience in such matters.

All reasonable arguments, it seemed, but not ones that Nicaragua would have difficulty countering with logic and precedent of its own. Nicaragua's lawyers would surely decry as a distinction without a difference the U.S. attempt to portray its yanking back of the Court's jurisdiction as a "modification" but not a "withdrawal." To the assertion of reciprocity, Nicaragua's lawyers would argue that the law permits the termination or modification of a treaty only in accordance with its terms, and that there need be nothing symmetrical about it; that the fact that Nicaragua had not voluntarily imposed upon itself a six-months' notice requirement was beside the point. To the argument that the ICJ lacked jurisdiction because the Security Council or the OAS was the proper forum for Nicaragua's complaint, Nicaragua could argue that the jurisdictions of the Security Council and the OAS encompassed political decisions and that it was asking for a legal resolution of the matter. Finally, as for the charge that the ICJ lacked competence in fact-finding, it seemed Nicaragua would have little trouble in persuading the Court that it had both the competence and authority to proceed in this area. No institution likes to have the breadth of its powers curbed, and the International Court was no exception.

My skepticism about our chances of success came up against a wall of optimism. I suggested, therefore, that if we were committed to going to The Hague we should at least lay a foundation for minimizing the damage in case of defeat; that we begin now to make the press and the public aware of the political nature of the International Court, and point out that its members are elected by majorities of the General Assembly and Security Council. That idea was rejected; there was to be no attack on "the integrity" of the International Court. The question of how we would proceed if we lost the jurisdictional argument was deferred to another day. The meeting was adjourned. Faith in the capacity of marshalled facts and reasoned arguments to carry the day pushed aside considerations of politics and prejudice.

With the question of whether to go to the Court on the jurisdictional issue having been decided, I reconciled myself to working with the team preparing the U.S. defense. I also assumed that sniping against the Administration by editorial writers, columnists, and various Congressmen on the charge of having "abandoned" the "rule of law" in walking away from the International Court would subside as they realized that the United States had not, in fact, taken any dispositive action. What, after all, could be more lawful and American than making a claim and presenting it to a court for adjudication? Lawyers in every court in every state of the Union did this every day of the week. I was, therefore, doubly surprised when a new attack came from a totally unexpected quarter—Senator Daniel Patrick Moynihan; worse, it was directed at me personally.

Delivering the commencement address to the graduating class at Syracuse University in May 1984, Senator Moynihan lashed out against the Administration for its response to the complaint Nicaragua filed before the International Court. This, he said, was an example of the new type of thinking taking root in the Administration, one disrespectful of established procedures and contemptuous of the rule of law in international affairs. He singled me out for criticism. Referring to an opinion piece, "U.S. Acts Lawfully," which I had published in the *New York Times* earlier that month,[14] Senator Moynihan accused me of "ignorance" not merely of the law, but of the "history of our country."

That was quite a charge. I had written that the notion that "we can bring the rule of law to bear on an unruly world if we but set an example by unilateral compliance" was "pious nonsense." I said that Nicaragua's contention rested on the concept "that because the level of Nicaragua's aid and assistance to the Salvadoran guerrillas is not quantitatively significant, El Salvador's right to defend itself is accordingly diminished." On this theory, since only 'modest' amounts of arms shipments and training occur, only 'modest' violations of El Salvador's borders result. And because any strong response by El Salvador to these violations might engender a larger war in the region, El Salvador must therefore tolerate violations of its territorial rights. This "turn the cheek" philosophy was, I concluded, nonsensical and without "any acceptance in international law."[15]

Apparently my observations did not sit well with Senator Moynihan. A few days later, on May 28, his remarks at Syracuse were quoted, with emphatic endorsement, by *New York Times* columnist Anthony Lewis.[16] As journalists do not usually make a practice of scouring commencement addresses for their material, it seemed that either Senator Moynihan or someone on his staff had forwarded his address for Anthony Lewis' use.

Why, I wondered, did my comments evoke such a hostile reaction from Senator Moynihan? He had also chosen to publish a letter to the editor in the *New York Times* attacking the position I had espoused in my earlier opinion piece as "baffling." "Clearly," he asserted, "the World Court is empowered to adjudicate such cases."[17] I responded by a letter to the editor stating that it seemed peculiar that the Senator from New York saw fit to prejudge the merits of the U.S. claim before his own government had an opportunity to present its reasons in court.[18]

No doubt Senator Moynihan was mirroring the feelings of many Americans who felt that America's commitment to international law and international organizations had been undermined by the Administration's decision to distance itself from the International Court. His remarks reflected the conviction that whether other nations did or did not adhere to the jurisdiction of the World Court was irrelevant to the U.S. commitment. Indeed, whether the Court might be capable of objective judgment seemed beside the point. What mattered, he seemed to be saying, was that the United States set a good example. In time other nations would follow suit, allow the International Court to adjudicate their disputes, and eventually the Court would have to live up to the high standards expected of it.

Here was Senator Patrick Moynihan, who as UN ambassador at the time of passage of the 1975 Zionism equals racism resolution, put his arms around the Israeli ambassador, Chaim Herzog, pointed to the others assembled in the chamber and by his own account, said, "Fuck 'em!"[19] But the International Court of Justice seemed somehow radically different. Moynihan felt compelled to rise to its defense, unable to accept the idea that the International Court of Justice might have become politicized like the UN General Assembly and the UN Security Council.

But Moynihan during his short tenure at the United Nations had not witnessed election of World Court judges by the UN General Assembly. He had not seen, as we had, how Egypt's erudite UN representative, Dr. Esmet Abdel Meguid—nearly universally acknowledged as the ideal candidate for a judgeship on the International Court—had been passed up in favor of the Non-Aligned Movement candidate, Algeria's Mohammed Bedjaoui. Abdel Meguid had been considered "too moderate" by the General Assembly, while Bedjaoui, who was so much less accomplished, had the advantage of tending to go along with the radical political rhetoric of the UN majority.

True, Bedjaoui's election was not itself indicative of an anti-American bias by the Court. He was only one of 15 judges. There were a number of Western judges on the bench who could hardly be accused of being the products of Third-World political machinations against the United States. But it wasn't a matter of individuals being ideologues. It was that on a political issue splitting East from West, the World Court as an institution would reflect the dominant politics in the General Assembly. Those politics—seen in the most charitable light—favored Nicaragua; the case would be viewed as that of a small, beleaguered nation fighting for freedom from American hegemony.

The first blow to U.S. hopes for a favorable judgment from the Court came on October 4 when the Court's President, Judge T.O. Elias, ruled that El Salvador would not be permitted to intervene in the case as an interested party to present its side of the story.[20] To American lawyers committed to the idea of due process this came as the first major blow to their faith in the International Court as capable of objective judgment, untainted by the politics at issue. True, El Salvador—which claimed to be the true victim in the Central American crisis—was accorded an opportunity to intervene later to show Nicaragua's support for subversion of El Salvador's government and explain its call upon the United States to assist in self-defense. But that intervention could come only at the merits phase, after the United States had lost the jurisdictional arguments. By then the damage would already be done.

It wasn't that El Salvador's intervention would result in arguments that the U.S. team could not present. The contention would be the same: that El Salvador, like other Central American states, was the victim of attacks supplied, directed, and aided by command and control facilities in Nicaragua. But had El Salvador been permitted to be present in the Court to make the argument, the case would have taken on another dimension: not as the strong against the meek, but as one Third-World state against another, each backed by its own superpower sponsor.

Davis Robinson was shaken by the Court's interim decision. Yet, he remained confident that the United States would prevail. Preparation of the case began to consume nearly all of his time. The pile of materials on his desk related to the case—documents of filings in the 1920s with the Court's clerks, learned commentary on the procedures of the Court—continued to grow higher, becoming as it did a stack of chips on which would ride America's chances of success against Nicaragua's complaint, and Robinson's standing within the State Department.

His chance came in September 1984. As the chief U.S. advocate, Robinson opened the U.S. defense. It was—not by Robinson's choice—to be an exceedingly narrow one. Within the circles of government, he had argued for a defense which would take note of political context. It would have portrayed the dispute as part of a contest between the United States and the Soviet Union, with the U.S. aim being the curbing of subversion in Central America by the Soviet's surrogate, Nicaragua. Robinson was, however, overruled. Nicaragua's pursuit of "revolution without frontiers" could be mentioned; the fact that it was the Soviets' supply of offensive weapons to Nicaragua which made that ambition achievable could not.

Nor was he permitted to dwell on the fact that without the Soviet Union being made a party to these proceedings an inherently unfair situation had been created. Information from U.S. files—those of the Pentagon, the White House, and presumably even those of the CIA dealing with U.S. support for the Contras—might be subpoenaed. By contrast, Soviet files dealing with support for Nicaragua were immune from examination. Those higher up than Robinson in the State Department and White House hierarchy had decided that the proceedings at The Hague were not to be turned into an arena for U.S.–Soviet confrontation. The faint stirrings of rapprochement and the glint of a thaw in U.S.–Soviet tensions were not to be disturbed by confrontation at The Hague.

On November 26, 1984, in an 11–5 decision (the 16-judge ruling came about as the result of a rule that a party has a right to nominate an additional judge to hear a dispute when its adversary has a national of its own sitting on the bench), the International Court of Justice ruled against the United States' contention that the Court had jurisdictional basis to hear Nicaragua's complaint. Several of the judges filed dissenting and separate opinions to complain that the Court's majority decision reflected sloppy and hasty reasoning.[21] At the State Department there was widespread disappointment. Even stalwart supporters of the Court perceived politics and prejudice in the decision.

The Court's ruling left the United States pondering what to do next. It now seemed clear that were the United States to proceed to argue the merits of the case, the overwhelming probability was that it would lose. It would likely face a judgment requiring it to cease all military and paramilitary activity in the area, and to honor Nicaragua's demand for billions of dollars in reparations. Were the United States to refuse to comply with the judgment, it would face international opprobrium as a lawless nation. Or, alternatively, the United States could choose to walk away from the Court entirely, and ignore its ruling on jurisdiction.

It took until January 18, 1985, for the State Department to make up its mind.[22] It would, it announced, walk away: "neither the rule of law nor the search for peace in Central America" would be served by further U.S. participation, said the State Department spokesman. Furthermore, he claimed that the objectives of the International Court were being subverted by the efforts of Nicaragua and its Cuban and Soviet sponsors to use the Court as a political weapon. If the Court wanted to be party to this and hear Nicaragua's complaint, that was its business, but the United States would have nothing more to do with the proceedings.

There could, however, be no walking away from the damage done. The Court's ruling, like the filing of Nicaragua's complaint, had its impact on Congress. Withdrawal of U.S. funding for military assistance to the Contras would soon follow in its wake. In its capacity to award or withhold legitimacy, the Court, like the United Nations, exercised its greatest power. For Congressmen and Senators wavering in their support for the Contras, the Court ruling, although it involved only the question of jurisdiction, was all that was needed to push them to oppose the Administration's request for funding for the Contras.

On October 7, 1985 the White House announced that the United States would no longer subscribe to the compulsory jurisdiction of the International Court.[23] It would agree to the jurisdiction of the Court under bilateral and multilateral treaties where the United States had specifically agreed to submit certain categories of disputes to the Court for resolution. In short, the United States could no longer be sued against its will, and never on an issue affecting its vital national security interests such as that presented by Nicaragua's complaint. The long love affair between the United States and the Court came to an end.

Several months later, on January 18, 1986, the State Department's bitter disappointment with the Court's decision was revealed on release of a harshly critical report, "Observations on the International Court of Justice's Judgment on Jurisdiction and Admissibility in

the Case of *Nicaragua v. United States of America*." Among its conclusions were the following:

> Each of the Court's holdings ignores or seriously misstates the evi-
> dence and law relevant to the issues before the Court. In brief, the
> Court:
>
> • Misconstrues the plain language of its own Statute.
> • Overrules its own prior holdings on at least two dispositive issues—
>   the meaning of the provision in the Court's Statute carrying over
>   acceptances of the compulsory jurisdiction of the Permanent Court of
>   International Justice to the present Court, and the necessity that a
>   State comply with the legal requirements set forth in the Statute in
>   order to accept the Court's compulsory jurisdiction.
> • Ignores the terms and unequivocal legal implications of Nicaragua's
>   own pleadings on two other issues—whether Nicaragua's claims
>   present a dispute involving an ongoing conflict, and whether the
>   Central American States other than Nicaragua will be affected by any
>   decision in the case.
> • Renders meaningless a reservation to the United States 1946 decla-
>   ration excluding certain multilateral disputes from the United States
>   acceptance of the Court's compulsory jurisdiction by deciding that
>   the meaning and applicability of the reservation can be determined
>   only after the case has been adjudicated on the merits.
> • Ignores the overwhelming weight of evidence and legal authority on
>   several key issues, although that evidence and authority were briefed
>   by the parties in extensive detail.

The Court proceeded to hear Nicaragua's case without U.S.
participation. On June 27, 1986, it delivered its ruling on the merits
of the complaint. The United States was found guilty of having violated international law in providing assistance to the Contras. By
contrast, Nicaragua's assistance to the rebels in El Salvador was determined not to be legally culpable because a quantitatively inferior
level of supplies was involved. El Salvador's recourse, the Court
ruled, was to go to the UN Security Council (where the deck was
stacked against it); it could not lawfully ask for U.S. help in resisting
Nicaraguan subversion.[24]

For international law scholars like Eugene V. Rostow the Court's
decision was a source of great anguish. A supporter of the Court, he
had long advocated reciprocal respect for its rulings and for its expanded jurisdiction as an essential component of world order. But to
him the Court's ruling in the Nicaragua case was a "tragic document."

Any hope he might still have harbored that the United States was capable of getting a fair hearing from it on issues of national security was eliminated. As for the lingering doubts that others might entertain about the wisdom of the U.S. withdrawal from the Court's jurisdiction, he deemed these "wistful deference to myth."[25] "The Court's decision," Rostow reluctantly concluded, "ranks in folly with that of the Supreme Court of the United States in the *Dred Scott* v. *Sandford* decision as an act of hubris and abuse of power."[26]

Explaining his disappointment, Rostow said that he found the Court's judgment incompatible with fidelity to law:

> The Court asserts that the shipment of arms to groups carrying on the insurrection against the government of a state is not in itself an armed attack against the state. This is hardly the view taken in volume after volume on the laws of neutrality, or by the leading case in the development of the customary international law on this branch of the subject. . . . Nor is it the view which governs the pattern of state practice today.[27]

Then turning his attention to those who would still support the Court despite its ruling, Rostow wrote:

> Some who view the Court's Nicaragua decision as a political rather than juridical event, may rejoice in the outcome on the grounds that as a practical matter the United States is the only possible victim of the doctrine the case proclaims. It is well that those of this persuasion recall that fashions change, and that the role of law in the social process is necessarily reserved for all seasons. . . . the precedent of the Court's judgment in the Nicaragua case can be read to excuse the shipments of arms and other forms of aid to opposition parties in the Communist states of Eastern Europe, and the Central Asian states of the Soviet Union, Cuba and other conquered provinces of the Soviet Union. . . .[28]

But in one respect Eugene Rostow erred. The International Court of Justice departed from international law only up to a point. Its ruling reflected and articulated a view of world law that had emerged at the United Nations in the last two decades. For the last twenty years the UN General Assembly had been redefining international law.[29] As early as 1975, the International Court of Justice had shown signs of having become increasingly oriented toward the position that UN General Assembly resolutions were to be treated as international law.[30] It had started with the General Assembly's 1970 Statement on

Principles of Friendly Relations. By the terms of that Statement, people had the right to resist a state which impeded their self-determination. The import of that formulation was, "Rather than defend itself, the state must refrain from any action that impedes the struggle, that is, it must refrain from action that would otherwise be characterized as self-defense. Third states are obliged to help the struggling groups, and cannot be held legally responsible by the targeted state for that help."[31] Thus international law, as articulated at the United Nations, had shifted from protection of the status quo towards a situation where "The state defending itself from change is now *per se* the law-breaker."[32]

The International Court of Justice's decision in the Nicaragua case gave explicit form and authority to this emerging international law. But the Court did even more than that. In its zeal it made history by going beyond even this new emerging "law"—daily articulated and hammered out at the United Nations—to insist that acts of violence by armed bands must "occur on a significant scale" before the right of self-defense could properly be invoked. And the Court excluded *by definition* from the category of armed attack "assistance to rebels in the form of the provision of weapons or logistical or other support."[33] Thus, a government targeted by another for low-intensity attack, in the form of supply of weapons or logistical support for guerrillas seeking to topple its regime, was deprived of any means to defend itself. It could not go to the Security Council or General Assembly to complain, as there the targeted state would be condemned for acting against groups struggling for independence and political freedom. The victim therefore became the villain; the state daring to respond to guerrilla attacks became itself the aggressor.

The Court's ruling was sobering. The American Society of International Law was shaken by the idea that the Court had chosen to go beyond what even Nicaragua's lawyers had asked of it. For the State Department it meant the removal of blinders and the realization that the International Court was part and parcel of the UN system and its politics. It was time to reassess the relationship.

From the start, Kirkpatrick had warned of what to expect from the Court. She was not trained in international law, nor was its language her own. But it took no special knowledge to understand that the struggle waged at the United Nations was over law and legitimacy, and that the International Court was but one significant manifestation of that struggle. No invisible shield separated developments in New York from pronouncements at The Hague. With the Court's ruling, what had been considered the maverick views of one woman moved to center stage. If the United Nations was not the new "Parliament" for man, neither was the International Court the forum for impartial rulings on matters that touched state sovereignty and affected the balance of power. The world wasn't constructed that way. No single vision of international law controlled; no singular allegiance to the rule of law prevailed. The kindest thing that could be said about the International Court's ruling in the Nicaragua case is that it led to the beginning of that wisdom.

17

Change of Guard

At the Republican National Convention in Dallas in August 1984, Jeane Kirkpatrick became a national star. Her chant and taunt to the Democrats—"The San Francisco Democrats" as she termed them, accusing them of always being ready to blame America first for the ills of the world—caught fire among the Convention crowd. I first heard the phrases while vacationing in Maine earlier that summer. I had called Kirkpatrick upon her return from southern France to offer help in preparing her speech. Then she tried out the lines on me.

> They (The San Francisco Democrats) said that saving Grenada from totalitarianism and terror was the wrong thing to do—they didn't blame Cuba or the Communists for threatening American students and murdering Grenadans—they blamed the United States instead. But then, somehow, they always blame America first.
>
> When our Marines, sent to Lebanon on a multinational peacekeeping mission with the consent of the United States Congress, were murdered in their sleep, the "blame America first crowd" did not blame the terrorists who murdered the Marines, they blamed the United States. But then, they always blame America first.
>
> When the Soviet Union walked out of arms control negotiations, and refused even to discuss the issues, the San Francisco Democrats did not blame the Soviet intransigence. They blamed the United States. But then, they always blame America first.
>
> When Marxist dictators shoot their way to power in Central America, the San Francisco Democrats do not blame the guerrillas and their Soviet allies, they blame United States policies of one hundred years ago. But then, they always blame America first.[1]

"What do you think?" she asked. That she had come a long way from the heavily analytic speeches of the past was clear. "This will be a stem-winder," I said. That it was polemical and an oversimplification was also clear, but then this was a political convention. It was a new phase for Jeane Kirkpatrick.

If the wrapping was new, the message was not. In her angry letter to Senator Hubert Humphrey in 1975 about the abandonment of Vietnam she had said much the same thing: America has nothing to apologize for. To the San Francisco Democrats she was prepared to say that they had misplaced their anger. This was to be a speech middle-America could relate to—bold, proud, and patriotic. Delivering it would be a different Kirkpatrick than the one who had come to the UN in plain academic garb ready to give speeches replete with "intellectual clarity"[2] but light on memorable punch lines.

After Dallas, life in New York and Washington seemed anticlimactic. The systems that at first had bewildered her had lost their mystique. If they were sordid at the edges, she was not above playing the game. She had earned the grudging admiration of her colleagues, could throw kisses at fellow ambassadors in UN halls and ballrooms and dazzle them at dinners. She was feted and honored by them even while saying that she would hold them responsible for what they said and how they voted. Joel Blocker, the ex-Paris *Newsweek* bureau chief and her press counselor for the last year, brought streams of carefully screened requests for newspaper, radio, and TV interviews. The media trailed her wherever she went; her pronouncements on foreign policy and domestic politics provided ready-made copy.

Agents besieged her to make deals for book contracts and speaking engagements. At lunch with the literary agent's agent, Swifty Lazar, she would be promised a seven-figure sum for her story. The Harry Walker agency in New York would guarantee her more than a million dollars' worth of bookings for at least her first year out of government service. The 1984 General Assembly session that followed the Dallas Convention seemed destined to offer few surprises, just a repetition of battles already fought. It was good that she had brought Dick Schifter to New York; he would be careful, keeping an eye on the numbers. She would be making plans to leave her UN post. The time had come to return to Georgetown University, where she would lecture one day a week; to the American Enterprise Institute, where she would be supplied with a spacious office, two secretaries, a travelling companion, an aide, and a research assistant; to write a syndicated column; to go on the national speaking circuit; and to see what the future might hold for her in national or state politics.

It was no secret throughout the fall of 1984 that she intended to leave her post after that term's General Assembly session. There were rumors that she might be interested in a new job within the Administration, if an important new role might be carved out for her. No one knew quite what that might be, but her conservative supporters campaigned nevertheless for the creation of a new post where she could help oversee U.S. foreign policy.

In mid-January came the announcement that had been expected for some time. The *Washington Post,* under the headline "Kirkpatrick to Quit Government," ran the following story by its ace reporters, John Goshko and Lou Cannon:

> U.N. Ambassador Jeane J. Kirkpatrick, tacitly conceding that President Reagan did not offer her the kind of job she considers necessary to exert strong conservative influence on the administration, announced yesterday that she is leaving government in order to 'speak out clearly' about her views on the proper course of American foreign policy.
>
> Administration sources, familiar with Kirkpatrick's thinking and the internal maneuvering about her future, said her remarks were intended as an acknowledgment and expression of concern about her belief that control of U.S. foreign policy had been captured by Secretary of State George P. Shultz and the administration's moderate wing.
>
> After a 35 minute private meeting with Reagan, Kirkpatrick ended weeks of speculation about her future. . . .
>
> Many administration officials believe that retired Lt. General Vernon A. Walters, the State Department's chief diplomatic troubleshooter, is the leading candidate to succeed Kirkpatrick.[3]

The predictions were correct. General Walters, a huge burly man in his mid-sixties who had made his way up the ranks as a translator and aide to every American President since President Eisenhower, and who had served as deputy chief of the Central Intelligence Agency under President Nixon, had informed his long-time supporter, Vice President George Bush, of his interest in being named Kirkpatrick's successor. He got his wish. In many ways he was custom-made for the job. He had lived the history of the post–World War II era. Wherever momentous events were occurring—in Europe at the formation of NATO; in Rio de Janeiro at the first postwar Pan-American Conference; in Teheran in 1951 at the transition of power to a pro-Western regime; in South America with Vice President Richard Nixon in 1958 at the time his car was stoned by an angry crowd; in Paris in 1960 with President Eisenhower at the summit conference which followed in the wake of the U2 incident— Vernon Walters was there. Later he served in Rome, as a military attaché during President Kennedy's term; as a military attaché in Rio and Paris during the term of President Johnson; and then as Deputy Director of the CIA, and facilitator of Secretary of State Henry Kissinger's secret talks with the North Vietnamese in Paris. Name any significant spot in the world, any leader of world stature; Walters had been there and had met that person.[4]

And yet the contrast between Jeane Kirkpatrick and Vernon Walters couldn't have been greater. She was an intellectual. He spoke eight different languages, but always remarked in a self-deprecating way that gave away too much that people said of him, "I speak in eight different languages but think in none." He had never graduated high school, had written no distinguished thesis or articles, had pronounced no ideas of his own relative to the management of U.S. foreign policy. He was of the military, but never really a commanding general. He took instructions, went on silent missions of others' choosing, and carried them out superlatively. He wanted to come to the United Nations not only to cap a distinguished career that had taken him many times over around the globe, but because he believed he could be useful there in making friends for the United States. Jeane Kirkpatrick's ambition on assuming the post of UN ambassador was to change policies and direction. Nothing could have been further from General Vernon A. Walters' mind. What they shared was an ability to forge bonds of loyalty and affection with those who worked closely with them.

The team he selected was as different from Kirkpatrick's as he was from her. While Kirkpatrick generally associated herself with younger men who had earned or worked toward Ph.D.s and had distinguished themselves in academic surroundings, Walters chose older men and one woman—Pat Byrne—who had had experience as foreign service officers or ambassadors. As Deputy U.S. Permanent Representative he chose Herbert Okun, a career foreign service officer of twenty years' experience who had previously served with distinction as the U.S. Ambassador to East Germany, and who, a decade earlier, had worked with Walters when posted in Rio as a consular officer. Hugh Montgomery, who replaced Harvey Feldman as head of the USUN Washington office, was a long-time associate of

Walters who had served with the Central Intelligence Agency in various posts throughout Europe and who had most recently been the Director of INR, the State Department's Bureau of Intelligence and Research. Pat Byrne, a career foreign service officer who had most recently been ambassador to Malaysia, assumed the role Bill Sherman had played at the Mission in overseeing its daily operations and host-country relations. Joseph Reed, formerly a chief aide to David Rockefeller at the Chase Manhattan Bank and most recently the U.S. ambassador to Morocco, was appointed the representative to ECOSOC, the post José Sorzano and then Alan Keyes had held. Richard C. Hottelet, a veteran correspondent who had covered the UN for CBS News for three decades, replaced Joel Blocker as Counselor for Press and Public Affairs. I was the only member of the Kirkpatrick team who was asked to stay on, retained in my capacity of legal counsel to the US Mission with the understanding that my role would again be a mix of personal, legal, and political counselor to the Ambassador.

It was not a smooth transition. Kirkpatrick had known Walters at the State Department, where she had occasion to work with him on Central American issues. She had grown to respect and admire his abilities. Walters complained frequently, however, that she had few kind words to say about him to ease his transition, and that he was left to his own devices to discover how to manage the Mission and its relationship with the State Department and the United Nations. At the State Department, Alan Keyes had been appointed Assistant Secretary of State for IO, the International Organizations Bureau. Dennis Goodman, who had worked with Keyes at the U.S. Mission, became his deputy. Together they would, perhaps through no fault of their own, make life unpleasant for Walters.

History began to repeat itself. The quarrel that had erupted in 1981 between Jeane Kirkpatrick and Elliott Abrams over who was to take orders from whom erupted with Walters vowing that he wouldn't let a 36-year-old State Department aide—Alan Keyes—or his cohort, Dennis Goodman, dictate to him what he should do. Called upon to mediate the dispute, I discovered it was not as much over receiving instructions as the manner in which they were delivered. It was not over the content of instructions—policy—or even over power, as was the case between Kirkpatrick and Abrams. Whatever voting instructions Alan Keyes delivered on behalf of his superior, Under-Secretary of State for Political Affairs Michael Armacost (Larry Eagleburger's replacement), or on behalf of the Secretary of State, were fine with

Walters. It was about respect. In time the tension would ease as Herbert Okun assumed the run of daily affairs of the Mission, maintaining nearly daily contact with Michael Armacost at State. What would not be fulfilled was Walters' desire for contact, and the respect he thought his due, on a higher level. Secretary of State George Shultz would frustrate that wish, never meeting with him alone, one-to-one, but always in the presence of one or two of his ubiquitous aides, Charlie Hill or Nick Platt.

And so Walters was left to concentrate on using his enormous personal appeal to make "friends" at the United Nations, to converse with other delegates in one of the eight languages he spoke fluently, to spend time in the Delegates Lounge adjacent to the UN General Assembly hall (an activity for which Kirkpatrick had neither the time nor the inclination), and to exchange stories and pleasantries. The delegates couldn't help but like what they saw. He was friendly (he would even smile and joke in Spanish with the new Nicaraguan representative), noncombative, nonfixated, straightforward in manner, accessible, and easy to get along with. Some, however, even while welcoming the change, felt rueful about Kirkpatrick's absence. They had become accustomed to looking forward to hearing her speeches which, although disagreeable, could be counted on to be fresh, provocative, carrying the stamp of her intellect, and of proximity to the highest echelon of U.S. power.

But the nostalgia, such as it existed, did not extend to content. Walters fitted in with a perceptible new climate of declining East-West tension. Mikhail Gorbachev had assumed the premiership of the Soviet Union; "glasnost" and "perestroika" were the codewords. Espousal of terrorism was moving out of fashion. Soviet client states such as Syria and Cuba would now introduce "anti-terrorism" resolutions although retaining the fine print exempting national liberation struggle from the new strictures. The US delegation would applaud the move as a major advance, a sign of the UN's promise for the future. It was the beginning of a new world, or so it seemed.

If the United Nations in 1985 had lost some of the vitriol which marked it in the earlier years, much was due to its desperate financial straits.[5] Runaway UN spending over the last decade had come up against spiraling inflation and delinquencies in payments of assessed UN contributions. The greatest threat came from the United States Government. In Congress, Senator Nancy Kassebaum had introduced and secured enactment of an amendment mandating a reduction of 20 to 25 percent in UN funding unless U.S. voting on UN budgetary matters was given greater weight in proportion to the amount of the U.S. assessment. Additional cuts in UN funding were required to satisfy the spending cuts mandated by the Gramm-Rudman-Hollings Bill. At a time of financial crisis, with the United States threatening even greater cutbacks, attacking the United States was no longer the free-for-all it had once been. Besides, it was not consonant with the warming trend in super-power relations.

Still, there would be enough shocks to go around to show that the old way of thinking was merely in a state of hibernation. For Walters the revelation came in April of 1985. I accompanied him across the street for his first "informal Security Council consultations" on an Arab-Israeli related matter: Israel's administrative detentions, arrests, and the threats of deportation—steps it was taking to deal with incidents of rock-throwing directed against Israeli military targets and civilians in the occupied West Bank. One delegate after another took the floor to condemn Israel for "Nazi-like behavior," "Nazi-fascist terror," and Gestapo tactics, and to assign responsibility for the "genocide" of Palestinians. Walters, who had seen diplomatic and military service on nearly every corner of the globe, was unprepared for, and indeed bewildered, by what he witnessed. It was not what he had expected. This was the Security Council, the most important arm of the UN peace-keeping system, operating in its inner sanctum like a crazed gang after prey, using words that defied their true meaning. He asked to address the informal chamber and in a voice that rose to a near bark said: "Gentlemen, I fought in World War II. I know what Nazi-like behavior is, and so should you. It is unacceptable and irresponsible to hear that term used as it has been today. The analogy simply doesn't apply." The delegates around him were stunned. They had overplayed their hand. Walters might not be Jeane Kirkpatrick, but there would be no going back to the business-as-usual of another time.

The great issues that were there during Jeane Kirkpatrick's term—Cyprus, Namibia, the Iran-Iraq war, the Arab-Israeli conflict, South Africa, Kampuchea (Cambodia), and Nicaragua—would still be there, not moving perceptively forward toward resolution. Additional votes would be gained in the effort to stave off the ritual of rejecting the credentials of Israel's delegation. Additional votes would be gained in favor of the annual General Assembly resolution calling on the Soviet Union (without directly naming it), to depart from Afghanistan. These would be hailed as victories by the Walters team, and in the context of the UN they were.

But it would be the conciliatory gesture, not the bark, which would characterize General Walters' term. In late 1985 he would help lay the groundwork for an eighteen-nation "Group of High Level Intergovernmental Experts to Review the Efficiency of the Administrative and Financial Functioning of the United Nations." Its purpose would be to aid the United Nations in engineering necessary financial and administrative reform. Much attention would be devoted to this matter. Attention would also be focused on getting the UN Security Council and the office of the Secretary General to become involved in seeking a withdrawal of the Soviet Union from Afghanistan, and to mediating an end to the war between Iran and Iraq.

Gone, however, would be the effort to change direction and policy from the office of the U.S. Permanent Representative to the United Nations. Even if there had been the ambition, there was no access to the President to make possible its fruition. Shortly after he assumed his new position, Walters realized that he was not being given the same access to the President his predecessor had enjoyed. He asked that I brief him about his legal rights as the U.S. Permanent Representative. He ended up writing President Reagan thanking him for the confidence he had placed in him, while assuring him that he would act in accordance with the powers vested in his office by the relevant legislation. But access to power is measured by the strength of personal relationships, not formal entitlements. Here changed international conditions, differences of personality and approach, and the obstinacy of a bureaucracy anxious to guard its prerogatives were to combine to assure that Jeane Kirkpatrick's relative independence and ability to influence policy and direction from her twin bases in New York and Washington would be an aberration, a relic of the past.

The denouement to the struggle over the role of the American ambassador to the United Nations in shaping the direction of U.S. policy would come after General Walters' departure with the appointment in March 1989 of his successor, Thomas R. Pickering, a career Foreign Service officer. Since the time of Henry Cabot Lodge the appointment as U.S. Ambassador to the United Nations carried with it Cabinet rank and invitations to attend sessions of the National Security Council. Thomas Pickering's assumption of the office was conditioned on a renunciation of these prerogatives. There would be a return to traditional diplomacy, with the emphasis on the development of personal relations and the careful execution of instructions. The formulation of policy would be left to others in the State Department, and to the White House. The post of the U.S. Permanent Representative to the United Nations would no longer be joined to the center of power in Washington. There would be little chance for the emergence of another Jeane Kirkpatrick.

Epilogue

A decade ended as it began—with Iraq. Dominating the attention of the United Nations in 1981 was Israel's bombing of Iraq's nuclear reactor, which was condemned as a violation of international law, and Abu Eain's attack on Israeli civilians, which was lauded as the use of "all necessary means" to end colonial, racist, and alien rule. By contrast, in 1991 an America-led multinational force demolished, among other targets, Iraqi nuclear weapons facilities in pursuance of a UN Security Council mandate to use "all necessary means" to liberate Kuwait. A dramatic transformation had taken place in the course of a fateful era—in the world at large, and in the place where change comes terribly slowly, United Nations headquarters in New York.

Only once before—in 1950—had collective military force been used to implement a UN resolution. Then, an assortment of national armies, but predominantly those of the United States, fought under the UN's aegis to turn back North Korea's aggression. But the Soviet Union was not a party to that decision, having made the error of stepping out of the UN Security Council's deliberations. When it returned, the matter had moved to the UN General Assembly, where a procedurally suspect "Uniting for Peace" resolution sought to bypass the UN Security Council and the prospect of a Soviet veto. By contrast, in 1990, U.S.-Soviet cooperation within the UN Security Council made possible the landmark resolution authorizing the use of force to free Kuwait.

The first major test of post-Cold War Super-Power cooperation thus proved successful. In its wake, the United Nations has been lauded as having shed both the ineffectiveness and the wretched excesses that characterized so much of its performance in the 1980s. Indeed, President George Bush has been in the forefront of those who have spoken of a rehabilitated United Nations able to assume

the role envisioned by its founders. Certainly no other American
president has labored as assiduously for UN support for U.S. policies.

To this end President Bush exhibited a remarkable penchant for
building consensus. It led to three-hour meetings of reconciliation in
Geneva with President Hafez al-Assad of Syria; to promises to the
perpetrators of the Tiananmen Square massacre; to secret deals with
Malaysians, Zairians, and Ivory Coasters when their support in the
UN Security Council proved crucial; to flights by Secretary of State
James Baker III to Saana, Yemen to lobby for an extra vote; to Ber-
muda, to keep the Canadians in line; and to meetings outside Moscow
to map strategy with the top Soviet leadership.

In 1981, when President Ronald Reagan and his ambassador in
New York, Jeane Kirkpatrick, began their work, the United Nations
was not to be confused with the "real world." In the real world the
United States had power; in the United Nations it was impotent. In
late 1990 and early 1991 the real world and the United Nations
meshed, one becoming the vehicle for the other in the implementation of U.S. policy in the Persian Gulf.

The phrase "new international order" had come easily to President Bush. Early in the Iraq crisis—on August 20, 1990—addressing
the Veterans of U.S. Foreign Wars, Bush spoke interchangeably of
America's commitment to "our friends when imperiled" and to the
new "international order." On September 11, in addressing a joint
session of Congress, Bush revealed that he had a fifth objective for
sending U.S. troops into the Gulf. Previously he had listed four:
protecting the Saudis from Iraqi attack, securing the release of American hostages, restoring the ousted Emir of Kuwait, and securing the
withdrawal of Iraq's forces from Kuwait. Then he proclaimed another,
presumably one for which Americans should be prepared to sacrifice
their lives: the promotion of a new world order, "a new era—freer
from the threat of terror, stronger in the pursuit of justice, and more
secure in the quest for peace, an era in which the nations of the
world, East and West, North and South, can prosper and live in
harmony."

At the center of that vision was the revamped role contemplated
for the United Nations. Thus Secretary of State James Baker, in
Moscow on November 7, 1990 for talks with Soviet President Mikhail
Gorbachev and Foreign Minister Eduard Shevardnadze, announced
that the United States would seek a UN Security Council resolution

authorizing the use of force to liberate Kuwait. At stake in the crisis was, he said, "the credibility of the United Nations."

A few years earlier that statement would have strained credibility. Then, the United Nations was hardly considered a serious agent for resolution of conflict. What change had taken place within the confines of the United Nations to warrant that new-found confidence?

The biggest change at the United Nations since Ronald Reagan's first term has been the attitude and conduct of the Soviet Union. By 1987 the "new thinking" which had taken place inside the Soviet Union had begun to show itself at the United Nations. Gorbachev announced that the Soviet Union would remit UN dues it had long refused to pay. The Soviet Foreign Office presented nearly one hundred different proposals for improving the effectiveness of the International Court of Justice. The Soviet campaign of "UN Charter reform" directed at rewriting the UN Charter to favor their view of world order—unwavering support of national liberation movements provided it was liberation of non-Socialist states—came to an end. After years of opposing the idea that the UN Secretary General could play an independent peace-making role, preferring that such matters be kept exclusively within the province of the UN Security Council where they exercised veto power, the Soviets suddenly began to laud the Secretary General's role.

One thing led to another. The enhancement of the powers of the UN Secretary General's office made possible mediation to end the Iran-Iraq war, negotiations for Soviet withdrawal from Afghanistan, and resolution of the Cambodia conflict. UN election observers were dispatched to ensure Namibia's peaceful transition to independence. And, in the euphoria over the prospect of renewed life for the UN, a most unexpected Nobel Peace Prize was awarded in 1988 to the UN's blue-helmeted peace-keeping forces.

Thus, when the Gulf crisis of 1990 broke, the prospect of a rehabilitated United Nations working in tandem with the Soviet Union and the United States had taken on an air of reality. It offered the particular, if somewhat nebulous, advantages of "legitimacy." It would enable Bush to mollify critics accusing him of rushing headstrong and unilaterally to war; it would give Gorbachev breathing room from the pressures of the military, the KGB, and the old thinkers who would castigate him for collaborating against a former Arab client. The "new world order" had become not only fashionable, but politically provident.

To be sure, it was not the world order the founders of international law—Grotius, Puffendorf, Vattel—envisioned. It was not a
closed system of "like-minded" states. Yet it was close to what the
founders of the UN system had in mind—a world based on the principle of sovereign equality of states. Thus the quality of a regime—
whether despotic or beneficent, democratic or totalitarian—would be
irrelevant to the right of all nations to live in peace, free from the use
or threat of force against their territorial integrity or independence.

For over forty years, nearly since the creation of the United
Nations, that vision had failed. The Soviet Union and the United
States harbored mutually incompatible visions of world order, each
based on the presumed moral superiority of one's values over those of
the other: proletarian revolution and "national liberation" versus the
promotion of human rights and democracy. With the end of the Cold
War, as the Soviet vision of order gave way to that of the West, the
Soviet Union and the United States became more "like-minded."
Still, the Security Council is composed of 15 member nations, and the
General Assembly of 159. What of these other nations? Had they
become more "like-minded" too?

Early in the Iraq crisis Secretary of State Baker had the opportunity to discover quickly that the UN system had not changed all that
much, not, at least, in dealing with the Arab-Israeli conflict. And the
UN's failure to deal successfully with that conflict is symptomatic of
all that continues to ail the political organs of the United Nations.

In mid-October 1990, America's best-laid plans for keeping the
members of the UN Security Council focused on Iraq went awry. The
shooting deaths of more than fifteen Palestinians by Israeli forces at
Jerusalem's Temple Mount—in response to rioting, the burning of a
police outpost, and the stoning of Israeli worshippers at the Western
Wall below—led to the introduction of a PLO-sponsored resolution.
Its aim: to keep the UN Security Council permanently engaged in
monitoring Israel's treatment of Palestinians, thus diverting its members' attention from the Iraq crisis. Flushed with its success in gaining
UN Security Council endorsement for its earlier proposals, the Administration hit upon the idea of doing something that the United
States hadn't done in more than twenty years: introduce a Security
Council resolution condemning Israel. In charging Israel with having
exercised "excessive use of force" at the Temple Mount, a three-fold
effect was anticipated: Arab states would be grateful for America's
introduction of a draft resolution condemning Israel; the Europeans
would laud American efforts to play within the UN system; and Israel

might grudgingly appreciate that the United States rescued it from the certainty of an even stronger resolution of condemnation.

The PLO draft had called for a Security Council commission to report back to the Council by October 20th with "recommendations on ways and means of ensuring the safety and protection of the Palestinian civilians under occupation." The American draft proposed instead a fact-finding team under the aegis of the Secretary General, whose mandate would be limited to the facts of the incident. Secretary Baker was confident that the American draft would pass without too much difficulty.

He was disappointed. A campaign was launched to enlist the Europeans (France didn't need any prodding) and others on the Council to defeat the American draft and to force the United States into a veto. As a senior State Department official put it at the time, "The Secretary is dismayed and very unhappy. He initiated a major policy decision at substantial domestic risk and thought they would be grateful."

When it dawned on the Administration that the "new" United Nations was playing its old game, President Bush intervened to ask President François Mitterand of France to stand with him. But Mitterand reportedly offered only the suggestion that the president be more "statesmanlike," and less parochial in his leanings.

As the eleventh hour approached, however, Non-Aligned support for the PLO draft weakened. The prospect of a U.S. veto augured badly for the Non-Aligned Movement, which had begun to look to the United Nations to play a more responsible role in world affairs. The British delegation then helped save the day. They proposed that the Security Council would authorize the Secretary General's team to do exactly the same work as the Security Council commission the PLO had called for: to go beyond fact-finding to an examination of the situation of Palestinians under Israeli occupation, and to report back regularly on its findings to the Security Council. The change would be neatly tucked away in a preambular paragraph of the resolution, through reference to a statement made the previous day by Britain's Permanent Representative in his capacity as the President of the Security Council. That statement had used language identical to that of the PLO draft in referring to the mandate for the Secretary General's "fact-finding" team.

With that "minor" change, the draft U.S. Security Council resolution was adopted. Such was the stuff of multilateral diplomacy which occupied nearly the full attention of the U.S. Secretary of

State, and occasioned direct involvement by the President, for a full
week during the height of the Iraq crisis.

Meanwhile, as debate over the Temple Mount resolution raged,
Syria's forces consolidated control over its neighbor, Lebanon, without a peep of protest, or cautionary note, from Washington. At the
same time, in the United States, those who supported the principle
enunciated by the International Court in the Nicaragua case—that
the victim of a little aggression has no recourse but to turn the other
cheek—began to argue with increasing support that the Administration was prohibited by law from undertaking military action on behalf
of the liberation of Kuwait without express authorization by the U.N.
Security Council.

It is a new world order, far different from the one Ronald Reagan
had to confront on the assumption of his presidency. The United
Nations has reflected that new reality. Still, what has characterized
the success of the United Nations in dealing with the Iraq crisis is its
capacity to skirt its normal processes. Through the personal diplomacy of President Bush and Secretary of State Baker, arrangements
were reached in various capitals on the foreign minister level which
could not be renegotiated in New York at the United Nations. But
this degree of investment of time and energy by the President and
Secretary of State can hardly serve as a model for action in other less
pressing crises. Indeed, perhaps nothing is so instructive about the
role of the United Nations when left to its own devices as the fact that
on the eve of allied military action against Iraq, the Security Council
was commencing a general debate, at the request of the PLO, on the
situation in the Israeli occupied territories.

The experience of the 1980s remains instructive. The attitudes
and alliances that then prevailed—the continuation of war by other
means, to use the inverse of von Clausewitz's famous maxim—still
dominate discussion of the Arab-Israeli conflict at the United Nations.
Inside the UN's walls the new international reality—the awareness
that democracy is preferable to tyranny, and that aggression cannot
be appeased—has begun to seep in. The United Nations can play a
role in shaping that new reality. But, as the Iraq crisis has demonstrated, without the resolve of the United States nothing more than
one or two anodyne UN Security Council resolutions might have
been expected to pass before the delegates disbanded to deal with
less pressing matters.

What is left to be done? Jeane J. Kirkpatrick, the embattled U.S.
representative, said it well in June 1983: "It is not too late to hope

that in the United Nations system we can produce, if not all, then at least some of the constructive contributions to peace and justice that the founders of the UN system hoped and planned for. It is just this expectation of possible constructive outcomes, and the prevention of negative, destructive, extreme, peace-endangering outcomes, that makes the United Nations today worth our participation."[1]

Notes

Introduction

1. Hannah Arendt, *The Origins of Totalitarianism* (New York: Harcourt, Brace, and World, 1968).
2. See Franz Neumann, *Behemoth: The Structure and Practices of National Socialism 1933–44* (New York: Oxford University Press, 1944).
3. Jeane J. Kirkpatrick, *Political Woman* (New York: Basic Books, 1974); *Leader and Vanguard: A Study of Peronist Argentina* (Cambridge, Mass.: Massachusetts Institute of Technology, 1971); *The New Presidential Elite: Men and Women in National Politics* (New York: Russell Sage, 1976).
4. Jeane J. Kirkpatrick, "Dictatorships and Double Standards," *Commentary*, November 1979, pp. 34–45.
5. See "Lecturer for the U.N.," *Time*, January 9, 1981, pp. 61–62. "Democrat for the United Nations," *Newsweek*, January 9, 1981, p. 18. A. Wolfe, "Jeane's Designs," *Nation*, February 7, 1981, pp. 133–34; P. Stoler and G.H. Wierzynski, "Squabbling Over Statecraft," *Time*, July 6, 1981, p. 11.

1. The Call

1. U.N. Security Council Resolution 487 (1981).
2. See William Claiborne, "Begin Backpedals on Threatening Imminent Strike at Syrian Missiles," *Washington Post*, June 19, 1981, p. A20.
3. For example, the representative of Syria, speaking before the 1985 session of the UN Special Political Committee, stated: "Palestinians are the victims of Zionism, the real heir to Nazism, which not only professes its racism but to this day also exploits the painful memory of the victims of Nazism to justify its crimes and atrocities against the Arab citizens suffering under the yoke of Zionist occupation." Quoted in Allan Gerson, "The United Nations and Racism: The Case of the Zionism as Racism Resolution as Progenitor," *Israel Yearbook on Human Rights* 17 (1987), 68–69.

   Appearing before the UN AESAN Regional NGO Symposium, May 2, 1985, Soviet Representative Roman Akhramovitch stated: "Zionist organizations in the countries of the West behave irresponsibly trying to carry out noisy anti-Palestine propaganda, based on gross slander, and on the criminal idea of racism and genocide. . . . [This is] the way the modern Zionist-Nazis want it." Cited in *supra*, p. 70.
4. Corfu Channel case (United Kingdom v. Albania), [1949] International Court of Justice Reports 4, 28 (hereafter I.C.J. Reports).
5. Myres S. McDougal and Harold D. Lasswell, "The Identification and Appraisal

of Diverse Systems of Public Order," *American Journal of International Law* 53:1 (1959); reprinted in Myres S. McDougal and W. Michael Reisman, eds., *International Law Essays* 15 (Mineola, N.Y.: Foundation Press, 1981).

6. Hugo Grotius, *De Jure Belli Ac Pacis* (The Rights of War and Peace: Including the Law of Nature and of Nations) (Westport, Conn.: Hyperion Press, 1985; reprint of 1901 ed.).

7. See Kenneth Love, *Suez: The Twice Fought War* (New York: McGraw Hill, 1969), pp. 519–20; Robert R. Bowie, *Suez 1956* (London: Oxford University Press, 1974). Geoffrey Marston, "Armed Intervention in the 1956 Suez Canal Crisis: The Legal Advice Tendered to the British Government," *International and Comparative Law Quarterly* 37 (October, 1968), 773–817.

8. See text of President Carter's Inaugural Address, *New York Times*, February 21, 1979, p. 13.

9. Eugene V. Rostow, "Peace as a Problem of Law," in Eugene V. Rostow, *Peace in the Balance: The Future of American Foreign Policy* (New York: Simon and Schuster, 1972), pp. 283–317.

10. "We are under a Constitution, but a Constitution is what the Judges say it is." Address, Elmira, New York, May 3, 1907; quoted by F.D. Roosevelt, March 9, 1937; cited in George Seldes, *The Great Quotations* (New York: Pocket Books, 1968), p. 225.

11. McDougal and Lasswell, op.cit.

12. Allan Gerson, "Management and Disposition: Israel, the West Bank, and the Rule of International Law," doctoral dissertation on reserve at Yale Law School Library; published in a revised version as *Israel, the West Bank, and International Law* (London: Cass, 1978).

2. Encounter

1. *New York Times*, October 26, 1962, pp. 1, 16.

2. *Time*, December 8, 1975, pp. 11–12. See also *Department of State Bulletin* 73 (December 1, 1975), pp. 790–95.

3. See chapter 11, note 3.

4. *Time*, March 17, 1980, pp. 37–38.

5. See Francis W. Carpenter, *Men in Glass Houses* (New York: McBride, 1951), p. 97; George T. Mazuzan, *Warren R. Austin at the U.N., 1946–1953* (Kent, Ohio: Kent State University Press, 1977), p. 99.

6. "Joining the Jackals?" *Jerusalem Post International Edition*, week of July 7–14, 1981.

7. Daniel Patrick Moynihan, "Joining the Jackals: The U.S. at the United Nations 1977–80," *Commentary*, February 1981, pp. 23–31.

8. See chapter 1, note 4.

9. Marian Christy, interview with Jeane Kirkpatrick, *Boston Globe*, July 20, 1981.

3. The PLO "Observer" Mission

1. United States of America v. Iran, 1980 I.C.J. Reports p. 5.

2. UN Participation Act of 1945, 22 USCA, Section 287.

3. Allan Gerson, *Israel, the West Bank, and International Law*, p. 81.

4. For policy statements on the aims of the Camp David accords, see Harold H.

Saunders, "Middle East: Challenges and Opportunities for Peace in the Middle East" (speech delivered in Boston, Mass., January 29, 1979), *Department of State Bulletin* 79 (March 1979), pp. 48–51.

5. U.N. Participation Act of 1945, op.cit.
6. U.N. Charter, Articles 3–6.
7. Ibid., Article 6.
8. See *U.N. Monthly Chronicle* 11:11 (December 1974), pp. 37–44.
9. *U.N. Monthly Chronicle*, op.cit.
10. Sergei Khrushchev, *Khrushchev on Khrushchev* (Boston: Little, Brown, 1990).
11. *U.N. Monthly Chronicle*, op.cit., pp. 80–82.
12. Harris O. Schoenberg, *A Mandate for Terror* (New York: Shapolsky, 1989), p. 70.
13. U.N. General Assembly Resolution 3375, November 10, 1975.
14. U.N. General Assembly Resolution 3379. For discussion of the Zionism as Racism resolution, see Allan Gerson, "The United Nations and Racism. The case of the Zionism as Racism Resolution as Progenitor," and Anthony Astrachain, "The Twilight of Reason: The UN's Holy Alliance," *Present Tense*, Winter, 1976, pp. 36, 38–40; Bernard Lewis, "The Anti-Zionist Resolution," *Foreign Affairs*, October, 1976, pp. 54–64.
15. See *U.N. Monthly Chronicle* 12:11 (December 1975), 10.
16. M. McDougal and F. Feliciano, *Law and Minimum World Public Order* (New Haven: Yale University Press, 1961).
17. See *United States Participation in the UN: Reports by the President to Congress, 1983–1990* (Washington, D.C.: Department of State).
18. See Articles 7 and 14 of the Report of the Intl. Law Comm. to the General Assembly on Relations Between States and Intl. Governmental Organizations, Doc. 2/8410/Rec. 1 (1971).
19. For a description of PLO involvement at the UN, see William Korey, "The PLO's Conquest of the U.N.," *Midstream*, November 1979, pp. 10–15.
20. Jeane J. Kirkpatrick, "U.N. Security and Latin America," *Commentary*, January, 1981, pp. 29–40.
21. Jeane J. Kirkpatrick, "The Method of Harold Lasswell," unpublished address, American Political Science Association (1979).
22. U.N. Participation Act of 1945, op.cit.
23. Henry Kissinger, *Years of Upheaval* (Boston: Little, Brown, 1982), p. 1197.

4. UN Finding, Congress, and the Restraints of International Law

1. Daniel P. Moynihan with Suzanne Weaver, *A Dangerous Place* (Boston: Little, Brown, 1978).
2. *U.N. Statistics Committee*, (New York: United Nations, July 1981).
3. Eugene V. Rostow, *Peace in the Balance* (New York: Simon & Schuster, 1972).
4. U.N. Charter, Articles 2:4, 33, 51, 52.
5. Myres S. McDougal and Harold D. Lasswell, "The Identification and Appraisal of Diverse Systems of Public Order," in McDougal and Reisman, pp. 15–42.
6. Dean Acheson, "The Arrogance of International Lawyers," *International Lawyer* 2 (1968) p. 591.
7. Allan Gerson, *Management and Disposition*
8. 1962, I.C.J. Reports 151.
9. "Certain Expenses Case of the United Nations," International Court of Justice,

Advisory Opinion of July 20, 1962, in Louis B. Sohn, ed., *Recent Cases on United Nations Law* (Brooklyn: The Foundation Press, 1963), pp. 25–55.

10. See Tables IIa and IIb in chapter 4, on "Estimated Withholding by Member States from United Nations Emergency Force (UNEF) and United Nations Disengagement Force (UNDOF) and United Nations Interim Force in Lebanon (UNIFIL)," and "Estimated Withholding by Member Nations from the Regular Budget of the United Nations Projected to 31 December 1982."

11. See essays on the U.S. role in the United Nations in "The U.N. Under Scrutiny," *Heritage Lectures,* Number 15 (Washington, D.C.: Heritage Foundation, 1982).

5. High Noon over Geneva Convention No. 4

1. Geneva Convention Relative to the Protection of Civilian Persons in Time of War, August 12, 1949, U.S.T. 3516, T.I.A.S. No. 3365, 75 U.N.T.S. 287.

2. U.N. Charter, Preamble.

3. Many of the nations involved in these wars have violated both the Fourth Geneva Convention of 1949 and the 1925 Protocol Prohibiting the Use of Asphyxiating, Poisonous, or Other Gases. In the mid-1960s Egypt employed chemical agents during its intervention in North Yemen. In the early 1980s Russia was accused of using chemical weapons in Afghanistan. In addition, chemical weapons were used by both Iran and Iraq in the Persian Gulf War and by Libya in its confrontation with Chad in 1987. See Item 54 of the preliminary list of the thirty-seventh session of the United Nations General Assembly, "Chemical and Bacteriological Weapons," May 21, 1982. See also W. Seth Carus, "Chemical Weapons in the Middle East," *Policy Focus,* Number 9, Washington Institute for Near East Policy, Washington, D.C., December 1988.

4. See chapter 1, note 3.

5. See *United States Participation in the UN: Report by the President to Congress for the Year 1981* (Department of State Publication 9340, released March 1983), p. 13.

6. "All Available Means"

1. *U.N. General Assembly: Provisional Verbatim Record of the One Hundred and First Meeting,* December 16, 1981, p. 56.

2. *New York Times,* August 23, 1979, p. A25.

3. *Eain v. Wilkes,* 641 F2d 504 (7th cir. 1981); *cert. den.* 454 U.S. 894, 102 S.C. 390.

4. Ibid.

5. Ibid.

6. ECOSOC, 1981/42, May 8, 1981.

7. *Yearbook of the United Nations* 35 (1981), p. 967.

8. U.N. General Assembly Resolution 36/171.

9. *Yearbook of the United Nations* 35 (1981), p. 910.

10. Daniel Patrick Moynihan, "Joining the Jackals: The U.S. at the United Nations 1977–80," *Commentary,* February 1981, pp. 23–31.

11. "Letter Bomb," *Time,* October 26, 1981, p. 24.

12. See Dorothy Rabinowitz, "Testing Haig's Resolve Against Terrorists: The Case of

Abu Eain," *New Republic*, December 16, 1981, pp. 12–14. See also James Kelly, "Furor over an Extradition: An Accused Arab Terrorist Is Sent Back to Israel for Trial," *Time*, January 4, 1982, p. 64.

7. Terror at the Dome of the Rock

1. See *Washington Post*, April 12, 1982, p. A1.
2. "Twenty-one injured as Anti-Israel Protests over Mosque Attack Spread," *Washington Post*, April 13, 1982, p. A12; and "Moslems Observe General Strike," *New York Times*, April 15, 1982, p. A6.
3. *New York Times*, April 15, 1982, p. A6.
4. Terzi was quoting "At the Dome of the Rock," *Washington Post*, April 13, 1982, p. A18.
5. These debates are summarized in the *U.N. Monthly Chronicle* 19:5 (June 1982), pp. 25–31.
6. Louis B. Sohn, *Cases on International Law* (Brooklyn: Foundation Press, 1967).
7. Menahem Milson, "How to Make Peace with the Palestinians," *Commentary*, May 1981, pp. 25–35.
8. *New York Times*, April 14, 1982, p. A1.
9. Ibid.
10. U.N. Security Council Draft Resolution S/14985.
11. *New York Times*, April 15, 1982, p. A6.
12. For a detailed description of the events that occurred at Hama, see Thomas L. Friedman, "Hama Rules," *From Beirut To Jerusalem*, (New York: Farrar Straus Giroux, 1989), pp. 76–105; and Wilhelm Dietl, "Death in Hamah," *Holy War* (New York: Macmillan, 1984), pp. 130–140.
13. *New York Times*, April 15, 1982, p. A6.
14. Ibid.
15. *U.N. General Assembly Official Records, Thirty-Sixth Session*, Supplement No. 35 (A/36/35).
16. *U.N. Security Council Provisional Verbatim Record of the Two Thousand Three Hundred and Fifty Sixth Meeting*, s/pv. 2356, April 19, 1982, pp. 3–5.
17. Ibid., pp. 6–17.
18. Ibid., pp. 23–28.
19. Ibid., pp. 22–41.
20. Ibid., pp. 41–45.
21. Ibid., pp. 46–50.
22. Ibid., pp. 48–50.
23. Ibid., pp. 58–61.
24. Ibid., pp. 61–62.
25. Ibid., p. 66.
26. *U.N. Security Council Provisional Verbatim Record of the Two Thousand Three Hundred and Fifty Seventh Meeting*, S/PV. 2357, April 20, 1982, p. 6; draft resolution s/14985.
27. Ibid., p. 7.
28. Ibid., pp. 8–11.
29. Ibid., pp. 11–18.
30. Ibid., pp. 16–20.
31. Ibid., pp. 21–22.

32. Ibid., p. 22.
33. Ibid.
34. Ibid., p. 30
35. Ibid., pp. 31–32.
36. Ibid., pp. 32–35.
37. Ibid., pp. 33–35.
38. Ibid., pp. 36–38.
39. Ibid., pp. 39–41.
40. Ibid., pp. 41–43.
41. Ibid., p. 46.
42. M. Orth, "Woman Capable of Reason," *Vogue*, July 1981, pp. 180–81.
43. *U.N. General Assembly Official Records, Thirty-Sixth Session*, Supplement No. 35 (A/36/35).
44. *Organization of American States Official Records, Twentieth Meeting*, Consultation of Ministers of Foreign Affairs, April 26, 1982.

8. "Malvinas, Malvinas"

1. Kirkpatrick, "U.S. Security and Latin America," pp. 29–40.
2. See "Argentina Seizes Falkland Islands: British Ships Move," *New York Times*, April 3, 1982, p. A1.
3. Alberto R. Coll and Anthony C. Arend, eds., *The Falklands War: Lessons for Strategy, Diplomacy and International Law* (Boston: George Allen & Unwin, 1985), p. 123.
4. U.N. Security Council Resolution 502.
5. Quoted in Max Hastings and Simon Jenkins, *The Battle for the Falklands* (New York: W.W. Norton, 1983), p. 109.
6. Kirkpatrick, "Dictatorships and Double Standards," pp. 34–45.
7. U.N. Security Council Report S-G S/15151; the full text can be found in *U.N. Monthly Chronicle* 19:7 (July 1982), 2, 4–5.
8. Ibid.
9. "Painful Lessons for All," *US News & World Report*, May 17, 1982, pp. 24–27.
10. *U.N. Security Council Provisional Verbatim Record of the Two Thousand Three Hundred Sixtieth Meeting*, S/PV. 2360, May 21, 1982, p. 12.
11. Ibid., pp. 12–32.
12. Ibid.
13. Ibid., pp. 32–51.
14. Ibid., pp. 68–76.
15. Ibid., pp. 79–80.
16. For the full text of the report, see *U.N. Monthly Chronicle* 19:7 (July 1982), 27.
17. *U.N. Security Council Provisional Verbatim Record of the Two Thousand Three Hundred and Sixty First Meeting*, S/PV. 2361, May 21, 1982, p. 8–12.
18. U.N. Security Council Draft Resolution S/15122.
19. *U.N. Security Council Provisional Verbatim Record of the Two Thousand Three Hundred Sixty Eighth Meeting*, S/PV. 2368, May 26, 1982, pp. 39–40.
20. Ibid., pp. 27–31.
21. Ibid., pp. 42–45.

22. Ibid., p. 37.

23. U.N. Security Council Draft Resolution S/15156/Rev. 2.

24. See "Britain Announces Argentine Surrender to End the Ten-Week War in the Falklands," *New York Times*, June 15, 1982, p. A1.

25. *U.N. Security Council Provisional Verbatim Record of the Two Thousand Three Hundred Seventy Third Meeting*, S/PV. 2373, June 4, 1982, pp. 4–5.

26. Ibid., pp. 6–7.

27. Ibid., p. 22.

28. Thomas M. Franck, "Dulce et Decorum Est: The Strategic Role of Legal Principles in the Falklands War," *American Journal of International Law* 77:1 (January 1983) pp. 112–28.

29. Peter Calvert, *The Falklands Crisis: The Rights and the Wrongs* (New York: St. Martin's Press, 1982), p. 79.

30. Alexander M. Haig, Jr., *Caveat: Realism, Reagan, and Foreign Policy* (New York: Macmillan, 1984), p. 298.

9. High-Stakes Poker

1. See generally, regarding plans for and execution of Israel's Lebanon operation, Avner Yaniv, *Dilemmas of Security* (New York: Oxford University Press, 1987), and Zeev Schiff, *Israel's Lebanon War* (New York: Simon & Schuster, 1984).

2. Yaniv, op.cit., pp. 137–40.

3. Ibid., pp. 92–112.

4. "Israel's Controversial Defense Chief: Architect of the Strike on Lebanon," *Washington Post*, June 11, 1982, pp. A21–22.

5. U.N. Security Council Draft Resolution S/15171: passed as Resolution 509, June 6, 1982.

6. M. Orth, op.cit.

7. See "U.N. Lebanon Plan Is Vetoed by U.S.," *New York Times*, June 27, 1982, p. A1.

8. U.N. Security Council Report S-G S/15178.

9. U.N. Security Council Draft Resolution S/15185.

10. Jeane Kirkpatrick, "The U.S. Role in the United Nations," reprinted in *Vital Speeches of the Day* 48:20, August 1, 1982.

11. James Reston, "Changing the Guard," *New York Times*, June 9, 1982, p. A27.

12. Russell Baker, "The Phony War," *New York Times*, June 9, 1982, p. A27.

13. "Amateurs on Parade," *New York Times*, June 9, 1982, p. A26.

14. "Jeane Denies She Intends to Leave U.N.," *New York Daily News*, June 9, 1982 p. A5.

15. David Broder, "Pulling Rank on the U.S. Envoy," *Washington Post*, June 9, 1982, p. A23.

16. Drew Middleton, "Israel: Intervention Poses Both Temptation and Peril for Syria," *New York Times*, June 7, 1982, p. A12.

17. "Israel's Goal, and America's," *New York Times*, June 11, 1982, p. A30.

18. William Safire, "The Liberation of Lebanon," *New York Times*, June 11, 1982, p. A31.

19. Edward Said, "Begin's Zionism Grinds On," *New York Times*, June 11, 1982, p. A15.

20. Moshe Arens, "What We Want in Lebanon," *Washington Post*, June 11, 1982, p. A15.
21. Thomas L. Friedman, "Palestinians Say Invaders Are Seeking to Destroy PLO and the Idea of a State," *New York Times*, June 11, 1982, p. A18.
22. Amos Perlmutter, *New York Newsday*, June 10, 1982.
23. Stephen Rosenfeld, "Crushing the Palestinians," *Washington Post*, June 11, 1982, p. A15.
24. See "Israel's Statement on the Cease-Fire," *New York Times*, June 12, 1982, p. A5.
25. See "Two High Aides' Wives in Africa for Two Weeks," *New York Times*, June 24, 1982, p. 7.
26. U.N. Security Council Document S/15248.
27. David Ottaway, "Arafat's Dilemma," *Washington Post*, June 24, 1982, pp. A1, 25.
28. Alexander M. Haig, Jr., *Caveat: Realism, Reagan, and Foreign Policy*, p. 315.
29. Rowland Evans and Robert Novak, "Why the Vicar Fell," *Washington Post*, June 28, 1982, p. A13.
30. Document S/15255. For the text of the resolution, see *New York Times*, June 27, 1982, p. 12.
31. Leslie Gelb, "U.S. Working on New Peace Plan to Broaden Camp David Accords," *New York Times*, August 12, 1982, p. A1. For a detailed analysis of post–Camp David relations between Egypt and Israel, see *Policy Paper Series Number Seven*, Washington Institute for Near East Policy, Washington, D.C. See also Boutros-Ghali, "The Foreign Policy of Egypt in the Post-Sadat Era," *Foreign Affairs*, Spring 1982, pp. 769–88.
32. The Reagan Plan called for 1) full autonomy, under Jordanian supervision, for Palestinians in the West Bank and Gaza Strip; 2) a freeze on Jewish settlement in the occupied territories; and 3) negotiations to bring about an undivided Jerusalem. For a full text of the Reagan Plan see *New York Times*, September 2, 1982, p. 14.

 See also William F. Buckley, Jr. "Reagan and the Mideast," *National Review*, October 1, 1982, pp. 1240–41.

10. Defining "Illegitimate" Purposes

1. See UN General Assembly Document A/37/563. For a historical overview of Israel and the UN, see "The United Nations' Campaign Against Israel," *Heritage Foundation Backgrounder*, United Nations Assessment Project Study, June 16, 1983.
2. For an assessment of U.S.-UN relations, particularly the U.S. financial commitment to the United Nations, see "The United States and The United Nations: A Balance Sheet," *Heritage Foundation Backgrounder*, United Nations Assessment Project Study, January 21, 1982.
3. See *New York Times*, October 7, 1982, p. A8.
4. See "U.S. Vows to Halt U.N. Ties If Israel Is Denied Its Seat," *New York Times*, October 17, 1982, p. A1. Shultz announced that "If Israel were excluded from the General Assembly, the United States would withdraw from participation in the Assembly and would withdraw payments to the United Nations until Israel's right to participate [was] restored." For the full text of the speech, see *New York Times*, November 19, 1982, p. A20.

5. See "House Backs Israel at U.N.," *New York Times*, November 19, 1983, p. 8.
6. Leigh S. Ratiner, Deputy Chairman of the U.S. Delegation to the final negotiating session of the Third United Nations Conference on the Law of the Sea, provides a review of the treaty in "The Law of The Sea: A Crossroads for American Foreign Policy," *Foreign Affairs*, Summer 1982, pp. 1006–1021. For additional background on the Law of the Sea, see Ryan C. Amacher and Richard James Sweeney, eds., *The Law of the Sea: U.S. Interests and Alternatives* (Washington, D.C.: American Enterprise Institute, 1976), and Guy M. Hicks, "The Law of the Sea Treaty: A Review of the Issues," *Journal of Social, Political and Economic Studies* 6 (Summer 1981), pp. 107–18.
7. Elisabeth Mann Borgese, "Law of the Sea," *Scientific American*, March 1983, p. 47. As cited in Bernard H. Oxman, David D. Caron, and Charles L. O. Buderi, eds., *The Law of the Sea: U.S. Policy Dilemma* (San Francisco: Institute for Contemporary Studies, 1983).
8. On January 29, 1981 President Reagan announced that the U.S. would return to the Law of the Sea negotiations. "The world's oceans are vital to the United States and other nations in diverse ways," said Reagan. "They represent waterways and airways essential to preserving the peace and to trade and commerce. They are major sources for meeting increasing world food and energy demands and promise further resource potential. They are a frontier for expanding scientific research and knowledge; a fundamental part of the global environmental balance; and a great source of beauty, awe, and pleasure for mankind. . . . The United States remains committed to the multilateral treaty process for reaching agreement on law of the sea." *Department of State Bulletin*, March 1982, pp. 54–55.
9. See *New York Times*, July 10, 1982, p. A5.
10. Jennifer Seymour Whitaker, "Outside The Mainstream: Reagan's Refusal to Sign the Law of the Sea Treaty May Make Vital Navigation Rights Hard to Obtain in the Future," *Atlantic*, October 1982, pp. 18–26.
11. U.S. Participation in the UN, Report by the President to the Congress, 1965, p. 108. That statement was reiterated at a meeting of the UN Special Committee on Peace-Keeping Operations. See M. Whiteman, *Digest on International Law*, Vol. 13, 1968, p. 331. Also U.N.G.A.O.R. 19th Session Annex No. 21, A/5916/ Add. 1, pp. 86–87.
12. See chapter 4, notes 10–11.
13. Quoted in testimony by Ambassador Jeane J. Kirkpatrick before the U.N. Senate Subcommittee on Foreign Operations, October 3, 1983, p. 10.
14. Ibid.
15. Letter provided by Arthur J. Goldberg to the U.S. Mission to the UN on the interpretation of the so-called "Goldberg Reservation." See "U.S. Will Not Pay a U.N. Assessment," *New York Times*, December 31, 1982, pp. A1–2.

11. "It's 1979 All Over Again"

1. See *New York Times*, March 20, 1982, p. A1.
2. "U.N. Mugging Fails," *New York Times* op-ed, March 31, 1983.
3. See *New York Times*, August 16, 1979, pp. 1, 14. For a detailed account of the Andrew Young affair, see Schoenberg, op.cit., pp. 351–73.

12. Reaching Bottom

1. *New York Times*, September 2, 1983, p. A1.
2. See *New York Times*, September 1, 1983, p. A1; September 2, 1983, sect. I, p. 1.
3. See, generally, Craig A. Morgan, "The Shooting of Korean Air Lines Flight 007: Responses to Unauthorized Aerial Incursions," in W. Michael Reisman and Andrew R. Willard, eds., *International Incidents: The Law That Counts in World Politics* (Princeton: Princeton University Press, 1988).
4. *U.N. Security Council Provisional Verbatim Record of the Two Thousand Four Hundred and Seventieth Meeting*, September 12, 1983, pp. 13–26.
5. "Ambassador Kirkpatrick's Statement, UN Security Council, September 6, 1983," USUN press release 70/1.
6. U.N. Security Council draft resolution S/15966/Rev. 1, September 12, 1983. The resolution received 9 votes in favor (France, Jordan, Malta, the Netherlands, Pakistan, Togo, the United Kingdom, the United States, and Zaire), and 2 against (Poland and the USSR), with 4 abstentions (China, Guyana, Nicaragua, and Zimbabwe). Since the Soviet Union, a permanent member of the Security Council, cast a veto, the resolution was not adopted.
7. Kirkpatrick, "UN Mugging Fails."
8. *Department of State Bulletin* 83 (October 1983), p. 11.
9. "Destruction of Korean Air Lines Boeing 747 Over Sea of Japan, 31 August 1983," Report of International Civic Aviation Organization Fact-Finding Investigation, December 30, 1983.
10. *Department of State Bulletin*, op.cit., p. 3.

13. Grenada, and the Emergence of a Reagan Doctrine

1. A. Bemins, "Blood and Terror in Beirut," *Newsweek*, May 2, 1983, pp. 22–25.
2. See M. Schwartz, "Jeane Kirkpatrick: Our Macho U.N. Ambassador," *National Review*, January 21, 1983, p. 46 ff.; and A. Goldberg, "Right to Heckle," *Nation*, April 12, 1983, p. 387.
3. See *New York Times*, October 14, 1981, p. A1.
4. See Walter Isaacson, "Feelings of Hurt and Betrayal", *Time*, October 31, 1983, pp. 29–30; and "The Lady or the Team Player," *Newsweek*, October 24, 1983, pp. 25–26.
5. See *Washington Post*, October 23, 1983, p. 1.
6. Ibid.
7. See account of events leading up to invasion of Grenada in Mark Whitaker, "A Crisis in the Carribbean," *Newsweek*, October 31, 1983, pp. 40–42; and Steven Strasser, "Grenada's Palm-Tree Putsch," *Newsweek*, October 24, 1983, p. 50.
8. Interview with Eugenia Charles, Prime Minister of Dominica, March 21, 1987. See also *New York Times*, October 27, 1983, p. A19.
9. Ibid.
10. For the full text of President Reagan's announcement of the invasion, see *New York Times*, October 26, 1983, p. A16.
11. Constantine C. Menges, *Inside the National Security Council* (New York: Simon and Schuster, 1988), p. 82.
12. See Note 7, Chapter I.

13. See U.N. Security Council Document S/16077/Rev.1.
14. "Gunboats to Grenada," *New Republic*, November 14, 1983, pp. 10–11.
15. See John Norton Moore, *Law and the Grenada Mission*, published by the American Bar Association Standing Committee on Law and National Security, January 18, 1984.
16. Ambassador Kirkpatrick's Statement, UN Security Council, October 27, 1983. *Department of State Bulletin*, December 1983, pp. 75–76. Emphasis added.
17. Draft resolution S/16077/Rev.1. The eleven countries voting in favor were: China, France, Guyana, Jordan, Malta, the Netherlands, Nicaragua, Pakistan, Poland, Soviet Union, and Zimbabwe. One vote against: United States. Three abstained: Togo, Great Britain, Zaire. The resolution was not adopted due to the negative vote of the United States.
18. See Nicholas Henderson (British Ambassador to Washington during Falklands War), "Behind the British Anger over Grenada," *Washington Post*, November 6, 1983; also see Anthony Lejeune, "Margaret Thatcher's No-No," *National Review*, November 25, 1983, pp. 1476–77.
19. Jeane J. Kirkpatrick, "The UN and Grenada: A Speech Never Delivered," *Strategic Review*, Winter 1984, p. 11.
20. Michael Jay Robinson, Maura Clancey, and William C. Adams, "Grenada Update," *Public Opinion*, February/March, 1984, pp. 51–55. This survey gives an overview of public opinion surrounding the Grenada invasion, of U.S. citizens, Grenadians, and those Americans who were on the island attending St. Georges Medical School at the time of the invasion.
21. "Goliath in Grenada," *New York Times*, October 30, 1983, IV, p. A18.
22. Ibid.
23. For a legal perspective on the invasion, see Laura Wheeler, "The Grenada Invasion: Expanding the Scope of Humanitarian Intervention," *Boston College International and Comparative Law Review*, 8 (Summer 1985), pp. 413–30; see also John Norton Moore, *op. cit.* and material cited therein.
24. "Squaring International Law with Political Imperatives," *New York Times*.
25. Reprinted in Moore, *Law and the Grenada Mission*, p. 25.
26. "Remarks at the Conservative Political Action Conference's Twelfth Annual Dinner," *Weekly Compilation of Presidential Documents* 21, March 8, 1985, p. 243.
27. Jeane J. Kirkpatrick and Allan Gerson, "The Reagan Doctrine, Human Rights, and International Law," *Might v. Right* (New York: Council on Foreign Relations, 1989), pp. 19–36.

14. Winding Down

1. For text of President Reagan's address before the 39th session of the UN General Assembly in New York on September 24, 1984, see *New York Times*, September 25, 1984, p. A10.
2. *New York Times*, September 10, 1984, p. A13.
3. Rowland Evans and Robert Novak, "America's Mideast Malaise," *Washington Post*, September 26, 1984, p. 3.
4. See Title V, Section 528 of the Foreign Assistance and Related Programs Appropriation Act, 1987, as contained in Public Law 99-500 calling upon the President to submit an annual UN country-by-country voting report to Congress; and

Section 117 of Public Law 98-164 calling upon the Secretary of State to do likewise.

15. Legitimating Terrorism Once Again

1. Many of these observations are presented in Douglas J. Feith, "Law in the Service of Terror—The Strange Case of the Additional Protocol," *National Interest*, Fall 1985, pp. 36–47.
2. The United Kingdom representative expressed "surprise" at the text of the amendments:

> The various arguments had presented no convincing case for considering an internal struggle as an international one. Moreover, it was a basic principle of the Geneva Conventions, The Hague Regulations and other instruments that legal and humanitarian protection should never vary according to the motives of those engaged in a particular armed struggle. Deviation from that principle would mean damaging the structure of The Hague and Geneva Conventions and would involve the need to reconstruct the whole of humanitarian law. Moreover, to discriminate between the motives of those engaged in the struggle would violate essential principles of human rights.

> As cited in Levie, *ibid.* at 7.
3. For a detailed discussion of the 1977 Geneva Protocols see the "Symposium on The 1977 Geneva Protocols," *Akron Law Review*, 19:4, (Spring 1986), and material therein cited.
4. *New York Times*, February 16, 1981, p. A19.
5. *New York Times*, February 17, 1987, p. A27.

16. The Last Illusion

1. For a detailed discussion of the International Court of Justice's functions, organization, procedures, and decisions, see the outstanding work by Shabtai Rosenne, *The Law and Practice of the International Court of Justice* (Norwell, Mass: Klewer, 1985), and *Documents on the International Court of Justice* (New York: Oceana, 1979).
2. David J. Brewer, "A Better Education—the Great Need of the Profession," in American Bar Association, *Report of the Eighteenth Annual Meeting*, August 27–30, 1985, pp. 454–56.
3. For a discussion of the positive attributes of the World Court, see Arthur W. Rovine, "The National Interest and the World Court," in Leo Gross, ed., *The Future of the International Court of Justice*, volume 1 (Dobbs Ferry, N.Y.: Oceana Publications, 1976).
4. Denna Frank Fleming, *The United States and the World Court, 1920–1966* (New York: Harper and Brothers, 1962), p. 48.
5. Customs Regime Between Germany and Austria, Advisory Opinion, 1931, P.C.I.J. Series A/B, No. 41, p. 37.
6. Harry S. Truman, *Memoirs by Harry S. Truman: Year of Decisions*, volume I (Garden City, N.Y.: Doubleday, 1955), p. 286.
7. United Nations Information Organizations and the U.S. Library of Congress, *Documents of the United Nations Conference on International Organization* 14 (1945), p. 166.

8. As cited in Fleming, op.cit., p. 195.

9. Hearings on S. Res. 196 before sub-committee on Sen. Comm. on For. Relations, 79th Cong., 2nd Sess. 45, 1946.

10. Ibid., p. 44.

11. The Right of Passage over Indian Territory (Portugal v. India) 1954; Southwest Africa (Ethiopia and Liberia v. South Africa) 1960; and Northern Cameroons (Cameroons v. United Kingdom) 1961.

12. The 1946 declaration of China was repudiated by the Government of the Peoples' Republic in 1972. See 1986–1987 I.C.J.Y.B. 59 note 1. The 1947 declaration of France was replaced by new declarations in 1959 and 1966, and was terminated in 1974. See 1959–1960 I.C.J.Y.B. 240; 1966–1967 I.C.J.Y.B. 52; and 1973–1974 I.C.J.Y.B. 49. The United Kingdom revised its declaration twice in 1955, and also in 1957, and in 1969. See 1955–1956 I.C.J.Y.B. 184–85; 1957–1958 I.C.J.Y.B. 211 (1958); 1958–1959 I.C.J.Y.B. 225–26; 1986–1987 I.C.J.Y.B. 90–91. The present British declaration, by its terms, may be further modified or terminated at will. The Soviet Union has never submitted a declaration.

13. Australia and New Zealand v. France, 1974 I.C.J. 253.

14. Allan Gerson, "U.S. Acts Lawfully," New York Times, May 4, 1984, p. A31.

15. Ibid.

16. Anthony Lewis, "When Lilacs Last . . ." New York Times, May 28, 1984, p. A19.

17. Daniel P. Moynihan, New York Times, May 19, 1984.

18. Allan Gerson, New York Times, June 6, 1984, p. A26.

19. Moynihan, A Dangerous Place, p. 185.

20. 1984 I.C.J. Reports 215.

21. 1984 I.C.J. Reports 392.

22. Richard Falk, "Curbing a Lawless Government," Progressive, June 1984, p. 13.

23. New York Times, October 8, 1985, p. A5.

24. 1986 I.C.J. Reports 14.

25. Eugene V. Rostow, "Disputes Involving the Inherent Right of Self-Defense," in Lori Fisher Damrosch, ed., The International Court of Justice at a Crossroads (Dobbs Ferry, N.Y.: Transnational Publishers, 1987), p. 278.

26. Ibid.

27. Ibid., p. 284.

28. Ibid.

29. M. V. Reisman, "Old Wine in New Bottles: The Reagan and Brezhnev Doctrines in Contemporary International Law and Practice," Yale Journal of International Law 13:1 (Winter 1988), pp. 171–98.

30. Ibid., p. 190, number 51.

31. Ibid., p. 192.

32. Ibid., p. 194.

33. Ibid., p. 196.

17. Change of Guard

1. Vital Speeches of the Day, (September 15, 1984).

2. Seymour Maxwell Finger, former Ambassador and senior adviser at the U.S. Mission to the United Nations from 1956 to 1971, wrote that Jeane Kirkpatrick "represented a dramatic change in style and approach from her immediate predecessors" at the U.N. and particularly in "her confrontational predilections."

See "The Reagan-Kirkpatrick Policies and The United Nations," *Foreign Affairs* (Winter 1983–1984), pp. 436–57.

3. John Goshko and Lou Cannon, "Kirkpatrick to Quit Government," *Washington Post*, January 31, 1985, p. A1.

4. Vernon A. Walters, *Silent Missions* (New York: Doubleday, 1978); Michael Massing, "America's Top Messenger Boy," *New Republic* (September 16–25, 1985) pp. 21–25.

5. See Joanne Turnbull, "Hard Times at the UN," *Newsweek*, October 6, 1986, p. 35.

Epilogue

1. Address before the Institute for Comparative Economic and Political Studies, Georgetown University, Washington, D.C., June 14, 1983. Reprinted in Jeane J. Kirkpatrick, *Legitimacy and Force*, volume 1: *Political and Moral Dimensions* (New Brunswick, N.J.: Transaction Books, 1988), p. 221.

Index